Sense and Nonsense about Crime, Drugs, and Communities

SEVENTH EDITION

Sense and Nonsense about Crime, Drugs, and Communities

SEVENTII EDITION

SAMUEL WALKER
University of Nebraska, at Omaha

WADSWORTH
CENGAGE Learning™

Australia • Brazil • Japan • Korea • Mexico • Singapore • Spain • United Kingdom • United States

WADSWORTH
CENGAGE Learning

Sense and Nonsense about Crime, Drugs, and Communities, Seventh Edition
Samuel Walker

Senior Acquiring Sponsoring Editor, Criminal Justice: Carolyn Henderson-Meier

Assistant Editor: Erin Abney

Editorial Assistant: John Chell

Associate Media Editor: Andy Yap

Senior Marketing Manager: Michelle Williams

Marketing Coordinator: Jillian Myers

Marketing Communications Manager: Laura Localio

Content Project Management: Pre-PressPMG

Creative Director: Rob Hugel

Executive Art Director: Maria Epes

Print Buyer: Linda Hsu

Rights Acquisitions Account Manager, Text: Roberta Broyer

Senior Rights Acquisitions Account Manager, Image: Dean Dauphinais

Production Service: Pre-PressPMG

Art Editing: Pre-PressPMG

Copy Editor: Cindy Bond

Illustrator: Frank Irwin

Cover Designer: Riezebos Holzbaur/Angelyn Navasca

Compositor: Pre-PressPMG

For product information and technology assistance, contact us at **Cengage Learning Customer & Sales Support, 1-800-354-9706**.

For permission to use material from this text or product, submit all requests online at **www.cengage.com/permissions**. Further permissions questions can be e-mailed to **permissionrequest@cengage.com**.

Library of Congress Control Number: 2010925062

ISBN-13: 978-0-495-80987-6

ISBN-10: 0-495-80987-X

Wadsworth
20 Davis Drive
Belmont, CA 94002-3098
USA

Cengage Learning is a leading provider of customized learning solutions with office locations around the globe, including Singapore, the United Kingdom, Australia, Mexico, Brazil, and Japan. Locate your local office at **www.cengage.com/global**.

Cengage Learning products are represented in Canada by Nelson Education, Ltd.

To learn more about Wadsworth, visit **www.cengage.com/Wadsworth**

Purchase any of our products at your local college store or at our preferred online store **www.cengagebrain.com**.

Printed in the United States of America
2 3 4 5 6 7 14 13 12 11

Brief Contents

Contents

PART V   The Drug Problem   301

Propositions

Foreword

Shortly after its initial publication, Samuel Walker's *Sense and Nonsense about Crime* was recognized as an important new book, a substantive contribution to the literature on crime and justice. Over the years, he has reworked its themes and developed its arguments in five more editions (updating the title to reflect an expanded discussion of drugs and drug policy in the third edition), and the field's appreciation of this book has only increased. Today, it is a major text in the study of crime and justice; some call it a nascent classic work in its field. It is a respected argument about our knowledge base for crime and justice, and it is one of those rare books that are deeply respected by scholars and policymakers alike.

It is, therefore, with extraordinary pleasure that I welcome the Sixth Edition to the Wadsworth Contemporary Issues in Crime and Justice Series. The series is devoted to giving detailed and effective exposure to important or emerging issues and problems that ordinarily receive insufficient attention in traditional textbooks. The series also publishes books meant to provoke thought and change perspectives by challenging readers to become more sophisticated consumers of crime and justice knowledge. If you are looking for a book that will make you an informed student of crime and justice policy and practice, you could not do better than the one you are now holding.

Why is this book so important? There are two reasons. First, so much of what is commonly believed about crime—and so much of what shapes public policy on crime—is nonsense. Second, Walker's book was the first (and is still the most effective) book written to point that out. The book provides a masterful critique of the American penchant for short-sighted, metaphorical strategies to prevent crime (boot camps are a good example) or feel-good rhetoric about crime priorities (end poverty, end crime) that have, over the years, not gotten us very far in our pursuit of a safer society. Today, we are enjoying a welcome, sustained national drop in crime rates. But this drop still leaves us with higher rates of crime than we want, and (perhaps more to the point) the source of the drop is more of a mystery to us than a lesson in crime prevention policy.

The contribution of this book—what makes this book special—is its willingness to show evenhandedly how favorite strategies of diverse political agendas have as their foundation some degree of "nonsense." If there is a lesson that this book brings to us repeatedly, it is that cherished images of crime and justice are flawed, inaccurate, and doomed to fail for particular reasons of the more or less well-known facts that we so often want to ignore to sustain our favorite ideologies. This book challenges us where we need to be challenged: in our willingness to ignore reality in order to nurture our frequently inadvisable pet ideas about crime and crime fighting.

You want your police to be tough, to chase dangerous criminals, to make life-saving arrests? Well, Professor Walker points out that you have to contend with the fact that police spend very little of their time acting in this way, and even when they do, not much in the way of crime control seems to result. You want your judges to lock 'em up and throw away the key? Walker shows all the ways that this belief is expensive and ineffective, even counterproductive. You think we need to save money through closer surveillance of the people convicted of crime? Make our lives safer by treating juveniles as though they were adults? End drug abuse through an all-out war on drugs? Here again, the book sheds cool light on hot emotions, showing how such strategies can backfire.

This book is not, however, just about nonsense in crime and justice. Perhaps nonsense gets the majority of the attention because so much of what we do is based on faulty thinking. But Walker is willing to tell us what makes "sense" as well. Big proposals lack much support, and politically popular proposals may be downright silly. But there are smaller, less ambitious ways in which we can contribute to a safer society, and we can do so without suspending our constitutional rights or giving up our public freedoms. One way we have learned to be smarter about crime is through the philosophy of evidence-based practice. This approach asks hard questions about criminal policy, seeking to base crime strategies on established studies that show those policies will work. Professor Walker applies the evidence-based criterion to his review of crime and justice policy: what emerges is a powerfully dispassionate analysis that gives us a carefully crafted challenge to start "making sense" in the way in which we talk about crime and develop policies to cope with it.

If you are getting ready to read this book, chances are you are contemplating a career in the field of criminal justice. At the very least, you have an informed citizen's interest in the problems of crime and justice. In either case, you have come to the right place to become more knowledgeable in your pursuits. After you read this book, you will join a large number of its alumni, dedicated to crime policies that make sense. I commend you.

Todd R.Clear
Series Editor

Preface

The Seventh Edition marks the twenty-fifth anniversary of *Sense and Nonsense about Crime*. Much has changed over that quarter of a century, in American society and in criminal justice. It has been an exciting challenge to keep pace with those changes and make sure that this edition is relevant to current developments.

When the first edition appeared, crack was just beginning to appear on the streets of America. One result was an epidemic of gun violence among young men. Some criminologists predicted that youth homicides would continue to soar. They didn't. Instead, serious crime, including homicide, began a completely surprising decline that is unprecedented in America. In New York City and other cities, violent crime has dropped to levels not seen since the early 1960s. Keeping track of these changes, and attempting to explain them, has been an important but necessary task. When the first edition of this book appeared, policymakers and criminologists were in the midst of a fierce debate over "career criminals." The questions of the day were how to identify that small group of offenders and what would be the impact of different policies that targeted them. You don't hear much about career criminals today, however. Policies that were hot new ideas twenty-five years ago did not work out, criminological research undermined most of the underlying assumptions, and the policy debate has moved on.

The Seventh Edition of *Sense and Nonsense* has a new subtitle, *Crime, Drugs and Communities*. This is the second change in the subtitle since the First Edition, as I have attempted to keep the book relevant to a changing world. The focus on communities began with the Sixth Edition and is now incorporated into the subtitle. As you will learn in this edition, the most important innovations in crime policy have a community focus: community policing, community prosecution, and prisoner reentry programs that look at the environment to which people leaving prison return.

The new edition continues the "nonsense" theme of the First Edition. We continue to have crime policies that are not supported by empirical evidence and which, in many cases, only make matters worse. Chapter 7 has a new section on sex offender registration and notification laws, which often include restrictions on where sex offenders can live. As you will learn, these requirements cover many offenders who are not going to be dangerous predators; As a result, law enforcement and corrections officers carry huge caseloads and struggle to focus on the few offenders who really do pose a possible risk to the community.

At the same time, the Seventh Edition is somewhat different from earlier editions because it puts a greater emphasis on the "sense" theme. There is growing evidence that some programs actually do work, in large part because they are solidly rooted in the best criminological research. People often ask if academic research ever makes a practical contribution to crime policy. The answer is that yes, some of it does. As you will learn, there is an emerging consensus that some— but not all—problem-oriented policing programs, drug courts, and community prosecution programs can be effective. Most interesting, as you will learn in Chapter 6, is that some of the programs may actually make deterrence work in ways that traditional programs have not.

This is an exciting development, and future editions of this book will assess whether this promise is fulfilled in practice.

New elements in the Seventh Edition include the following:

- Chapter 1 discusses the resource crisis in criminal justice, where the economic recession of 2008–2010 has cut government budgets and made it difficult for agencies to either maintain their current programs or develop innovative ones.

- Chapter 2 discusses the horrific Garrido kidnapping and rape case in California, which raises serious questions about the effectiveness of sex offender registration laws and the capacity of the system to identify and monitor repeat predators.

- Chapter 2 also discusses the parole crisis in California, which involves a hidden system of "back-end" sentencing where more people enter California through parole revocation than a court sentence.

- Chapter 3 has new material on wrongful convictions.

- Chapter 4 replaces the outdated emphasis on career criminals with a more relevant focus on the prediction problem in criminal justice.

- Chapter 5 has brand new material on closed circuit television (CCTV) cameras as a crime prevention tool. They are presented here as a form of police "patrol."

- Chapter 6 has an important new discussion of how some problem-oriented policing programs may deliver a message of deterrence far more effectively than traditional programs.

- Chapter 7 has new material on sex offender notification and registration laws, with special emphasis on how they deliver a false promise of security to the public.

- Chapter 8 examines the impact of plea bargaining reforms and looks at whether they really change anything.

- Chapter 9 has a revised discussion of the failure of states to implement their own victim's rights laws, with reference to the discussion of the courtroom work group in Chapter 3.

- Chapter 10 includes a discussion of the Supreme Court decision in *District of Columbia v. Heller* that declared the Washington, DC, ban on guns unconstitutional, and how the decision affects other gun control efforts.

- Chapter 11 has a greatly expanded examination of drug courts, and a discussion of why they are often more effective than other treatment programs.

- Chapter 12 offers new evidence for the growing interest in procedural justice and whether it can reduce crime by getting more people to obey the law.

- Chapter 13 includes new material on the impact of the Mexican drug cartels on crime and violence in the United States.

- Chapter 14 continues and expands the discussion begun in the Sixth Edition that ties together promising new developments in different areas of the criminal justice system.

ANCILLARIES

eBank Instructor's Resource Manual with Test Bank. The manual includes learning objectives, key terms, a detailed chapter outline, discussion topics, and a test bank. Each chapter's test bank contains questions in multiple-choice, true false, fill-in-the-blank, and essay formats, with a full answer key. The test bank is coded to the learning objectives that appear in the main text, and includes the page numbers in the main text where the answers can be found. Finally, each question in the test bank has been carefully reviewed by experienced criminal justice instructors for quality, accuracy, and content coverage. The manual is available for download on the password-protected website and can also be obtained by e-mailing your local Cengage Learning representative.

DEDICATION

I would like to dedicate this book to Mary Ann Lamanna, who has been a wonderful companion over the past quarter of a century. As I am completing this Seventh Edition, she is working on the Eleventh Edition of her book (so I guess I have some work to do). But despite the demands of publishing deadlines, she knows that there is always time for a movie.

ABOUT THE AUTHOR

Samuel Walker is Isaacson Professor of Criminal Justice at the University of Nebraska, Omaha, where he has taught for over thirty years. He is the author of thirteen books on policing, criminal justice history and policy, and civil liberties. His most recent books include *Police Accountability* (Wadsworth, 2001) and *The New World of Police Accountability* (Sage, 2005). His current research involves police accountability, focusing primarily on citizen oversight of the police, and police early warning (EW) systems. Professor Walker currently serves on the Panel on Policing of the National Research Council of the National Academy of Sciences.

Samuel Walker

PART I

Thinking Clearly about Crime

1

Crime and Policy:
A Complex Problem

CRIME AT A 30-YEAR LOW

Crime in America hit a 35 year low in 2008. The National Crime Victimization Survey (NCVS) reported that in 2008 rates of both violent crimes and property crime reached the lowest level recorded since the NCVS was initiated in 1973. The NCVS data marked a continuation of the dramatic crime drop that began in 1993. The reduction in crime occurred in all major categories of both violent and property crime. The robbery rate fell from 6.2 per 1,000 in 1992 to 2.2 in 2008. The household burglary rate fell from 58.7 to 26.3 per 1,000 in the same period (Figure 1.1 presents the NCVS trends from 1973 to 2006).[1]

This great decline in crime is a historic event. Even though crime has edged up in some cities, Americans are much safer today than they were 15 or 20 years ago. The meaning of the crime drop becomes clearer when we look at certain cities. In New York City, murders fell from an astonishing 2,245 in 1990 to only 461 in 2009, the lowest total since the 1960s. On the West Coast, Los Angeles had the lowest number of murders in 2009 since 1967. The 2008 murder rate in San Diego was almost one-quarter of what it had been in 1991 (4 per 100,000 vs. 15), and was almost as low as it had been in the 1960s. The robbery rate in San Diego had gone up slightly since 2002, but was still one-third of the 1991 rate (1.50 per 1,000 vs. 4.72).[2]

The crime drop seems like a miracle to many Americans. For the first time in a generation, there is good news about crime and violence. Since crime rates began to soar around 1963, crime has ripped the social fabric of the United States and has been a major issue in American politics. In addition to the harm inflicted by particular crimes—murder or rape—crime devastates our communities, instilling fear and causing people to move out of their neighborhoods. And in politics, the issue of "crime" has been intertwined with race and has contributed to the racial polarization of American society.

Illustration by Frank Irwin, © Wadsworth, Cengage Learning.

Is the Crime Drop Genuine?

Initially, some skeptics wondered if the crime drop was genuine, a fluke, a temporary blip, or the product of a statistical artifact. These questions are no longer valid. All of the evidence indicates that it is indeed real. Most important, despite some small increases, and some variations from city to city, serious crime has not returned to its former levels.

Rate of violent victimization pre- and post-methodological redesigns

Rate of property victimization pre- and post-methodological redesigns

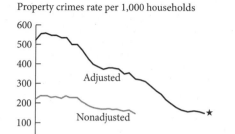

FIGURE 1.1   Victimization Trends, 1973–2006.

SOURCE: Bureau of Justice Statistics, Criminal Victimization 2006 (Washington, DC: Department of Justice, 2007).

Several factors indicate that the drop is genuine. First, the NCVS is regarded as a very reliable measure of criminal victimization. No one has ever suggested that the data are manipulated or methodologically flawed. See the many NCVS reports on the website of the National Criminal Justice Reference Service [NCJRS].) Second, the trends in the NCVS data have continued for 15 years, and so cannot be dismissed as a temporary phenomenon. Third, even though the FBI's Uniform Crime Report (UCR) uses a different methodology, and does not measure crimes committed, it too has reported significant declines in crime over the past 15 to 20 years.

Additionally, many other social indicators have also moved in a positive direction over the past 20 years. Decreases in teenage pregnancy and infant mortality (Table 1.1), for example, suggest a general improvement in the quality of life in American society as the result of subtle but important changes in people's behavior in areas of life apart from criminal behavior. The most worrisome social indicator, however, is the unemployment rate. The healthy American economy in the 1990s was an important contributor to all of these trends, including the reduction in crime. Yet, the recession of 2008–2009 led to the highest unemployment rates in many decades. This is a very worrisome factor for future crime trends.[3]

Explaining the Crime Drop

How do we explain the great American crime drop? Why did it happen? What are the causes? American criminologists and policy analysts have hotly debated these questions. The advocates of particular policies all argue that it was their favored approach: increased incarceration, community policing, a decline in the use of crack cocaine, a stronger economy, and so on. Franklin Zimring threw a monkey wrench into this debate with the simple but basic idea of taking a look outside the United States and examining crime trends in other countries. What he found puts the great American crime drop in very useful perspective.

TABLE 1.1   Positive trends in two U.S. social indicators: Teenage births and infant mortality, 1970–2003

Teenage births Births to women, ages 15–17 per 1,000		Infant mortality Deaths per 1,000 live births	
1972	39	1970	20.0
1977	33.9	1975	16.1
1982	32.2	1980	12.6
1987	31.7	1985	10.6
1992	37.6	1990	9.2
1997	31.4	1995	7.6
2003	22.4	2000	6.9

SOURCE: U.S. Census Bureau, *Statistical Abstract of the United States: 2007* (Washington, DC: Department of Commerce, 2007).

Zimring found that in the decade of the 1990s several countries experienced declines in crime. The most important example is Canada, where crime went down in six of the seven UCR categories. Canada is a very useful comparison. It is contiguous to the U.S., shares a common language (with the partial exception of French-speaking Quebec) and culture, and has very close economic relations. If crime trends in the two countries are so similar, the changes in the U.S. cannot be readily explained by unique American factors. Let's take a closer look at this issue.[4]

We should quickly emphasize that the two countries began the decade of the 1990s with very different levels of crime, especially violent crime. The murder and robbery rates in the U.S. were far higher than in Canada. That is a basic fact about crime in America: it has very high levels of violent crime compared with other industrialized countries. Nonetheless, whatever the starting point, it is the similarity in the declines that commands our attention.

With respect to possible causes, the most important comparison involves imprisonment. The prison population in the U.S. soared in the decade, increasing 57 percent, while it *dropped* 6 percent in Canada. While they do not settle the debate, these data raise very serious questions about the role of incarceration in the great American crime decline. How could Canada get roughly the same results by moving in the opposite direction on imprisonment? A similar problem arises with regard to the number of police. The COPS program provided federal funds to increase the number of police officers in the U.S. by something like 60,000 to 75,000 (see Chapter 5). Some analysts estimate that this represented a 14 percent increase in the police-population ratio. In Canada, meanwhile, the ratio *fell* by an estimated 10 percent. These data make it difficult to argue that increasing the number of police officers contributed to the American crime drop. A similar problem exists with regard to economic factors. While the Canadian economy improved just as it did in the U.S., unemployment was consistently higher than in the U.S. throughout the period.[5]

How then do we explain the "extraordinary parallels" in crime trends in the two countries? The "central puzzle," Zimring argues, lies in the fact that Canada experienced a greater decline "than could be explained by any visible causes." He concludes that it might involve broad changes in behavior that are beyond the reach of social science to explain. In short, there are no "easy explanations."

The main point of Zimring's analysis is that we should always take a very broad view of a social trend, whether it is crime or another issue. Take a good look at long-term historical trends. Use a comparative perspective: compare the U.S. to other countries, and compare crime trends with other social indicators. Be careful about jumping to conclusions based on short-term data, and be very wary of anyone claiming that their favorite crime policy is responsible for some recent good news.

Blumstein and Wallman, in their collection of articles in *The Crime Drop in America*, reach a conclusion roughly similar to Zimring's, arguing that "no single factor can be invoked as *the* cause of the crime decline in the 1990s."[6] Criminologist Richard Rosenfeld suggests a general cultural shift away from violence that might explain the improvement in other social indicators besides crime.[7]

It is too early for us to throw up our hands and say we can't explain anything. We should not give up just because there are no easy, immediate answers. One of the major goals of this book, after all, is to clear away the nonsense about crime policy. Consequently, we have to look more closely at the various explanations that have been offered for the crime drop. We will find some plausible reasons to explain at least part of the crime drop in some of these arguments. There is fairly persuasive evidence, for example, that the dramatic decline in the use of crack had a major impact on crime trends. We will look at this in detail in Chapter 13. At the same time, there is some promising evidence regarding the impact of recent innovations in policing—community policing, problem-oriented policing, "hot spots" policing—although we should not exaggerate their impact on national crime rates.

Contextual vs. Policy Factors

Our task is to sort through different factors that might explain the great crime drop. The most intelligent short discussion is in an Urban Institute paper, *Reflections on the Crime Decline: Lessons for the Future?*[8] Jeremy Travis and Michelle Waul make an important distinction between contextual and policy factors that affect crime.

Contextual factors include demographic changes, the rise and fall of the crack cocaine epidemic, and changes in labor markets. The increase in the proportion of crime-prone young people in the population in the 1960s (the famous "baby boom" era) explained much of the great crime wave of the 1960s, but the influence of demography has been far more complicated in the last 20 years. A demographic analysis failed to predict the great increase in violent crime in the mid-1980s, as well as the sharp decline after 1993. The changing popularity of crack provides a much better explanation. The rise in violent crime coincided with the arrival of crack, and the crime drop has coincided with its waning popularity. Travis and Waul suggest that a younger generation saw the devastating effects of crack and decided that the drug was just not cool. With respect to changing labor markets, the Urban Institute paper cites data showing that the real wages (actual wages adjusted for inflation) of low-skilled workers declined by almost 25 percent from the early 1980s to 1993, when it bottomed out (from $9.00/hr to $6.74). The economic prosperity of the 1990s included a rise in real wages, and this coincided with the great crime drop.

The *criminal justice policies* that the Urban Institute paper considers most relevant include several gun control policies (which we will examine in detail in Chapter 10), the increase in incarceration and consequent incapacitation of offenders (Chapter 7), and innovations in policing (Chapters 5 and 15). After considering all these, the Urban Institute paper concludes that *no single factor* can explain the great crime drop. Instead, it is probably the *interplay* of different factors, including both contextual factors and criminal justice policies, that best explains it. If this is true, one of the challenges in this book is for us to identify which of those factors contributed to the crime drop, and the relative importance of each one.

Looking ahead, one of the arguments in this book is that no single policy is likely to be the main factor in reducing crime. A *sensible approach* is that effective crime reduction is likely to be the result of several different policies working together. Consequently, our analysis shifts the focus from specific policies or components of the justice system (e.g., police, sentencing) to the communities where the impact of different policies are felt.

A Word About the Possible Impact of Abortion

In one of the more controversial arguments about the crime drop, a number of economists have argued that the legalization of abortion by the 1973 *Roe v. Wade* decision played a major role. (It is interesting that this debate has been largely dominated by economists rather than criminologists, who have stayed away from it.) The basic argument is simple: legalized abortions, about 1.5 million from the 1980s to recent years, created a cohort of so-called "unborn offenders." As a group, they would have begun entering their high crime years (15–24 years) in the early 1990s; however, because they did not exist, they are responsible for part of the crime drop that began in the early 1990s. The argument further adds that abortions were disproportionately high among women whose children would be most at risk for criminal behavior.[9]

Because it involves a highly sensitive and controversial argument, many criminologists have shied away from this issue. Still, it needs to be considered, and that is exactly what Franklin Zimring did in his book on the crime drop. In his analysis, the theory of the "unborn offender" collapses. Most important, he looks at the data on actual live births in the U.S. from the 1960s to the present. The data indicate that despite 1.5 million annual abortions, the annual number of live births actually increased slowly but steadily after *Roe v. Wade*. In short, there was no reduction of the number of youths in the high crime cohort. It gets worse. The percentage of those born to single mothers increased significantly in the period. This is extremely important, because the "unborn offender" argument holds that a significant number of the abortions involved mothers whose children would be at high risk for criminality (including single mothers, especially). The data indicate that the number of births in this high risk category actually increased rather than decreased. Finally, there is the matter of timing. The number of abortions began to increase beginning in 1974 (allowing for a lag following the Supreme Court decision). The first wave of unborn offenders would have been 15 in 1989, and there were at least three more cohort years before crime began to decline. Unfortunately, the late 1980s and early 1990s were the years when youth violence, and gun violence in particular, peaked (causing much alarm about young "predators"). Thus, the expected impact of abortion did not begin to occur when it should have.[10]

THE PURPOSE OF THIS BOOK

This book is a search for effective crime policies. It attempts to answer one basic question: *What works?* What criminal justice policies are effective in reducing serious crime? We will review some of the major crime control proposals and evaluate their effectiveness in light of what we know about crime and justice. Previous editions of this book, written when crime rates were high, sought to determine what *might* work. Now, in the face of the great crime drop, we have to turn the question around: What *has worked?* Did certain crime policies contribute to the reduction in crime? If so, which ones? Why exactly were they effective? And can the lessons from one success story be transferred to other programs in other parts of the criminal justice system?

THE NEW STANDARD: EVIDENCE-BASED
CRIME POLICY

A new standard has emerged for evaluating the effectiveness of crime policies. It is a far higher and demanding scientific standard than has been used in the past. Evidence-based policymaking is extensively used in health care policy and has become one of the most important developments in criminology. This approach requires policies to be based on a solid foundation of evidence drawn from the best research. The relevant questions are: What is the evidence? Does the evidence indicate that a policy works? Does the research meet the highest scientific standards? Have the findings been replicated in other studies?

Evidence-based policy originated in England with the Cochrane Collaboration, which examined the effectiveness of health care policies. It has spread to health care policy in this country. There is now a large and growing network of evidence-based medicine (EBM) centers, websites, journals, tutorials, and other readily available resources. Governments are adapting the principles of evidence-based policy to crime control. In England, the Home Office (the equivalent of our Department of Justice) is aggressively promoting evidence-based crime reduction and has published a report, *Working Out What to Do: Evidence-Based Crime Reduction.*[11]

In January 2003, the Justice Department and the Coalition for Evidence-Based Policy initiated a joint effort to promote evidence-based crime and substance abuse policy. It recommended that "federal agencies develop a concise, uniform, user-friendly set of principles on what constitutes 'rigorous evidence' of an intervention's effectiveness," and that "agency crime/substance-abuse grant programs, where appropriate, require applicants to provide a concrete strategy for implementation of evidence-backed interventions with fidelity."[12] The movement for evidence-based crime policy was formally launched in the United States with the founding in February 2000 of the Campbell Collaboration in Philadelphia (named for the psychologist Donald Campbell, whose work is familiar to many criminal justice students through their research methods class).

Why the Need for Evidence-Based Crime Policy?

The Traditional Lack of Evidence to Support Crime Policies. The movement for evidence-based crime policy has added a refreshing, demanding—and long overdue—element of scientific rigor to policy debates. The former director of the Office of Justice Programs, Deborah Daniels, declared: "In the past, criminal justice practitioners operated on instinct and assumption, not science. They tried new approaches, if they did so at all, because they sounded as though they should be effective. But it did not occur to the practitioners to examine the research before they instituted a particular practice, or to measure its effectiveness as they deployed it."[13] In short, good intentions are not enough; sound policies require solid evidence.

Even worse than the lack of evidence, many policies have been continued—at great expense—despite the fact that good research has found them to be ineffective. Daniels cites the example of the Drug Abuse Resistance Education program, or DARE, the highly popular school-based drug prevention initiative. It has operated in as many as 75 percent of all school districts in some years at a cost of about $200 million a year. The General Accounting Office (GAO) reviewed evaluations of DARE and in 2003 reported that there were "no statistically significant differences in illicit drug use between students who received DARE lessons in the fifth or sixth grade, referred to as intervention groups, and students who did not—the control groups."[14]

Not Just Ineffective, But Actually Harmful. Some crime reduction policies are not merely ineffective, but actually cause harm. Can this be possible? Can it be that programs designed to help people actually leave them worse off? Sadly, the answer is yes. The noted criminologist Joan McCord identified several examples of programs where the outcomes were harmful.[15]

The famous Cambridge-Somerville (Massachusetts) Youth Study from the 1930s to 1945 (with follow-up reports on the original subjects through the early 1980s) matched boys under the age of 10 who received treatment, with control group boys. The treatment consisted of professional counselors, referral to specialists for particular problems, tutoring, and activities such as summer camps. McCord found that among the 103 pairs of youths who had different outcomes, those in the treatment group were actually *more likely* to have been convicted of a UCR Index crime, to have died at a younger age, or to have been diagnosed as alcoholic, schizophrenic, or manic depressive than those boys not receiving treatment. Even worse, the adverse effects were greater among those boys who received longer and more intensive treatment.

A Michigan Volunteers in Probation (VIP) program involved volunteers who counseled probationers in juvenile court. The VIP program, of course, sounds wonderful: eager volunteers providing additional assistance to young delinquents, and at no cost to the state. What could be better? Unfortunately, delinquents who received the VIP counseling did *worse* than those who did not. In short, the kids would have done better with no treatment at all.

Scared Straight is a popular program designed to frighten kids out of criminal behavior by exposing them to the terrible conditions in prison. The Scared Straight idea was popularized by a 1979 television documentary and was eventually adopted in 38 states. An evaluation of the San Quentin (California) Squires program found that after 12 months, 81 percent of the treatment group had been arrested, compared with only 67 percent of the control group. (We look at Scared Straight in more detail in Chapter 6).[16]

The disturbing news is that well-intentioned treatment can sometimes harm. Evidence-based policymaking is designed to guard against this possibility by requiring a review of program evaluations (and accepting only those evaluations that meet scientific standards).

The New Standards of Evidence-Based Crime Policy

The evidence-based policy movement defines very specific standards. First, it demands empirical evidence of the effectiveness of a policy. This rules out hope, wishful thinking, and good intentions. It also excludes policies whose assumptions are extrapolated from other evidence (e.g., since we know that X works in the context of Y, we can assume that it will also work in the context of Z).

Second, it sets a very high requirement of experimental or quasi-experimental research design in which subjects are randomly assigned to treatment and control groups. This includes an assessment of the quality of the research design of studies. The 1997 University of Maryland report *What Works?* was probably the first to use the method in American criminal justice, rating studies on a scale of 1 to 5. Thus, when we ask whether there is any evidence of effectiveness in a program or policy, it makes a difference whether a study gives it a rating of 2 or 5. A rating of 2 may mean that the research design was so weak that we can't be sure of the findings.[17]

A third element of evidence-based policy is the requirement of replication. It is not sufficient that the effectiveness of a policy be validated by one study; the findings need to be confirmed by similar studies replicating it. This has been a serious problem for criminal justice policymaking. Many policies have been based on only one study. The Kansas City Preventive Patrol Experiment (see Chapter 5) has been enormously influential in developing policy, but it was never replicated.

Similarly, the Minneapolis Domestic Violence Experiment had a huge influence on the growth of mandatory arrest policies for domestic violence. It was replicated, but only later, and when the replications found mixed support for mandatory arrest, they were largely ignored.[18] Part of the problem is that experiments such as the one in Kansas City are enormously expensive, to the point where replications are almost impossible.

Finally, the findings of available evaluations need to be subject to systematic reviews of studies, or what are called *meta-analyses*. To determine whether or not a policy is effective, policy analysts should systematically review *all* of the available studies. It is no longer sufficient that a policy be based on one study that finds it effective.

Not everyone is completely happy with the movement for evidence-based crime policy. Its aggressive insistence on experimental designs with random assignment tends to devalue other important forms of criminological research. But with respect to policy-related research—which is only one part of the larger field of criminology—it has injected a necessary and healthy element of scientific rigor.

Our Approach to Evaluating Crime Policies

As the evidence-based policy movement argues, there are many policies that are either unsupported by any evidence of effectiveness or that have been found to be either ineffective or actually harmful. One of the major obstacles to finding sensible crime policies is that there are so many *bad ideas*. Especially when crime rates were high and rising even higher, people grasped desperately at any idea that seemed to offer hope. Politicians have eagerly obliged public opinion, offering simplistic solutions that promise quick and dramatic results. One of the most popular policies in the 1990s was the so-called "three strikes" law, providing mandatory life prison sentences to persons convicted of a third felony. Such laws were enacted by 15 states between 1993 and 1994 alone.[19] As we shall see in Chapter 7, however, there is no conclusive evidence that it has been effective in reducing crime, and some evidence that it has simply created new problems.

As we proceed through our examination of crime policy, we will frame our conclusion in terms of a series of propositions. Our first proposition is this:

> ## PROPOSITION 1
> Most current crime control proposals are nonsense.

UNDERSTANDING THE AMERICAN
CRIME PROBLEM

The main reason why most crime policies are nonsense is because people do not understand the nature of the crime problem in this country or how the criminal justice system works. One of the main goals of this book is to help people understand crime and criminal justice so that we can begin to think clearly about crime policy. In a review of public opinion surveys, the Sentencing Project found that the public "consistently misjudges" trends in crime; in the 1990s people continued to believe that crime was rising, even though it was actually falling dramatically. The Sentencing Project also found that people consistently believe that the criminal justice system is far more lenient than it really is.[20] The Gallup Poll consistently finds that only 20 percent of the American people had confidence in the criminal justice in 2008. This was even lower than television news (24 percent) and the public schools (33 percent).[21] A major part of the lack of confidence is that people simply don't know how it really operates. The disconnect between what most people believe and how the justice system actually works is an important point that will arise throughout this book.

America's Two Crime Problems

Your risk of being a crime victim depends a lot on who you are. Most important are your race or ethnicity and your income. The victimization rate for robbery in 2007 was 1.9 per 1,000 for white Americans and 4.9 for African Americans. The burglary rate was 57.6 per 1,000 for the poorest Americans (annual income of less than $7,500), compared with 17.2 for the wealthiest (income of $75,000 or more). Data on homicides provide especially dramatic evidence of the racial disparity in victimization. The number of murders nationally reached an all-time high of 26,250 in 1992. While the national homicide rate has fallen by 33 percent since the early 1990s (from 9.8 per 100,000 in 1991 to 5.6 in 2007), African Americans are still six times more likely to be murdered than whites (19.8 versus 3.3 per 1,000).[22]

In short, many analysts believe that the United States has *two* crime problems: one that affects most white, middle-class Americans and another that affects people of color, the poor, and young people of color in particular.

Very poor neighborhoods have been overwhelmed by crime and drugs. For their residents, whom some analysts call the *underclass*, the quality of daily life worsened significantly in the 1980s. In some neighborhoods the drug trade completely takes over the streets, with open drug use and selling. And despite the crime drop, many of these neighborhoods are still filled with unacceptable levels of violent crime, disorder, and community breakdown.

B o x   1.1   Crime, Race and Ethnicity: Data Problems

One problem that limits our understanding of crime and justice in America is the lack of data on ethnicity. The U.S. Census classifies people by race and also by ethnicity. It is possible to be white by race, and either Hispanic or non-Hispanic in terms of ethnicity. You can also be African American by race, and either Hispanic or non-Hispanic by ethnicity. Both the NCVS and the UCR still use the category of "race," which they divide into "white" and "black." Following traditional practice, Latino Americans are classified as whites. Thus, we do not have data of criminal victimization by ethnicity, and for Latino Americans in particular. The distinctions are important. We know that our behavior varies by race and ethnicity, but we don't have good data on this critical issue.[23]

Elliott Currie, citing the evidence from two different surveys of drug use, extends this point by arguing that we have two drug problems: one involving the majority of the population and the other concentrated in the inner cities.[24] The National Survey on Drug Use and Health (formerly called the National Household Survey on Drug Abuse) reports decreases in drug use since the 1970s. Those data reflect the general population. The Drug Abuse Warning Network (DAWN), which surveys hospital emergency room admissions, reported soaring "mentions" of cocaine use in the late 1980s and persistently high rates in later years. These data, by contrast, reflect the heavy use of certain drugs by particular segments of the population.[25] These data suggest a very serious drug problem for one segment of the population but not for the nation as a whole. (In Chapter 13 we will discuss the different sources of data on drug use in more detail.)

Criminologists Franklin Zimring and Gordon Hawkins argue that the American crime problem is primarily one of violent crime, particularly lethal crime.[26] Comparative victimization surveys consistently indicate that the victimization rates for property crimes in many European countries are actually higher than those in the United States. The burglary and theft rate for England and Wales in 2003–2004 was 3.5 per 1,000, compared with 2.5 in the United States. England and Wales were also higher on assaults and threats (5.8 per 1,000) than the U.S. (4.3 per 1,000).The United States ranked first in sexual assaults in the ICVS data, however, with a rate of 1.4 per 1,000, compared with 0.9 for England and Wales and 0.4 for Germany. The real difference is with *lethal* violence. In 2006, the U.S. homicide rate was more than three times that of Canada (down from four times 15 years earlier), and over six times the rate for Germany. And despite the recent crime drop, the United States still has extremely high rates of lethal violence. Zimring and Hawkins argue that we need to focus our attention on murder rather than burglary, drug use, or other crimes.[27]

B o x 1.2   Lethal Violence: The U.S. vs. The U.K.

The New England Coalition to Prevent Gun Violence has illustrated the extraordinary level of gun-related lethal violence in the U.S. compared with Great Britain. In 2008 there were a grand total of 42 gun-related deaths in Great Britain. The population of the U.S is about five times that of Britain (61 million), so when we multiply their gun deaths by five, we get 210. Compare this with 30,364 gun-related deaths in the U.S. (for 2005), which includes homicides, suicides, and accidental deaths.

$$U.K.: 210 \times 5 = \quad 210 \text{ (Estimated deaths, assuming equal populations)}$$
$$U.S.: \qquad\qquad 30,364 \text{ (Actual deaths)}$$

England, meanwhile, *does* have a crime problem. The International Crime Victim Survey found that it ranked first among all surveyed countries in 2003–2004, with a rate of 3.5 per 1,000, while the United States ranked eighth, with a rate of 2.5 per 1,000. To repeat, other countries have crime problems; the United States is unique with respect to *lethal* violence.

SOURCES: New England Coalition to Prevent Gun Violence, *Great Britain vs. United States in Gun Deaths*, http://necpgv. blogspot.com/. Jan van Dijk, John van Kesteren, and Paul Smit, *Criminal Victimisation in International Perspective: Key Findings from the 2004–2005 ICVS and EU ICS* (New York: United Nations, Office on Drugs and Crime, 2008).

TABLE 1.2   Sorting fact from fiction: Sex offender rearrest rates

MYTH: Violent sex offenders have high recidivism rates
DATA: Released Felony Defendants Rearrested Prior to Case Disposition, 2004

Criminal Charge	Percent Rearrested	Felony Rearrest	Misdemeanor Rearrest
Murder	39	29	10
Rape	6	3	2
Robbery	21	12	9
Burglary	25	18	7
Drug Trafficking	21	14	7

EVIDENCE: Sex offenders (rape, at least) have the lowest reoffending rates
POLICY IMPLICATIONS: Laws designed to control sex offenders through closer surveillance (e.g., sex offender registration laws; community notification) on the assumption that they have high reoffending rates are based on erroneous assumptions

SOURCE: Bureau of Justice Statistics, *Felony Defendants in Large Urban Counties, 2004* (Washington, DC: Department of Justice, 2008).

The Bait and Switch Problem

Zimring and Hawkins also argue that the failure to understand the specific aspects of the American crime problem results in "bait and switch" crime policies. Many policies are simply unrelated to the most serious parts of the crime problem. They are advertised as solutions to the most serious crimes (meaning murder, armed robbery, and rape) but in practice have their most serious impact on less serious crimes (particularly burglary and assaults). The term *bait and switch* comes from the area of consumer fraud, where a retailer advertises a low-priced item to draw customers, but then will not sell the item to them, usually claiming that it is "sold out," and tries to steer them toward buying a higher-priced item. The National Criminal Justice Commission agrees with the bait and switch criticism, pointing out that the war on crime has promised to attack *violent* crime but has mainly resulted in the imprisonment of more nonviolent offenders. Take a look at the data on registered sex offenders in Table 1.2. Sex offenders have the lowest rearrest rate. In California, two-thirds of the "sex-related" parole violations involved victimless offenses, such as not registering as a sex offender or missing a meeting.[28]

As we examine different crime policies in the chapters ahead, we want to make sure that they have an impact on their intended target. This consideration has important implications for incapacitation as a crime control policy, which we will examine in Chapter 7.

WAGING WAR ON CRIME

For almost half a century we have been waging "war on crime." President Lyndon Johnson first declared war on crime in 1965. President Richard Nixon then announced his own war in 1969, and President George H. W. Bush (father of George W. Bush) declared war on drugs on September 5, 1989.[29] Other politicians and policymakers have followed their lead and used the rhetoric of "war" to characterize our crime policy. In the 2000 and 2004 elections, presidential candidates from both major parties were still promising to get tough on crime.

The consequences of the war on crime and drugs have been enormous. The number of prisoners has increased over eightfold, from 196,429 in 1970 to 1,600,00 by 2008. Add in the 730,000 people in local jails, and we have over 2.3 million behind bars. The United States has been on an imprisonment orgy, and as Figure 1.2 indicates, the last 30 years represent a radical break with the past. The incarceration rate rose from 96 per 100,000 in 1970 to 738 in 2006 (state and federal prisoners). This compares with incarceration rates of 107 per 100,000 in Canada, 126 in Australia, and 62 in Japan.[30]

Prisons, as we have indicated, are only part of the story. The national jail population increased almost fivefold between 1979 and 2008, rising from 153,394 to 730,000 inmates. (One reason for the increase in the jail population is that prisons are overcrowded, and local authorities send convicted offenders to jail rather than to prison.) The number of people on probation grew from 1,079,258 adults in 1976 to 4,215,361 by 2007, and the number of adults on parole soared from 156,194 to 799,875 by 2007. Thus, the total number of people "under correctional supervision" by 2007–2008 was almost 7 million.[31]

Several forces have contributed to the imprisonment boom, including some major crime policies that we will look at in this book: mandatory imprisonment laws; "truth in sentencing" laws that require prisoners to serve, for example,

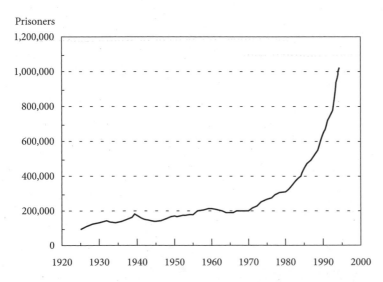

FIGURE 1.2 Sentenced prisoners in state and federal institutions on December 31, 2006.

SOURCE: Bureau of Justice Statistics, Sourcebook of Criminal Justice Statistics—2006. (Washington, DC: Government Printing Office, 2006), p. 551.

85 percent of the sentence; and restrictions on prisoner good time that limit early release. A special problem exists in California where more people enter prison every year because of parole revocation rather than a sentence from a court. These policies all reflect the very punitive pubic attitudes about crime, criminals, and drugs. Most of the growth in prison populations, moreover, is the result of an increase in drug arrests.[32]

The impact of the war on crime on society, and on racial and ethnic minority communities in particular, is one of the main themes of this book. Has the war contributed to the crime drop? Or has it made things worse, increasing the alienation of African American young men in particular? Are harsh punishments for crime morally justified and socially effective, as conservatives such as John J. DiIulio argue, or are they counterproductive as the Sentencing Project and others argue?[33]

Race, Ethnicity, and the War on Crime

Elliott Currie, Jerome Miller, the Sentencing Project, and others argue that the war on crime has made things worse: it has not deterred crime, it is racially biased, and it has contributed to the destruction of inner-city communities and consequently increased the likelihood of juvenile violence. The war on crime has also weighed heavily on the Latino community, with young Latino men being stereotyped as gang members, drug dealers, and illegal immigrants.

Currie and others argue that the war on drugs has been waged primarily against young African American men. The Sentencing Project found that African Americans represented 13 percent of the population, but 35 percent of all people arrested for drug offenses, 55 percent of those convicted, and 74 percent of those sentenced to prison for drug offenses.[34] Yet, the National Survey of Drug Use and Health found only modest differences in reported illicit drug use by race and ethnicity. In 2008, for example, 8.2 percent of whites reported using drugs in the past month compared with 10.1 percent of African Americans. This small difference is far out of line with the huge disparities in arrests and convictions. Meanwhile, only 6.2 percent of Latinos reported using drugs in the past month. The huge disparities in arrest and incarceration for drug offenses, in short are way out of line with the differences in reported illegal drug use.[35]

Jerome Miller characterizes the war on crime as a case of "search and destroy" directed at young African American men.[36] The National Center on Institutions and Alternatives estimates that on any given day, 42 percent of the young black men (ages 18 to 35) in Washington, DC, are under the control of the justice system: either in prison or jail or on probation or parole. The figure for Baltimore was 56 percent. About 75 percent of the Washington, DC, black men were likely to be arrested before they reached age 35.[37] In short, a huge number of African American men are acquiring arrest records as a result of the war on drugs. By 1990, more black men were in prison than in college.

One of the most profound consequences of the war on crime is the loss of the right to vote. Virtually every state strips a convicted felon of the right to vote. The impact on the African American community is enormous, considering that an estimated 10 percent of the adult African American population is under correctional supervision at any given moment. The Sentencing Project estimates that in 2009 about 5.3 million Americans could not vote because of a felony conviction at some point in their lives. In the city of Atlanta, to take just one example, one in seven African American men, or 14 percent, were disenfranchised.[38] We will take a closer look at disenfranchisement and other restrictions imposed on ex-offenders in Chapter 14. The disparate impact of the war on crime has been profound on attitudes toward the justice system, and the result is a deep distrust of the justice system among African Americans.

Discrimination and the *perception* of unfairness contribute to the crime problem. As we will see in Chapter 12, Tom Tyler and other experts on procedural justice argue that a perception of unfairness undermines the legitimacy of the legal system. People are more inclined to obey the law if they feel that the law and legal institutions are fair and treat them with respect. The sense of unfairness and alienation from the justice system, meanwhile, leads to disrespect for the law and a greater likelihood of lawbreaking.[39]

The War on Crime and the Resource Crisis in Criminal Justice

The American criminal justice system faces a serious crisis of resources that affects our ability to effectively reduce crime. The war on crime has overloaded the criminal justice system. "Getting tough" has actually backfired across the country.[40]

Common sense tells us that to be effective, a crime policy has to have sufficient resources. That is true regardless of what your goals. If you believe that police patrol deters crime, you have to have enough officers and patrol cars to effectively accomplish that goal. If you believe that drug treatment programs reduce crime, you have to have enough treatment programs, with enough staff and beds (for residential programs) to get the job done.

The resource crisis appears in almost every part of the criminal justice system.

Public Defenders Offices.   Across the country, public defenders carry an excessive caseload. Many have over 100 cases at any one time, which means that they cannot provide adequate legal representation as required by the Constitution. In Osceola-Orange County, Florida, with the busiest criminal courts in the state, the public defenders office lost 40 positions, including 10 attorneys in recent years. Some costs are also being shifted to defendants. Felony defendants are now charged a $200 fee. A study in Kentucky found that prosecutors have a budget that exceeds $130 million for handling cases involving the indigent; public defenders have only $56 million for the same cases. In Harris County, Texas (Houston), the prosecutor's office has 30 investigators, while there are none for defense attorneys being paid by contract.[41]

What are the consequences of this lack of resources? Public defenders don't have time to work with their clients, seek out potential witnesses, or examine the evidence carefully. (In Missouri in 2004, public defenders had to handle an average of 6.6 cases every working day.) They cannot negotiate plea bargains as well as they should. They make mistakes. Some innocent people are convicted, with the result that the real offenders remain free. People lose trust in the system.

Drug Treatment Programs.   An Urban Institute study found that of 1.5 million offenders at risk for drug abuse or dependency, only about 55,000 actually receive treatment. That is only 3.8 percent of the need. The cost of providing that treatment was estimated at $1 billion—a huge cost, to be sure. But studies have estimated that drug courts and related treatments save $2.21 for every $1.00 invested. The savings are estimated on the basis of the dollar cost of the number of crimes a nontreated offender would commit (including cost to victims, cost of arrest, cost of detention and adjudication, and cost of the sentence). Thus, the $1 billion investment would save $2.21 billion, for a net savings to society of about $1.2 billion annually.[42]

California's Prison and Parole Crisis.   Prisons across the country are overcrowded, some of them dangerously so. The crisis in California is simply the worst in any state by far. California prisons, with 167,000 prisoners in mid-2009, were at almost double their official capacity. A federal judge finally ordered the state to reduce its number of prisoners by 41,000. A state expert panel on adult offender rehabilitation found that among those leaving prison, 50 percent had not participated in any work or rehabilitation program and did not have a work assignment for their entire prison term. Things do not get better on parole. An estimated 56 percent of parolees do not participate in any rehabilitation program.[43]

The resource crisis in California extends to parole officers who had case loads averaging 70 parolees per officer. This is up from 45 per officer in the 1970s; the American Probation and Parole Association recommends 50 per officer. As a result, many parolees receive absolutely no meaningful supervision whatsoever. About 80 percent of the parolees have two 15-minute, face-to-face meetings per month with their parole officers. In the system's least restrictive supervision category, parolees "report" by mailing a post card to their parole officer.[44]

California only makes the situation worse for itself. Because of the combined effect of its determining sentencing law (see Chapters 6 and 7) and parole regulations, most people entering prison every year are parole violators. But 20 percent of them are back in prison for only one month! And many are there for only four months. This is meaningless as "punishment" and creates a huge dollar cost in terms of processing them first as parole violators and then sending them to prison through a revolving door.

Shortages in Police Officers.   The 1994 Violent Crime Control Act provided federal funds to hire 100,000 additional police officers around the country. In the end, about 70,000 were probably hired. This was during a time of economic prosperity, however. The recession of 2008–2009 has had a major impact on local governments, particularly police departments. Many cities have not been able to hire new officers. Justice Department data indicate that the national police population ratio shrank from 2003 to 2007 (from 3.1 to 3.1 per 1,000). To be sure, the decline is statistically small, but it has increased as a result of the 2008–2009 recession, which has hit cities very hard. The Chicago Police Department was 500 officers below its authorized strength in the fall of 2009, for example. In addition, a number of officers who are in the National Guard have been called to duty in the wars in Iraq and Afghanistan. That has produced additional shortages.[45]

Finally, the enormous cost of the war on crime has drained tax dollars from other social needs, such as education, public health, and the economic infrastructure of roads and bridges. In California, for example, state expenditures for corrections were only half the amount spent on higher education in the early 1980s; by 1994, they were equal, at $3.8 billion. Prison budgets had risen dramatically, whereas the state colleges and universities had suffered drastic cuts. If education has historically been an investment in the future of society, then the cuts in education to finance prison represent a *dis*-investment in the future.

A very basic lesson is apparent here: The justice system can handle only so much business. When it is overloaded, serious problems arise. The system does not "collapse" like a building, however. It keeps on going, but only through adjustments that are often undesirable and counterproductive with respect to effective crime control.

The Futility of Waging "War" on Crime.

"War" is the wrong metaphor for crime policies. First, it raises unrealistic expectations, promising a "victory" and an end to the "war." In fact, we will never completely eliminate crime. At best, we will succeed in reducing it, hopefully to the point where it does not destroy entire communities. For the same reason, many medical experts do not like the idea of declaring "war" on cancer or other diseases. Whether the problem is crime or cancer, a realistic and sensible goal is to get it down to some tolerable level.[46]

The war metaphor is also wrong because it suggests that we are fighting a foreign enemy. This leads people to demonize criminals as people apart from the rest of us. To a great extent, this tendency to demonize has encouraged racial and ethnic stereotypes and aggravated the racial polarization of American society. Additionally, the "us versus them" attitude encourages police officers to regard suspects as people who do not have the same rights as other American citizens. Community policing, which emphasizes close working relations between police and citizens, is a far more appropriate approach for a democratic society. Finally, as we have already seen, the current war on crime has had a terrible effect on American society, particularly on racial and ethnic minority communities. These facts lead us to the following proposition:

PROPOSITION 2
Waging "war" is the wrong way to fight crime.

The truth is, we do not face a foreign enemy. We are up against ourselves. We need to deal with our own social institutions, our own values, our own habits, and our own crime control policies. Criminologists Steven F. Messner and Richard Rosenfeld argue that "the sources of crime" in this country lie "in the very same values and behaviors that are conventionally viewed as part of the American success story." The values of material success and individual advancement work for many people, but for others the opportunity to achieve the "American Dream" is blocked. They argue that to deal effectively and responsibly with the crime problem we cannot demonize criminals as "others," but instead need to reexamine how well our institutions serve all people.[47]

The American response to the crime problem resembles the way many people deal with being overweight—by "diet binging." Just as people go on crash diets, lose weight, put it all back on, and then take up another diet fad a year later, so we tend to "binge" on crime control fads. In the 1980s it was "selective incapacitation"; in the 1990s boot camps and "three strikes" laws; today it is offender reentry programs (see Chapter 14). And so it goes. Typically, everyone forgets yesterday's fad without examining whether it really worked. The solution to a weight loss problem does not lie in a miracle cure; instead, it involves difficult long-term changes in one's own behavior: eating less, eating less fattening food, and exercising more. By the same token, we will reduce crime when we make basic changes in all of our social policies that affect families, employment, and neighborhoods. There is no quick, easy, "miracle" cure for crime.

CRIME POLICY: A PLAGUE OF NONSENSE

Americans have trouble thinking clearly about crime. The result is a lot of crime control proposals that are nonsense. Why? The main reason is that we have been overwhelmed by violent crime. Even with the great crime drop, we still have far more violent crime than any other industrialized country. (The qualification about violent crime is important. Many countries have higher rates of property crime: theft, pickpocketing, etc.).[48]

Fear of crime pervades our daily lives like a plague, affecting the way we think, the way we act, the way we respond to one another. Almost half (46 percent) of Americans in 2008 reported that they worried about their home being burglarized when they were not there.[49] (And this is despite the fact that the NCVS reports a steady decline in the household burglary rate over the past 17 years.) It has a corrosive effect on interpersonal relations, making us wary of small acts of friendliness toward strangers. It also distorts the political process, with politicians offering quick-fix solutions that have no realistic hope of reducing crime. Fear and frustration about crime produce irrational thinking. Almost every year some new proposal promises to reduce crime by 30–50 percent. Most of these proposals, we argue, are nonsense.

Even some of the most informed experts on criminal justice are overwhelmed by the problem. When Jerome Miller first sent the manuscript of his book *Search and Destroy* to the publisher, his editor wrote back that it was "too pessimistic"; it had no optimistic recommendations on how to solve the crime problem. Miller admitted that his editor was right; he did not "have many suggestions— and those I do have, aren't likely to be taken."[50] Many other people have had the same problem: an inability to formulate sensible, realistic proposals for reducing crime.

But as we shall see in this book, Miller was indeed too pessimistic. A number of different crime reduction policies have proven to be successful. The results are still modest, and we need more evaluations, but there are some promising approaches. The challenge is to identify policies that work and put them together into a comprehensive approach in which they reinforce each other.

We need to make an important distinction regarding the goals of different reform proposals. Many sensible proposals involve reducing the *harm* done by the criminal justice system. Many experts have made proposals for reducing the harm done by our current sentencing practices. In *Malign Neglect* Michael Tonry offers a specific proposal for reducing racial disparities in sentencing. The Urban Institute has a report with recommendations for treating drug offenders more effectively and reducing crime.[51] Harm reduction, meaning reducing the harm done by the criminal justice system, is a very important and laudable goal. After all, we shouldn't make a bad criminal justice problem worse. The focus in this book, however, is on policies that will reduce *crime*, particularly serious crime.

The Ground Rules

The goal of this book is to identify sensible and effective crime policies. Let's begin by establishing the ground rules. First, we will focus on crime control. We are concerned with policies that will reduce the level of serious crime. We will consider questions of justice and fairness as constraints on crime policy, but those issues are not our primary focus. Effectiveness—defined as reduction in crime—is not the only criterion for a sensible crime control policy. We have limits to what we can do. A democratic society respects the rule of law and standards of justice and fairness, unlike totalitarian societies, which are based on the principle of unlimited government power. It might reduce crime if we just shot all robbers and drug dealers on sight. When an Islamic rebel group took power in Kabul, the capital of Afghanistan, in 1996, the group restored punishments such as stoning to death people guilty of adultery and cutting off the hands of thieves. One criminal was driven through the streets on a truck with an amputated hand and heavy weights holding his jaw open. Such practices, however, violate our standards of decency and due process.

Second, we will focus primarily on the crimes of robbery and burglary. This limited focus helps impose some discipline on our thinking. Too many people evade the hard questions about crime by changing the subject. Liberals often find it difficult to talk about robbery and burglary, changing the subject to victimless crimes such as gambling, marijuana use, and unconventional sexual behavior. Conservatives, meanwhile, focus on celebrated cases (particularly extremely vicious crimes) that have little to do with the routine felonies of robbery and burglary. We will discuss celebrated cases and how they distort our understanding of how the justice system works in Chapter 2.

At several points along the way, we will consider some other crimes to illustrate certain points. An entire section is devoted to drunk driving because this subject provides very useful insights into such issues as police crackdowns, sentencing reform, and deterrence. Domestic violence also illustrates some issues related to deterrence. Chapter 13 covers drugs because it is impossible to talk about crime policy today without addressing drugs and their impact on public attitudes, arrests and prison populations.

Third, this book concentrates on crimes committed by adults. Juvenile crime and delinquency are serious problems that warrant attention, but the world of juvenile justice is a special realm, with its own unique problems, that deserves a separate critical inquiry.

Thinking Clearly about Crime Prevention

As the 1997 University of Maryland report on *Preventing Crime* argues, many people are confused about the term *crime prevention*. The report points out that "the national debate over crime often treats 'prevention' and 'punishment' as mutually exclusive concepts, polar opposites on a continuum of 'soft' versus 'tough' responses to crime."[52] As we explain shortly, this dichotomy generally defines conservatives as the advocates of "tough" policies and liberals as the advocates of "soft" policies.

The Maryland report persuasively argues that this is a false dichotomy. Regardless of their label, all crime policies are designed to prevent crime. Particular policies are simply different means to that end. An allegedly soft treatment program (e.g., outpatient drug abuse counseling) is intended to prevent crime no less than is an allegedly tough sentencing policy (e.g., a three-strikes law). From the standpoint of effective crime prevention, the real issue is not one of intentions or methods but consequences. Which policies reduce crime?

The Question of Reasonable Goals

Our search for sensible and effective crime policies raises a difficult question of criteria. What do we mean by *effective?* Let us say we find a policy that would reduce crime by 5 percent without doing any serious harm. Is that a goal worth pursuing? A 5 percent reduction is not much, given the size of our crime problem. We would still be swamped by murder, robbery, rape, and drug abuse. It would be easy to dismiss that policy as hardly worth the effort, but we should not leap to that conclusion too quickly.

The issue here is one of reasonable goals. In his discussion of gun crimes, Gary Kleck makes a persuasive case in favor of modest goals. We should not expect quick and dramatic changes. Unreasonable expectations lead to disappointment and frustration. Kleck advises thinking in terms of modest goals that can be achieved.[53] In the long run, a sensible approach to crime will probably include a series of different policies, each one focusing on a different aspect of the larger problem and each one producing a modest reduction in crime. The best example, which we will discuss in Chapter 6, involves traffic fatalities. The rate of traffic fatalities has gone down steadily since the 1920s. This is not the result of any single policy (e.g., a tough sentencing law for drunk drivers) but a combination of improvements in roads, automobile design, seat belts, and other changes.

The New Focus on Communities and Crime

The title of Todd Clear's 2007 book makes the point: *Imprisoning Communities.* Judges sentence individuals to prison, but the large impact of America's imprisonment boom is on the communities where convicted offenders lived before going to prison.[54] The most important new development in thinking about crime policy is a focus on the community context. Community policing obviously emphasizes community, as do most problem-oriented policing programs. They are now joined by community prosecution programs that stress the impact of crime on the quality of life in neighborhoods. In the field of corrections, offender reentry programs focus on the community factors that influence ex-offenders' reintegration into society. Successful reentry, moreover, requires the involvement of public and private social service agencies to help ex-offenders become law abiding citizens. Finally, all of these programs are supported by new perspectives in theoretical criminology that examine the collective efficacy of communities to deal with crime through informal means and through partnerships between neighborhood groups and criminal justice agencies.

Clear argues that our policy of mass incarceration has had a devastating impact on communities, and African American communities in particular. Sending so many men from particular neighborhoods to prison breaks up families, weakens the critical social control function of parents, removes positive role models, damages the economic health of communities which are already distressed (by removing potential breadwinners), and undermines the legitimacy of the criminal justice system, which in turn contributes to further law breaking. As crime rises in particular communities, moreover, employed and law-abiding families move out, thereby removing positive role models for those who remain.[55]

All of these factors combine to undermine the *collective efficacy* of neighborhoods: the capacity of ordinary people to work together to solve neighborhood problems. Criminologists increasingly emphasize the importance of informal controls over crime (for that matter, all behavior): intimate partnerships, families, friendship networks, neighborhood ties, and so on. The important point is that the formal criminal justice system is really a last resort when these informal mechanisms fail. This shifts the focus of our inquiry away from the traditional emphasis on police, courts, and corrections and on to families and communities. This argument does not mean that the institutions of the criminal justice system have no immediate role at all. It does mean that we should look at how, for example, the police can strengthen collective efficacy, and how we can end policies that actively damage the critical informal social controls.

Because the new community-focused programs share common elements, we will examine them together in Chapter 14. These common elements include undertaking careful planning and bringing in outside experts, working closely with community groups, developing partnerships with other criminal justice and non–criminal justice agencies, using nontraditional and often non–criminal justice responses (such as civil law remedies), and conducting rigorous evaluations to determine effectiveness. Keep these elements in mind as we examine traditional crime policies in Chapters 5 through 13. The new community-focused programs learn from the weaknesses and failures of those traditional approaches.

GUILTY: LIBERALS AND CONSERVATIVES

Nonsense about crime is politically nonpartisan. Both liberals and conservatives have been guilty of making extravagant promises about crime reduction. In 1967, the President's Crime Commission, representing a liberal perspective, promised "a significant reduction in crime" if its recommendations were "vigorously pursued." In 1975, the conservative James Q. Wilson offered a program that he claimed would reduce serious crime by 30 percent.[56] Neither of these promises were realistic. And over the years other liberals and conservatives have made equally ridiculous promises. Consequently, our third proposition is as follows:

PROPOSITION 3
Both liberals and conservatives are guilty of peddling nonsense about crime.

Crime policies are guided by certain underlying assumptions. Liberals and conservatives begin with different assumptions about crime, the administration of justice, and human nature. To make sense of different crime control proposals, it is helpful to analyze the underlying assumptions of each side.

CRIME CONTROL THEOLOGY

A serious problem with the debate over crime policy is that faith usually triumphs over facts. Both liberals and conservatives begin with certain assumptions that are almost like religious beliefs. Too often, these assumptions are not supported by empirical evidence. We call this phenomenon *Crime Control Theology*.[57]

Most conservatives, for example, believe that the death penalty deters crime. This view persists despite the fact that no evidence conclusively supports it. Most liberals, meanwhile, believe that "treatment" works as a cure for crime and drug abuse, despite considerable evidence on the limited effectiveness of treatment programs.

In *Point Blank*, Gary Kleck points out how people switch sides on the deterrence question to suit their beliefs. Conservatives believe that the death penalty deters crime but then argue that the exclusionary rule will not deter police misconduct. Liberals switch sides in the opposite direction, arguing that the death penalty does not deter crime but that the exclusionary rule does work.[58] This leads us to the following proposition.

PROPOSITION 4
Most crime control ideas rest on faith rather than facts.

Conservative Theology

Crime control theologies represent idealized worlds that express people's highest hopes and deepest fears. Conservative crime control theology envisions a world of discipline and self-control in which people exercise self-restraint and subordinate their personal passions to the common good, and their immediate desires to long-term interests. It is a world of limits and clear rules about human behavior.

Conservative crime control theology emphasizes personal responsibility. The problem is that criminals lack self-control. They succumb to their passions and break the rules. They kill because they cannot control their anger. They steal because they want something now and are unable to defer gratification. Poverty or other social conditions are no excuse for crime, in the conservative view. People remain poor because they lack the self-discipline to get an education, find a job, and steadily try to improve themselves. Conservatives are fond of pointing to the many individuals who were born in poverty but worked hard and became rich and successful.

Free will, rational choice, and moral responsibility reign supreme in conservative crime control theology. People are responsible for their own fate; they *choose* to commit crime. James Q. Wilson and Richard J. Herrnstein argue: "At any given moment, a person can choose between committing a crime and not committing it."[59] A good example of a policy based on rational choice theory is the "Just Say No" antidrug campaign. It assumes that all we have to do is persuade people to make the decision not to use drugs.

Rational choice theory holds that people weigh the relative risks and rewards of committing crime. If the risk of punishment is low or the punishments are relatively light, more people will tend to commit crime. If the chance of being caught and punished is high and the punishments are relatively severe, fewer people will choose to commit crime. Thus, the certainty and severity of punishment directly affect the crime rate.[60]

In conservative crime control theology, punishment has both a moral and a practical element. Because criminals choose to offend, they deserve punishment. They are morally responsible for their actions. Rules are the basis of a civil society, and rule breaking should be punished. This is called *retribution*, or *desert*. James Q. Wilson summed it up in a frequently quoted statement: "Wicked people exist. Nothing avails except to set them apart from innocent people."[61] Conservatives also believe that punishment shapes future behavior through the process of *deterrence*. There are two categories of deterrence. *Specific* deterrence is directed at the individual offender, teaching him or her that bad actions have unpleasant consequences. *General* deterrence is directed at the general population, teaching by example.

Conservatives are deeply ambivalent about the role of government in controlling crime. William J. Bennett, John J. DiIulio, Jr., and John P. Walters argue that the "root cause" of crime is "moral poverty" (as opposed to material poverty). Too many children grow up not learning right from wrong. Moral health, they argue, is nurtured primarily by strong, two-parent families, religious training, and social institutions that reinforce the right values. "Can government supply manner and morals?" they ask. "Of course it cannot," they answer. People are socialized into law-abiding behavior primarily by private institutions, beginning with the family. But, these conservatives argue that, government does have an important role to play in providing effective examples of holding people responsible for their behavior. Thus, the swift, certain punishment of offenders helps breed moral health. Moral poverty is fostered by the failure of the criminal justice system to punish criminals. Thus, while government cannot do everything, it can do something.[62]

Underlying conservative crime control theology is an idealized image of the patriarchal family. Punishment resembles parental discipline. Minor misbehavior is greeted with a gentle warning, a second misstep earns a sterner reprimand, and serious wrongdoing receives a severe punishment. The point is to teach the wisdom of correct behavior by handing out progressively harsher sanctions and threatening even more unpleasant punishment if the behavior continues.

The real world of crime and justice, unfortunately, does not work like this idealized family. It is filled with some very incorrigible children. Some are so deeply alienated from society that they do not respect the overall structure of authority. Punishment, in fact, may only distance them further, undermining the legitimacy of the system (see Chapter 12). Some observers believe, for example, that arrest and imprisonment are such common experiences in some poor racial and ethnic minority neighborhoods that they have lost whatever deterrent threat they might have once had.[63]

John Braithwaite's provocative book *Crime, Shame, and Reintegration* offers a useful perspective on this problem. Braithwaite describes the process of "reintegrative shaming" as being very much like the way a family handles someone who breaks the rules. But his theory also clearly indicates that informal sanctions work when close social bonds link the sanctioner and the sanctioned, and where no great differences in values exist in the community—that is, when the relationship more closely resembles a family.[64]

This is the heart of the problem. The family analogy breaks down in the real world because we have a heterogeneous and fragmented society, characterized by great differences in wealth, race, ethnicity, religion, and lifestyles. Our society is anything but a tightly knit community with shared values. Braithwaite's theory, in fact, is a good explanation of why informal, family-style sanctions do not work in our society. His description of the conditions under which a system of reintegrative shaming can work is actually a very accurate description of a seventeenth-century New England village, where that approach to crime control was used very effectively.[65]

The limits of reintegrative shaming lend further support to the importance of a community orientation and the interdependency of institutions and policies emphasized by the University of Maryland *Preventing Crime* report. Effective reintegration requires a reasonably healthy community. Achieving a healthy community, in turn, probably requires a series of crime prevention programs directed toward a number of different institutions: families, schools, the local labor market, and so on.

Conservatives explain the failure of punishment to work by focusing on problems in the criminal justice system. Punishment, they say, is not certain or severe enough. Too many loopholes allow criminals to beat the system: the exclusionary rule, the Miranda warning, the insanity defense, plea bargaining, and so on. The idea that many criminals "beat the system" and "get off easy" is an article of faith in conservative crime control theology. Close these loopholes, ensure certainty of punishment, and we can reduce crime. Longer prison terms and the death penalty, meanwhile, will increase the deterrent effect and reduce crime. We will take a close look at this idea in several of the chapters ahead.

Liberal Theology

Liberal crime control theology emphasizes the social context of crime. According to liberals, criminal behavior is largely the result of social influences such as the family, the peer group, the neighborhood, economic opportunities, and discrimination. Much criminological theory, such as Shaw and McKay's social disorganization theory, reflects this view.[66]

Liberal crime policy seeks to alter social influences that are associated with crime. Rehabilitation programs, for example, are designed to provide a structured set of influences—job counseling, substance abuse treatment—designed to encourage law-abiding behavior. Liberals favor community-based alternatives to imprisonment because they represent a normal social environment compared with the abnormal environment of prison.

Liberals are as guilty of wishful thinking as are conservatives. A fundamental article of faith in liberal crime control theology is the optimistic belief that people's behavior *can* be reshaped through some kind of formal treatment program. The history of prison and correctional reform is the story of a continuing search for the Holy Grail of rehabilitation: a program that will truly reform offenders. The people who invented the prison in the nineteenth century thought that that institution would do the job.[67] When it had obviously failed, reformers invented parole and the indeterminate sentence, advertising them as the magic keys to rehabilitation. When these measures did not solve the problem of crime, reformers came up with new variations (group counseling, intensive supervision, and so forth). None of these programs has demonstrated consistent effectiveness.

If conservatives refuse to face the facts about the failure of punishment, liberals refuse to look at the sad history of the failure of rehabilitation. Faith continues to survive in the face of repeated failure. It is also an article of faith among liberals that the United States is the most punitive country in the world. We do, in fact, lock up more people than any other country. Our current incarceration rate of 738 per 100,000 leads the world (including both prisons and jails). James Lynch's research offers a valuable comparative perspective on this figure. Using arrests as a baseline, he notes that the probabilities of an offender's going to prison are only slightly different in the United States, Canada, England, and West Germany. In this regard, we are no more punitive than most other countries. We do, however, give much longer prison sentences. Our incarceration rate is greater primarily because we have more serious crime than these other countries.[68]

If conservatives believe that most of our problems are the result of loopholes that let too many people off easy, liberals are guilty of blaming everything on overly harsh punishments.

Liberals are ambivalent on the question of individual responsibility. Although they emphasize the importance of social conditions in causing crime and reject the conservative preoccupation with individual responsibility, they cannot completely ignore the role of individual choice. Rehabilitation programs, in fact, are designed to influence individuals to make different (and better) choices. In the realm of the public policy debate, however, liberals tend to downplay the element of individual responsibility.

A Word about Rules

One way to distinguish between conservatives and liberals with respect to crime policy is their attitude toward *rules*. Everyone believes in rules and their application in a consistent fashion. This is what people mean when they refer to the "rule of law."

Conservatives and liberals mainly disagree over which set of rules to emphasize. In criminal justice, we have two basic sets: criminal law and criminal procedure. The substantive *criminal law* is a set of rules governing everyone's behavior. It defines certain behavior as criminal and specifies the penalty for breaking the rules. *Criminal procedure*, on the other hand, is a set of rules governing criminal justice officials. It tells them what they may not do (e.g., conduct unreasonable searches and seizures) and what they must do (e.g., bring the suspect before a magistrate without unnecessary delay).[69]

Conservatives emphasize the rules of the criminal law. Harming a person or taking someone else's property violates the basic standards of a decent society. Anyone who violates these rules should be punished. Liberals tend to emphasize the rules of criminal procedure. A free society is one that strictly limits the potentially awesome power of government officials.

One way to understand the difference between liberal and conservative attitudes toward rules is to recognize what each side sees as its worst nightmare. For conservatives, unchecked criminality leads to anarchy and the death of freedom.

For liberals, unchecked government power leads to tyranny and the death of freedom. The difference is really a question of what represents the greatest threat to freedom. Both sides are ambivalent about rule breaking. Conservatives tend to be willing to excuse violations of the rules of procedure to control crime. They will overlook the unreasonable search if it helps convict a criminal. Liberals, on the other hand, are more concerned about official rule breaking. They are willing to see a criminal suspect go free if a police officer or some other official has made a serious mistake. These differences are not absolute, of course. They are really matters of emphasis. Conservatives do not endorse gross abuses by the police, and liberals do not endorse crime.

The classic statement of the difference between conservatives and liberals on this issue is Herbert Packer's essay on the "two models of the criminal process."[70] Conservatives embrace the *crime control model*, which puts a high priority on the effective control of crime. To this end, they are willing to grant officials considerable leeway, not restricting them with a lot of rules. Liberals prefer the *due process model*, in which the highest priorities are fair treatment and the presumption of innocence. Formal rules (due process guarantees) are designed to achieve these goals.

Ideological Confusion: Switching Sides

The conservative/liberal dichotomy is a useful way to think about crime policy. It helps identify the basic assumptions that underlie different policies. In the last few years, however, this dichotomy is not quite as sharp as it was a few years ago. Strange things have been happening. Some conservatives have adopted traditional liberal policies, and many liberals have embraced traditional conservative ideas. Understanding the crime debate today requires sorting our way through this ideological confusion.

One major change involves the issue of legalizing drugs. Decriminalization has traditionally been a proposal by liberals. They have argued that we should not criminalize behavior that does not harm others. Moreover, criminalizing a lot of behavior often tends to make things worse, by overloading the criminal justice system, encouraging corruption, and failing to respond effectively to what are really social and medical problems. Surprisingly, many prominent conservatives endorse legalizing drugs. The most prominent is the writer and television talk show host William F. Buckley. We will examine the arguments in favor of drug legalization in Chapter 13. For the moment, it is important to note that some conservatives have switched sides and adopted a traditional liberal position.

Also, the conservative administration of George W. Bush has strongly supported offender reentry programs (see Chapter 14), which involve the traditional liberal idea of reintegrating offenders into society.

Meanwhile, many liberals have adopted some conservative crime control proposals. The best example is former President Bill Clinton. The 1994 Violent Crime Control Act, which he supported, calls for more police and longer prison sentences. In the 1996 presidential election campaign, political observers said that Clinton had moved to the right and embraced the traditional Republican position on crime. In short, the ideological lineup on crime control policies has become very muddled. Nonetheless, it is still possible to identify a set of crime policies that, because of their underlying assumptions, can be classified as conservative and another set that can be classified as liberal. These categories will help us analyze the different policies we will consider in this book.

CONCLUSION

Crime is a serious problem in the United States. The recent dramatic reductions in the crime rate still leave a problem of violent crime that is far higher than in other industrialized countries. Unfortunately, we do not have many good ideas about how to solve the crime problem. In this initial chapter, we have tried to sketch out some of the complexity of the U.S. crime problem. We have also indicated briefly why so many crime control policies are worthless. In the chapters that follow, we will develop these themes in more detail. The next two chapters take a closer look at how the criminal justice system actually works. Then we will turn our attention to specific crime control proposals. As we already indicated, our basic goal is to find some crime control policies that make sense and that are supported by persuasive evidence.

NOTES

1. Bureau of Justice Statistics, *Sourcebook of Criminal Justice Statistics Online*. Check the most recent data at "Estimated Number and Rate of violent and property victimizations." www.albany/sourcebook/pdf.

2. San Diego Police Department, "San Diego Historical Crime Rates per 1,000 Population, 1960–2008." www.sandiego.gov/police/. "Homicides Near Record Low Rate in New York City," *New York Times*, December 29, 2009. "L.A. is Latest City to See Crime Drop," The Wall Street Journal, January 8, 2010.

3. Although a little dated, the best summary of these trends is Marc Miringoff and Marque-Luisa Miringoff, *The Social Health of the Nation: How America Is Really Doing* (New York: Oxford University Press, 1999). Check the *Statistical Abstract of the United States* (annual), or other Web resources for the most recent data.

4. Franklin E. Zimring, *The Great American Crime Decline* (New York: Oxford University Press, 2007). See especially Chapter 5, "Which Twin Has the Toni? Some Statistical Lessons from Canada," pp. 107–134.

5. Ibid., pp. 120–121.

6. Alfred Blumstein and Joel Wallman, eds., *The Crime Drop in America* (New York: Cambridge University Press, 2000), p. 11.

7. Ibid.

8. Jeremy Travis and Michelle Waul, *Reflections on the Crime Decline: Lessons for the Future?* (Washington, DC: Urban Institute, 2002). Available on the Urban Institute website.

9. Steven D. Levitt, "Understanding Why Crime Fell in the 1990s: Four Factors That Explain the Decline and Six That Do Not," *Journal of Economic Perspectives*, 18 (Winter 2004): 163–190.

10. Zimring, *The Great American Crime Decline*, pp. 85–103.

11. Nick Tilley and Gloria Laycock, *Working Out What to Do: Evidence-Based Crime Reduction* (London: Home Office, 2002). www.homeoffice.gov.uk.

12. Coalition for Evidence-Based Policy [CEBP], *Bringing Evidence-Driven Progress to Crime and Substance-Abuse Policy: A Recommended Federal Strategy* (December 2003). Available on the CEBP website.

13. *Remarks of the Honorable Deborah J. Daniels, Assistant Attorney General of Justice Programs, at the National Forum on Evidence-Based Crime and Substance Abuse Policy*, Washington, DC, June 14, 2004.

14. General Accounting Office, Letter to Senator Richard Durbin, January 15, 2003, "Subject: Youth Illicit Drug Use Prevention: DARE Long Term Evaluations and Federal Efforts to Identify Effective Programs." www.gao.gov/new.items/do3172r.pdf.

15. Joan McCord, "Cures That Harm: Unanticipated Outcomes of Crime Prevention Programs," in David Weisburd, Anthony Petrosino, and Cynthia Lum, eds., "Assessing Systematic Evidence in Crime and Justice: Methodological Concerns and Empirical Outcomes," Special Issue, *The Annals* 587 (May 2003): 16–30.

16. Ibid. James O. Finckenauer, *Scared Straight and the Panacea Phenomenon* (Englewood Cliffs, NJ: Prentice-Hall, 1982).

17. Lawrence W. Sherman, Denise C. Gottfredson, Doris L. MacKenzie, et al., *Preventing Crime: What Works, What Doesn't, What's Promising* (Washington, DC: Government Printing Office, 1997), pp. 2. NCJ 171676.

18. Lawrence W. Sherman, *Policing Domestic Violence* (New York: The Free Press, 1992). Christopher D. Maxwell, Joel H. Garner and Jeffrey A Fagan, *The Effects of Arrest on Intimate Partner Violence: New Evidence from the Spouse Assault Replication Program* (Washington, DC: Justice Department, 2001). NCJ 188199.

19. Ashley Nellis and Ryan S. King, *No Exit: The Expanding Use of Life Sentences in America* (Washington, DC: The Sentencing Project, 2009).

20. The Sentencing Project, *Crime, Punishment and Public Opinion: A Summary of Recent Studies and Their Implications for Sentencing Policy* (Washington, DC: The Sentencing Project, n.d.). Available on the Sentencing Project website.

21. Bureau of Justice Statistics, *Sourcebook of Criminal Justice Statistics Online*, Table 2.10.2008.

22. Check the NCJRS website for the most recent victimization survey data. Highlights and past data are also available in the *Sourcebook of Criminal Justice Statistics Online*. www.albany.edu/sourcebook/.

23. These issues are discussed at greater length in Samuel Walker, Cassia Spohn and Miriam DeLone, *The Color of Justice: Race, Ethnicity, and Crime in America*, 4th ed. (Belmont, CA: Thomson, 2007), pp. 5–16.

24. Elliott Currie, *Reckoning: Drugs, the Cities, and the American Future* (New York: Hill and Wang, 1992).

25. Department of Health, Education, and Welfare, *Drug Abuse Warning Network, 2006: National Estimates of Drug-Related Emergency Department Visits* (Washington, DC: SAMSA, 2008).

26. Franklin E. Zimring and Gordon Hawkins, *Crime Is Not the Problem: Lethal Violence in America* (New York: Oxford University Press, 1997). James Lynch, "Crime in International Perspective," in James Q. Wilson and Joan Petersilia, eds., *Crime* (San Francisco: ICS Press, 1995), pp. 11–38.

27. Jan van Dijk, John van Kesteren, and Paul Smit, *Criminal Victimisation in International Perspective: Key Findings from the 2004–2005 ICVS and EU ICS* (New York: United Nations Office on Drugs and Crime, 2008). Zimring and Hawkins, *Crime Is Not the Problem*, chapter 4.

28. Ryken Gratter, Joan Petersilia, and Jeffrey Lin, *Parole Violations and Revocations in California* (Washington, DC: Department of Justice, 2008). www.ncjrs.gov/pdffiles1/nij/grants/224521.pdf.

29. Samuel Walker, *Popular Justice: A History of American Criminal Justice*, 2nd ed. (New York: Oxford University Press, 1998), pp. 180–211.

30. Christopher Hartney, *U.S. Rates of Incarceration: a Global Perspective* (Oakland, CA: National Council on Crime and Delinquency, 2006).

31. Bureau of Justice Statistics, *Probation and Parole in the United States, 2007: Statistical Tables* (Washington, DC: Department of Justice, 2009). www.ojp.usdoj.gov/bjs/pub/pdf/ppus07st.pdf.

32. Gratter, Petersilia, and Lin, *Parole Violations and Revocations in California.*

33. William J. Bennett, John J. DiIulio, Jr., and John P. Walters, *Body Count* (New York: Simon and Schuster, 1996). Marc Mauer, *Lessons of the "Get Tough" Movement in the United States* (Washington, DC: The Sentencing Project, 2004).

34. Jerome G. Miller, *Search and Destroy: African American Males in the Criminal Justice System* (New York: Cambridge University Press, 1996).

35. U.S. Department of Health and Human Services, *Results from the 2008 National Survey of Drug Use and Health: National Findings* (Washington, DC: SAMSA, 2009).

36. Miller, *Search and Destroy*, p. 7.

37. National Center on Institutions and Alternatives, *Hobbling a Generation: African American Males in the District of Columbia's Criminal Justice System* (Alexandria, VA: National Center on Institutions and Alternatives, 1992).

38. The Sentencing Project, "Request for a Thematic Hearing on the Discriminatory Effects of Felony Disenfranchisement Laws, Policies and Practices in the Americas," September 8, 2009. www.sentencingproject.org.

39. Tom R. Tyler, *Why People Obey the Law* (New Haven: Yale University Press, 1990).

40. Marc Mauer, *Lessons of the "Get Tough" Movement in the United States* (Washington, DC: The Sentencing Project, 2004).

41. The Constitution Project, *Justice Denied: America's Continuing Neglect of Our Constitutional Right to Counsel* (Washington, DC: The Constitution Project, 2009).

42. Avinash Singh Bhati, John K. Roman, and Aaron Chalfin, *To Treat or Not to Treat: Evidence on the Prospects for Expanding Treatment to Drug-Involved Offenders* (Washington, DC: The Urban Institute, 2008). http://www.urban.org/url.cfm?ID=411645.

43. Gratter, Petersilia, and Lin, *Parole Violations and Revocations in California.*

44. Ibid.

45. Check the *Sourcebook* for data on police-population ratios. http://www.albany.edu/sourcebook/.

46. One of the best early discussions of the harmful effect of declaring "war" on crime is the classic essay, Egon Bittner, "The Police and the 'War on Crime,'" in Egon Bittner, *Aspects of Police Work* (Boston: Northeastern University Press, 1990), pp. 89–232.

47. Steven F. Messner and Richard Rosenfeld, *Crime and the American Dream*, 3rd ed. (Belmont, CA: Wadsworth, 2001).

48. See the reports from the International Crime Victimization Survey [ICVS]. www.unodc.org.

49. Gallup Poll data, "Respondents Reporting Concern About Crime Victimization," 2008, cited in *Sourcebook of Criminal Justice Statistics Online*.

50. Jerome G. Miller, *Search and Destroy: African American Males in the Criminal Justice System* (New York: Cambridge University Press, 1996).

51. Michael Tonry, *Malign Neglect* (New York: Oxford University Press, 1995). Bhati, Roman, and Chalfin, *To Treat or Not to Treat: Evidence on the Prospects for Expanding Treatment to Drug-Involved Offenders*.

52. Sherman et al., *Preventing Crime*.

53. Gary Kleck, *Point Blank: Guns and Violence in America* (New York: Aldine de Gruyter, 1991), pp. 432–433.

54. Todd R. Clear, *Imprisoning Communities: How Mass Incarceration Makes Disadvantaged Neighborhoods Worse* (New York: Oxford University Press, 2007).

55. Ibid. See especially Chapter 7 on "The Impact of Incarceration on Community Safety," pp. 149–174.

56. President's Commission on Law Enforcement and Administration of Justice, *The Challenge of Crime in a Free Society* (Washington, DC: Government Printing Office, 1967), p. vi. James Q. Wilson, *Thinking About Crime*.

57. George C. Thomas and David Edelman, "An Evaluation of Conservative Crime Control Theology," *Notre Dame Law Review* 63 (1988): 123–160.

58. Kleck, *Point Blank*.

59. James Q. Wilson and Richard J. Herrnstein, *Crime and Human Nature: The Definitive Study of the Causes of Crime* (New York: Simon and Schuster, 1985), p. 44.

60. But see the article Wilson coauthored with Allan Abrahamse, "Does Crime Pay?" *Justice Quarterly* 9 (September 1992): 359–377.

61. Wilson, *Thinking About Crime*, p. 209.

62. Bennett, et al., *Body Count*, p. 205.

63. See the discussion of this point in Daniel S. Nagin, "Criminal Deterrence Research at the Outset of the Twenty-First Century," in Michael Tonry, ed., *Crime and Justice: A Review of Research*, vol. 23 (Chicago: University of Chicago Press, 1998), pp. 4–5.

64. John Braithwaite, *Crime, Shame, and Reintegration* (New York: Cambridge University Press, 1989). John Braithwaite, "Restorative Justice: Assessing Optimistic and Pessimistic Accounts," in Michael Tonry, ed., *Crime and Justice: A Review of Research*, vol. 25 (Chicago: University of Chicago Press, 1999), pp. 1–127.

65. Clifford R. Shaw and Henry D. McKay, *Juvenile Delinquency in Urban Areas* (Chicago: University of Chicago Press, 1942).

66. Lawrence M. Friedman, *Crime and Punishment in American History* (New York: Basic Books, 1993). Walker, *Popular Justice*, chap. 1.

67. David J. Rothman, *The Discovery of the Asylum* (Boston: Little, Brown, 1971).

68. Lynch, "Crime in International Perspective."

69. On the subject of rules and discretion, see Samuel Walker, *Taming the System: The Control of Discretion in American Criminal Justice, 1950–1990* (New York: Oxford University Press, 1993).

70. Herbert L. Packer, "Two Models of the Criminal Process," in *The Limits of the Criminal Sanction* (Stanford, CA: Stanford University Press, 1968), chap. 8.

2

Models of Criminal Justice

The triumph of faith over facts requires a willful disregard of the realities of crime and criminal justice. Many people believe what they want to believe, regardless of the facts. Part of the problem is that the American criminal justice system is so complex. We actually have over 50 separate criminal justice systems (50 state systems, the federal system, Native American justice systems), which include 18,769 separate state and local law enforcement agencies. Our state court systems are all structured differently. Take a look at the Bureau of Justice Statistics (BJS) report *State Court Organization*.[1] In addition, criminal codes vary across the country. Punishments for different crimes are not the same. Assisted suicide is a crime in most states, but not in Oregon. Same-sex marriage is against the law in most states, but it is legal in Iowa and several other states.

The day-to-day administration of justice is even more complex than the formal machinery of the justice system. To the casual observer, things often seem chaotic. Many important decisions are made in informal, "low-visibility" settings—the arrest on the street, the plea bargain negotiated in the court hallway. Even many experts are mystified by some of the important features of our criminal justice system. After several decades of research, we now have a reasonably good picture of police discretion and plea bargaining, but other important decisions are still hidden. We have only recently gained a good picture of traffic stop decisions. What factors go into the decision? The driving behavior alone? The condition of the car? The setting, such as the neighborhood? The race, ethnicity, or gender of the driver? Or just some hunch or feeling that something is not right? The lack of good data and analysis leads to misunderstanding and myth. Consequently, our next proposition is as follows:

PROPOSITION 5
**Most crime control ideas are based on false assumptions
about how the criminal justice system works.**

Illustration by Frank Irwin, © Wadsworth, Cengage Learning.

Two attitudes dominate thinking about the administration of criminal justice: the Old Idealism and the New Cynicism. Neither helps explain how the system works.

The Old Idealism is the classic civics-book picture of justice. In this scenario, diligent and hardworking officials enforce the law as it is written in the statutes; a person who commits a crime is duly arrested and prosecuted for that offense; if convicted, he or she receives the prescribed punishment. It is an adversarial system of justice that determines the truth of guilt or innocence through a public contest between prosecution and defense, overseen by an impartial judge. Although inspiring, this version of the criminal process does not describe the reality of our justice system.

The New Cynicism is a mirror image of the Old Idealism. It portrays a chaotic criminal justice system in which there is neither law, nor order, nor justice. Police discretion is completely out of control: Officers arrest whomever they want, use force without provocation, and so on. Prosecutors plea bargain wildly, letting guilty people get off while innocent people are railroaded into prison. Defense attorneys and prosecutors are friends and cut deals to suit each other's needs.[2] Sentencing is totally arbitrary: There is no rhyme or reason why some people go to prison and others get probation. Parole boards grant or deny release without any rational or scientific basis for their decisions. Finally, the New Cynicism holds that the entire criminal justice system is pervaded with discrimination against people of color.[3]

The New Cynicism comes in two versions. Conservative cynics see irrational decision making undermining effective crime control. Criminals are not punished for their crimes: Either they are not arrested, or they get their charges dropped, or they obtain early parole release. Crafty defense lawyers manipulate the rules of criminal procedure to beat the system. Liberal cynics, on the other hand, believe that the apparent chaos of the system hides systematic discrimination. The poor are punished while "respectable" offenders get off easy; African Americans and Hispanic Americans are the victims of systematic discrimination.

In our search for effective crime policies, our challenge is to reject old myths and to find the truth about the justice system. Undeniably, much decision making *is* irrational. Many offenders *do* escape punishment: The risk of being arrested even for drunk driving, for example, is extremely low. There is racial discrimination in the system: The African American who murders a white person is far more likely to be sentenced to death than the white person who murders an African American.

But neither version of the New Cynicism adequately explains how the justice system handles *routine cases on a day-to-day basis*. That is the unrelenting focus of our inquiry. This chapter argues that most of the time, the system operates in a fairly consistent and predictable manner. Not necessarily in a good manner; just a predictable one. Much criminal justice research supports this view. Donald Black and others, for example, have found predictable patterns in police arrest discretion. Studies of plea bargaining have found that about 80 percent of the outcomes were predictable if the seriousness of the offense and the defendant's prior record were known in advance.[4]

Despite a high degree of predictability, the justice system is filled with paradoxes and inconsistencies. There is much truth in the comment that "the problem is not that our system is too lenient, or too severe; sadly, it is both."[5] Years ago, Norval Morris and Michael Tonry argued that we simultaneously send too many people to prison and give others meaningless forms of probation with little supervision: "We are both too lenient and too severe."[6] This paradox is a key to understanding how our criminal justice system really works.

Policing offers a concrete example of the contradictions in the administration of justice. In the same city, in the same precinct, on the same night, within the space of an hour, a pair of police officers both *over*enforce and *under*enforce the law: They may be overly aggressive toward a young African American man hanging out on a street corner, and then within an hour not make an arrest in a domestic violence incident a few blocks away, denying the victim the protection of the law.[7] Sentencing offers additional examples. Some people with multiple drunk driving convictions manage to avoid mandatory prison terms, while someone arrested for possession of a small amount of drugs is sentenced to 25 years in prison. In terms of the relative harm to society of the two offenses, this inconsistency makes no sense, but it does happen.

THE CRIME COMMISSION'S MODEL

To help understand how the justice system works, social scientists have constructed models of the system. The first and most famous model (Figure 2.1) was developed over 40 years ago by the President's Crime Commission (officially the President's Commission on Law Enforcement and Administration of Justice).[8]

The Commission's most important contribution was to introduce the "systems" approach to the study of criminal justice. Today, we take it for granted, but it was something very new back in 1967. Previously, people thought in terms of separate justice agencies that had little relationship to each other. The systems approach helps us understand how different parts of the justice system interact with each other in complex ways.

The Crime Commission's model accomplished exactly what models are designed to do: provide a conceptual framework, or paradigm, that helps (1) identify general patterns, (2) define problems, and (3) focus research and policy planning. The systems model focuses attention on the flow of cases among agencies, the interrelationships among agencies (or "components" of the system), and the pervasiveness of discretionary decision making throughout the system.[9] Once the model identified the pervasiveness of discretion, researchers studied the factors that influence those decisions. Today we have a better understanding of why things happen the way they do. To take one example, we now understand that plea bargains are not the result of "bad" people, but the result of sociological factors such as managing the case workload. The systems approach also emphasizes the dynamic relationship among components of the system and how decisions at one point (say, the prosecutor) affect decisions "upstream" (the police) and "downstream" (the judge).

One of the best recent examples of how one part of the system affects decisions in another part involves California parole revocations. More than half of the California county jails have "caps" on the number of inmates. Until 2009, the state prisons did not. Thus, when parolees commit new crimes, many of the cases are handled by parole revocation—which sends the parolees back to state prison—rather than by the prosecution, which would have the parolees spend time in the local jail awaiting trial.[10]

The Crime Commission's model has serious limitations, however. Research on criminal justice suggests an alternative model.

THE CRIMINAL JUSTICE WEDDING CAKE

The major shortcoming of the Crime Commission's model is that it portrays a single justice system that handles all cases alike. Our alternative model is a four-layer wedding cake that focuses our attention on important variations in how cases are handled according to their seriousness (Figure 2.2). The wedding cake model was first developed by Lawrence Friedman and Robert V. Percival in *The Roots of Justice,* a history of criminal justice in Alameda County, California, between 1870 and 1910. Additional support, based on contemporary evidence, is found in Michael and Don Gottfredson's *Decision Making in Criminal Justice.*[11]

The wedding cake model emphasizes two points. First, there are significant differences *between* types of cases, based primarily on the seriousness of the offense, the offender's prior record, and the relationship between the victim and the offender. Second, there are fairly consistent patterns of disposition *within* each category.

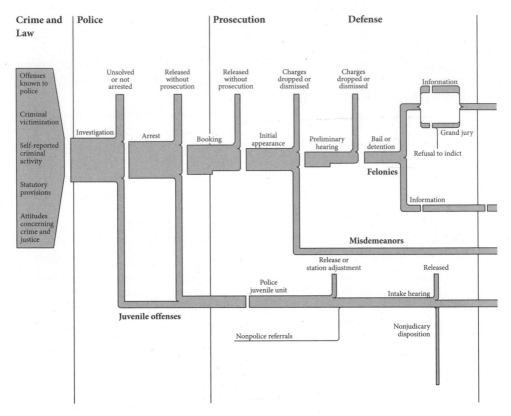

FIGURE 2.1 The Crime Commission's model of the criminal justice system.

SOURCE: President's Commission on Law Enforcement and Administration of Justice, Task Force Report: Science and Technology (Washington, DC: Government Printing Office, 1967) pp. 58–59.

Celebrated Cases: The Top Layer

At the top of the wedding cake is a very small layer of "celebrated cases." Every year the news is dominated by a celebrated case involving either a famous person or a particularly gruesome crime. In 2009, the country was horrified by the case of Philip Garrido, who kidnapped 11-year-old Jaycee Lee Dugard in 1991, held her prisoner for 18 years in his back yard, raped her, and fathered her two children. We will examine shortly the questions raised by this terrible case.

Celebrated cases are different from other cases in several respects. First, they usually involve the *full criminal process,* including that rare event, the criminal trial. (One of the most famous examples is O. J. Simpson's 1995 trial for murdering his wife.) In a trial, we get to see fundamental issues contested in public view: the sanity of the defendant; the admissibility of the evidence; the credibility of the witnesses; and the competence of the prosecutor, defense attorney, and judge. Trials are dramatic events, filled with tense cross-examination and suspense about the outcome. They are very rare events, however. Most criminal cases never go to trial, and in fact many are dismissed without prosecution.[12]

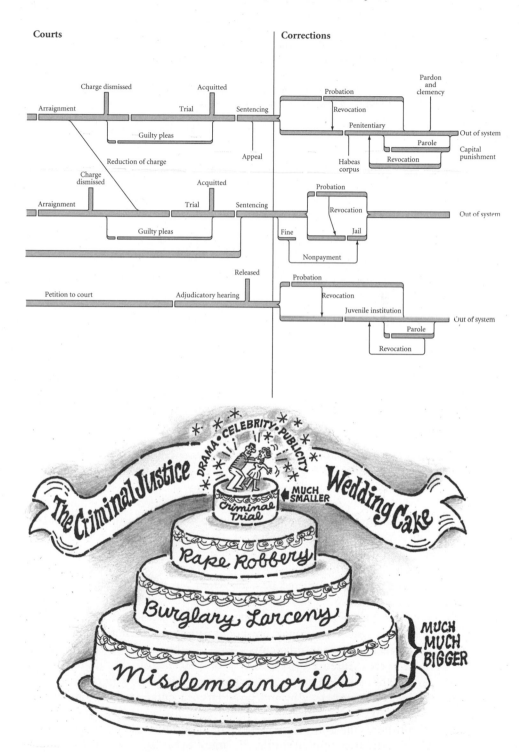

FIGURE 2.2   The criminal justice wedding cake.

Illustration by Frank Irwin, © Wadsworth, Cengage Learning.

B o x 2.1   Fact vs. Fiction: How Dangerous are our Schools?

Celebrated cases are very rare, but they distort our perceptions of how the justice system works. Ask yourself, How often is someone kidnapped, raped, and held prisoner for 18 years? The shocking Columbine High School massacre on April 20, 1999, in which two students shot and killed 13 students and faculty, left a deep imprint on public consciousness. Many people believe that schools are violent and dangerous places and that violence is increasing. The 2008 BJS study of School Crime and Safety presents a very different picture. The number of students murdered between 1992 and 2007 has fluctuated from year to year, but remained basically stable, ranging from a high of 34 in 1992 to a low of 13 in 1999, and then back up to 27 in 2007. True, there are many thefts, some bullying, and a lot of drug dealing, but our public schools, with over 50 million students enrolled, are not pervaded by criminal violence.[13]

Second, celebrated cases receive an enormous amount of *publicity,* usually because of the nature of the crime itself (typically something ghastly, like the Garrido case) or the fame of the person involved (O. J. Simpson, for example). A few cases become celebrated because they result in landmark Supreme Court rulings. The famous *Miranda* case is an excellent example because of the importance of the decision (requiring police to advise suspects of their rights) and its lasting impact on police procedures.

Third, as we have already mentioned, the publicity surrounding celebrated cases *distorts public perceptions* about criminal justice. People mistakenly assume that they are typical of all cases.

One of the main arguments of this book is that we should look at the facts before jumping to conclusions about how the system works. The famous 1995 O. J. Simpson murder trial provides an excellent example of how systematic data can dispel myths. Simpson's acquittal led many people to conclude that spouse murderers "beat the system" all the time. Even worse, it led many whites to believe that African American jurors will not convict an African American defendant. Both of these perceptions are grossly wrong. In response to the Simpson trial outcome, the BJS analyzed its data on spouse murders from the 75 largest counties in the country for 1988. This included a total of 540 cases.[14] As Figure 2.3 indicates, very few accused spouse murderers beat the system. In fact, only 2 percent of the husbands were acquitted. Wives were more likely to win acquittal (14 percent) because there were more likely to be mitigating circumstances, such as killing in self-defense. The system was tough on spouse murder defendants at every stage. Only 13 percent were not prosecuted. And of those who were convicted, 71 percent were sentenced to prison (81 percent of the husbands and 57 percent of the wives). This is an excellent example of how good, systematic data can debunk popular myths and provide an accurate picture of how the system really works.

Unfortunately, the BJS data set does not report the racial composition of juries. Because the data come from the 75 largest urban counties in the country, however, it is a safe assumption that racial minorities were well represented.

THE GARRIDO KIDNAPPING AND RAPE: A CLASSIC CELEBRATED CASE

One of the most shocking crimes in recent memory was discovered in the summer of 2009. Philip Garrido, with the cooperation of his wife, had kidnapped and held Jaycee Lee Dugard prisoner for 18 years. Dugard was only 11 in 1991 when she was kidnapped. During her detention, Garrido raped her and fathered her two children (who were 15 and 11 when they were discovered and released).

Philip Garrido has had a long and serious criminal record. He served 10½ years in federal prison, and was paroled in 1988. In 1993, he was rearrested for a parole violation. Later, he served another seven months in prison in Nevada on an abduction charge. At the time of his 2009 arrest he was a registered sex offender under California law.

The case raises a number of questions about how the criminal justice system works— or fails to work. We will look closely at most of them in this book:

- How often do appalling cases like this occur? Are they common, or is this truly a celebrated case?

- Why did Garrido serve only 10½ years of his original 50-year sentence? What was the basis for his parole in 1988?

- Most important, do we have diagnostic instruments that allow us to identify dangerous offenders who should not be released?

- Given Garrido's prior record, why did he only serve seven months on the later charge in Nevada? Was his record checked?

- How effective is parole in controlling dangerous criminals? What exactly did Garrido's parole "supervision" consist of?

- As a registered sex offender, was Garrido monitored? Didn't officials notice the make-shift prison he had in his backyard? How effective are sex offender registration laws in controlling repeat offenders? Is there any actual monitoring and supervision?

- Why did police fail to investigate a tip about Garrido in 2006?

- Didn't the people living in Garrido's neighborhood notice anything strange?

- Did Garrido keep slipping through the cracks because the system was so overloaded with relatively minor offenders that officials couldn't concentrate on more serious offenders?

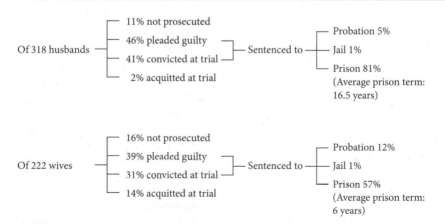

FIGURE 2.3 Dispositions of spouse murder defendants.

Thus, there is probably no truth to the idea that minority jurors refuse to convict minority defendants. These data, in fact, indicate no real difference in the conviction rates between whites (81 percent) and African Americans (79 percent).

The great value of the BJS data set is that it reflects the routine, day-in, day-out administration of justice. It gives us a far more accurate picture of how the system operates than celebrated cases such as the O. J. Simpson trial. To understand how routine robberies and burglaries are handled, we need to turn our attention to the second and third layers of the wedding cake. The lesson is clear: beware of celebrated cases. Sure, they are great fodder for gossip, but they do not reflect how the system works for most cases.

Serious Felonies: The Second and Third Layers

In their original version of the wedding cake, Friedman and Percival put all felony cases in one layer. The Gottfredsons made an extremely important refinement by dividing felonies into two categories based on the seriousness of the offense. In our wedding cake, the more serious felonies (rape, robbery) go into the second layer and the less serious felonies (burglary, larceny) go into the third.

A large body of research supports the view that criminal justice officials consistently use several factors to define the seriousness of an offense: (1) the nature of the crime, (2) whether a weapon was used, (3) whether the victim was injured, (4) the suspect's prior record, and (5) the relationship between the victim and the offender. Jeffrey T. Ulmer's study of sentencing under the Pennsylvania sentencing guidelines found that most of the departures from the guidelines were based on considerations of seriousness (prior record, offense type, severity).[15]

The process of classifying cases is *informal;* there is no actual checklist of factors. (This is not always true anymore. Some prosecutors' offices have formal guidelines that embody considerations of seriousness. Minnesota and some other states have sentencing guidelines that are based on both seriousness of the crime and the defendant's prior record.)[16] Essentially, officials ask themselves, "How much is this case worth?" or "How bad is this offender?" The everyday language of police and prosecutors reveals a lot about how cases are handled. They refer to "heavy" cases and "real" crimes as opposed to the "garbage" or "bullshit" cases. A study of California probation officers found that they used the same definitions of "heavy duty" and "lightweight" cases that judges and prosecutors used.[17]

These judgments about seriousness are shared by all the members of the *courtroom work group.* As we will see in Chapter 3, the courtroom work group is one of the most important factors in determining how the system works. The work group consists of criminal justice officials who work together day in and day out. For the sake of efficiency, they develop shared understandings about how to handle routine cases. This approach has two important consequences. First, it means that individual discretion is controlled *informally,* through shared understandings and expectations (as opposed to formal rules). Second, it produces a high degree of consistency *within* each layer of the wedding cake. The shared definition of seriousness facilitates rapid disposition of a high volume of cases. Prosecutors and defense attorneys do not spend a lot of time arguing over particular cases; they know that an armed robbery where the victim was injured is a very serious case. Actually, as we will see in Chapter 8, the whole idea of plea "bargaining" is misleading. The criminal court is not like a Middle Eastern bazaar, where people haggle over the price of each item. Instead, as Malcolm Feeley argues, it resembles a modern supermarket, with set prices and high volume.[18] The "fixed prices" reflect the shared assumptions about how much cases are "worth."

Ulmer's study of sentencing in three Pennsylvania counties also found, however, that the degree of shared understandings can vary. One county court system had a high degree of stability among prosecutors, defense attorneys, and judges, and as a result had very collegial relations and shared understandings. A large urban county, on the other hand, had a high degree of turnover in the district attorney's office, which resulted in conflict between prosecutors and defense attorneys and a low level of collegiality and understanding between defense attorneys and judges.[19] In short, while *most* court systems operate under shared understandings, there are important *variations* depending on the composition and culture of the local courtroom work group. We will discuss the work group in more detail in Chapter 3.

Robbery illustrates how officials distribute cases between the second and third layers. Because robbery is generally considered a very serious crime, most such cases end up in the second layer. About one-third of all robberies, however, are between acquaintances. These are often private disputes: a disagreement over borrowed money or tools where the "offender" takes back his or her property by force.[20] These robbery cases tend to end up in the third layer because they are not considered as serious as robberies by strangers. If, however, the offender has a long prior record of arrests and convictions, the case might remain in the second layer.

The Complexity of the System: "Back-End Sentencing" in California. In California, two-thirds of all the people entering prisons are parole violators rather than newly sentenced offenders. Officials have called it "back-end sentencing," because parole officials are doing what we think judges should do: send people to prison. Among other things, this process contributes to the serious prison overcrowding in the state.

The process is a result of some unique aspects of California sentencing and parole laws. Under California's Determinate Sentencing Law (which we discuss in Chapter 7), all but a few prisoners are automatically released on parole. The parole laws, meanwhile, require parole officers to report parolees for a wide range of parole violations. About 66 percent are sent back to prison within three years (about 60 percent for parole violations rather than for a new crime). In another irrational twist, many spend only one to four months in prison. (We will discuss that issue in Chapter 11.) It gets worse. Some parolees commit new offenses. Rather than prosecute them, however, local authorities simply revoke their parole. Parole revocations require a lower standard of proof (preponderance of the evidence) rather than proof beyond a reasonable doubt, and thus are considered a "sure thing." In addition, parole revocation sends the person to a state facility rather than a local jail. Most local jails are overcrowded, and in 2006 more than half had "caps" on the number of inmates.[21]

T A B L E   2.1   Percentage of defendants sentenced to prison by prior record

Prior Record	Percentage Sentenced to Prison
More than one prior felony conviction	53%
Only one prior felony conviction	37%
Prior misdemeanor one or more prior conviction	20%
No prior convictions	22%

SOURCE: Bureau of Justice Statistics, *Felony Defendants in Large Urban Counties, 2004–Statistical Tables* (Washington, DC: Justice Department, 2008), Table 30.

The Impact of Prior Record

The BJS report on *Felony Defendants in Large Urban Counties, 2004* provides powerful evidence on the impact of prior record in the disposition of cases. As Table 2.1 indicates, the percentage of defendants convicted of a violent offense sentenced to prison dropped from 75 percent for those with two or more prior felony convictions to only 40 percent for those with no prior convictions (felony or misdemeanor). A similar pattern exists for persons convicted of a property offense.

The Impact of the Victim/Offender Relationship

A Vera Institute study of felony arrests in New York City illustrates the tremendous impact of the relationship between the offender and the victim. Figure 2.4 indicates that 88 percent of the stranger robberies resulted in conviction. Moreover, prosecutors were not lenient in plea bargaining: 77 percent of those convictions (68 percent of the original arrests) were on felony charges. Nearly three-quarters (74 percent) of those convicted were incarcerated, and half of them did time of a year or more. This is hardly the picture of a system "soft" on crime.[22]

The prior-relationship robberies are a completely different story. Only about a third (37 percent) of the suspects were convicted, and only 13 percent of them (5 percent of the number originally arrested) were convicted on felony charges. Slightly more than half (56 percent) of those convicted were incarcerated, but none did a year or more.

The powerful effect of prior relationships is also evident in rape cases. About half of the sexual assaults in the Vera Institute study were committed by men who knew the victim. Sixty percent of these cases were dismissed; another 20 percent ended in a guilty plea with only minor punishment. All of the stranger-rape cases, however, went to trial. Three-quarters of these resulted in conviction and imprisonment, and two-thirds of the prison terms exceeded 25 years.

The most important point that emerges from this analysis is that the criminal justice system is very tough on second-layer felonies. Offenders who have committed a serious crime, committed it against a stranger, and have a long prior record are very likely to be (1) prosecuted on the top charge, (2) convicted, and (3) given a relatively severe sentence (usually prison).

The third layer of the criminal justice wedding cake is a different story. The less serious cases are regularly dismissed; defendants are often allowed to plead

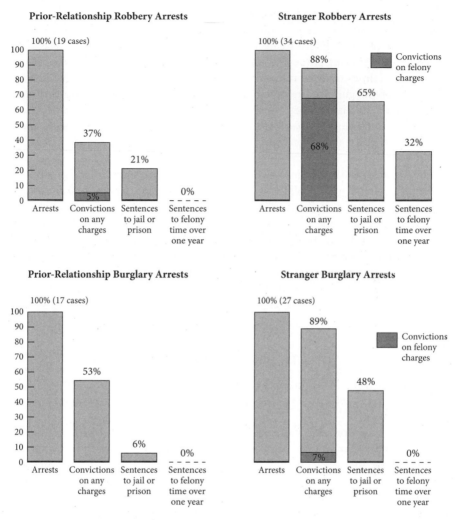

FIGURE 2.4 Outcomes of stranger and nonstranger robberies and burglaries, New York City.

SOURCE: Vera Institute, Felony Arrests, rev. ed. (New York: Longman, 1981), pp. 68, 86. Reprinted with permission.

guilty to lesser offenses; and, if convicted, defendants are placed on probation. Outcomes are less predictable in the third layer because there is less consensus about the seriousness and the appropriate response than in the second layer.

In their classic study of the jury, Harry Kalven and Hans Zeisel explain this lack of consensus in terms of a "liberation" hypothesis. Under certain circumstances, they argue, jurors are "liberated" from normal constraints.[23] Applying this hypothesis to the wedding cake, we can say that in the third layer the lack of consensus about the seriousness of the crime or the offender's prior record liberates prosecutors and judges from the conventional shared understandings of seriousness. This allows them to base their decision on other factors. In some instances, the defendant's race or other personal attribute becomes a factor.

Spohn and Cederblom explored the <u>liberation hypothesis in</u> a study of 4,655 violent felony cases in Detroit from 1976 to 1978.[24] They found that African Americans were more likely to be incarcerated than whites. But this was true only in the less serious crimes: in assaults rather than more serious felonies, in acquaintance crimes, and in cases in which there were no prior violent felony convictions or no gun was involved. The outcomes in the more serious crimes (that is, the second-layer cases) were more consistent, with whites and African Americans treated equally harshly. In the less serious (e.g., third-layer) cases, there was less consensus about how much these cases were "worth," and this allowed extralegal factors such as race to come into play.

We might note that crime *victims* make the same distinctions about seriousness as do criminal justice officials. The National Crime Victimization Survey consistently finds that victims report the more serious crimes at a higher rate than less serious ones. In 2006, victims reported 59.8 percent of all completed robberies, but only 32 percent of all completed thefts. They only reported 50.8 percent of attempted robberies, however, indicating their view that this crime is not as serious as a completed robbery. The gap is even wider with regard to rape. Victims report 49.2 of completed sexual assaults, but only 25.7 percent of attempted ones. For all crimes, the more serious the crime, the higher the reporting rate.[25]

Prior Relationship: A Policy Dilemma

The role of the prior relationship between victim and offender presents a major policy dilemma. At issue is whether it is legitimate to use this role as a factor in decision making.

In the area of domestic violence, research has found that police traditionally have taken into account the nature of the relationship. The more intimate the relationship, the less likely the police are to make an arrest.[26] Thus, they are less likely to arrest the abusive husband than the abusive boyfriend or lover. In response to protests from women's groups, many police departments have adopted mandatory arrest or arrest-preferred policies that either require an arrest in a felonious domestic assault or advise officers that arrest is the preferred disposition. The intent is to ensure equal enforcement of the law and to eliminate discrimination based on marital status.

Along the same lines, Susan Estrich argues that all sexual assaults should be prosecuted with equal vigor. Rapes between acquaintances should not be treated less seriously than stranger rapes. Estrich describes her conversation with a local prosecutor who explained that he used the prior-relationship criterion in *all* criminal cases, not just rape. He was accurately describing how officials generally handle criminal cases.[27]

What would happen if we did eliminate prior relationship as a decision-making factor in all criminal cases? At the arrest stage, it would produce more domestic violence arrests. (In fact, some evidence suggests that the police have been making more domestic violence arrests in recent years. The FBI's arrest data indicate that aggravated-assault arrests have been increasing since the 1970s compared with other felony arrests.) At the prosecution stage, it would move a large number of cases from the third to the second layer of the wedding cake. This would, in turn, result in more offenders being sentenced to prison.

This outcome presents us with a policy dilemma. Eliminating prior relationship as a decision-making factor would produce greater equality in the administration of justice—a desirable outcome. At the same time, however, it would increase the overall punitiveness of the justice system. Is that a desirable result?

A general lesson can be learned here. Significant changes in criminal justice policy often involve major trade-offs. The gains on one side of the equation need to be considered in light of the consequences on the other side.

Hard or Soft on Crime? Unraveling the Paradox

Is the criminal justice system hard or soft on crime? Our wedding cake illuminates the paradox noted by Zimring, Morris, and Tonry: The system is *simultaneously harsh and lenient*. A great deal depends on the seriousness of the case. The system is very hard on second-layer cases, such as robberies committed by people with long prior records. But it is relatively soft on assaults by offenders with no prior records. It is hard on stranger rapes but more lenient on acquaintance assaults.

Additional support for the distinction between the second and third layers of the wedding cake is found in some career-criminal prosecution programs. We will look at these in detail in Chapter 8. These programs are designed to concentrate prosecutorial resources on a special class of cases involving career criminals to make sure they are convicted and sentenced to prison. The San Diego Major Violator Unit succeeded in convicting 91.5 percent of the career criminals it handled. But 89.5 percent of the career criminals were being convicted before the program began. Under the program, 100 percent of the convicted career criminals were incarcerated, but the rate had been 95.3 percent beforehand. In short, criminals deemed "serious" by commonsense criteria were already being taken very seriously. As Diana Gordon, former director of the National Council on Crime and Delinquency, put it, "Being tough doesn't work because being lenient is not the source of the problem."[28]

The idea that our criminal justice system is tough on serious crime comes as a surprise to many people. A Sentencing Project report found that most people believe that the system is much softer than it actually is.[29] There are two reasons for this misperception. First, as we have already explained, celebrated cases that are not typical of general patterns have a powerful impact on public attitudes. Second, because official data usually aggregate sentences into general categories, they obscure the important distinctions between serious and less serious crimes. Aggregate data give the *appearance* of softness because relatively few cases end up in the second layer. Violent crimes represent only 10 percent of all felonies reported to the police. Larceny, the least serious felony, accounts for 54 percent of the total. The wedding cake model allows us to focus on how the system responds to the most serious crimes, those in the second layer.

The Lower Depths: The Fourth Layer

The fourth layer of the wedding cake is a world unto itself. The lower criminal courts handle all of the misdemeanors in most jurisdictions. The volume of cases is staggering, far outnumbering felonies. The eight Part I Index crimes accounted for only 17 percent of the nearly 10.7 million arrests in 2007. About half of the Part II Index crime arrests involved "public order" offenses: disorderly conduct, breach of the peace, drunkenness, and so on. In fact, the largest single arrest category in 2007 was "All other offenses (except traffic)," with a total of almost 3 million. Under the criterion of seriousness, these cases are not considered to be "worth" much at all. Few of the defendants are regarded as real threats to public safety.

Because of the huge volume of cases and their relative lack of seriousness, relatively little concern is shown for the formalities of the felony process. In an excellent study of the lower courts of New Haven, Connecticut, Malcolm Feeley concludes that these institutions remain virtually untouched by the due process revolution.[30] To enter these courts is to step back in time 80 years. None of the defendants in the 1,640 cases he examined insisted on a jury trial. Half never had an attorney. Even for those that did, the lawyer's contribution was minimal. Even more shocking, by our standards of due process, defendants were arraigned en masse, in assembly-line fashion. Sentences were extremely light. Half of the defendants received a fine of $50 or less, and only 4.9 percent were sentenced to jail.

Feeley concludes that the "process is the punishment": Simply being brought into the lower courts is the real punishment, quite apart from the eventual outcome of the case. Insisting on your "rights" only increases the "punishment." A private attorney, for example, would charge $200 to handle a case (about $800 at today's rates). This is four times the fine were you simply to cop a plea at the earliest possible moment. Moreover, because most defendants in the lower courts are hourly wage earners rather than salaried professionals, the lost wages involved in fighting a case would generally exceed the potential fine. (Each case in Feeley's study averaged three court appearances. Fighting the case would only increase the number and length of court dates.)

The closer we look, however, the more complicated the picture becomes. A study of the Philadelphia lower courts offers a different view and illustrates the hazards of generalizing about American criminal justice. Stephen J. Schulhofer found that in Philadelphia's two lower courts—Municipal Court and the Court of Common Pleas—about half (48 percent) of all cases went to trial, virtually all defendants had legal counsel, and the punishments meted out to the guilty were relatively significant. Nearly a quarter (22 percent) of the convicted offenders received a jail sentence, and 17.4 percent received fines (which ranged as high as several hundred dollars). Schulhofer argues that Feeley overstated the "process" costs of contesting a case in the lower courts. The price of the likely penalty, at least in Philadelphia, makes the case worth fighting. The main reason appears to be that penalties are significantly stiffer in Philadelphia than in New Haven.[31]

We do not need to resolve the differences between Feeley's and Schulhofer's findings here. The basic points are that (1) the lower courts are very different from the upper courts and (2) there are significant differences between courts in different jurisdictions.

CONCLUSION

Our wedding cake model of the criminal justice system is designed to help us make sense of the administration of justice in action. As we go along, the most important thing to keep in mind is that we should not be distracted by celebrated cases. They make great stories for the tabloids, but they interfere with our understanding of routine operations in criminal justice. In particular, we want to be very skeptical of any policies that are based on celebrated cases. And because we are primarily concerned with the control of serious crime—robbery and burglary in particular—we need to keep our eyes focused on the second layer of the wedding cake.

NOTES

1. Bureau of Justice Statistics, *State Court Organization, 1998* (Washington, DC: Department of Justice, 2000). NCJ 178932.

2. This interpretation is vividly captured in "The Practice of Law as a Confidence Game," in Abraham Blumberg, *Criminal Justice*, 2d ed. (New York: New Viewpoints, 1979), pp. 242–243.

3. For a reasonable review of the evidence, see Samuel Walker, Cassia Spohn, and Miriam DeLone, *The Color of Justice: Race, Ethnicity, and Crime in America*, 4th ed. (Belmont, CA: Wadsworth, 2007).

4. Donald Black, *The Manners and Customs of the Police* (New York: Academic Press, 1980). Peter F. Nardulli, James Eisenstein, and Roy B. Flemming, *The Tenor of Justice: Criminal Courts and the Guilty Plea Process* (Urbana: University of Illinois Press, 1988).

5. Franklin Zimring, Sheila O'Malley, and Joel Eigen, "Punishing Homicide in Philadelphia: Perspectives on the Death Penalty," *University of Chicago Law Review* 43 (Winter 1976): 252.

6. Norval Morris and Michael H. Tonry, *Between Prison and Probation: Intermediate Punishments in a Rational Sentencing System* (New York: Oxford University Press, 1990), p. 3.

7. Walker et al., *The Color of Justice*, chap. 4.

8. President's Commission on Law Enforcement and Administration of Justice, *Task Force Report: Science and Technology* (Washington, DC: Government Printing Office, 1967), pp. 58–59.

9. On the origins of the systems perspective, see Samuel Walker, "Origins of the Contemporary Criminal Justice Paradigm: The American Bar Foundation Survey, 1953–1969," *Justice Quarterly* 9 (March 1992): 201–229.

10. Ryken Grattet, Joan Petersilia, and Jeffrey Lin, *Parole Violations and Revocations in California* (Washington, DC: Department of Justice, 2008).

11. Lawrence M. Friedman and Robert V. Percival, *The Roots of Justice: Crime and Punishment in Alameda County, California, 1870–1910* (Chapel Hill: University of North Carolina Press, 1981). Michael R. Gottfredson and Don M. Gottfredson, *Decision Making in Criminal Justice: Toward the Rational Exercise of Discretion*, 2d ed. (New York: Plenum, 1988).

12. Jeffrey Toobin, *The Run of His Life: The People vs. O. J. Simpson* (New York: Random House, 1996).

13. Bureau of Justice Statistics, *Indicators of School Crime and Safety: 2008* (Washington, DC: Department of Justice, 2009).

14. Bureau of Justice Statistics, *Spouse Murder Defendants in Large Urban Counties* (Washington, DC: Department of Justice, 1995). NCJ 153256.

15. Jeffrey T. Ulmer, *Social Worlds of Sentencing: Court Communities Under Sentencing Guidelines*. (Albany: State University of New York Press, 1997), pp. 60–62.

16. William F. McDonald, *Plea Bargaining: Critical Issues and Common Practices* (Washington, DC: Government Printing Office, 1985).

17. The informal language is reported in several studies: Lynn Mather, "Some Determinants of the Method of Case Disposition: Decision Making by Public Defenders in Los Angeles," *Law and Society Review* 8 (Winter 1974): 187–216. David Sudnow, "Normal Crimes: Sociological Features of the Penal Code in a Public Defender Office," *Social Problems* 12 (Winter 1965): 255–276. John Rosecrance, "Maintaining the Myth of Individualized Justice: Probation Presentence Reports," *Justice Quarterly* 5 (June 1988): 235–256.

18. Malcolm M. Feeley, "Perspectives on Plea Bargaining," *Law and Society Review* 13 (Winter 1979): 199.

19. Ulmer, *Social Worlds of Sentencing: Court Communities Under Sentencing Guidelines*.

20. Donald Black, *Toward a General Theory of Social Control*, vol. 2 (Orlando, FL: Academic Press, 1984), pp. 1–28.

21. Grattet, Petersilia, Lin, *Parole Violations and Revocations in California*.

22. Vera Institute, *Felony Arrests*, rev. ed. (New York: Longman, 1981).

23. Harry Kalven, Jr., and Hans Zeisel, *The American Jury* (Boston: Little, Brown, 1966), pp. 164–166.

24. Cassia Spohn and Jerry Cederblom, "Race and Disparities in Sentencing: A Test of the Liberation Hypothesis," *Justice Quarterly* 8 (September 1991): 306.

25. Bureau of Justice Statistics, *Criminal Victimization in the United States, 2006: Statistical Tables* (Washington, DC: Justice Department, 2008).

26. Black, *The Manners and Customs of the Police.*

27. Susan Estrich, *Real Rape* (Cambridge, MA: Harvard University Press, 1987).

28. U.S. Department of Justice, *An Exemplary Project: Major Violator Unit – San Diego, California* (Washington, DC: Department of Justice, 1980). Diana R. Gordon, *Toward Realistic Reform: A Commentary on Proposals for Change in New York City's Criminal Justice System* (Hackensack, NJ: National Council on Crime and Delinquency, 1981), p. 16.

29. The Sentencing Project, Crime, Punishment, and Public Opinion: A Summary of Recent Studies and Their Implications for Sentencing Policy (Washington, DC: The Sentencing Project, nd).

30. Malcolm M. Feeley, *The Process Is the Punishment* (New York: Russell Sage Foundation, 1979).

31. Stephen J. Schulhofer, "No Job Too Small: Justice Without Bargaining in the Lower Criminal Courts," *American Bar Foundation Research Journal* (Summer 1985): 519–598.

3

The Going Rate

EVALUATING THE SYSTEM

We now turn our attention to the question of how the criminal justice system works on a day-to-day basis. How effectively does it control crime? How successful is it in catching, prosecuting, and punishing dangerous criminals? Is the system fair? Is there a pattern of discrimination against people of color?

Great controversy surrounds these questions. In a book subtitled *The Collapse of Criminal Justice,* Judge Harold Rothwax bluntly declares, "The long arm of the law is somewhat fractured these days."[1] Rothwax describes case after case of criminals who committed serious crimes not being punished because of some loophole in the system. Other experts see different problems. The Sentencing Project, for example, sees the system breaking down because of the resource crisis (see Chapter 1). It is overloaded by bad policies: too many prisoners; not enough drug treatment programs; excessive parole case loads. Still others see a pattern of pervasive race discrimination. One result, as we argue in Chapter 12, is a loss of legitimacy for the justice system; and one consequence of that is greater lawbreaking.[2]

Where does the truth lie? Is the system too weak or too harsh? Is the system completely out of control or are there understandable patterns in how decisions are made? Evaluating the performance of our criminal justice system is a difficult task. As we have already learned, on some questions we do not have good data. It is only recently that the controversy over "driving while black" prompted the first studies of police traffic enforcement. Even where reasonably good data are available, experts disagree over what they mean. There is much debate over the traffic stop data we now have. Most have found racial disparities, but do those disparities represent discrimination?[3] A similar debate exists over punishment. What is harsh?; what is soft? Is a three-year prison sentence for burglary "tough" or "lenient"? Experts disagree.

It is possible to identify some general features of the criminal process in this country. In virtually every local jurisdiction, there is a *going rate* for crime. The going rate is defined as the standard and predictable punishment for a crime.

"THE LONG ARM OF THE LAW..."

Illustration by Frank Irwin, © Wadsworth, Cengage Learning.

Some scholars argue that if you know the offense and the defendant's prior criminal record, you can probably predict the outcome of about 80 percent of all cases. Plea "bargaining," in the sense of haggling over the final result as you would at a flea market, actually has very little impact on case outcomes.[4]

THE FUNNEL

To understand the going rate, a good place to begin is the analysis by the President's Crime Commission of the flow of cases through the system (Figure 3.1). These data are from the 1960s, but they are a useful starting point for understanding some general patterns in the administration of justice. And in fact, the general patterns still hold today. The Crime Commission found that despite 6 million reported and unreported crimes, only 63,000 offenders were sentenced to prison. This led to the conclusion that only 1 percent of all criminals go to prison—a figure that many people have cited as evidence that the criminal justice system fails to punish offenders. We argue that these data present a very distorted picture, creating a serious misunderstanding of how the system works.

In a sharp critique, Charles Silberman argued that the Crime Commission's analysis was "grossly misleading."[5] Reanalyzing the same data (Figure 3.2), he pointed out that about 260,000 (35.7 percent) of the original 727,000 arrests involved juveniles whose cases were transferred to juvenile court. What happens to those juveniles is, of course, extremely important but not our concern here.

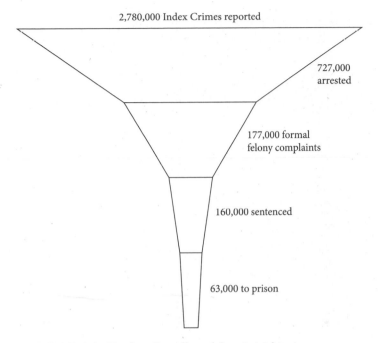

2,780,000 Index Crimes reported

727,000 arrested

177,000 formal felony complaints

160,000 sentenced

63,000 to prison

FIGURE 3.1   The funneling effect of the criminial justice system.

SOURCE: President's Commission on Law Enforcement and Administration of Justice, Task Force Report: Science and Technology (Washington, DC: Government Printing Office, 1967), p. 61.

To remain consistent with our ground rules, however, we will concentrate on the adults.

Subtracting the juveniles leaves 467,000 adult arrests. Silberman argued that this is the proper baseline for assessing the performance of the adult criminal justice system. About 27 percent of these arrests (128,000) were dismissed, leaving 339,000 prosecuted adults. This results in a prosecution rate of 73 percent, which is hardly a sign of softness on crime. Then, about half (48 percent) of these defendants pled guilty to a misdemeanor. These cases were not "lost," as many people believe. The defendants were convicted of a crime and acquired a criminal record. They also experienced the costs in time and money required by the case, along with the humiliation of it all. We might disagree about the severity of punishment, but the fact is that they were convicted of a crime.

Subtracting the misdemeanor convictions leaves 177,000 adult felony complaints. Of these, 90 percent were convicted: 130,000 by a guilty plea and 30,000 by trial. This is an extremely impressive conviction rate. When we combine the 177,000 felony convictions with the 162,000 misdemeanor convictions, we have a total of 332,000 adults convicted. This represents 69 percent of the adults arrested and 95 percent of those prosecuted. This is a picture of a fairly tough criminal justice system.

The Crime Commission and Silberman both used 1960s data. Have things changed in the past 40 years? The BJS report *Felony Defendants in Large Urban*

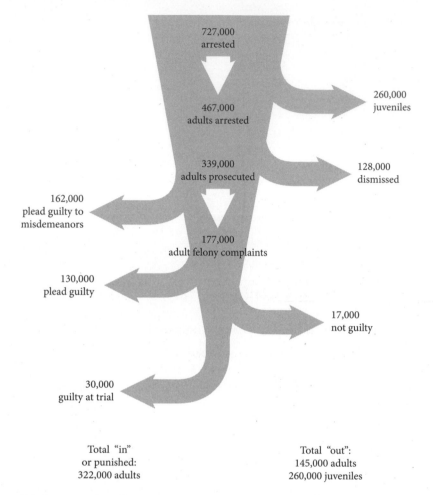

FIGURE 3.2   Silberman's recalculation of the Crime Commission's funnel.

SOURCE: Charles Silberman, *Criminal Violence, Criminal Justice* (New York: Random House, 1978), pp. 257–261.

Counties, 2004 indicates that 68 percent of all felony arrests presented to prosecutors resulted in a conviction (up slightly from 64 percent in 2000); 59 percent were convicted of a felony and 9 percent were convicted of a misdemeanor. These patterns are not radically different from the 1960s.[6]

When we apply our wedding cake model to the analysis, we find interesting patterns. Conviction rates vary by the type of crime. In 2004, 71 percent of all murder defendants were convicted, while 62 percent of rape and 69 percent of robbery defendants were convicted. (Be careful to note that these are total conviction rates. Of the rape defendants, 54 percent were convicted of a felony and 8 percent were convicted of a misdemeanor.) The lowest conviction rate was for assault defendants (56 percent overall; 45 percent for a felony). Looked at from this perspective, this is not a system that is soft on crime. What happens to felony defendants who are convicted? The BJS report indicates that in 2004, 75 percent

T A B L E   3.1   Probable outcomes of felony arrests and felony convictions, 2004

	Likelihood of felony arrest leading to felony conviction	Likelihood of felony conviction resulting in prison sentence
Murder	41%	91%
Robbery	47	71
Aggravated assault	23	42
Burglary	50	46
Drug trafficking	80	42

SOURCE: Bureau of Justice Statistics, *Felony Sentences in State Courts* (Washington, DC: Department of Justice, 2004). NCJ 206916.

were incarcerated; 36 percent went to prison; and 40 percent went to jail. The overall incarceration rate represents an increase in punitiveness since the days of the President's Crime Commission in the 1960s.

It is important to disentangle the data. An incarceration rate of 75 percent is pretty high. If you focus on the fact that only 36 percent go to prison, the system appears to be a lot softer on crime. But remember, jail is not a pleasant experience. And most jails have fewer programs than do prisons, so in some respects it is even a less pleasant place to spend time. Thus, it is easy to manipulate the debate, depending on whether you cite the 75 or the 36 percent figure. It is also a matter of judgment as to how harsh you think a term in jail is. Bear in mind that all of those going to jail have a criminal conviction, many with a felony conviction, that will limit their opportunities in life for years to come (especially getting a job), and perhaps for the rest of their lives.[7]

The picture gets even more complicated when we step back and take a broader view. The BJS data on felony defendants do not tell the whole story of what happens to people who are arrested. The data represent cases that are presented to prosecutors. This omits many cases of people who are arrested but have the charges dismissed early by the police or even rejected by prosecutors. It is necessary, therefore, to take a look at rejections and dismissals.

Arrest Data, Rejections and Dismissals

Another measure of the harshness or leniency of the system involves your chances of going to prison or jail (that is, any incarceration) if you are arrested. This issue introduces some hidden complexities in the criminal justice system involving the nature of official arrest data and the rejection and dismissal of cases. Using these data, BJS estimates that if you are arrested for robbery, your chances of incarceration are 40 out of 100; for burglary they are 33 out of 100. From this perspective, the system begins to look fairly weak. But there is more to the story, as we shall see.[8]

The BJS estimate uses official arrest data as reported to the FBI. These data, however, do not accurately report all the people who were actually arrested. We have to examine carefully what is meant by an "arrest." A Police Foundation report found that police departments did not report arrests in a comparable fashion. Many people who are taken into custody are not officially *recorded* as being arrested.[9] This illustrates the crucial difference between arrests as a matter of law and official data on arrests. If you are stopped and detained on the street by a police officer, you are legally under arrest (in the sense that you are not free to go). Some departments record these incidents as an arrest, but many do not. If you are taken to police headquarters, questioned, and then released, you were legally arrested. But not all of these cases are recorded. In some cases an arrest is made and officially recorded but then dismissed by the police themselves (because of insufficient evidence, the arrest of a different suspect, etc.). In short, your actual chances of incarceration are less (possibly much less, we don't know, and it varies with each police department) than estimated by BJS.

Police discretion in dismissing arrests is another important hidden decision point in the criminal justice system. Joan Petersilia found that about 11 percent of all arrests in California were dropped by the police.[10] These cases never even reach a prosecutor's desk, and consequently are not reported in many data sets, including the BJS felony defendant report. In short, the "true" number of persons arrested in any given year is much larger than official data indicate.

After a case reaches the prosecutor's desk, it can either be *rejected* by the prosecutor or *dismissed* by a judge. These are two distinct stages in the process. We need to inquire into why cases are rejected or dismissed. Table 3.2 presents BJS data on the reasons for rejections and dismissals in New York and San Diego. (These data are a little old, but the general patterns still hold today.) Evidence problems—either insufficient evidence or lack of any evidence—account for most of the rejections by prosecutors: 61 percent in New York and 51 percent in San Diego. Witness problems are the second most important reason: 18 percent of the rejections in New York and 19 percent in San Diego. For most crimes against persons (robbery, rape, assault), the testimony of the victim or a witness is the primary evidence. These data indicate that evidence and witness problems account for about 70 to 80 percent of all rejections.

Evidence and witness problems are also important factors in the dismissal of cases, accounting for 33 percent of the dismissals in New York City and 20 percent in San Diego. The lack of evidence or witnesses is a legitimate reason for dropping a case. A prosecutor cannot win a case without them. Dismissing cases for this reason does not mean that the system is soft on crime. Officials are simply doing what circumstances force them to do. In short, rejections and dismissals are not a loophole.

A closer look reveals that the term *dismissal* is misleading. Many of these cases are not really "lost," as some critics of the system argue. In San Diego, for example, almost half of the "dismissals" involved some form of action by the system: 11 percent were diverted, 27 percent were referred for other prosecution, and 10 percent were covered by another case. In short, these defendants were still in the hands of the criminal justice system and liable for some kind of sanction.

The data on rejections and dismissals have very important policy implications. Most important, they clearly indicate that due process problems—illegal

T A B L E 3.2   Why felony arrests are declined for prosecution

Manhattan, New York 1988

Most serious charge	Diversion	Other prosecution	Evidence	Arrests declined due to:				
				Witness	Due process	Interest of justice	Covered by other case	Other
Percentage of declinations	0%	3%	61%	18%	2%	10%	0%	6%
Murder and manslaughter	0	0	75	25	0	0	0	0
Rape	0	0	30	40	0	30	0	0
Robbery	0	8	63	22	0	3	0	4
Aggravated assault	0	3	33	40	0	13	0	11
Burglary	0	0	79	21	0	0	0	0

San Diego, California 1988

Most serious charge	Diversion	Other prosecution	Evidence	Arrests declined due to:				
				Witness	Due process	Interest of justice	Covered by other case	Other
Percentage of declinations	0%	0%	51%	19%	13%	11%	3%	4%
Murder and manslaughter	0	0	50	3	0	30	0	17
Rape	0	0	30	60	0	8	1	2
Robbery	0	0	49	36	1	6	0	7
Aggravated assault	0	0	39	46	2	9	1	3
Burglary	0	0	59	15	8	8	5	5

(continued)

59

T A B L E   3.2   Why felony arrests are declined for prosecution (*continued*)

Manhattan, New York 1988

Most serious charge	Diversion	Other prosecution	Evidence	Cases dismissed due to:				
				Witness	Due process	Interest of justice	Covered by other case	Other
Percentage of declinations	0%	0%	19%	14%	0%	10%	6%	51%
Murder and manslaughter	11	1	17	15	0	2	14	39
Rape	0	0	13	33	0	4	3	47
Robbery	0	0	18	21	0	4	4	53
Aggravated assault	1	0	10	26	0	13	3	48
Burglary	0	0	15	11	0	13	6	54

San Diego, California 1988

Most serious charge	Diversion	Other prosecution	Evidence	Cases dismissed due to:				
				Witness	Due process	Interest of justice	Covered by other case	Other
Percentage of declinations	11%	27%	14%	6%	0%	7%	10%	25%
Murder and manslaughter	0	20	20	0	0	30	0	30
Rape	0	4	22	22	0	31	4	18
Robbery	0	17	27	27	1	4	3	22
Aggravated assault	2	26	21	17	0	5	5	23
Burglary	2	25	12	10	0	6	13	32

SOURCE: Bureau of Justice Statistics, *The Prosecution of Felony Arrests, 1988* (Washington, DC: Government Printing Office, 1992).

searches or coerced confessions—are not a major reason why cases are not prosecuted. They accounted for only 15 percent of the rejections and none of the dismissals in San Diego. Equally important, due process problems arose primarily in drug and weapons cases. They accounted for only 1 percent of the rejections of robbery cases and 8 percent of the burglary rejections. In short, thousands of criminals are not "beating the system" in the early stages of prosecution because of legal "technicalities" or loopholes. Judge Harold Rothwax's attack on the rights of criminal suspects in his book *Guilty* is a classic example of using only celebrated cases and ignoring the general patterns in the administration of justice. We will look more closely at some other alleged loopholes in the system in Chapter 8.

One unresolved question remains, however. The BJS data indicate that many cases are dismissed in the "interest of justice." What exactly does this mean? It may mean that the offense is not that serious, or that the victim and offender know each other, or that some form of private settlement has been worked out. Until more detailed research is done on this question, we do not know whether these dismissals are appropriate or represent a covert pattern of bias in the system.

The decision to reject or dismiss a case is a highly discretionary one. Most of these decisions are made very quietly, and the prosecutor does not really have to account to anyone for them. An important question is whether a pattern of racial and ethnic bias is apparent in these decisions. Cassia Spohn and her colleagues found that women and white defendants were more likely to have their cases rejected than males and minorities. The racial and ethnic disparities were strongest at the rejection stage only. This may result from the fact that the decision to reject is much less visible than the decision to dismiss. Once a case has been accepted for prosecution, it becomes known to a wider range of people, and this visibility may act as a constraint on prosecutors and judges.[11]

Joan Petersilia's analysis of racial disparities found that African American defendants in California were more likely to have their cases rejected and dismissed than whites. This apparent favored treatment, however, may be a result of discrimination at the arrest stage. Some research suggests that police arrest African Americans on weaker evidence than whites. When these weak evidence cases reach the prosecutor, they are more likely to be dismissed or rejected. In short, discrimination takes place, but at an earlier point than that identified by Spohn and her colleagues.[12]

Sentencing Offenders

As we have seen, once the weak cases have been weeded out, the criminal justice system becomes extremely punitive. Overall conviction and incarceration rates are fairly high. And as we point out above, some of those incarcerated go to prison and some go to jail. Jail terms are typically short—less than one year. To understand whether the system is tough or soft, we now have to look at prison sentences. There are two separate aspects of prison sentences. First, there is the sentence imposed by the judge at sentencing, and there is the amount of time actually served. Many people argue that sentences are too short, while others argue that sentences in America are too long, far longer than other countries. Then, many people argue that prisoners get out too early and are returned to the streets. Others argue that the percentage of sentences actually served has gotten much higher in the last few decades.

BJS has estimated that in 2004 convicted murderers received an average sentence of 268 months (or just over 22 years), robbers got an average of 101 months (8 years and 5 months), and burglars an average of 55 months (4 years and 7 months). Interestingly, the BJS data report zero percentage of people convicted of murder or rape receiving a sentence of two years or less. All of these sentences, it should be noted, were longer than reported in 2000 by BJS, indicating that the trend toward longer sentences had continued.[13]

The actual time served by a convicted offender is the most realistic estimate of how punitive the criminal justice system is. Most offenders sentenced to prison are released early as a result of good-time reductions and parole. And in a particularly significant development, the system has become steadily more punitive. The percentage of sentences actually served increased from 32 percent in 1988 to 45 percent in 1996 and 55 percent in 2000 (the most recent data available). The estimated time served by robbers increased from 38 months in 1988 to 48 months in 1996 and 55 months in 2000. The time served by burglars increased from 22 to 25 to 29 months in the same period. These increases were the result of several developments: the abolition of discretionary parole in some states; mandatory sentencing laws that have increased sentences; sentencing laws that deny good-time reductions for some offenses; and a general attitude of punitiveness that has led judges to hand out longer prison sentences.[14]

How Do We Compare?: An International
Perspective on the Going Rate

How does the going rate for crime in the United States compare with its counterpart in other countries? A standard liberal criticism is that our criminal justice system is far more punitive than that of any other country. Conservatives, meanwhile, argue that we are too lenient and fail to punish criminals. James Lynch's careful analysis of comparative data suggests that both liberals and conservatives are clinging to their favorite myths on this question.[15]

On one hand, we do lock up a lot of people. We already have the highest incarceration rate in the world (750 per 100,000, including both the prison and jail populations).[16] And as our previous discussion indicates, we are fairly tough on those offenders whom we manage to arrest. From this perspective, it is hard to say that we are soft on crime.

At the same time, however, our high incarceration rate is mainly the result of our high rates of violent crime. At one point, the American murder rate was 4 times higher than Canada's and 10 times higher than England's and West Germany's. Our robbery rate was five times higher than those of England and

West Germany. These differences have narrowed in recent years because of the great crime drop, but our rates of violent crimes are still much higher than those of other industrialized societies. Violent crimes, moreover, were more likely to result in prison sentences, and armed robbery was more likely to result in a prison sentence than unarmed robbery. Lynch points out that a far higher proportion of robberies in the United States are armed than in other countries. In other words, we have a high incarceration rate in large part because we have such high rates of those crimes that typically send an offender to prison.[17]

The relevant question becomes: Is the going rate for particular crimes significantly higher in the United States than it is in other countries? Lynch estimated the chances of going to prison for a person arrested for murder, robbery, burglary, and larceny/theft in the United States, England, Canada, and West Germany. He found that a robber's chance of going to prison was 36 percent in the United States, 41 percent in Canada, and 39 percent in the United Kingdom. The odds were lower only in West Germany. The odds of going to prison were also roughly the same for murder, burglary, and larceny in the three English-speaking countries. In terms of the tendency to send convicted offenders to prison, then, the United States is not that much more punitive than other countries.[18]

In terms of time served, however, the United States is significantly more punitive, especially for property crimes. Lynch found that the average number of months served in prison for murder in the United States (50.5) was slightly higher than in England and Wales (43) but lower than in Canada (57). (Because of different methodologies, these estimates for the United States vary slightly from the ones cited earlier in this section.) Average time served for robbery was somewhat higher in the United States and substantially higher for both burglary and theft. Burglars in the United States, for example, served an average of 16.06 months, compared with 5.23 in Canada and 6.72 in England and Wales. The gap was even greater for theft. Convicted thieves in America served an average of 12 months, compared with only 2 in Canada and 4.65 in England and Wales.

A separate BJS report comparing crime and punishment in the United States and in England and Wales between 1981 and 1996 found that the United States and England incarcerated an equally high percentage of convicted murderers, robbers, and rapists but that the United States imprisoned a far higher percentage of burglars, assaulters, and auto thieves. The BJS data also indicate that American incarceration rates have risen dramatically since the 1960s, particularly in the late 1980s, and these trends hardly indicate that the American criminal justice system is "collapsing" in the sense of failing to punish convicted offenders.[19]

Lynch's comparative research highlights the fact that the going rate consists of two components. The first is the tendency to imprison serious offenders. On this point, the American going rate is very similar to other industrialized countries'. The second is the amount of prison time actually served. Here, the United States is more punitive—but primarily for property, not violent, crimes. Lynch did not study drug offenses, but the United States is likely comparatively very punitive, in terms of both incarceration and length of sentences.

THE COURTROOM WORK GROUP

The going rate is established and maintained by the people who work in the criminal justice system. The phrase "the system" implies some impersonal entity, but in fact it is a *process* involving people who make a series of discretionary decisions day in and day out.[20] A police officer decides to make an arrest; a prosecutor rejects a case; a judge sentences an offender to prison, and so on. Prosecutors, defense attorneys, judges, and to some extent police officers make up the *courtroom work group,* or what some refer to as the *local legal culture.* To understand how the system works, we need to examine how they go about their work: the decisions they make, the reasons why they make them, how they adjust to changes in the law or the workload, how they respond to people who challenge their established going rate.

In perhaps the best study of this phenomenon, Nardulli, Eisenstein, and Flemming characterized local courthouses as communities. "After spending an enormous number of hours in various county courts," they observed, "we became convinced that the concept of a courthouse community can be an immensely useful tool in trying to understand them."[21] In this context, "community" means that a group of people work together and have a mutual interest in getting the job done as efficiently as possible.

The bureaucratic setting of the courtroom work group exerts a major influence on the decisions of individual officials. All criminal justice officials exercise enormous discretion, but there are important differences in the settings in which they work. Police officers generally work alone or in pairs, often with no witnesses. For this reason, police work has been characterized as a "low-visibility" activity. To be sure, if an officer makes an arrest, it will be reviewed by others: a supervisor will sign off on it and prosecutors and defense attorneys will review it. But if the officer does not make an arrest, that decision is not reviewed by anyone. Prosecutors, defense attorneys, and judges, on the other hand, work in the highly visible setting of the courthouse. Their actions also leave a paper trail that enhances accountability. The news media and the public are potential witnesses to decisions that occur in open court. Finally, other members of the work group constrain the decisions of individual members. A truly outrageous decision by a prosecutor is likely to be challenged by a defense attorney or judge. Bail amounts and plea agreements are, in fact, negotiated among work group members. As a result, the actions of courtroom officials are constrained by other officials.

Working together every day, members of the courtroom work group reach a general consensus about how different kinds of cases should be handled. This involves a shared understanding about how much cases are "worth." There are "heavy" cases (that is, serious violent crimes) and "garbage" cases (relatively minor theft). This valuation allows them to move cases along quickly.

An Administrative System of Justice

Conflict between prosecution and defense is the exception rather than the rule. In theory we have an *adversarial* system of justice. The bedrock principle of the

Anglo-American system of justice is that a person is innocent until proven guilty and that the state has to prove guilt beyond a reasonable doubt. Additionally, the defendant has a right to challenge the prosecutor's case, with the assistance of counsel, in a public trial overseen by a neutral judge. This is different from the *inquisitorial* system of justice, where there is a presumption of guilt and the rights of defendants are not protected the way they are in the American system.

The reality of American criminal justice, however, is that we have an *administrative* system of justice. Few cases (about 10 percent) are settled through a public trial. There is no public clash between prosecution and defense. That occurs only in the few celebrated cases. In our administrative system of justice, decisions are negotiated among members of the courtroom work group, with a high degree of consensus and cooperation. A study of nine courts by the National Center for State Courts found that work group members in each court shared a "norm of proportionality," that is, of how much different cases are worth. Experts on plea bargaining describe the process as a "supermarket," with set prices and a high volume of business.[22] (We will discuss plea bargaining in detail in Chapter 8.)

Frederic Suffet's study of bail setting offers an excellent illustration of the consensus and cooperation that prevail in the courtroom work group. Only 3 percent of the cases he examined involved any conflict over the bail decision; some disagreement arose in another 9 percent.[23] Over the years, the members of this work group had developed a shared understanding about how much bail to set for different kinds of cases—in other words, how much each case was worth. In her study of plea bargaining, Alissa Pollitz Worden found a high degree of judicial agreement with prosecutorial sentence recommendations. She speculated that going rates "may be so predictable that a prosecutor need not make a formal recommendation in order to ensure that a sentence bargain will be honored by the court."[24]

Another example is John Rosecrance's study of presentence investigation (PSI) reports by probation officers. In theory, the PSI is an independent evaluation of a convicted offender's social history, taking into account criminal record, employment history, family status, and so on. Yet Rosecrance found that probation officers (POs) classified offenders very quickly on the basis of their offense and prior record. Even more important, they based their recommendations on what they thought judges and prosecutors wanted. The California POs he studied were in regular contact with prosecutors and discussed their cases with them. They rarely challenged plea agreements, which often included an understanding about the sentence. As one PO put it, "It's stupid to try and bust a deal.... Who needs the hassle? ... Everyone, including the defendant, has already agreed."[25]

Nardulli, Eisenstein, and Flemming add the important point that courtroom work groups vary from jurisdiction to jurisdiction. Each courtroom community has its own "distinctive character." Typically, one person plays "a dominant role ... by virtue of personality, professional skills (or reputation), political power, longevity, or some other attribute."[26] Ulmer's study of three Pennsylvania courts found important differences related to the stability of the membership in local work groups. In the wealthy suburban court system ("Rich County"), there was a high degree of membership stability and a culture of understanding and collegiality. In the large urban court ("Metro County"), on the other hand, there was considerable turnover in the prosecutor's office, which resulted in conflict between prosecutors and defense attorneys and close relations between the defense attorneys and judges. The Metro County example illustrates the extent to which other members of a courtroom work group adjust to some kind of disruption arising from one member of the group.[27]

Interestingly, the National Center for State Courts study found that the ability of local criminal courts to process cases efficiently was not necessarily related to caseloads and resources. It is a widespread belief that heavy case loads are the cause of delays in the courts. The Natonal Center found that courts that handled cases faster than other courts were characterized by a sense of mutual respect among work group members. That is, prosecutors and defense attorneys regarded each other as competent and well prepared. Even when they challenged each other over issues related to evidence they respected the other side's professionalism. In the slower courts, work group members regarded each other as not fully competent. The lack of respect led to questions and misunderstandings that slowed down the processing of cases. The respect that work group members have for each other, in short, is a major part of the local work group culture. And professionalism, not low case loads, leads to efficient case processing.[28]

The Limits of Reform

The courtroom work group has enormous power to limit, frustrate, or even block reforms in the justice system. A state legislature might pass a new law, or the Supreme Court might issue a landmark ruling, but that does not guarantee that the process will really change. Our capacity to make significant changes in how the system works is extremely important. Remember, we are searching for policies that will help reduce crime. Assuming we find some policies that do work, we have to be able to implement them and change how the system works. A few examples illustrate the power of the courtroom work group to frustrate reforms.

- The Supreme Court ruled in 1967 that defendants in juvenile court have a constitutional right to an attorney (*In re Gault*). Barry Feld, however, found that only half (47.7 percent) of the kids in Minnesota juvenile courts in 1984 actually had legal counsel. State officials simply did not comply with the law.[29]

- The Supreme Court ruled in 1963 (*Gideon v. Wainwright*) that adult felony defendants have a constitutional right to an attorney. A recent report by the Constitution Project, however, found that because of the resource crisis in criminal justice (see Chapter 1), many public defenders offices are overwhelmed with cases and cannot provide meaningful representation for their clients. Some public defenders have even threatened to or actually have refused to accept more cases.[30]

- Congress passed a "speedy trial" law in 1974, and several states enacted similar laws. Malcolm Feeley, however, found that these laws had almost no effect on the flow of cases. All members of the courtroom work group—judges, prosecutors, and defense attorneys—had their own reasons for delaying cases. The laws permit exceptions to the requirement, and officials take advantage of them. As one judge explained, "Our court has figured out ways to deal with the [speedy trial] act that don't cause us to change our practices at all."[31]

- Many states passed "three strikes" laws in the 1990s, but with the exception of California, prosecutors in most states were simply not using the law. Wisconsin had used it only once in a year and a half, whereas five other states had not used it at all. Even in California, use of the law varies tremendously by jurisdiction. Out of 8,381 inmates serving a third strike sentence in California in 2008, 3,140 (or 37 percent) were sentenced in Los Angeles County. San Diego County had sent on 659, and San Francisco County only 39.[32] Passing a law, in short, does not guarantee that it will be used or used even handedly in the same state. This is not the whole story about three-strikes laws, however. The Sentencing Project argues that three-strikes laws are being used enough in several states to account for a significant part of the prison population growth. About 20 percent of all California prisoners are serving three strike terms.[33]

We should not be completely cynical about the prospects for change. Some reforms have been implemented. A few examples illustrate this point.

- The "defense of life" rule was designed to reduce police use of deadly force. As a result, the number of persons shot and killed by the police fell from 559 in 1975 to 300 in 1987, and the racial disparity between African Americans and whites shot and killed was cut in half.[34]

- The Minnesota sentencing guidelines enacted in 1980 had the explicit goal of limiting the use of imprisonment. To a great extent this strategy has worked, and Minnesota has maintained the lowest incarceration rate of any state (with the possible exception of South Dakota).[35]

- The federal sentencing guidelines imposed harsher sentences and limited the discretion of judges. While some judges have found ways to get around the guidelines' strict requirements, there has been a significant increase in imprisonment for federal crimes.

The Dynamics of Reform

In short, some reforms are successfully implemented and some are not. What makes the difference? A great deal depends on the nature of the reform itself. Some experts believe that modest reforms, which require only slight changes in how the courtroom work group operates, are more likely to succeed than sweeping changes. Raymond T. Nimmer argues that "the probability of system change is inversely related to the degree of change sought by a reform." Eisenstein, Flemming, and Nardulli agree, concluding that "the more radical a proposed change the less likely is its adoption."[36] The three-strikes laws represent radical disruptions of established going rates and probably for that reason have been ignored in most jurisdictions.

In their study of rape law reform, on the other hand, Cassia Spohn and Julie Horney found significant changes in only one of six jurisdictions. They speculated that the new Michigan rape law was so comprehensive that it forced changes in the attitudes and behavior of courtroom work group officials, whereas the minor reforms in the other five jurisdictions had little impact.[37]

In the conclusion of their study of courts and their communities, Eisenstein, Flemming, and Nardulli offer some other sobering conclusions about the possibilities for reform. On one hand, changes mandated from *outside* the courtroom work groups face serious obstacles. They agree with Feeley that work groups have enormous ability to resist change. At the same time, however, change initiated from *within,* by the work group itself, also faces major obstacles. Efforts by judges to speed up trials may be blocked by prosecution and defense attorneys.[38]

In short, *some* things work. We should not adopt the cynical view that *nothing* works, or the naive view that *everything* works. The important point here is that the power of the courtroom work group to frustrate reform is extremely relevant to our search for sensible and effective crime policies. Even if we found a good policy, officials could not implement it.

An evaluation of the implementation of three-strikes laws explained that "[t]o some degree, sentencing policies and reforms involve a tug-of-war between the judicial, executive, and legislative branches of government for control over criminal justice matters."[39] The courtroom work group has enormous power to limit or frustrate reforms, but it does not have total control. When the legislature directs a major change—as in the case with sentencing guidelines—the courtroom work group can adapt and offset some of the intended change but cannot completely nullify it.

While there is tremendous stability and continuity in the criminal justice system, it is also true that the going rate does change over time. Take another look at the trends in the American prison population (Chapter 1, Figure 1.2). The prison population exploded as a result of sentencing policy changes: mandatory imprisonment laws, longer mandatory minimums, three-strikes laws, "truth in sentencing laws," and restrictions on prisoner good time. At the same time, there can also be *unplanned* developments. The impact of the post–World War II baby boom on crime was not planned by anyone. A significant increase in the workload of the justice system, meanwhile, produces adaptations. Arrests for public order offenses, for example, declined significantly between the 1960s and the 1990s.[40] As serious crime increased, police simply shifted their priorities and gave less attention to relatively minor crimes.

Criminal Justice Thermodynamics

The systems perspective on the administration of justice helps us see how changes in one part of the system affect decisions in other parts. Malcolm Feeley suggests that a major change may set off a "chain reaction throughout the entire system," forcing other officials to adapt and in some cases creating new and unanticipated problems.[41] We explain this chain reaction effect in terms of "criminal justice thermodynamics." You may remember from a physics class that the law of thermodynamics says that every action has an equal and opposite reaction. The justice system works in much the same way: actions produce reactions.

Our law of criminal justice thermodynamics states:

> An increase in the severity of the penalty will result in less frequent application of that penalty.

Our law has an important corollary:

> The less often a severe penalty is applied, the more arbitrary will be the occasions when it is applied.

The death penalty is an excellent example of the law of criminal justice thermodynamics. Because it is the ultimate penalty, it exerts enormous pressure on the courtroom work group. Many devices are used to evade its application (plea bargaining to a second-degree murder charge, demanding a jury trial, using the insanity defense, appealing on every potential issue, requesting pardon or commutation, and so forth). Thus, the action of the prosecutor in filing first-degree murder charges (making the case eligible for the death penalty) causes a reaction by the defense.

Because the death penalty is rarely used, its application is very arbitrary. In the landmark case of *Furman v. Georgia* (1972), the Supreme Court characterized the application of the death penalty as being so rare that it is "freakish" and akin to being "struck by lightning."[42]

Three-strikes laws are another excellent example. These laws provide very severe sentences for people convicted of a third felony (part of the California law also applies to people with certain kinds of second felonies)—typically, life or a very long mandatory prison term. Every study, however, has found that prosecutors rarely if ever use the law. And even in California, where it is used most often, it is primarily used by prosecutors only in certain counties.[43]

Pamala L. Griset's study of correctional practices in New York illustrates how an increase in severity can produce adaptations that, in many respects, undermine the original intent of getting tougher with criminals. New York adopted a series of mandatory sentencing laws in 1973 and 1978, followed by several early release programs in 1987 and 1989. The result was an odd mix of indeterminate and mandatory sentencing policies. The prison population began to increase, but because of financial constraints, the state did not build all of the planned new prisons.[44]

The three new early release programs—shock incarceration, "earned eligibility" for parole, and CASAT (Comprehensive Alcohol and Substance Abuse Treatment)—gave correctional officials enormous discretion over offenders' eligibility for early release. They began using these programs to reduce prison populations. Under earned eligibility, inmates gained a "presumption of release" for merely participating in a treatment, educational, or work program. Thus, they received a reward for what in the past had been considered minimal good conduct. The net effect was to release them early and to undercut the intent of mandatory minimum sentencing laws. Meanwhile, many offenders released under work release programs were allowed to live at home and report in twice a week. Over one-third of the participants in this "day reporting" program had been convicted of violent crimes. Here, also, correctional officials gained a vast amount of hidden discretion and used it to undercut the supposedly tough sentencing laws.

Wrongful Convictions: How Many Mistakes?

Since the administration of justice is a human process, involving day-in, day-out decisions by members of the courtroom work group, it is inevitable that there will be mistakes. The question is, How frequent are they? How often are innocent people wrongfully convicted? The issue of wrongful convictions has received a lot of publicity recently because of advances in DNA technology, which makes it possible to positively link a suspect with a crime and also to positively clear someone.

In 1992 Barry Scheck and Peter Neufeld established the Innocence Project at Cardozo Law School in New York City to provide legal assistance to convicted offenders on DNA issues. By 2009, 244 convicted offenders had been exonerated and released. They had served an average of 12 years in prison before their release. Seventeen had been sentenced to death; others were serving sentences of life in prison. Larry Mayes, for example, served 18 1/2 years in prison in Indiana after being wrongfully convicted of rape and robbery and sentenced to 80 years in prison. Local Innocence Projects have been established in 41 states and the District of Columbia.[45]

How can an innocent person be convicted of murder and sentenced to death or life in prison? The Innocence Project has identified several causes. The most important are false identification, police or prosecutor misconduct, bad lawyering by defense counsel, and incorrect scientific analysis of evidence.

Errors such as these raise disturbing questions about the courtroom work group. If the police or prosecutor engaged in misconduct, why didn't the defense attorney or judge notice and blow the whistle? If a defense attorney was grossly incompetent, why didn't the judge intervene? The answer to these questions goes to the very nature of the courtroom work group. The basic norms of the group emphasize cooperation and not challenging other members of the group. While this facilitates efficient handling of cases in the vast majority, the cases handled by the Innocence Project indicate that it can also cover up willful misconduct or incompetence—and send an innocent person to death row.

Most of the Innocence Project cases were celebrated cases to begin with: usually gruesome murders or rape and robbery crimes. Exoneration through DNA evidence automatically moved all of them into the celebrated case category. The question for us is, How often do mistakes happen in routine cases? How often do they occur in run-of-the-mill burglary and robbery cases? What is the overall error rate? Are there just a few celebrated cases, or do miscarriages of justice happen all the time?

C. Ronald Huff and his colleagues developed an ingenious method for estimating the number of wrongful convictions. They surveyed 229 Ohio criminal justice officials (judges, prosecutors, public defenders, police), along with attorneys general from all states, and asked for *their* estimate of the frequency of wrongful convictions. After eliminating the extremely high and low estimates, they concluded that errors occur in slightly less than 1 percent of all felony cases.[46]

What are we to make of this estimate? From one perspective, an error rate of less than 1 percent is very good. We should all be so successful in whatever we do. It compares very favorably with the false positive and false negative rates we will encounter with the prediction problem in Chapter 4. But Huff and his associates projected this error rate to the national level and estimated 5,729 wrongful convictions in 1981 (one-half of 1 percent of the total of 1,145,780 convictions). Six thousand innocent people convicted of a felony every year is a shocking fact to contemplate.

As for the death penalty, Hugo Bedau and Michael Radelet estimated that for every 20 persons executed in this country since 1900, at least 1 innocent person was convicted of a capital crime. They found a total of 343 persons mistakenly convicted of capital crimes; 25 were actually executed, while many of the others served prison terms of up to 25 years.[47]

In short, serious mistakes do occur in the criminal justice system. Some innocent people are in fact convicted and sent to prison—in some cases for long prison terms. We need to be ever-vigilant to guard against such mistakes and develop appropriate policies that will help prevent them. Nonetheless, if Huff's 1 percent estimate is correct, mistakes are extremely rare. The focus of this book is on the routine processing of cases in the 99 percent of cases free of serious error.

CONCLUSION

A going rate for crime exists in the United States. If you are convicted of a certain crime and have a certain prior record, it is possible to predict the outcome of your case with a high degree of accuracy. The going rate does vary between jurisdictions but is fairly stable within each one. It is established and maintained by the members of the courtroom work group, who work together daily.

The concept of the going rate is extremely important for our search for sensible and effective crime policies for two reasons. First, many proposed policies are based on mistaken assumptions about how the system works. They do not take into account the fact that the administration of justice is very stable, consistent, and predictable and that it is relatively tough on those offenders who are caught and prosecuted. Second, many proposed reforms would have trouble being implemented. The going rate is determined by the courtroom work group, which has tremendous power to adapt and either ignore or evade the intent of a new law or policy. Simply passing a new law does not necessarily mean that the intended changes will occur.

NOTES

1. Judge Harold J. Rothwax, *Guilty: The Collapse of Criminal Justice* (New York: Random House, 1996), p. 25.

2. Marc Mauer, *Lessons of the "Get Tough" Movement in the United States* (Washington, DC: The Sentencing Project, 2004). Jerome G. Miller, *Search and Destroy: African-American Males in the Criminal Justice System* (Cambridge: Cambridge University Press, 1996), p. xii. Tom R. Tyler, *Why People Obey the Law* (New Haven: Yale University Press, 1990).

3. Samuel Walker, Cassia Spohn, and Miriam DeLone, *The Color of Justice: Race, Ethnicity, and Crime in America,* 4th ed. (Belmont, CA: Wadsworth, 2007). Michael Tonry and Matthew Melewski, "The Malign Effects of Drug and Crime Control Policies on Black Americans," in Michael Tonry, ed., Crime and Justice: A Review of Research (Chicago: University of Chicago Press, 2008), pp. 1–44.

4. Excellent discussions of the going rate are in James Eisenstein, Roy B. Flemming, and Peter F. Nardulli, *The Contours of Justice: Communities and Their Courts* (Boston: Little, Brown, 1988), and Peter F. Nardulli, Roy B. Flemming, and James Eisenstein, *The Tenor of Justice* (Urbana: University of Illinois Press, 1988). Also see Jeffrey T. Ulmer, *Social Worlds of Sentencing* (Albany: State University of New York Press, 1997).

5. Charles Silberman, *Criminal Violence, Criminal Justice* (New York: Random House, 1978), p. 258.

6. Bureau of Justice Statistics, *Felony Defendants in Large Urban Counties, 2004* (Washington, DC: Department of Justice, 2008). NCJ 221152.

7. See the discussion of the barriers faced by prisoners reentering society in Joan Petersilia, *When Prisoners Come Home: Parole and Prisoner Reentry* (New York: Oxford University Press, 2003).

8. Bureau of Justice Statistics, *Sourcebook of Criminal Justice Statistics Online,* Table 5.0002.2004. www.albany.edu/sourcebook.

9. Lawrence W. Sherman and Barry Glick, *The Quality of Police Arrest Statistics* (Washington: The Police Foundation, 1984).

10. Joan Petersilia, *Racial Disparities in the Criminal Justice System* (Santa Monica, CA: Rand, 1983), p. 21.

11. Cassia Spohn, John Gruhl, and Susan Welch, "The Impact of the Ethnicity and Gender of Defendants on the Decision to Reject or Dismiss Felony Charges," *Criminology* 25 (1987): 175–191. For a provocative discussion on whether sentencing guidelines achieve their designed result of increasing the visibility or "transparency" of the sentencing process, see Ulmer, *Social Worlds of Sentencing.*

12. Petersilia, Racial Disparities in the Criminal Justice System, pp. 20–30.

13. Bureau of Justice Statistics, *Felony Sentences in State Courts, 2004.*

14. Bureau of Justice Statistics, *Felony Sentences in State Courts, 2000* (Washington, DC: Department of Justice, 2003). NCJ 198821.

15. James Lynch, "Crime in International Perspective," in James Q. Wilson and Joan Petersilia, eds., *Crime* (San Francisco: ICS Press, 1995), pp. 11–38.

16. Pew Center on the States, *1 in 100: Behind Bars in America 2008* (Washington, DC: Pew Foundation, 2008). www.pewtrusts.org.

17. Lynch, "Crime in International Perspective."

18. Ibid. A more recent and more thorough analysis is Bureau of Justice Statistics, *Cross-National Studies in Crime and Justice* (Washington, DC: Department of Justice, 2004). NCJ 200988.

19. Bureau of Justice Statistics, *Crime and Justice in the United States and in England and Wales, 1981–1996* (Washington, DC: Department of Justice, 1998). NCJ 169284.

20. Samuel Walker, *Taming the System: The Control of Discretion in Criminal Justice, 1950–1990* (New York: Oxford University Press, 1993). Michael R. Gottfredson and Don M. Gottfredson, *Decision Making in Criminal Justice,* 2nd ed. (New York: Plenum, 1988).

21. Nardulli et al., *Tenor of Justice.*

22. Brian J. Ostrom and Roger A. Hanson, *Efficiency, Timeliness, and Quality: A New Perspective from Nine State Criminal Trial Courts* (Williamsburg, VA: National Center for State Courts, 1999). Available on the National Center for State Courts website. Malcolm Feeley, "Perspectives on Plea Bargaining," *Law and Society Review* 13 (Winter 1979): 199.

23. Frederic Suffet, "Bail-Setting: A Study in Courtroom Interaction," *Crime and Delinquency* 12 (1966): 318–331.

24. Alissa Pollitz Worden, "The Judge's Role in Plea Bargaining: An Analysis of Judges' Agreement with Prosecutors' Sentencing Recommendations," *Justice Quarterly* 12 (June 1995): 273.

25. John Rosecrance, "Maintaining the Myth of Individualized Justice: Probation Presentence Reports," *Justice Quarterly* 5 (June 1988): 235–256.

26. Nardulli et al., *Tenor of Justice,* p. 41.

27. Ulmer, *Social Worlds of Sentencing,* especially Table 8.1.

28. Ibid.

29. Barry C. Feld, *Justice for Children: The Right to Counsel and the Juvenile Courts* (Boston: Northeastern University Press, 1993), p. 55.

30. National Right to Counsel Committee, *Justice Denied: America's Continuing Neglect of Our Constitutional Right to Counsel* (Washington, DC: The Constitution Project, 2009).

31. Malcolm Feeley, *Court Reform on Trial* (New York: Basic Books, 1983), p. 173.

32. Ashley Nellis and Ryan S. King, *No Exit: The Expanding Use of Life Sentences in America* (Washington, DC: The Sentencing Project, 2009).

33. Ibid.

34. William A. Geller and Michael S. Scott, *Deadly Force: What We Know* (Washington, DC: Police Executive Research Forum, 1992), p. 503. Bureau of Justice Statistics, *Policing and Homicide, 1976–98: Justifiable Homicide of Felons by Police and Murder of Police by Felons.* (Washington, DC: Department of Justice, 2001). NCJ 180987.

35. Terance D. Miethe and Charles A. Moore, *Sentencing Guidelines: Their Effect in Minnesota* (Washington, DC: Department of Justice, 1989). Bureau of Justice Statistics, *Sourcebook of Criminal Justice Statistics Online.* Available on the SUNY Albany website. Information about the Minnesota sentencing guidelines is available on the Minnesota Sentencing Guidelines Commission website.

36. Raymond T. Nimmer, *The Nature of System Change* (Chicago: American Bar Foundation, 1978), p. 181. Eisenstein et al., *Contours of Justice,* p. 294.

37. Cassia Spohn and Julie Horney, *Rape Law Reform: A Grassroots Revolution and Its Impact* (New York: Plenum, 1992), pp. 171–173.

38. Ibid., pp. 291–305.

39. Peter W. Greenwood, Susan S. Everingham, Elsa Chen, Allan F. Abrahamse, Nancy Merritt, and James Chiesa, *Three Strikes Revisited: An Early Assessment of Implementation and Effects* (Santa Monica, CA: Rand, 1998). Schiraldi, Colburn, and Lotke, *Three Strikes and You're Out: An Examination of the Impact of 3-Strike Laws 10 Years after their Enactment.* Available on the Justice Policy Institute website.

40. See the annual arrest data reported by the Uniform Crime Reports; go to the FBI website for the most recent reports. The best compilation is *The Sourcebook of Criminal Justice Statistics,* available on the SUNY Albany website.

41. Malcolm Feeley, *Court Reform on Trial,* p. 184.

42. *Furman v. Georgia,* 408 U.S. 238 (1972). Raymond Paternoster, *Capital Punishment in America* (Lexington, MA: Lexington Books, 1991).

43. Ashley Nellis and Ryan S. King, *No Exit: The Expanding Use of Life Sentences in America* (Washington, DC: The Sentencing Project, 2009).

44. Pamala L. Griset, "The Politics and Economics of Increased Correctional Discretion over Time Served: A New York Case Study," *Justice Quarterly* 12 (June 1995): 307–323.

45. The Innocence Project. www.innocenceproject.org.

46. C. Ronald Huff, Arye Rattner, and Edward Sagarin, "Guilty Until Proven Innocent: Wrongful Convictions and Public Policy," *Crime and Delinquency* 32 (October 1986): 518–544. C. Ronald Huff, Arye Rattner, and Edward Sagarin, *Convicted but Innocent* (Beverly Hills, CA: Sage, 1996).

47. Hugo Adam Bedau and Michael L. Radelet, "Miscarriages of Justice in Potentially Capital Cases," *Stanford Law Review* 40 (November 1987): 21–179.

4

The Prediction Problem

S everal examples illustrate the prediction problem—a critical phenomenon that runs through the entire criminal justice system.

- A convicted drug offender comes before the judge for sentencing. It is his first drug offense, involving intent to sell a small amount and possession of a small amount of drugs. He does have a prior record: two arrests as a juvenile and a burglary (where he took only a few items) as an adult. What sentence should he receive? Probation or a short prison term?

- A convicted robber comes before the judge next. He has a longer record: several arrests as a juvenile (but with no incarcerations), two burglaries (probation), and a prior robbery for which he received a short prison sentence. Prison or probation?

- A young woman is convicted of possession of stolen property. The property actually belonged to her boyfriend, who was convicted and sentenced to prison for a series of household burglaries. Should she go to prison or be placed on probation?

- A 22-year-old has been convicted of an armed robbery while on parole. He has a fairly extensive criminal record, both as a juvenile and an adult. He was on parole at the time after going to prison for a robbery. Prison or probation?

These are fairly typical cases. All involve a sentencing decision by the judge. As we have emphasized, sentencing is a critical discretionary decision. (For the sake of the discussion, we are assuming this is not a sentencing guidelines state, where the judge would be required to give a prison sentence in some of these cases.) In this chapter we want to look at the decisions as *predictions*—predictions about the offender's future behavior. Is this offender likely to commit additional crimes, such as robbery or burglary? If that is the prediction, then imprisonment would serve to prevent those crimes through incapacitation. Or is the person likely to mature out of criminal activity? If that is the prediction, then supervised probation might be the best choice.

The criminal justice system is pervaded by discretionary decisions that involve predictions about future behavior. A police officer does not arrest someone in a domestic disturbance in the belief that the underlying problem is not very serious and the assailant is not likely to do it again. (Here we are assuming there is no mandatory arrest law or police department policy that applies.) A judge orders an arrested person held without bail because of a long history of repeat offenses. A probation officer writes a presentence investigation (PSI) that recommends probation rather than prison because the offender's social history suggests that he or she is not likely to become a repeat offender. A judge sentences an offender to prison in the belief that his prior record indicates a high probability of reoffending. A parole board denies release on parole because it finds no evidence that the offender is ready for release and therefore is likely to reoffend.

The central question is whether these predictions have any validity. Are they based on solid evidence (for example, about the offenders probability of reoffending), or just the beliefs of the decision maker? Is it possible to improve our decision making by developing better instruments of diagnosis and evaluation? As we will see, this is especially relevant for sentencing. Sending only serious repeat offenders to prison would have a significant crime reduction effect. Not sending dangerous offenders to prison would save tens of millions of dollars and be more just to the individuals involved. A lot rides on these prediction decisions. In some respects, police officer decisions are even more consequential. If the officer decides to not arrest someone, there is never any case at all.

In this chapter we will look at the evidence on our ability to predict future criminal behavior. We begin with a review of the subject of career criminals. This was a hot criminal justice issue in the 1980s, and the research it stimulated provides some very good evidence for our discussion. To understand the interest in career criminals we need to begin with the project that initially inspired policy makers, Marvin Wolfgang's birth cohort study.

THE CAREER CRIMINAL

The career criminal was a major focus of crime control policy for many years. It is not quite the hot topic it was in the 1980s. It is another example of the fad syndrome in criminal justice policy, where a new idea arises, generates a lot of excitement and policy development, and then fades as research slowly undermines the assumptions.

Even though it is no longer a leading issue, the career criminal is very relevant for our inquiry. Several important crime control policies that we will examine in this book—preventive detention, major-offender prosecution programs, selective incapacitation—are aimed at the so-called career criminal. All of these programs assume that if we could identify and effectively respond to these offenders—through incapacitation, treatment, or another method—we could make significant reductions in crime. After three decades of research, experimentation, and program evaluation, we have a reasonably good idea of whether targeting the career criminal actually works. This chapter reviews that evidence.

WOLFGANG'S BIRTH COHORT

In the past, people have always talked about "hard-core" criminals, "repeaters," or "chronic recidivists," but these terms were based largely on myth and stereotypes. We are indebted to Marvin Wolfgang, Robert Figlio, and Thorsten Sellin for giving us a detailed profile of these people. Wolfgang and his colleagues' landmark study, *Delinquency in a Birth Cohort*, one of the most important pieces of criminal justice research in the last 30 years, has had a profound influence on thinking about crime policy.[1] Wolfgang's birth cohort included all the males born in Philadelphia in 1945 and traced their careers through their eighteenth birthday in 1963. Using official records, such as police and school records, the study reconstructed the criminal careers of a sample of 9,945 juveniles. The principal finding was that a small percentage of delinquents were responsible for a majority of all crimes and for about two-thirds of all violent crimes.

As Table 4.1 indicates, 35 percent of the cohort had at least one *officially recorded contact* with the police. Of that group, 46 percent had no more contacts. Wolfgang labeled them "one-time offenders." He divided the remaining 1,862 juveniles into two groups. The 1,235 with two, three, or four contacts were labeled the "nonchronic recidivists." The remaining 627 with five or more contacts were the "chronic delinquents." They represented 6 percent of the original cohort and 18 percent of the 3,475 delinquents. These 627 are the so-called career criminals.

Several comments about Wolfgang's data are in order. Most important, he measured delinquency in terms of officially recorded police contacts. Obviously, many delinquents were never caught, and the actual prevalence of criminal behavior was undoubtedly higher than 35 percent. Some had contact with the police, but the officer chose not to record it. Some of those with a recorded police contact, meanwhile, may have been picked up by mistake and should not be considered "offenders." Also, many of the "one-time delinquents" committed other illegal acts but were never caught. And, finally, some "nonchronic delinquents" committed more than four crimes.

Despite these limitations, however, the cohort study highlighted some important patterns in delinquency. It gave us the first clear picture of the prevalence of delinquency: that is, the percentage of any group of males who commit crime.

T A B L E 4.1   Wolfgang's birth cohort

	Number	Percentage of original sample	Total criminal offenses	Percentage of total offenses
Original sample	9,945			
Delinquents	3,475	34.9%	10,214	
One officially recorded contact with police	1,613	16.2	1,613	15.8%
Two to four contacts	1,235	12.4	3,296	32.3
Five or more contacts	627	6.3	5,305	51.9

SOURCE: Marvin Wolfgang, Robert M. Figlio, and Thorsten Sellin, *Delinquency in a Birth Cohort* (Chicago: University of Chicago Press, 1972).

Second, it gave us a good picture of the percentage we can consider "career criminals." Finally, it documented the fact that most delinquents stop committing illegal acts at some point, and most of them stop relatively early. We do not know what makes them stop. Some "mature out." Others may be deterred by their contact with the police. Still others may be helped by the treatment program included in their juvenile court disposition. All we know for sure is that most eventually stop.

Wolfgang's most important finding, and the one that excited policymakers, was the small group of 627 chronic recidivists that was responsible for more than half (52 percent) of all the crimes committed by the entire cohort and 63 percent of all the Index crimes (71 percent of the murders, 73 percent of the rapes, and 82 percent of all the robberies). The one-time offenders committed only 16 percent of the total; the nonchronic recidivists, the remaining 32 percent.

The policy implications of these data are obvious: If we could successfully identify and effectively respond to that 6 percent, we could achieve a major reduction in serious crime. And the point is relevant for both liberal and conservative crime policies. If you are a liberal who believes in rehabilitation, identifying and successfully treating that 6 percent would achieve a huge reduction in crime. If you are conservative, you will get a tremendous crime reduction by successfully incapacitating in prison that same 6 percent.

OTHER COHORT STUDIES

Wolfgang's original findings have been confirmed by other cohort studies. He and his associates conducted a follow-up study of males and females born in Philadelphia in 1958. This was a larger cohort (28,338 subjects) and more representative in terms of race and sex. Following the cohort's criminal careers between 1968 and 1974 (ages 10 to 18), they found a similar pattern in criminal behavior: 33 percent had at least one recorded contact with the police, whereas the chronic recidivists represented 7.5 percent of the total cohort (compared with 6.3 percent in the original study).[2]

The 1958 cohort did commit more crimes. Remember, this study covered the late 1960s, when the crime rate soared. The murder rate was three times higher and the robbery rate five times higher than for the 1945 cohort. Thus, about the same percentage of cohort members became delinquent, but those who did committed more crimes and far more serious ones.

Some people might question whether Philadelphia is representative of the rest of the country. Lyle Shannon studied three cohorts in Racine, Wisconsin, tracing the careers of 6,127 persons born in 1942, 1949, and 1955. Unlike Wolfgang, he followed his subjects into adulthood. Members of the 1942 cohort were 33 years old when the study ended. Shannon found that most of his subjects had at least one contact with the police: 68 percent of the 1942 group, 69 percent of the 1949 cohort, and 59 percent of the 1955 cohort (but the members of this last cohort were only 22 years old when the data collection ended, so it missed part of their high-crime years). These figures may seem frightening until we learn that most of the arrests were for relatively minor crimes. Part I Index crimes represented only 12.7 percent of all the arrests for the 1942 cohort and 15.9 and 24.6 percent for the 1949 and 1955 cohorts, respectively. These data confirm what criminologists have long known: that most males in this country break the law at some point in their lives but that most of the lawbreaking involves minor crimes such as vandalism.[3]

The career criminal patterns in Racine closely resembled those in Philadelphia. Shannon found that 9.5 percent of the 1942 cohort had 51 percent of the police contacts, 8 percent of the 1949 group had 50.8 percent of the contacts, and 5.8 percent of the 1955 group had 50.8 percent of that group's police contacts. Looking at felony arrests only, he found that people with four or more contacts represented 0.6 percent of the 1942 cohort but accounted for 27.1 percent of the felony arrests. For the 1949 group, 1.7 percent of the cohort had four or more contacts and were responsible for 44.1 percent of the felony contacts; for the 1955 group, 3.5 percent of the cohort had four or more and accounted for 63.8 percent of the felony contacts.

The fact that the Racine findings parallel those from Philadelphia is very significant. Racine is a relatively small midwestern community, with a population of only 71,000 in 1950 and 95,000 in 1970. Racial minorities constituted only 11 percent of the population in 1970. Philadelphia in 1970 was the third largest city in the country, with a minority population of 33.6 percent. The Racine study suggests that Wolfgang's most important finding holds true for other communities. Additional support comes from David Farrington's study of young men in London. Farrington found that 6 percent of his sample accounted for 49 percent of all the criminal convictions in the cohort.[4] In short, there appears to be a near-universal pattern in which a small group of offenders account for a very high proportion of all the crimes committed by their cohort.

DEFINING OUR TERMS AND CONCEPTS

Before going any further, it is useful to clarify some of the terminology used in career criminal research.[5] First, we can distinguish *criminal careers* from *career criminals*. Every offender has a criminal career. Some have short ones; others have long ones. Everyone who goes to school has an academic career. If you drop this and every other course tomorrow and never return to school, you have had an academic career—a very short one. The kid who commits one act of minor vandalism has a criminal career—a short one. The career criminal is the person with a long criminal career.

Another basic concept is the *prevalence* of criminality. We define this in terms of *participation,* which distinguishes between those who commit at least one crime and those who do not commit any. As we mentioned previously, the Philadelphia cohort study found that 35 of the original cohort had a contact with the police. To identify the real career criminals, we need to know the *frequency* of offending—that is, the rate at which active criminals commit crimes. As we will learn later, this issue has extremely important implications for crime policy. If the frequency is about five felonies a year, imprisoning offenders will have a certain crime reduction effect through incapacitation. But if the frequency is 144 felonies per year, the crime reduction effect will be much greater. Obtaining an accurate estimate of the frequency, then, is extremely important for assessing the impact of incapacitation. Determining the *seriousness* of offending is also important, because we want to identify those who commit the more serious crimes. The beginning of a criminal career is referred to as the *onset*. Do career criminals begin earlier than one-time offenders? If they do, we might be able to spot them that way. *Persistence* refers to continuing criminal activity and *desistance* to stopping. The amount of time between onset and desistance is the *career length*.

FROM RESEARCH TO POLICY

Wolfgang's original birth cohort study generated an enormous amount of excitement, stimulating further research and influencing the development of crime policies. The study was published at a politically opportune moment. By 1972, crime rates had been rising dramatically for a decade. The public was disillusioned with the liberal rehabilitation-oriented policies of the 1960s and was ready for programs that promised to "get tough" with hard-core criminals.[6] Wolfgang's data suggested that it might be possible to identify that small group.

This book examines some of the specific policies inspired by the career criminal research. They include police programs that target suspected career criminals for intensive surveillance (Chapter 5), pretrial detention of allegedly "dangerous" offenders (Chapter 7), career criminal prosecution programs (Chapter 8), and selective incapacitation for repeat offenders (Chapter 7). Many of the treatment-oriented crime control policies proposed by liberals are also designed to deal with particular classes of offenders. Intensive probation programs (Chapter 11) are designed for "high-risk" offenders, whereas boot camps are designed for special categories of offenders.

The data in Table 4.1 make it look simple: Spot the chronic recidivists and either treat or punish them accordingly. The problem, however, is that nothing is simple in the real world of criminal justice. Ideas that sound good in theory do not necessarily work out in practice. Let us look at some of the problems that arise when we try to translate Wolfgang's birth cohort research into crime control policy.

APPLICATION PROBLEMS

As is so often the case with path-breaking research, *Delinquency in a Birth Cohort* raised more questions than it answered. It was a major breakthrough to learn that we needed to focus on 6 percent of a cohort, but it was only the beginning.

Criminologists have devoted an enormous amount of time and energy to answering some basic questions. First, exactly who are the career criminals? Second, when do they begin their criminal careers, and can we identify them early in their careers before they commit most of their crimes? Third, how much crime does each one commit? (As we will see shortly, this question is particularly important.) Fourth, what kinds of crime do they commit? Fifth, how long do they remain active criminals? Sixth, when do they stop? Seventh, why do they stop? Is it the result of some criminal justice policy or do they simply mature out? All of these issues are related to the bottom line question: Are there criminal justice programs or interventions that cause them to stop earlier than they otherwise would?

The basic challenge confronting any policy directed toward career criminals is to identify and control these offenders *and only them*. It is a waste of time and money to imprison one-time offenders who do not commit more crimes. Traditionally, criminal justice officials believed that they could identify the repeat offenders or the truly dangerous criminals. Judges denied bail to defendants they "knew" were dangerous. Judges granted some convicted offenders probation because they "knew" they were not going to commit more crimes. Most of these decisions were based on hunch, guesswork, or just plain bias. At best, they relied on the seriousness of the immediate offense and the offender's prior record.

This issue is illustrated by the famous story about how one Supreme Court justice defined pornography. In the *Jacobellis* case (1964), Justice Potter Stewart admitted that he could not define "hard-core pornography" but said, "I know it when I see it."[7] Many criminal justice officials believe that they know a career criminal when they see one.

In the real world of criminal justice, career criminal programs run into two serious problems. The first is correctly identifying the career criminal and not mistakenly identifying low-rate offenders. We call this the *prediction problem*. The second is accurately estimating how much crime these career criminals actually do (the frequency of offending)—and thus how much crime we will prevent by either imprisoning or treating them. Let us look at both of these problems in detail.

CONFRONTING THE PREDICTION PROBLEM

Identifying someone as a career criminal is essentially a prediction. We are predicting that they will commit many crimes in the future. In this discussion, we are looking at the problem from the standpoint of the decision maker: the judge or the parole board. This is very different from the perspective of the social scientist. The researcher may find very strong correlations: e.g., between prior drug involvement plus low income and reoffending. Correlations tell us a lot about general patterns of behavior. A judge, however, is not interested in general patterns. He or she has to make a decision about the convicted offender standing in front of the bench to be sentenced.

We can use three basic methods for predicting criminal behavior. The first is an *actuarial* approach that relies on patterns of behavior among individuals with similar characteristics. Insurance companies use this method. The data indicate that young drivers have more accidents than middle-age drivers and that young men have much worse records than young women. Thus, insurance companies charge higher insurance rates for young people.

A second approach uses the *prior history* of the individual. Someone has committed many crimes in the past, and so we predict that this behavior will continue in the future. Or, in education we say that you flunked the first test in this course and, therefore, we predict that you will flunk the next one. As we learned in Chapter 3, criminal justice officials typically use prior criminal record to assess offenders. Sentencing guidelines build prior record into the matrix, assigning more points for each offense.

A third approach is *clinical evaluation*. Here, predictions about future behavior are based on the assessments of trained experts. A psychologist or social worker, for example, might conduct a personal interview, review the individual's social history (family, employment record, and so forth), and possibly administer a psychological test. Presentence investigations by probation officers are an example of clinical evaluations based on an offender's social history.

The Wenk Study

The question is, Can these techniques be used to successfully predict future criminal behavior? A good test was conducted on behalf of the National Council on Crime and Delinquency by Ernst A. Wenk, James O. Robison, and Gerald W. Smith. The results were not reassuring. Wenk and his colleagues began with a sample of 4,146 youths committed to the California Youth Authority (CYA). Of this group, 104 subsequently became "violent recidivists." Wenk and his colleagues sought to develop a prediction instrument that would have identified these 104 individuals if it had been used in advance. Their instrument involved a combination of prior record and clinical assessment, using each juvenile's prior criminal record and history of violence and substance abuse, among other factors. Clinical assessments were based on psychological tests and interviews.[8]

Table 4.2 indicates the results. As is obvious, the method successfully identified only half (52) of the 104 who subsequently committed a violent act. This group, referred to as the *true positives,* was correctly and positively identified as likely to commit a violent act. The other 52 slipped through the net, however. We call them the *false negatives.* They were falsely (or incorrectly) predicted not to be violent. From this perspective, the prediction instrument was only 50 percent accurate; it missed half of those who actually became violent.

There is an additional problem, however. As Table 4.2 indicates, 404 people were incorrectly predicted as likely to become violent. These are referred to as the *false positives.* What this means is that the method used by Wenk and his associates incorrectly identified about eight people for every one who was successfully identified as likely to become violent. From this perspective, the prediction instrument is accurate only about 12 percent of the time (52 out of the total of 456 predicted to be violent). To translate this figure into real-world terms, it would mean imprisoning eight nonrecidivists for every violent recidivist

TABLE 4.2   Number of youths predicted to be violent and nonviolent who proved to be violent and nonviolent, California, 1972

	Predicted violent	Predicted nonviolent
Actual violent	True positives: Violent persons correctly identified as and incarcerated 52	False negatives: Violent persons incorrectly identified as nonviolent and not incarcerated 52
Actual Nonviolent	False positives: Nonviolent persons incorrectly identified as violent and needlessly incarcerated 404	True negatives: Nonviolent persons correctly identified as nonviolent 3,638

SOURCE: Ernst A. Wenk, James O. Robison, and Gerald W. Smith, "Can Violence Be Predicted?" *Crime and Delinquency* 18 (October 1972): 393–402.

correctly identified. Obviously, the costs in terms of dollars and unnecessary deprivation of liberty would be enormous.

The Wenk study reveals the difficulty in predicting human behavior. Even with the extensive data available, the study's method produced large numbers of both false positives and false negatives. Even though many people think that they "know" career criminals "when they see one," in fact it is very difficult to predict future behavior accurately.

We can illustrate the prediction problem by applying it to Wolfgang's birth cohort. If juvenile court officials used the same prediction instrument to identify the 627 chronic recidivists, they would miss half of them (313) and then needlessly lock up 2,500 juveniles who would not become chronic recidivists. The same problem bedevils all prediction schemes, and as we shall see that it affects both conservative-oriented incapacitation policies and liberal-oriented rehabilitation programs.

The Texas Death Row Inmate Study

A more recent test of predicting dangerousness was conducted by the Texas Defender Service, the agency that represents death row inmates. It reviewed 155 cases in which prosecutors in recommending the death penalty had used experts to predict a defendant's future dangerousness. It then examined the prison disciplinary records of these inmates with respect to violent behavior. The predictions of dangerousness were *wrong in 95 percent of the cases*. Only 8 of the 155 predicted dangerous inmates had records of "seriously assaultive behavior." In fact, 20 percent of the inmates ($n = 31$) had no disciplinary violations of any sort. The remaining 75 percent had some record of disciplinary actions, but none involved serious assaults. Sixty-seven of the 155 inmates had been executed and had spent an average of 12 years on death row. Forty currently reside on death row and have been incarcerated an average of eight years. Forty-eight inmates had their sentences reduced and had served an average of nearly 22 years.[9]

The Federal Sentencing Guidelines

The 1987 law creating the federal sentencing guidelines also established the U.S. Sentencing Commission with a staff and a mandate to evaluate the implementation and impact of the guidelines. Since one of the goals of the guidelines is to reduce crime through incapacitation, the commission attempted to evaluate whether they were accurately predicting future criminal behavior. In a 2004 report, the commission found that the guidelines system of criminal history scores was positively correlated with recidivism rates. As offender criminal history scores increased, so did recidivism rates. Only 13.6 percent of the offenders with the lowest scores (Criminal History Category [CHC] I) recidivated in the first two years, compared with 55.2 percent of those with the highest scores (CHC VI). The Sentencing Commission concluded that the guidelines were accurately predicting future criminal behavior.[10]

The problem with the Sentencing Commission approach is that its prediction system relies on very broad categories based on prior record and does not attempt to predict the future behavior of individuals within a particular criminal history category. And in fact, the federal sentencing guidelines were intended to severely limit the discretion of judges in sentencing and prevent them from sentencing on the basis of individual factors (that is, making predictions about individual offenders). The sentencing guidelines can be properly seen as a "justice model" of sentencing, in which sentences are based on the seriousness of the offense and prior record. All the Sentencing Commission report tells us is that in general, people with longer criminal histories are more likely to commit more crime in the future than people with less serious criminal histories.

In the end, the evidence clearly indicates that the prediction problem is a recurring issue in criminal justice. We will encounter it again in Chapter 7 with regard to bail setting and incarceration, and in Chapter 11 with respect to probation and parole decision making.

The Rand Selective Incapacitation Study

A second exercise in prediction was conducted by the Rand Corporation in its report *Selective Incapacitation*.[11] The Rand Inmate Survey (RIS) involved self-report interviews in California, Texas, and Michigan in which prison inmates were asked how many crimes they had committed between arrests. While far from perfect, this self-report method yields a reasonably good estimate of the undetected crime committed by these offenders.

Then, using the actuarial method of prediction, the Rand researchers correlated the self-reported criminal activity with the social histories of the 2,190 inmates. They identified 13 characteristics that were correlated with high rates of criminal activity. Only those characteristics that were legally relevant and appropriate were used. An offender's race is not a legally appropriate factor, for example. Rand then used these data to develop a seven-point prediction scale (Table 4.3). Offenders with four or more points were then predicted to be high-rate offenders; those with two to three points were predicted to be medium rate, and those with only one or no points were low-rate offenders.

T A B L E 4.3   Seven-point scale of factors affecting prediction of offense rates

1.   Prior conviction for the instant offense type

2.   Incarcerated more than 50 percent of preceding two years

3.   Conviction before age 16

4.   Served time in a state juvenile facility

5.   Drug use in preceding two years

6.   Drug use as a juvenile

7.   Employed less than 50 percent of the preceding two years

SOURCE: Peter W. Greenwood, *Selective Incapacitation* (Santa Monica, CA: Rand, 1982), p. 50.

In the next stage, Rand retrospectively correlated the prediction scores with inmates' actual reported criminal activity. The results appear in Table 4.4. The prediction device was correct only 51 percent of the time. This represents the combination of the predicted low-risk offenders who proved to be low risks (14 percent), the predicted medium risks who proved to be medium risks (22 percent), and the predicted high risks who actually proved to be high risks (15 percent). A 51 percent accuracy rate is not very good. You could do as well flipping a coin.

At the same time, the prediction device was *grossly* wrong in 7 percent of the cases: the 4 percent who were predicted to be high risks but who turned out to be low risks (false positives) and the 3 percent who were predicted to be low risks but proved to be high risks (false negatives). The prediction device was only *moderately* wrong in the remaining 42 percent of the cases. (Consider for a moment the real-world implications of the 4 percent error rate for those incorrectly predicted to be high risks. Given our current prison population, that translates into about 50,000 people needlessly imprisoned.)

We can hardly expect any system to be perfect. The relevant question is whether the Rand prediction device is *better than existing sentencing practices.* Recall our discussion of goals in Chapter 1. We should not seek perfection, only an improvement over what we have been doing. If it leads to a substantial improvement, even though less than perfect, it would be useful. Peter Greenwood took his sample of offenders and categorized them as low, medium, or high risks

T A B L E 4.4   Predicted versus self-reported offense ratio for robbery and burglary

Score on prediction scale		Self-reported offense rates (%)			
		Low	Medium	High	Total
Low	(0–1)	14	10	3	27
Medium	(2–3)	12	22	10	44
High	(4–7)	4	10	15	29
Total		30	42	28	100

SOURCE: Peter W. Greenwood, *Selective Incapacitation* (Santa Monica, CA: Rand, 1982). p. 59.

Illustration by Frank Irwin, © Wadsworth, Cengage Learning.

according to the sentences they had actually received. These sentences were "correct" 42 percent of the time. That is, in 42 percent of the cases, the sentencing judges had correctly identified the high-rate offenders and sentenced them to long prison terms and correctly identified low-rate offenders and sentenced them to short terms. Meanwhile, the judges were grossly wrong 12 percent of the time. In short, the extremely sophisticated Rand prediction device was only slightly better than what judges had in fact already done with these offenders (51 percent versus 42 percent).

Several years later, Rand researchers made another attempt at predicting career criminals. They used two samples. One group included 2,700 men who had been committed to the CYA as juveniles between 1966 and 1971. The second group included 200 RIS inmates who had been incarcerated for either burglary or robbery and had been released at least two years before the new study. Rand used the original seven-point prediction scale for the RIS group and a modified five-point scale for the CYA group.[12]

The results of this study are expressed in the subtitle of the Rand report: *Why the High-Rate Offenders Are Hard to Predict*. The authors concluded that "high rate offenders cannot be accurately identified, either prospectively or retrospectively, on the basis of their arrest rates alone,"[13] and they conceded that the earlier Rand conclusions about the ability to identify high-rate offenders and reduce crime by selectively incapacitating them were "overly optimistic."[14]

B o x 4.1   Discussion: The Prediction Problem and the Garrido Case

In conclusion, it appears that we do not have the diagnostic tools that would allow us to predict with much accuracy the future behavior of a particular criminal. Remember that this is what a judge is up against. One way to look at this problem is to consider the horrible Garrido kidnapping and rape case we discussed in Chapter 2. When Garrido was first released from prison, was it possible to predict that he would go on to commit terrible crimes? Based on his record to that point, including his behavior in prison, did he look much different from the many other offenders who had similar criminal careers? One answer says that officials missed the obvious and made a terrible mistake. An alternative answer says that there was nothing special about his record compared with that of similar offenders, and that based on the information they had available to them at that time, they did not make a mistake.

HOW MUCH CRIME DO THEY COMMIT?

A critically important problem in translating career criminal research into crime policy involves estimating how many crimes the average high-rate offender commits. The estimate has important practical ramifications. How many crimes will we prevent if we lock up an armed robber for five years? How much safer will we be compared with the robber's completing a three-year sentence? Criminologists have devoted considerable energy to developing estimates of the *annual offending rate* for career criminals.

The RIS attempted to estimate annual offending rates through interviews with inmates in three states. It was one of the most influential studies, and its findings have been widely used. The self-report method was a major advance because official records (e.g., arrest reports) do not provide a complete picture of a criminal's criminal behavior. Many crimes are not reported, and obviously, most crimes do not result in an arrest.

The RIS estimated high rates of criminal activity, but with some important variations. California robbers averaged 53 robberies per year, compared with 77 for Michigan robbers but only 9 a year for those in Texas. The RIS also found that criminals did not specialize in one type of crime. California robbers also averaged 90 burglaries, 163 thefts or frauds, and 646 drug offenses each year. Texas robbers, meanwhile, averaged 24 burglaries and 98 thefts each year.[15]

The variations in annual offending rates among the three states are striking. Why were the rates so much higher for Michigan and California compared with Texas? The best explanation is that Texas judges sent more robbers to prison, regardless of their actual criminal histories. As a result, the Texas sample included a higher proportion of low-rate offenders than the Michigan and California samples did, thereby dragging down the group's average. California judges were being more selective, incarcerating only the worst robbers, with the result that the inmates in that state had much higher annual crime rates.

The difference in the annual offending rates may seem like a minor technical point, but it has tremendous practical consequences. We need a precise estimate of the annual offending rate to calculate the amount of crime reduction we will get. The annual offending rate is expressed as *lambda*. If the lambda is large, then we can expect a substantial reduction in crime for every career criminal who is imprisoned or rehabilitated. But if the lambda is low (that is, if the average career criminal commits relatively few crimes each year), then the payoff will be much lower.

Estimates of lambda by respected scholars vary enormously. Alfred Blumstein and Jacqueline Cohen estimated that adult arrestees committed an annual average of 3.4 robberies and 5.7 burglaries in Washington and 4.7 robberies and 5.3 burglaries in Detroit. The National Youth Survey estimated that active offenders committed an average of 8.4 robberies and 7.1 burglaries per year.[16] At the other end of the scale, Edwin W. Zedlewski, in *Making Confinement Decisions,* used an estimate of 187 felonies per year.[17] The practical implications of these different estimates are obvious. If we accept Zedlewski's figure, we could expect a great reduction in crime. But if we accept Blumstein and Cohen's figure, we will get a much smaller payoff for locking up each offender. When we discuss incapacitation as sentencing policy in Chapter 7, we will take a critical look at Zedlewski's use of his 187 figure.

A major part of the problem here is the concept of *average* offending rates. The RIS data clearly indicate that there is no such thing as an "average" career criminal. The median annual robbery rate for the RIS inmates was 5 per year. The top 10 percent, however, averaged 87 robberies per year. It is important to remember that the RIS inmates were a pretty select group: They got caught and were sent to prison because judges regarded them as dangerous offenders. The top 10 percent of the RIS sample, then, were the worst of the worst.

From a practical standpoint, to get some real payoff in terms of crime reduction, it is necessary to identify this small group from among all the other "serious" offenders. Say, for example, that you wanted to send most robbers (5 robberies per year) to 5-year prison terms and give the really high-rate robbers (87 robberies per year) 15 years. You would have to make very precise predictions.

We will examine this subject again in Chapter 7 when we discuss incapacitation as a crime control strategy. It is worth pointing out, however, that despite all the initial excitement about the possibilities of applying career criminal research through *selective* incapacitation, we have in practice abandoned that goal and adopted a policy of *gross* incapacitation. The prison population has soared because we are locking up lots of people without making fine distinctions.

CONCLUSION

The prediction problem is an excellent example of the difficulties of translating research into policy. Additionally, Wolfgang's original finding about the fact that a small group of offenders is responsible for a huge percentage of all crime focuses our discussion. *If* we could correctly identify the small number of serious repeat offenders, and then incarcerate them, we could achieve a significant reduction in crime. The Garrido kidnapping and rape case is a classic celebrated case that also focuses our attention on the prediction problem. *If* his future criminal conduct could have been predicted, we could have spared his victim tremendous suffering.

The key word here, of course, is *if*. Research on the prediction problem indicates that it is difficult, if not impossible, to precisely identify in advance the small group of high-rate offenders. This difficulty is compounded by the fact that estimates conflict on how much crime these high-rate offenders actually do. If the averages are in fact low, we will not get that much payoff in terms of crime reduction.

The problems we have identified here have a direct impact on many of the crime control policies we will examine in the chapters ahead. As we mentioned earlier, the administration of justice consists of a series of discretionary decision points. Many of those decisions involve predictions about who is and who is not dangerous.

NOTES

1. Marvin Wolfgang, Robert M. Figlio, and Thorsten Sellin, *Delinquency in a Birth Cohort* (Chicago: University of Chicago Press, 1972).

2. Paul E. Tracy, Marvin E. Wolfgang, and Robert M. Figlio, *Delinquency in Two Birth Cohorts* (Chicago: University of Chicago Press, 1985).

3. Lyle W. Shannon, Judith L. McKim, James P. Curry, and Lawrence J. Haffner, *Criminal Career Continuity: Its Social Context* (New York: Human Sciences Press, 1988).

4. The findings of all the longitudinal studies are reviewed in David P. Farrington, Lloyd E. Ohlin, and James Q. Wilson, *Understanding and Controlling Crime: Toward a New Research Strategy* (New York: Springer, 1986), see especially pp. 50–52.

5. Alfred Blumstein, Jacqueline Cohen, Jeffrey Roth, and Christy A. Visher, eds., *Criminal Careers and "Career Criminals"* (Washington, DC: National Academy Press, 1986).

6. Samuel Walker, *Popular Justice: A History of American Criminal Justice*, 2nd ed. (New York: Oxford University Press, 1998).

7. *Jacobellis v. Ohio*, 378 U.S. 184, 197 (1964).

8. Ernest A. Wenk, James O. Robison, and Gerald W. Smith, "Can Violence Be Predicted?" *Crime and Delinquency* 18 (October 1972): 339–402.

9. Texas Defender Service, *Deadly Speculation: Misleading Texas Capital Juries with False Predictions of Future Dangerousness* (Austin: Texas Defender Service, 2004). Available on the Texas Defender Service website.

10. U.S. Sentencing Commission, *Measuring Recidivism: The Criminal History Computation of the Federal Sentencing Guidelines* (Washington, DC: Author, 2004).

11. Peter W. Greenwood and Allan Abrahamse, *Selective Incapacitation* (Santa Monica, CA: Rand, 1982).

12. Peter W. Greenwood and Susan Turner, *Selective Incapacitation Revisited: Why the High-Rate Offenders Are Hard to Predict* (Santa Monica, CA: Rand, 1987).

13. Ibid., p. x.

14. Ibid., p. 49.

15. The data are in Greenwood and Abrahamse, *Selective Incapacitation*. The original report is Joan Petersilia, Peter W. Greenwood, and Marvin Lavin, *Criminal Careers of Habitual Felons* (Santa Monica, CA: Rand, 1977).

16. Alfred Blumstein and Jacqueline Cohen, "Estimating Individual Crime Rates from Arrest Records," *Journal of Criminal Law and Criminology* 70 (1979): 561–585. Blumstein et al., *Criminal Careers and "Career Criminals."*

17. Edwin W. Zedlewski, *Making Confinement Decisions* (Washington, DC: Government Printing Office, 1987).

PART II

"Get Tough": The Conservative Attack on Crime

Conservatives argue that we can reduce serious crime if we just "get tough" with criminals. Their crime control agenda, which has not changed in 40 years, includes the following items. First, we can reduce crime if we would just unleash the cops and give them more power and resources. We will look at several strategies for unleashing the cops in Chapter 5. Second, we can deter crime through swifter, more certain, and more severe punishments. We will take a close look at the theory of deterrence and some deterrence-oriented programs in Chapter 6. Third, we should lock up more criminals by sending more to prison and for longer prison terms. This represents a strategy of incapacitation. We will look at several incapacitation programs in Chapter 7. Fourth, conservatives believe that too many criminals "get off" through loopholes in the criminal justice system. We will examine four proposals designed to close loopholes in Chapter 8. Conservatives and some policy analysts believe that the recent reduction in crime is a result of these policies.

5

Unleash the Cops!

Illustration by Frank Irwin, © Wadsworth, Cengage Learning.

Conservatives believe that we can reduce crime if we just "unleash" the cops. Give them more officers and expanded powers, they argue, and the police will deter crime more effectively and arrest more criminals. There are two basic strategies for increasing the crime fighting effectiveness of the police. The first involves more intensive police patrol. This can be accomplished in one of three ways: by simply putting more police officers on the street, engaging in an intensive "crackdown" on crime, or having them focus their efforts toward specific places or crimes. Focused efforts include many community policing and problem-oriented policing programs, some of which are known as "hot spots" policing. A modern variation on more cops involves the use of closed circuit television (CCTV) in certain areas. This is a relatively inexpensive technological approach to the old idea of greater surveillance. The second strategy involves giving the police more powers, specifically by removing constitutional restraints on obtaining evidence and confessions. Let's look at these and other proposals to see whether they are likely to reduce crime.

Thinking about more effective police efforts has evolved considerably in recent years. Much of the public clings to old and discredited ideas such as putting more cops on the street or removing constitutional restraints. This is another example of how people do not really understand how the criminal justice system works. Other ideas, however, are new and based on solid research. The idea of "hot spots" policing is a good example. The research foundation is the reason such programs are often labeled "working smarter." The lesson of this chapter is that effective police anti-crime efforts are not a matter of simply "more cops" or "working harder," but of attacking crime and disorder intelligently and using an evidence-based approach. David Bayley has characterized the last years of the twentieth century as perhaps the most innovative period in the history of policing.[1] There is a lot of solid evidence available at this point. Let's see how this evidence is being used in practice.

MORE COPS ON THE STREET

Before looking at the recent evidence-based police programs, it is useful to clear the deck of the old idea of simply putting more police on the street. This approach is still very popular with the public. When most people today say they want better policing, what they really mean is they want more cops in their neighborhood.

Routine police patrol represents the basic police strategy for fighting crime. Patrol is the core police function, and it is where most police officers are assigned. The idea that police patrol deters crime has been the bedrock principle of policing since Robert Peel created the London Metropolitan Police in 1829. We will look at the concept of deterrence in other criminal justice contexts in Chapter 6 (felony sentencing, the death penalty). Here we will take a close look at how deterrence is supposed to work in policing. The questions before us are simple: Does police patrol deter crime? Does more patrol deter crime more effectively? Are there particular strategies for addressing crime and disorder that are more effective than others?

The Police and Crime

Policing is a very complex operation, and there is a lot of mythology about the relationship between the police and crime. There are two sides to the deterrence process. On the one side, "putting more cops on the street" is more complicated than most people think. On the other side, we have to look closely at what people perceive and how they react to the police.

T A B L E   5.1   Police/population ratios, major cities, 2000

	Sworn officers per 1,000 population
Washington, DC	6.3
New York City	5.0
Philadelphia	4.6
Detroit	4.4
Los Angeles	2.5
Denver	2.7
San Diego	1.7
San Jose	1.6

SOURCE: Bureau of Justice Statistics, *Local Police Departments, 2000*
(Washington, DC: Government Printing Office, 2003).

The standard measure of the level of police protection is the police/population ratio: the number of officers per 1,000 people. Nationally, there were 2.3 sworn officers per 1,000 people in the United States in 2005. In the largest cities (250,000 or more people), however, the figure rose to 2.8 per 1,000, compared with only 1.9 in medium-sized cities (100,000 to 249,000 population). Table 5.1, however, indicates that police/population ratios vary enormously. All policing is local, as they say, and the variation among cities is striking. According to the most recent data, Washington, DC, has more than twice as much police protection as Los Angeles and almost four times as much as San Diego. This does not make Washington a safer city, however.

In practice, the police/population ratio is a virtually meaningless figure because it does not tell us how police departments *utilize* their officers. If a department does not put those officers on the street, or if it uses inefficient two-officer patrols, additional officers will not have any real impact. Table 5.2 illustrates the point by comparing two hypothetical police departments, one that is very efficiently operated and one that is not. Both are in cities with populations of 500,000. One has 900 sworn officers, the other 600. The department with 900 officers, however, assigns a lower percentage to patrol. Many officers are probably assigned to desk jobs. The department also does not assign its patrol officers according to a rational workload formula, leaving the busy evening shift understaffed. Finally, it employs two-officer patrol units, which are much less efficient than one-officer units. The net result is that the city with the higher police/population ratio actually has fewer patrol units on the street during the high-crime evening shift. The citizens are paying more for police protection but getting less. Simply adding more officers to a poorly managed department, in short, will be largely wasted.

Even more important than the number of officers on the street is the question of what those officers actually *do* out there. At the simplest lever, if the officers engage in little active police work—initiating contacts with citizens, intensively patrolling high-crime areas, for example—the public will not get much in the way of actual crime fighting—*even if those tactics were proven to be effective*. (We will

T A B L E 5.2   Deployment of patrol officers in two hypothetical cities

	City X	City Y
Population	500,000	500,000
Sworn officers	900	600
Percentage of officers assigned to patrol	50	70
Officers assigned to patrol	450	420
Percentage of patrol officers assigned to 4 P.M.–12 A.M. shift	33	50
Patrol officers, 4 P.M.–12 A.M. shift	148	210
One-officer patrols	20	190
Two-officer patrols	64	10
Total patrols, 4 P.M.–12 A.M.	84	200

look at this important question later.) In short, adding more cops to a department where the officers don't do much active policing is another waste.

Before we finish with this question, however, let's see what the evidence is. Are there lower crime rates in cities with more cops? In the most systematic review of the evidence, Eck and Maguire reviewed 27 studies of the relationship between the number of police officers and the crime rate. They found very mixed results. Only 20 percent of the studies found that more police was correlated with lower crime rates, while 30 percent found just the reverse: more police was correlated with more crime. (Keep in mind, the findings involved correlations and not causations.) By the standards of evidence-based crime policy, this is not persuasive evidence that increasing the number of police reduces crime.[2]

Hiring More Police: The COPS Program

The largest, most intensive and most expensive program to add more police officers in history was the federal Community-Oriented Policing Services (COPS) program. The 1994 Violent Crime Control Act, which launched COPS, provided over $8.8 billion between 1995 and 2000 to put a promised 100,000 more officers on the streets of America. COPS office funds paid for 75 percent of the cost of a new officer for three years.

There is a great deal of controversy over the COPS program. Two questions need to be considered. First, did the program actually result in 100,000 more officers on the street? Second, did those additional officers help reduce crime? Remember, the COPS program coincided with the great crime decline in the 1990s. Was it responsible for that decline? Or, was it partly responsible, supplementing other crime reduction factors? Or was the money simply wasted?

First we have to specify exactly what the program funded and how many new officers were added. The COPS office made three different kinds of grants. The Universal Hiring Program funded the hiring of new officers. Technology grants, meanwhile, funded equipment designed to free officers from administrative duties and make them available for street duty. Finally, innovative grants supported community-oriented policing programs. There is much controversy over how many additional police officers were actually hired because of the COPS program. The estimates are complicated because the COPS program counted officers freed for street duty through technology grants. The most reliable estimates range from a low of 69,000 to a high of about 90,000.[3]

Zhao, Scheider, and Thurman conducted a national evaluation of the impact of the COPS program. They studied 7,179 city police agencies that received COPS funding between 1994 and 1998 (omitting state police, county sheriffs, and other special purpose agencies, as well as 535 cities with populations of less than 1,000). They separately evaluated the three types of COPS grants. The grant data were lagged by one or more years (depending on the type of grant) to allow for implementation. Common sense tells us that it takes time for new officers to be recruited, trained, and placed on the street, so the effect, if any, will be delayed by a year or more.[4]

Analyzing official UCR data from 1994 to 1999, Zhao and his colleagues found that in cities with 10,000 or more people the hiring grants and the Innovative grants did reduce crime. They estimated that *one dollar in grant funding per city resident* for hiring (that is, $350,000 in a city of 350,000 people) resulted in a decline in 5.26 violent crimes per 100,000 people (e.g., about 18 violent crimes in a city of 350,000 people). Innovative grants, meanwhile, were associated with even greater reductions in violent crimes. No crime reductions were associated with the technology grants, however.

These findings were promising, but a cost–benefit analysis puts them in a different perspective. Let's take a hypothetical city of 350,000 people. COPS funding of $350,000 ($1 per resident in the Zhao analysis) would result in a re-duction of about 18 violent crimes (at the rate of 5 per 100,000). This comes to about $19,400 per violent crime. Let's assume that the city is Omaha, Nebraska (2000 population: 390,000). In 2003 Omaha had 2,627 reported violent crimes. The $350,000 would have purchased less than a 1 percent reduction in violent crime (0.68 percent, to be exact).

These data raise serious questions about the cost-effectiveness of the COPS program. It would require an expenditure of an additional $4 million dollars to achieve a 10 percent reduction in violent crime in a city of 350,000. Consider the implications of this for other cities. An additional expenditure of $1.3 million in Phoenix would produce a slightly less than 1 percent reduction in violent crime; and it would take more than an extra $13 million to approach a 10 per-cent reduction. Remember that the ground rules for our inquiry require that a program not just be effective but that it be consistent with our legal standards (e.g., not violate constitutional law) *and that it be practical*. This includes considera-tions of cost. The program has to be something we can realistically afford. It is not clear that the COPS formula meets the cost-effectiveness test.

A more recent analysis of the COPS program by Worrall and Kovandzic, which corrected for what it saw as some methodological problems with the Zao study, reached a very different and very pessimistic conclusion: "COPS grants had no discernible effect on serious crime during the period covered."[5]

In their discussion, they explored some of the practical problems in trying to reduce crime by spending money on police officers. When they analyzed the average annual COPS spending in terms of overall spending on police, they found that it represented only one-half of one percent of a typical police department's annual budget. That is a very small increase. Furthermore, they point out, as we do, that police are spread pretty thin out there on the street. (See our discussion of the Kansas City Patrol Experiment in the next section.) They estimate that because police are deployed in three shifts, no more than 10,000 new officers were out on the street at any one time. For the country as a whole, that's not many per city per shift. In short, all that money ($8.8 billion) does not—and cannot—increase the police presence in, for example, your neighborhood.

We should say, in fairness that measuring the impact of added police officers is extremely difficult. Many different variables potentially affect crime rates, and police staffing patterns vary considerably from department to department. As we will see, a similar problem affects attempts to measure the impact of different sentencing laws from state to state. The debate between the two major studies discussed here is likely to continue into the future.

The evidence on the COPS program leads to the following conclusion:

PROPOSITION 6

Adding police officers, in combination with community policing programs, may produce modest reductions in crime but is not cost-effective.

The Deterrent Effect of Patrol: Lessons of Kansas City

The idea that a *visible police presence* deters crime has been the core principle of modern policing since the days of Peel in London. For nearly 150 years everyone accepted this idea on faith, without any scientific evidence to back it up. The Kansas City Preventive Patrol Experiment (1972–1973), one of the most important research projects in police history, finally tested the deterrent effect of policing.[6]

The design of the experiment divided the South Patrol District into three groups of patrol beats. *Proactive* beats received two or three times the normal level of patrol. *Reactive* beats received no routine patrol: Police cars entered those areas only in response to a citizen's call for service; officers handled the call and then left the beat area. *Control* beats kept the normal level of patrol. Using a victimization survey, the experiment examined the effect of different levels of patrol on criminal activity and citizen perceptions of police protection. Unlike earlier experiments, they controlled for other variables that might affect the level of criminal activity: temporary or random changes in criminal activity, unreported crime, the possible displacement of crime into neighboring areas, and the reactions of both police officers and citizens to changes in police activity.

The Kansas City experiment found that the level of patrol had *no effect on either crime or citizen perceptions and fear of crime*. Crime did not increase in the reactive heats where there was less patrol and did not decline in the proactive beats where there was more patrol. Moreover, people did not seem to notice the differences in the level of patrol. Fear of crime did not go up in the reactive beats and did not go down in the proactive beats.[7]

It is important to emphasize that the experiment did *not* prove that patrol has absolutely no effect on crime. At no time were there beats with no police presence whatsoever. Patrol cars entered reactive beats to handle 911 calls, and officers in other units (e.g., juvenile, criminal investigation) entered them to handle their own assignments. Law-abiding citizens and potential criminals alike saw a marked police car and assumed that the police were patrolling the area. This phenomenon has been described as the *phantom effect* or *residual deterrence*. Even if there are no police around, patrol works if people believe that they are. Residual deterrence works in several ways. People who saw patrol cars in proactive beats probably assumed that there were patrol cars in reactive beats. Moreover, as a practical matter we all pass through different police beats as we go about our lives (from home to job, school, the store, and so on). When we see a patrol car in one beat, that impression stays with us as we move through other beats. Most important for our purposes, the experiment found that *more* police patrols did not *reduce* the criminal activity.

The Kansas City findings were partly confirmed by the subsequent Newark (New Jersey) Foot Patrol Experiment (1978–1979), which found that different levels of foot patrol had no effect on the crime rate. Interestingly, however, it also found that additional foot patrol officers reduced citizen fear of crime and improved attitudes toward the police department. This finding proved to be one of the keys to the development of community policing and problem-oriented policing. We will come back to it later.[8]

Understanding Deterrence and the Police

Why did adding patrol officers not reduce crime in either Kansas City or Newark? A major part of the answer lies in the underlying theory of deterrence. The theory assumes that the "treatment" (in this case, police patrol) communicates a threat of apprehension and causes people not to commit crime. It logically follows that more police patrol will communicate that threat more effectively and thereby have a greater crime reduction effect. Think about it in basic terms: two patrol cars in a neighborhood will communicate the threat to twice as many people, or to one potential criminal twice as often, as only one patrol car.

Deterrence, as we will discuss in Chapter 6, is a matter of social psychology. The target audience has to *perceive* the threat (in this case, more police patrol), *calculate* the increased risk (of arrest), *understand* that the consequences are unpleasant (prosecution and possible conviction and imprisonment), and then make a *rational decision* not to commit a crime.[9]

In the real world of policing, deterrence theory breaks down. First, police patrol is spread very thin even in the best of circumstances. A patrol car actually passes each point in its assigned beat very few times in any day or seven-day period. Doubling the number of patrol units (increasing the treatment or the "dose") may not represent a difference that people are likely to perceive. It is sort of like taking four aspirins instead of two for a serious health problem.

Second, many actual or potential offenders do not perceive police patrol as a meaningful threat. They simply don't think that they will be caught. The official clearance rate for burglary in 2008, after all, was only 12.5 percent, and the rate for robbery only 26.8. (And remember, these figures are based on reported crimes. Taking into account unreported crimes, the actual clearance rates are much lower.) Teenagers, moreover, have a sense of invincibility. Much crime is impulsive, with offenders not rationally calculating. Experienced criminals, meanwhile, are fatalistic and assume that sooner or later they will be caught. Analyzing the Rand Inmate Survey, James Q. Wilson and Alan Abrahamse found that most prison inmates were fatalistic and thought there was a good chance they would be arrested, convicted, or even injured as a result of doing crime. Nonetheless, almost all had committed repeat offenses. Clearly, the fear of adverse consequences did not deter them.[10]

Third, many crimes are inherently not suppressible by patrol. The majority of murders and assaults, and about half of all rapes, occur between people who know each other. Because they usually occur indoors and in the heat of passion, the level of police patrol out on the street has no effect on them. Robbery, burglary, and auto theft, on the other hand, occur outside, and are at least theoretically suppressible through patrol.

By the standards of evidence-based crime policy, both the Kansas City and Newark experiments provide persuasive evidence that simply adding additional patrol officers (and not changing how they patrol or what they do) does not increase the deterrent effect of patrol. The evidence leads us to the following proposition:

PROPOSITION 7
Increasing the level of traditional police patrol will not reduce crime.

THE ALL-SEEING EYE: CCTV

Many people are excited about using closed circuit television (CCTV) to monitor particular neighborhoods as a means of fighting crime. CCTV involves two strategies. First, many people believe that the presence of the cameras will deter crime. Second, the resulting video recordings will provide evidence that will lead to arrests.

CCTV is essentially a technological extension of police patrol: A continuous "eye" observing an area. Think of it as a lot of patrol officers assigned to specific locations. And since potential criminals presumably know the CCTV cameras are there, it theoretically represents a continuous deterrent. Our challenge is to determine if these assumptions are correct. CCTVs, of course, are widely used in particular locations: your bank, the local convenience store, the entrance to many apartments, and so on. In some cases they do provide useful images of robbers that are helpful in making an arrest. Robbers, of course, know the cameras are there, and this raises a serious question about the deterrent effect. A bank or store, however, is a specific location with a high probability of being a crime target.

That's why the owners install cameras. Our question is whether they are effective out in *public* places, on the streets, and whether they have a deterrent effect there.

CCTVs as a crime fighting tool are far more extensively used in England than the United States. Between 1998 and 2001 alone, the British government spent the equivalent of $250 million in American dollars on CCTVs. This was a huge investment in an area whose population is equal to California and Texas combined. New York City has an enormous CCTV network. The New York Civil Liberties Union, which is primarily concerned about privacy issues, estimated that the number of cameras in the Greenwich Village/SOHO area increased from 142 in 1998 to 2,227 in 2005. This is a huge number of cameras for such a relatively small part of the city.[11] Fortunately for us, the effectiveness of CCTVs has been evaluated by David Farrington, one of the world's top criminologists, and others. The evidence is very mixed.

Welsh and Farrington reviewed 22 studies of the effectiveness of CCTVs on violent and property crimes, particularly vehicle crimes. To qualify for their review, a study had to use comparable control areas without CCTVs. Among the 13 evaluations that involved a city center area or public housing area, the results were mixed. Five reported a positive effect on crime, five reported no effect, and three reported negative results (that is, an increase in crime). Four other studies involved public transportation systems, all of which were subways (three in London, one in Montreal). Some involved other crime-fighting innovations as well as the CCTVs. The evaluations found some overall reduction in crime, but no reduction in violent crimes. Another five evaluations involved automobile parking areas, and all included additional changes such as improved lighting. Four of the five evaluations reported reductions in crime, while one reported an increase in crime.[12]

In short, CCTVs are most effective in reducing property crime in parking areas, particularly when coupled with other improvements such as better lighting. This makes sense. Parking areas are fixed locations (much like convenience stores) that are likely targets. There is mixed evidence regarding crime in general public areas, and no evidence of a positive impact on violent crime. This too makes sense. Assaults and robberies on the street do not occur at fixed locations, but are randomly distributed without any pattern (apart from a general high crime area). Considering the enormous cost of CCTVs, the evidence raises questions about the cost-effectiveness of CCTVs as a crime-fighting strategy. Thus:

PROPOSITION 8

Closed circuit television (CCTV) is not an effective tool for reducing violent crime or property crime, except for specific locations.

POLICE "CRACKDOWNS" ON CRIME

So far we have discussed proposals to hire and place more officers on the street. This has involved simply the number of officers and not what they actually do. Now let's examine different police strategies and tactics for reducing crime. We will first look at several traditional strategies. Later we will examine some recent, research-based innovative strategies.

Traditional police "crackdowns" are a classic example of the "get tough" approach to policing. Essentially, a *crackdown* is a short burst of intensive law enforcement, involving many arrests, directed toward a particular area or a particular crime.[13]

One well-known antidrug crackdown was Operation Pressure Point (OPP) in New York City. In the early 1980s, OPP targeted an open-air drug market on the city's Lower East Side that had been described as a "drug buyer's paradise." An additional 240 officers flooded the area, dispersing crowds, stopping and questioning suspected drug buyers and sellers, writing traffic tickets, and making a high volume of arrests (more than 2,000 in the first month alone). Also, the police department ended its Desk Appearance Ticket (DAT) policy, which allowed persons charged with misdemeanors to be released immediately, and the U.S. attorney's office agreed to process many of the drug arrests in federal court, where the defendants would face harsher sentences.[14]

There are a number of serious questions about the process and impact of OPP, however. Particularly important, the evaluation did not control for the possible *displacement* of drug trafficking into other neighborhoods. (As we will see shortly, the issue of possible displacement of crime, and the possible diffusion of positive effects, is a major concern in recent innovations.) Moreover, drug dealers adapted to the crackdown with more sophisticated techniques, such as using lookouts and "steerers" to insulate the actual dealers from the police. *Adaptation* by offenders is another important issue. The cost-effectiveness of the large number of arrests was not evaluated. Finally, the evaluation mentioned but did not discuss in detail the implications of the police misconduct that the program encouraged. Officers disrupted drug dealing, for example, by harassing potential buyers and scaring them off. Another problem is the replacement effect. A drug crack down may well remove drug dealers from an area, but they may also be replaced by other individuals who see an opportunity to make money. As one police officer put it, for every person arrested "there is always a replacement."

One of the major problems with traditional crackdowns is that they are unfocused. They did not have a specific, evidence-based strategy for targeting particular offenders or problems. The recent innovations in police we will look at shortly do embody these characteristics, and the evidence on their effectiveness is much more hopeful. Also, traditional crackdowns have always been police-only efforts. The new thinking holds that effective strategies need to involve partnerships among criminal justice agencies, other government services, and community organizations.

FASTER RESPONSE TIME

Get to a crime in progress quickly, and catch the offender in the act. The belief in the effectiveness of fast response times is another popular myth. If the police could just get there a little faster than they do normally, they would arrest a lot more criminals and drive down the crime rate. Word of the likelihood of arrests, moreover, will spread and deter other potential criminals. Let's take a hard look at the belief in faster response times.

In practice, however, faster response time does not produce more arrests. The police are called to very few crimes in progress. At most, only about 30 percent of all patrol dispatches involve criminal activity. Some studies put the figure as low as 17 percent. Moreover, about 75 percent of these crime-related calls involve "cold" crimes: typically, a burglary that occurred many hours earlier. The offender is long gone, and it makes no difference whether the police get there in three minutes or three hours.[15]

The remaining crime-related calls are "involvement" crimes, meaning that a confrontation exists between the victim and a suspect. At most, they represent only 25 percent of crime-related calls and only 7.5 percent of all dispatches. Response time rarely makes a difference in these crimes, either. In many cases, the victim and offender are acquaintances. The victim can identify the suspect no matter when the police arrive. Equally important, crime victims usually do not call the police immediately. Traumatized and confused, they often try to compose themselves, decide whether to even call the police, and often call a friend or family member first. This delay in calling the police renders irrelevant the police travel time in terms of catching the offender. At best, faster police response might make a difference in a very small number of crime calls: about 3 percent, according to a study by the Police Executive Research Forum. Commercial robberies are the best example. If someone calls the police while the crime is in progress, a very quick response time might improve the chances of catching the offender at the scene. But these kinds of crime are rare events.[16]

The National Academy of Sciences report concluded that improving police response time does not reduce crime.[17] We agree.

PROPOSITION 9
Faster response time will not produce more arrests or lower the crime rate.

RESEARCH-BASED POLICE STRATEGIES

Most police experts agree that the traditional approaches of adding more police, conducting crackdowns, and trying to lower response times will not reduce crime. But they also agree that certain police innovations, such as problem-oriented policing (POP), and especially "hot spots" policing can be effective. The crucial difference is that these innovations involve carefully planned and focused police strategies that are solidly based on research evidence on what works and what does not work. The National Academy of Sciences report on policing concluded that while still preliminary, there is "a strong body of evidence suggesting that taking a focused geographic approach to crime problems can increase the effectiveness of policing."[18] Let's look at some of the programs that were the cause of the National Academy's optimism.

Problem-Oriented Policing. POP programs represent a more sophisticated kind of focused police activity. While they often involve an intensive law enforcement effort, they are far more complex than the traditional unfocused crackdowns we discussed earlier. Most draw upon four important new developments in policing.

First, the POP approach involves careful *planning,* utilizing the SARA model: scanning, analysis, response, assessment. The SARA model is an excellent example of the new research-driven approach to police crime fighting. Problem-oriented policing holds that instead of attacking "crime" in a global and unfocused way, the police should identify particular problems (e.g., open air drug dealing, graffiti, residential burglaries, and so on), examine the underlying causes, and develop strategies designed to address them.[19]

Second, many programs draw heavily on the concept of "hot spots." Lawrence W. Sherman's analysis of 911 calls in Minneapolis found the astonishing fact that 5 percent of the addresses in the city accounted for 64 percent of all 911 calls. A very few places, which he labeled hot spots, were consuming the vast majority of police time and effort.[20] The concept of hot spots has since become a major focus of research and policy development in policing. It also represents a research-based approach to policing: utilizing an important new concept from the world of social science; maintaining a sophisticated data base on calls for service and reported crimes; and analyzing those data to identify the true hot spots.

Third, they involve *partnerships* with other government agencies and private groups to address social problems that are associated with criminal activity. Police departments, for example, have developed working partnerships with local housing officials to help fix up deteriorated buildings.

Fourth, many programs use nontraditional responses, such as civil remedies rather than arrest. This involves, for example, restraining orders against known gang members or prostitutes, or housing authority orders forcing landlords to repair buildings they own.

SMART IN OAKLAND

The Specialized Multi-Agency Response Team (SMART) program was directed toward specific drug hot spots in Oakland, California. The police were, as the acronym spells out, part of a multiagency task force. In addition to increased law enforcement activity by the police (more patrol, field interrogations, arrests), SMART mobilized officials from the housing, fire, and public works departments to enforce local building codes and clean up the physical appearance of the neighborhoods. A training program for landlords was designed to help them screen prospective tenants and evict existing tenants for rules violations. Lorraine Green's evaluation of SMART found that it reduced the level of drug activity in the target areas. Moreover, not only did it not displace crime to nearby areas, but it had a "diffusion" effect of improving surrounding areas. We discuss the important concept of diffusion in more detail shortly.[21]

Three key factors, working in combination, distinguish the SMART program from the traditional police crime-fighting approaches. First, it represents a change in police *activity,* as opposed to the mere number of police officers. Second, it focuses narrowly on specific hot spots, as opposed to unfocused patrol of the entire community. Third, it enlists other agencies (e.g., the city housing agency) and uses non–criminal justice tactics (code enforcement) to address problems associated with crime.

The emerging consensus among crime policy experts is that not only must the police engage themselves with non–criminal justice agencies, but they also need to work closely with other criminal justice agencies and focus on the full range of problems in specific neighborhoods. We will discuss the community-focused approach to crime in more detail in Chapter 14.

Hot Spots in Lowell and Jersey City

A hot spots experiment in Lowell, Massachusetts, also followed the SARA model of planning and implementation. The scanning identified 34 separate hot spots of crime and disorder that represented only 2.7 percent of the area of the entire city, but about 30 percent of all violent crime calls to the police. The 34 areas were then distributed into 17 matched pairs. Police captains were then made responsible for developing POP programs in their areas. In practice, many of the POP efforts were not solidly based on an underlying analysis of the problems (the "A" in SARA). Many involved established POP tactics such as cleaning up vacant lots and improving lighting. The experimental areas also received additional police enforcement efforts, such as increased patrol, dispersing loiterers, public nuisance arrests, and so on. The weekly average of misdemeanor arrests in the treatment areas increased about 18 percent. Data collected for the experiment included traditional calls for service, and both photographs of the physical appearance and observations of social activities (e.g., the number of people engaging in disorderly activity) in each area.

Analysis of the data found that calls for service regarding violent crime went down significantly (42 percent for robbery and nondomestic assault incidents). Meanwhile, observed social disorder was reduced in 14 of the 17 treatment areas. Analysis of the catchment areas surrounding the treatment and control areas found that crime increased only very slightly and not to a statistically significant degree. In short, a few criminals may have moved a few blocks to escape more intensive police presence, but for the most part they did not.[22]

A hot spots experiment in Jersey City, New Jersey, was directed at illegal drug markets and prostitution. The anti-prostitution effort on Cornelison Avenue included three common POP tactics: increased enforcement in the form of arrests of prostitutes; cleaning up trouble spots by fencing off a wooded lot and closing one street to limit access for johns cruising for prostitutes; and finally working with community groups to help prostitutes deal with personal problems such as drugs. The tactics in the drug-infested area also included both traditional enforcement and innovative community partnerships. An evaluation found that the POP efforts not only reduced crime in the experimental areas but in neighboring areas as well. In short, crime was not displaced by intensive police efforts, and the crime reduction was in fact diffused to surrounding areas that did not receive the innovative treatment.[23]

The evidence from these innovative programs is very promising. The bottom line is that policing can make a difference in reducing crime and disorder. It is not a matter of more policing, but *smarter* policing, especially research-driven and focused police efforts. The main barrier to this innovative approach to police crime fighting is implementation. There have been many community policing and problem-oriented policing experiments over the past 25 years.[24] Unfortunately, many were poorly designed and/or poorly implemented. The department did not use the SARA model, or did not use it properly. The changes in police activities were not always appropriate for the underlying problems, or they were not maintained throughout the experiment. Innovative policing, in short, can make a difference, but it is a major challenge to design and carry out a successful program.

The evidence so far supports the conclusions of the National Academy of Sciences report, and our position is:

PROPOSITION 10

Carefully planned and focused problem-oriented policing strategies can be successful in reducing crime and disorder.

Zero Tolerance and COMPSTAT in New York City

New York City represents a special case regarding the impact of changes in policing on crime. By 2000 violent crime had fallen to a level not seen since the mid-1960s. As Franklin Zimring points out in a separate chapter on New York, the decline in crime in that city far exceeded even the significant declines in other big cities. The robbery rate, for example, declined 70 percent in the decade of the 1990s, compared with 32 percent in the rest of the U.S. without New York.[25]

At the same time, there were three major changes in policing that might have played some role in reducing crime. First, the size of the police department grew significantly, increasing by 35 percent (to 40,000 sworn officers), compared with a national average of 14 percent. Second, the department under Police Commissioner William Bratton adopted a policy of "zero tolerance" policing that involved vigorous enforcement of minor crimes (e.g., public urination, not paying fares on the subway). Advocates of zero tolerance argue that attacking minor crimes not only sends a message of deterrence but in many cases leads to an arrest on a major charge. Someone arrested for cheating the subway, for example, is found to possess a handgun. Critics, however, argue that such aggressive tactics aggravate police-community relations.[26] Third, the police department adopted COMPSTAT, a computerized system of crime analysis that provides timely data on crime in neighborhoods and holds precinct captains accountable for addressing patterns of crime.[27]

Did these developments, independently or in combination, contribute to the reduction in crime? The National Academy of Sciences report expressed considerable skepticism.[28] First, most cities have enjoyed comparable reductions in major crimes without any of the changes that the NYPD made. San Diego, for example, also experienced a return to the levels of crime of the 1960s, with only a modest increase in the number of officers, only one-third the police/population ratio, and no aggressive zero-tolerance policy.[29]

Second, Zimring argues that there are three special features of New York City that may have contributed to the effectiveness of changes in policing there. New York City began with very high absolute crime rates in the early 1990s. Special police efforts, therefore, confronted concentrated areas of crime unlike other cities. Additionally, the tremendous density of the population in New York City means that a change in policing in a particular neighborhood affects more people than would be the case in other, less densely populated cities. Finally, the handgun laws in New York City have been among the strictest in the country for years. When the police removed a gun, Zimring argues, it was not as easily replaced as it would be in other cities. (We examine guns and gun reduction strategies in Chapter 10.)[30]

Third, as the Urban Institute report on the crime drop argues, the decline in the prevalence of crack cocaine was particularly important in terms of reducing violent gun crimes among young men. Crack was a special problem in New York City, and the decline in its use coincided with the great crime drop.[31] The National Academy also pointed out that, in practice, zero-tolerance policing in New York was implemented in selected neighborhoods. As a result, it was really a geographically focused approach to crime (similar to the approach we discussed and endorsed above) and not a generalized, citywide policy.

The Urban Institute cautiously warns us that no single factor can explain fluctuations in the crime rate.[32] It would be wise to be skeptical about the claims made for zero-tolerance policing and instead think in terms of multiple factors acting in combination: a national decline in crime, an improving economy, the declining popularity of crack, and, finally, innovations in policing.

EVIDENCE-BASED STANDARDS FOR STUDYING POLICING AND THE CRIME DECLINE

In Chapter 1 we discussed the importance of evidence-based standards for evaluating all crime policies. In an analysis of the impact of COMPSTAT in New York City, and related innovations in Boston and Richmond, Virginia, Richard Rosenfeld, Robert Fornango, and Eric Baumer outline three standards that criminologists should demand of public officials who claim their policy—*and what they should demand of themselves in their own research*.

First, any reported reductions in crime must be "plausibly linked" to the intervention in question. In plain English, how exactly is this program or treatment likely to affect crime?

Second, any reduction in crime must have occurred when and where the intervention, or program or treatment, existed, and not where it was not in effect. In short, you cannot claim that a program reduced crime in one city if other cities also experienced declines in crime during the same period.

Third, the reported rate of reduction in crime must exceed the expected rate of decline. Thus, if crime has been trending downward for, say, a decade, a continued decline would be expected in the next few years. This factor is referred to as "history" in research methods.

Rosenfeld, Fornango, and Baumer argue that these three factors are the "minimum threshold" for giving credence to claims about the impact of an intervention, program or treatment.

SOURCE: Richard Rosenfeld, Robert Fornango, and Eric Baumer, "Did Ceasefire, COMPSTAT, and Exile Reduce Homicide?" *Criminology and Public Policy* 4:3 (2005): 419–450.

MORE DETECTIVES

Some people believe that adding more detectives, or making other improvements to detective work, will result in more arrests and thereby lower the crime rate. Let's look at the evidence on this popular belief.

Myths and Realities of Detective Work

Detective work is surrounded by myths that are perpetuated by the media and the police themselves. Movies and television cop shows portray criminal investigation as fast-paced, exciting, and dangerous work, with frequent shootings, car chases, and confrontations with dangerous criminals. In the classic television show from the 1950s, *Dragnet,* Sgt. Joe Friday (Jack Webb) always caught the offender. Today, the highly popular television show *CSI* emphasizes the forensic aspects of detective work. From *Dragnet* to *CSI,* however, the media image of detectives is pure mythology.

The reality of criminal investigation is very different from the myth. Most detective work is boring, unglamorous, and highly unproductive. Instead of kicking in doors, ducking bullets, and wrestling with dangerous sociopaths, detectives spend most of their time writing reports. The clearance rate (the percentage of crimes solved by arrest) for Part I Index crimes was 20 percent in 2002. It was highest for acquaintance crimes (homicide: 64 percent) and lowest for property crimes (burglary: 13 percent). A Rand study of criminal investigation found that the typical case gets an average of about four hours' work, and most of that involves paperwork.[33]

When the police do solve a crime, it is generally because the victim or a witness knows the offender or can provide a good lead to the first police officer who arrives on the scene.[34] In many acquaintance crimes (e.g., assaults, rapes) the offender is still there when the police arrive, so that no real "detective" work is required. This explains why between 60 and 80 percent of all arrests are made by patrol officers instead of detectives.[35]

The importance of having a good lead at the very beginning was documented almost 40 years ago by the President's Crime Commission. It analyzed 1,905 cases handled by the Los Angeles Police. As Figure 5.1 indicates, the LAPD cleared 86 percent of the 349 cases in which a suspect was immediately identified by the victim or witness. But they cleared only 12 percent of the remaining 1,556 cases in which no suspect was immediately identified.[36]

The key to solving crimes and making arrests, in short, is *information about a specific suspect.* When the police begin with little or no information to work with, the chances of clearing the crime are very low. In other words, the odds of solving a crime depend primarily on the characteristics of the crime rather than the number of detectives or the amount of hours they devote to a case. Increasing the number of detectives is not going to help if there is not a good lead at the outset. Detectives always complain about being overworked, and it is true that they are swamped with cases. Information rather than time is the critical factor.[37]

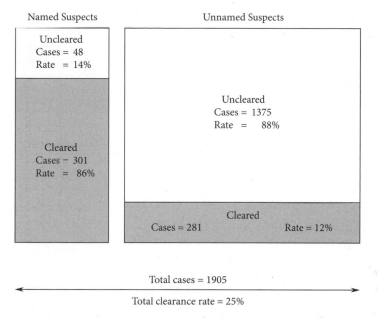

Named Suspects   Unnamed Suspects

Uncleared
Cases = 48
Rate = 14%

Cleared
Cases = 301
Rate = 86%

Uncleared
Cases = 1375
Rate = 88%

Cleared
Cases = 281   Rate = 12%

Total cases = 1905

Total clearance rate = 25%

F I G U R E 5.1 Clearance of crimes with named and unnamed suspects, Los Angeles Police Department, 1966.

SOURCE: President's Commission on Law Enforcement and Administration of Justice, Task Force Report: Science and Technology (Washington, DC: Government Printing Office, 1967), p. 8.

It is indeed true that detectives solve some crimes through exhaustive detective work. But these are rare events and not typical of most cases. They are in fact good examples of the celebrated cases we discussed in Chapter 2.

Better training for detectives is not likely to increase the clearance rate. Even the smartest and best-trained detective is not likely to solve a "cold" crime for which there are no leads. The Rand study of criminal investigation found that the quality of training made little difference in clearance rates between departments.[38] Training is not completely irrelevant, of course. An incompetent detective can easily lose a case by bungling the interrogation or mishandling the evidence. Skill does make a difference and training can improve skills. But this assumes that there is some evidence to begin with.

The Myth of Fingerprints

A great deal of mythology surrounds fingerprints. The FBI has elevated fingerprints to near-mythical status in the solving of crimes. The Bureau now has over 200 million fingerprint cards on file, representing about 79 million individuals. The mystique of fingerprints was designed to project an image of the Bureau as an incredibly efficient agency—efficient because it was backed by the massive weight of "science."

In reality, fingerprints are rarely the critical factor in solving crimes. It is extremely difficult to get usable prints from a crime scene. The New York City police obtain usable prints in only about 10 percent of all burglaries. And in only

3 percent of those cases do the prints help with the arrest. In Long Beach, California, a suspect was identified through fingerprints in only 1.5 percent of all cases.[39] The TV show *CSI* is great entertainment, but it seriously distorts the reality of police work. Fingerprints, blood samples, and hair specimens are not what solve most crimes. Information about a suspect does.

The Myth of DNA Sweeps

Some police departments have also tried to use DNA testing to identify criminal suspects. The science of DNA testing offers great opportunities in criminal justice, but only if it is used correctly. The greatest successes have involved exonerating mistakenly convicted offenders. In these cases, DNA evidence from the crime scene (even cases many years in the past) has proven that the convicted person was not the offender. Some police departments, however, have engaged in DNA "sweeps": taking samples from as many as 1,000 or even 2,000 people. The most celebrated case involved the so-called "BTK Killer" in Wichita, Kansas, where the police took DNA samples from several hundred people. But in this and other cases, there was no individualized suspicion about those tested. Consequently, there was much controversy over violations of the Fourth Amendment rights of the people tested. Even more important, a national survey found that DNA "sweeps" were extremely ineffective in solving cases. DNA evidence identified the perpetrator in only 1 out of the 18 cases that were located. DNA testing can clinch a case where there is a clear suspicion about a suspect, but it cannot identify a perpetrator where there is no individualized suspicion.[40]

Targeting Career Criminals

One of the hot ideas of the 1980s called for the police to target a small number of suspected career criminals. Like selective incapacitation and major-offender prosecution programs, these programs were based on Wolfgang's birth cohort study, which we examined in Chapter 4. The assumption was that if detectives succeeded in arresting this small group of high-rate offenders, a significant reduction in crime would follow.

The Repeat Offender Project (ROP, pronounced "rope") in the Washington, DC, police department involved a special unit of 60 officers targeting suspects whom they believed were committing five or more Index crimes a week. The list of suspects was developed by cross-indexing information from other units in the department, such as Investigation Services, the Career Criminal Unit, the Warrant Squad, the Court Liaison Division, the district commanders, and the Youth Division. ROP officers surveilled these suspects to arrest them for felonies.[41]

An evaluation of Washington's ROP program revealed mixed results. Around-the-clock surveillance of suspects quickly proved to be "time-consuming, frustrating, and unproductive." ROP officers got bored waiting and watching. As a result, ROP shifted its emphasis to suspects with arrest warrants on file. Eventually, half of the unit's time was devoted to this activity. In this respect, then, ROP essentially became an intensified warrant enforcement unit. Like many other supposed innovations, it called for officers to do what they always said they were doing.

The ROP unit officers succeeded in arresting 58 percent of their targeted group, significantly more than the 8 percent arrested among a control group of potential suspects. Nonetheless, the overall arrest productivity of ROP officers was less than that of a comparison group of officers. The 62 ROP officers produced 66 convictions by the end of the first year, or a little more than 1 per officer. Whether this was money well spent is a good question. Even more disturbing is the 37.2 percent conviction rate for ROP arrests (66 of 177). This seems to defy the basic rationale of career-criminal programs that supposedly target people who are believed to be active, high-rate offenders. You would expect a high conviction rate for these suspects. Given the cost of the program and the reduction of nonarrest activities (such as order maintenance) by ROP officers, the evaluation raised serious questions about the cost-effectiveness of the program.[42]

To sum up this section, arrest is the weakest point in the criminal justice system. As we explained in Chapter 2, only 20 percent of crimes are cleared by arrest, compared with about 50 percent of all arrests being prosecuted and about 90 percent of prosecuted cases resulting in conviction. Unfortunately, there does not appear to be any way to increase the clearance rate significantly. The ability of the police to solve crimes is determined primarily by the nature of individual crimes, and in particular whether there is a good lead about a suspect. The evidence leads to our next proposition:

PROPOSITION 11
More detectives, or other changes in detective work, will not raise clearance rates or lower the crime rate.

ELIMINATE THE "TECHNICALITIES"

Conservatives firmly believe that the courts have "handcuffed" the police with procedural rules that limit their power to investigate and solve crimes. According to this view, these "technicalities" of criminal procedure allow streetwise criminals to "beat the system" and avoid punishment. In a sweeping indictment of the criminal justice system, Judge Harold Rothwax of New York argues that the system is geared for "anything but the truth." Procedural rules designed to ensure "fairness" undermine the search for truth about guilt or innocence, with the result that "criminals go free."[43]

Conservatives direct their fire at the Supreme Court, particularly the Warren Court (1953–1969), which issued a series of decisions protecting the rights of suspects and limiting the powers of the police. The two most famous decisions, *Mapp* (1961) and *Miranda* (1966), coincided with the great increase in crime between the early 1960s and early 1970s. Consequently, many people blame the Court for our high rates of crime.[44]

Repeal the Exclusionary Rule

The Supreme Court established the exclusionary rule in the 1961 *Mapp v. Ohio* decision. The Court held that "all evidence obtained by searches and seizures in violation of the Constitution is, by that same authority, inadmissible in a state court."[45] Prosecutors cannot use evidence obtained in violation of the Fourth Amendment's guarantee of "the right of the people to be secure in their persons, houses, papers, and effects, against unreasonable searches and seizures." Evidence obtained illegally is "excluded," or inadmissible in court.

Mapp produced a storm of controversy that has continued for 40 years. Critics charge that the exclusionary rule has limited the ability of the police to gather evidence necessary to convict criminals. Actually, the exclusionary rule was nothing new in 1961. The Supreme Court had applied it to federal proceedings in 1914 (*Weeks v. United States*) and by 1961 it was already in effect in more than half of the states, mainly through decisions by state supreme courts. *Mapp* simply applied the exclusionary rule to all the states.

The exclusionary rule has three basic purposes: to protect the rights of individuals against police misconduct, to maintain the integrity of the judiciary, and to deter the police from misconduct. The rule has always evoked far more outrage than the equally famous *Miranda* warning. *Miranda* excludes confessions that have been obtained improperly. Even many law-and-order advocates concede that a coerced confession is wrong. But the *Mapp* exclusionary rule applies to physical evidence that speaks for itself, no matter how it was obtained. Therefore, they believe that it should be allowed as evidence.

The Exclusionary Rule and Crime Fighting

Several studies indicate that the exclusionary rule has virtually no impact on the crime-fighting capacity of the police. James J. Fyfe argues that the impact is "minuscule" and "infinitesimal."[46] Very few cases are "lost" because the evidence is excluded as a result of an improper search. Drug cases are the only area where the rule has any noticeable impact, and even there the effect is fairly small. Take another look at the data in Table 3.2 in Chapter 3, which indicate that due process problems account for a very small percentage of all rejections and dismissals and that not all of those due process problems involve the exclusionary rule.

When we consider the realities of police work, we can understand why the exclusionary rule has such a limited impact. As we pointed out earlier, the police solve crimes when they immediately obtain a good lead about a suspect, from either the victim or a witness. Physical evidence, independent of some other kind of identification of the suspect, is rarely the primary factor in making an arrest and convicting an offender.

The limited impact of the exclusionary rule is mainly confined to drug possession, weapons possession, and gambling cases. It is not hard to see why. The most important element of a drug possession case is whether the defendant actually had the drugs and how the police obtained the evidence. Robbery cases, on the other hand, are more likely to depend on eyewitness identification of the suspect. Physical evidence is rarely the crucial factor.

Once in court, few defendants try to use the exclusionary rule, and even fewer succeed. Procedurally, the defense attorney asks the court to exclude or suppress the evidence. Judges have the discretion to grant or deny the motion. Peter F. Nardulli found that motions to suppress physical evidence were made in fewer than 5 percent of all cases and were successful in only 0.69 percent of the total. A General Accounting Office study of the federal courts found that motions to suppress evidence were filed in only 11 percent of all cases and that between 80 and 90 percent were denied. Finally, a study of search warrants by the National Center for State Courts showed that only 5 percent of all motions to suppress were successful.[47]

Defense lawyers file motions to suppress evidence because they have a professional obligation to represent their clients' interests. Not filing such motions might raise questions about their competence. Most of the time, however, they are just going through the motions, if you will pardon the expression. They are not the "crafty" lawyers of popular folklore. Most felony cases are handled by public defenders who are conscientious but extremely overworked. They have little time to devote to any one case, and in some jurisdictions they meet their clients only moments before entering the courtroom.

Even when a motion to exclude evidence succeeds, the defendant will not necessarily go free. He or she can still be convicted on other evidence. If an appeals court overturns a conviction under the exclusionary rule, the prosecutor can refile charges on the basis of the remaining evidence. A study of search warrant cases found that 12 of the 17 defendants (70 percent) who succeeded in having evidence suppressed were subsequently convicted on other charges.[48]

Judges vary greatly in their willingness to invoke the exclusionary rule. Sheldon Krantz and his colleagues found in their study of Boston that one judge granted 45.4 percent of the motions to suppress, whereas another granted only 22.2 percent. Three judges denied all motions presented to them. Motions to suppress were successful in only 2 percent of all the gambling and drug cases that Krantz et al. studied.[49]

A controversial 1982 study by the National Institute of Justice produced a much higher estimate of the rule's impact. It found that in 520,993 felony arrests in California between 1976 and 1979 prosecutors rejected a total of 86,033 cases for various reasons. Illegally obtained evidence accounted for 4,130 of those rejections. The Justice Department claimed that the 4,130 represented 4.8 percent of the 86,033 rejections.[50] In a pair of stinging critiques, Thomas Y. Davies and James J. Fyfe argued that it was more accurate to consider the 4,130 rejections as a percentage of the original 520,993 cases. This produces a rejection rate of only 0.8 percent (a figure that is very close to some of the other studies).[51]

In short, the exclusionary rule does not let "thousands" of dangerous criminals loose on the streets, and it has almost no effect on violent crime. Judge Rothwax and other critics of the exclusionary rule are guilty of reacting to a few celebrated cases. Yes, some convictions are overturned, and some of those defendants who are factually guilty are released, but these are rare events. Research on the exclusionary rule has so conclusively found that it does not impede professional law enforcement that there has hardly been any new research in the last 20 years.

The evidence leads us to the following proposition:

PROPOSITION 12

Repeal or modification of the exclusionary rule will not help the police reduce serious crime.

The Positive Impact of the Exclusionary Rule.   Far from impairing police work, the exclusionary rule has played a major role in improving the professionalism of police work. Myron Orfield's study of narcotics officers in Chicago found that the exclusionary rule produced a number of significant reforms. The Chicago police and the Illinois state attorney's office developed a closer working relationship, the state attorney scrutinized applications for warrants more closely, and the police department improved its own training and supervision. The result was better police work. Interviews with Chicago narcotics detectives found that they supported the rule and were very concerned that weakening it would open the door to police abuse. Officers said that the experience of having evidence excluded in court was a valuable learning experience—the best on-the-job training they ever got.[52]

Response to the exclusionary rule depends on the professionalism of a police department. Craig Uchida and Tim Bynum studied the impact of the 1984 *Leon* decision, which allowed a "good faith" exception to the exclusionary rule. Like the earlier studies, they found that the overall impact of the exclusionary rule in seven jurisdictions was "slight." Less than 1 percent (0.9) of all motions to suppress evidence obtained by search warrants were successful. In three of the seven jurisdictions, no motions to suppress evidence were successful. Those sites had a high degree of cooperation between police and prosecutors that included training of police officers and supervision of warrants. In "River City," however, the police were less professional and had an antagonistic relationship with prosecutors. Motions to suppress were filed in 57 percent of all cases, and 14 percent of them were successful.[53]

Many thoughtful law enforcement executives now accept and even welcome the rule. Former FBI Director William Sessions said that "protections that are afforded by the exclusionary rule are extremely important to fair play and the proper carrying out of the law enforcement responsibility."[54] Most law enforcement experts believe that the exclusionary rule forces law enforcement agencies to be more professional, and that weakening the rule would permit lazy and unprofessional work. Because of the rule, law-abiding citizens do not have to fear overzealous and intrusive action by a cop, and so the police enjoy greater public respect.

Instead of abolishing the exclusionary rule altogether, some critics propose modifying it to permit good-faith searches: cases in which the officer made an honest mistake (as in getting a number wrong on a street address). As noted previously, the Supreme Court adopted the good-faith exception in *United States v. Leon* (1984), ruling that evidence could be admitted if it were obtained under a valid search warrant even though it was later found that there was not probable cause to issue the warrant.[55]

The good-faith exception, however, presents several problems. First, it complicates rather than simplifies search-and-seizure cases by opening the door to appeals based on whether the search was in good or bad faith and whether the officer made an honest mistake or a deliberate one. Fyfe argues that this makes the judge's job even harder. Second, the good-faith exception encourages police incompetence. It gives officers an incentive to claim that they made a minor mistake instead of prodding them to do a professional job in the first place. One of the main effects of the exclusionary rule has been to stimulate police professionalism.[56]

Finally, and the most important in terms of crime fighting, the good-faith search is not going to significantly increase the number of convictions because few convictions are being "lost" owing to the exclusionary rule's existence.

Abolish *Miranda*

The *Miranda* warning is the second major so-called technicality that conservatives believe handcuffs the police. The 1966 *Miranda v. Arizona* decision held that to ensure a suspect's Fifth Amendment protection against self-incrimination, the police must advise a criminal suspect of certain rights: Prior to any questioning, the person must be warned that he has a right to remain silent, that any statement he does make may be used against him, and that he has a right to the presence of an attorney, either retained or appointed.[57]

Conservatives have been angry about *Miranda* ever since. In the original decision, Justice Byron White dissented on the grounds that it "return[s] a killer, a rapist or other criminal to the streets and to the environment which produced him, to repeat his crime whenever it pleases him." Other opponents have repeated this criticism for 30 years.[58]

Almost 35 years later, the *Miranda* warning is the most widely known and probably most misunderstood element of police procedure. Hollywood and television writers love it. The warning adds a special dramatic complication to the plot. In one movie, a narcotics detective wrestles the suspect to the ground with one arm while reading from the *Miranda* warning card he holds in the other hand. Get it? The police have one hand tied behind their backs. A 1991 public opinion poll on the two-hundredth anniversary of the Bill of Rights found that while only 10 percent knew why it was originally adopted, 80 percent knew about their right to remain silent if arrested.[59] A recent book observed that "School children are more likely to recognize the *Miranda* warnings than the Gettysburg Address."[60]

Miranda in Operation. Does the *Miranda* warning really handcuff the police? Let us look at it in operation. First, let us clear up a few myths about the decision. The *Miranda* warning does not have to be given at the moment of arrest but only before questioning. If a suspect blurts out a confession ("Why did I do it?"), the confession is admissible. Also, a suspect can waive his or her rights by agreeing to talk and agreeing to do so without a lawyer. In fact, many suspects do waive their rights.

Paul G. Cassell, a strong critic of *Miranda,* and Bret S. Hayman properly raise the question of how we should measure the impact (or the "cost") of *Miranda*.

They make a persuasive argument that we should not look at the number of convictions overturned because of a *Miranda* violation but the number of confessions the police do not get. Surveying all of the studies done to date, they estimate that the rate of confessions has declined by 16 percent because of *Miranda*. But that is not the whole story, because some offenders are convicted even without a confession. The authors estimate that confessions are needed in about 24 percent of all cases. Thus, the net effect is that *Miranda* results in a "loss" of convictions in 3.8 percent of all cases (16 percent of 24 percent = 3.8 percent). Despite Cassell and Hayman's own claims, this is not a very significant impact.[61]

Stephen J. Schulhofer, moreover, argues that Cassell and Hayman's study suffers from a number of methodological flaws. One of the more serious is their failure to take into account the fact that confession rates were dropping in the years before *Miranda,* for reasons unrelated to the decision. Factoring in a continuation of this trend and adding in the effect of other methodological problems, Schulhofer estimates that the "loss" due to *Miranda* is not 3.8 percent but less than 1 percent (0.78). "For all practical purposes," he concludes, "*Miranda's* empirically detectable net damage to law enforcement is zero."[62]

The best study of *Miranda* in operation is Richard Leo's "Inside the Interrogation Room," in which he directly observed a total of 182 police interrogations in three police departments. Leo found that 78 of the suspects waived their *Miranda* rights and cooperated with the police. As a result, two-thirds (64 percent) made a full confession, a partial confession, or some incriminating statement. What tactics did the police use to get them to cooperate? In over 80 percent of the cases, the police either confronted them with evidence of their guilt or appealed to their self-interest (it will help you if you talk), or both.[63]

In short, the *Miranda* warning was no barrier to successful police work. In the vast majority of the cases, the police got suspects to waive their rights and confess or make an incriminating statement, and they did so through lawful means. It should be noted, however, that in 30 percent of the cases, the police lied by confronting the suspects with false information about their guilt, as in falsely telling them that their partner had confessed. This evidence supports keeping the *Miranda* warning.

Why do so many suspects waive their rights and confess? Why do only about 20 percent of suspects take advantage of their right to remain silent? The first point is that the police do not arrest very many suspects. They clear only about 26 percent of all robberies and 14 percent of all burglaries. Thus, they usually have some evidence against the few suspects they do arrest. This leaves a small group of cases in which there is reasonably strong evidence. And as Leo discovered, detectives confront 85 percent of all suspects with evidence of their guilt. The suspects in these remaining cases have powerful incentives to cooperate and confess. They know that they committed the crime, and they realize that the police have some fairly good evidence against them. A lot of them feel guilty about it. Leo found that detectives appealed to suspects' consciences in 23 percent of all cases. Some suspects who confess hope to get a better deal in a plea bargaining. The detectives in Leo's study appealed to the suspects' self-interest in 88 percent of the cases.[64]

The image of the tough, streetwise criminal who is skilled at manipulating the rules is another myth. Some suspects do invoke their *Miranda* rights, but the majority cooperate with the police. Felony suspects are typically young, poorly educated, and in many instances functionally illiterate. Most failed to learn how to manipulate the public school bureaucracy to their advantage, and they are not much more successful in the criminal justice system. The typical robber or burglar is so disorganized and impulsive that he does not even plan his crimes very well. The Rand Inmate Survey found that 40 percent of the juvenile robbers and 25 percent of the adults had not even intended to rob anyone when they left home. As one kid put it, "It was just a sudden thing. I didn't really mean to do it. I didn't plan nothing; it just happened." Among the adult career criminals, only 40 percent bothered to visit the sites of their crimes in advance, and as few as 22 percent made an effort to check on police patrol in the area.[65]

In custody, young offenders may strike a tough pose, but it is usually nothing more than that—a pose, an act. A skilled professional detective can get most suspects to talk.

Modifying Miranda.   In 1984, the Supreme Court finally accepted the conservative argument and created a "public safety" exception to the *Miranda* warning. In *New York v. Quarles,* the Court held that when the safety of an officer or a citizen is threatened, as by the presence of a gun, the officer may ask questions before advising a suspect of his or her rights.[66] The decision represents a major victory in the conservatives' 30-year campaign to reverse the rules laid down by the Warren Court. Given the limited impact of the *Miranda* warning on confessions, however, it is hard to imagine that this limited exception would result in many more arrests or any significant crime reduction. Consequently, the evidence leads to this proposition:

PROPOSITION 13
Repeal or modification of the *Miranda* warning will not result in more convictions.

CONCLUSION

The police are the front line of the criminal justice system. Patrol is the primary strategy for preventing crime, and arrest is the "gatekeeping" point for all criminal cases. Many people believe that we could reduce crime significantly if we would just "unleash" the cops: give them more resources and more powers. We have found that these ideas are not likely to reduce crime.

The good news is that promising programs that involve carefully planned, focused, evidence-based strategies, such as hot spots and problem-oriented policing programs, have proven successful in several experiments. The significance of these programs goes far beyond policing. As we will find in the chapters ahead, similarly focused, problem-oriented programs— such as drug courts and community prosecution—have also shown promising results. These successes provide the foundation for a potentially comprehensive approach to crime and disorder.

NOTES

1. David Bayley, *Police for the Future* (New York: Oxford University Press, 1994), p. 101.

2. John Eck and Edward Maguire, "Have Changes in Policing Reduced Violent Crime? An Assessment of the Evidence," in Alfred Blumstein and Joel Wallman, eds., *The Crime Drop in America* (New York: Cambridge University Press, 2000), pp. 210–214, especially Table 7.1.

3. The most recent and most sober analysis is John L. Worall and Tomislav V. Kovandzic, "Cops Grants and Crime Revisited," *Criminology* 45:1 (2007): 159–190.

4. Jihong "Solomon" Zhao, Matthew C. Scheider, and Quint Thurman, "Funding Community Policing to Reduce Crime: Have COPS Grants Made a Difference?" *Criminology and Public Policy* 2 (2002): 11.

5. John L. Worall and Tomislav V. Kovandzic, "Cops Grants and Crime Revisited," *Criminology* 45 (March 2007): 159–190.

6. George L. Kelling, Tony Pate, Duane Diekman, and Charles E. Brown, *The Kansas City Preventive Patrol Experiment: A Summary Report* (Washington, DC: The Police Foundation, 1974).

7. Ibid.

8. The Police Foundation, *The Newark Foot Patrol Experiment* (Washington, DC: The Police Foundation, 1981).

9. Franklin E. Zimring and Gordon J. Hawkins, *Deterrence: The Legal Threat in Crime Control* (Chicago: University of Chicago Press, 1973).

10. James Q. Wilson and Alan Abrahamse, "Does Crime Pay?" *Justice Quarterly* 9 (September 1992): 372–373.

11. New York Civil Liberties Union, *Who's Watching? Video Camera Surveillance in New York City and the Need for Public Oversight* (New York: NYCLU, 2006).

12. Brandon C. Welsh and David P. Farrington, "Effects of Closed-Circuit Television on Crime," *Annals* 587 (May 2003): 110–135.

13. Lawrence W. Sherman, "Police Crackdowns," in Michael Tonry and Norval Morris, eds., *Crime and Justice: An Annual Review of Research*, vol. 12 (Chicago: University of Chicago Press, 1990), pp. 1–48.

14. Lynn Zimmer, "Proactive Policing against Street-Level Drug Trafficking," *American Journal of Police* 9 (no. 1, 1990): 43–74.

15. William Spelman and Dale K. Brown, *Calling the Police: Citizen Reporting of Serious Crime* (Washington, DC: Department of Justice, 1984).

16. Ibid.

17. National Academy of Sciences, *Fairness and Effectiveness in Policing: The Evidence* (Washington, DC: National Academy Press, 2004), pp. 226–227.

18. Ibid., p. 235.

19. Herman Goldstein, *Problem-Oriented Policing* (New York: McGraw-Hill, 1990). Michael S. Scott, *Problem-Oriented Policing: Reflections on the First Twenty Years* (Washington, DC: Department of Justice, 2000).

20. Lawrence W. Sherman, Patrick R. Gartin, and Michael E. Buerger, "Hot Spots of Predatory Crime: Routine Activities and the Criminology of Place," *Criminology* 27 (1989): 27–55.

21. Lorraine Green, "Cleaning Up Drug Hot Spots in Oakland, California: The Displacement and Diffusion Effects," *Justice Quarterly* 12 (December 1995): 737–754.

22. Anthony A. Braga and Brenda J. Bond, "Policing Crime and Disorder Hot Spots: A Randomized Control Trial," *Criminology* 46:3 (2008): 576–607.

23. David Weisburd, Laura A. Wycoff, Justin Ready, John Eck, Joshua C. Hinckle, and Frank Gajewski, "Does Crime Just Move Around the Corner? A Controlled Study of Spatial Displacement and Diffusion of Crime Control Benefits," *Criminology* 44:3 (2006): 549–591.

24. Scott, *Problem-Oriented Policing: Reflections on the First Twenty Years.*

25. Franklin E. Zimring, *The Great American Crime* Decline (New York: Oxford University Press, 2007), pp. 149–150.

26. Bernard Harcourt, *Illusion of Order: The False Promise of Broken Windows Policing* (Cambridge, MA: Harvard University Press, 2001). George L. Kelling and Catherine M. Coles, *Fixing Broken Windows* (New York: Free Press, 1996). William J. Bratton and Peter Knoblach, *Turnaround* (New York: Random House, 1998).

27. Eli Silverman, *NYPD Battles Crime* (Boston: Northeastern, 1999). David Weisburd, Stephen Mastrofski, Ann Marie McNally, Rosann Greenspan, and James Willis, "Reforming to Preserve: COMPSTAT and Strategic Problem Solving in American Policing," *Criminology and Public Policy* 2 (July 2003): 421–456.

28. National Academy of Sciences, *Fairness and Effectiveness*, pp. 228–230.

29. Gary Cordner, "Problem-Oriented Policing vs. Zero Tolerance," in Tara O'Connor Shelley and Anne C. Grant, eds., *Problem-Oriented Policing: Crime-Specific Problems, Critical Issues and Making POP Work* (Washington, DC: Police Executive Research Forum, 1998), pp. 303–314.

30. Zimring, *The Great American Crime Decline*, pp. 156–158.

31. K. Jack Riley, *Crack, Powder Cocaine, and Heroin: Drug Purchase and Use Patterns in Six U.S. Cities.* NCJ 167265 (Washington, DC: Department of Justice, 1997); For an examination of the declining appeal of crack cocaine, see R. Terry Furst, Bruce D. Johnson, Eloise Dunlap, and Richard Curtis, "The Stigmatized Image of the 'Crack Head': A Sociocultural Exploration of a Barrier to Cocaine Smoking Among a Cohort of Youth in New York City," *Deviant Behavior*, 20 (1999): 153–181.

32. Jeremy Travis and Michelle Waul, *Reflections on the Crime Decline: Lessons for the Future?* (Washington, DC: Urban Institute, 2002). Available on the Urban Institute website.

33. Peter Greenwood, *The Criminal Investigation Process* (Santa Monica, CA: Rand, 1975).

34. Wesley Skogan and George Antunes, "Information, Apprehension, and Deterrence: Exploring the Limits of Police Productivity," *Journal of Criminal Justice* 7 (Fall 1979): 217–241.

35. Albert J. Reiss, *The Police and the Public* (New Haven, CT: Yale University Press, 1971), p. 104.

36. President's Commission on Law Enforcement and Administration of Justice, *Task Force Report: Science and Technology* (Washington, DC: Government Printing Office, 1967), p. 8.

37. John E. Eck, *Solving Crimes: The Investigation of Burglary and Robbery* (Washington, DC: Police Executive Research Forum, 1983).

38. Greenwood, *Criminal Investigation Process*.

39. Joan Petersilia, "Processing Latent Fingerprints—What Are the Payoffs?" *Journal of Police Science and Administration* 6 (June 1978): 157–167.

40. Police Professionalism Initiative, *Police DNA Sweeps Extremely Unproductive: A National Survey of Police DNA "Sweeps"* (Omaha: University of Nebraska at Omaha, 2004).

41. Susan E. Martin and Lawrence W. Sherman, "Selective Apprehension: A Police Strategy for Repeat Offenders," *Criminology* 24 (February 1986): 155–173; Susan E. Martin, "Policing Career Criminals: An Examination of an Innovative Crime Control Program," *Journal of Criminal Law and Criminology* 77 (Winter 1986): 1159–1182.

42. Martin and Sherman, "Selective Apprehension."

43. Harold J. Rothwax, *Guilty: The Collapse of Criminal Justice* (New York: Random House, 1996), p. 15.

44. Samuel Walker, *Popular Justice: A History of American Criminal Justice*, 2nd ed. (New York: Oxford University Press, 1998), pp. 180–193.

45. *Mapp v. Ohio*, 367 U.S. 643 (1961).

46. James J. Fyfe, "The NIJ Study of the Exclusionary Rule," *Criminal Law Bulletin* 19 (May–June 1983): 253–260.

47. Peter F. Nardulli, "The Societal Costs of the Exclusionary Rule: An Empirical Assessment," *American Bar Foundation Research Journal* 1983 (Summer 1983): 585–690; Comptroller General of the United States, *Impact of the Exclusionary Rule on Federal Criminal Prosecutions*, Report #GGD-79-45 (April 19, 1979); National Center for State Courts, *The Search Warrant Process* (Williamsburg, VA: National Center for State Courts, 1986).

48. National Center for State Courts, *Search Warrant Process*.

49. Sheldon Krantz, Bernard Gilman, Charles G. Benda, Carol Rogoff Hallstrom, and Gail J. Nadworny, *Police Policymaking* (Lexington, MA: Lexington Books, 1979), pp. 189–192.

50. National Institute of Justice, *The Effects of the Exclusionary Rule: A Study in California* (Washington, DC: Government Printing Office, 1982).

51. Fyfe, "The NIJ Study of the Exclusionary Rule"; Thomas Y. Davies, "A Hard Look at What We Know (and Still Need to Learn) about the 'Costs' of the Exclusionary Rule: The NIJ Study and Other Studies of 'Lost' Arrests," *American Bar Foundation Research Journal* 3 (Summer 1983): 611–690.

52. Myron W. Orfield, Jr., "The Exclusionary Rule and Deterrence: An Empirical Study of Chicago Narcotics Officers," *University of Chicago Law Review* 54 (Summer 1987): 1016–1055.

53. Craig Uchida and Tim Bynum, "Search Warrants, Motions to Suppress and 'Lost Cases': The Effects of the Exclusionary Rule in Seven Jurisdictions," *Journal of Criminal Law and Criminology* 81 (Winter 1991): 1034–1066.

54. Sessions quoted in *New York Times,* 5 November 1987.

55. *United States v. Leon,* 468 U.S. 897 (1984).

56. James J. Fyfe, "In Search of the 'Bad Faith' Search," *Criminal Law Bulletin* 18 (May–June 1982): 260–264.

57. *Miranda v. Arizona,* 384 U.S. 436 (1966).

58. An invaluable collection of articles on the subject is Richard Leo and George C. Thomas, III, eds., *The Miranda Debate: Law, Justice, and Policing* (Boston: Northeastern University Press, 1998).

59. "Poll Finds Only 33% Can Identify Bill of Rights," *New York Times,* 15 December 1991.

60. Paul G. Cassell and Bret S. Hayman, "Police Interrogation in the 1990s: An Empirical Study of the Effects of Miranda," *UCLA Law Review* 43 (February 1996): 860. Paul G. Cassell, "Miranda's Social Costs: An Empirical Reassessment," *Northwestern University Law Review* 90 (Winter 1996): 387–499.

61. Leo and Thomas, eds., *Miranda Debate,* p. xv.

62. Stephen J. Schulhofer, "Miranda's Practical Effect: Substantial Benefits and Vanishingly Small Social Costs," in Leo and Thomas, eds., *Miranda Debate,* p. 205.

63. Richard A. Leo, "Inside the Interrogation Room," *Journal of Criminal Law and Criminology* 86 (1996): 266–303. For a full discussion of interrogations and other "scientific" investigation techniques, see Richard A. Leo, *Police Interrogation and American Justice* (Cambridge: Harvard University Press, 2008).

64. Ibid.

65. Joan Petersilia, Peter W. Greenwood, and Martin Lavin, *The Criminal Careers of Habitual Felons* (Washington, DC: Government Printing Office, 1978).

66. *New York v. Quarles,* 467 U.S. 649 (1984).

6

Deter the Criminals

Cops on the streets deter criminals. More cops, therefore, must deter crime more effectively. Right? The threat of long prison sentences also deters criminals. Right? Maybe, or maybe not.

Deterrence is an article of faith among conservatives: Punishment deters crime; swifter, more certain, and more severe punishments will reduce crime even further. In Chapter 5 we discussed why routine police patrol does not deter crime as Robert Peel imagined it would. In this chapter we will look at deterrence in theory and practice. We are going to violate our own ground rules a little and discuss some issues that fall outside the scope of our inquiry: the death penalty, drunk driving crackdowns, and domestic violence. These crimes are not directly related to robbery and burglary, but they offer some important evidence about deterrence.

We will also examine some new and promising research about deterrence. Traditionally, research generally found little deterrent effect in the most popular crime policies. Recent research on some innovative programs, however, has found some positive results. We will take a look at what is new and different about these programs that appears to have some positive deterrent effect.

DETERRENCE THEORY

The theory of deterrence has a simple, intuitive appeal. People want to avoid unpleasant experiences, so if we make the punishment for crime more unpleasant, fewer people will commit crime. The basic theory of deterrence is simple, but in actual practice it is very complex, resting on a number of related assumptions that may not work in the real world of criminal justice.[1]

First, it is important to distinguish between the general deterrent effect of the criminal law and the criminal justice system on one hand and the more limited deterrent effect of particular policies or programs on the other.

The criminal law and the criminal justice system certainly have some general deterrent effects. The law defines the boundaries of acceptable behavior and specifies the consequences of crossing those boundaries. Social psychologist Tom Tyler, in the title of his book, investigates *Why People Obey the Law*. His answer is that people are more likely to obey the law if they regard it and the justice system as legitimate: it reflects their values.[2] (We will examine his theory of legitimacy in detail in Chapter 12.) Most of us do *not* commit serious crimes. We are not murderers, robbers, or burglars. Our socialization is mainly responsible for this: our parents, religious upbringing, education, peer group influence, etc. The justice system's threat of punishment reinforces our behavior, but mainly the criminal law expresses our society's values. In the most comprehensive review of the subject, Daniel Nagin concludes that "the collective actions of the criminal justice system exert a very substantial deterrent effect."[3]

Nagin explains that the real issue of deterrence is "whether a specific policy, grafted onto the existing structure, will materially add to the preventive effect."[4] That is the main point of our inquiry in this book: Are there policies that will reduce serious crime from its current level? Are there some policies that are more effective than others? On this issue, Nagin is very cautious. There is a lack of clear and convincing evidence about policies that, from a deterrence perspective, produce real, long-term reductions in crime. To understand why we should be skeptical about the added deterrent effect of any criminal justice policy, let's examine the assumptions underlying deterrence.

Assumptions Underlying Deterrence

The theory of deterrence involves a number of basic assumptions. As we noted in Chapter 5, the main line of deterrence theory operates in the realm of social psychology. It assumes the existence of an information loop involving potential offenders' knowledge and perception of the potential punishment. First, offenders have to be *aware* of the threat. They have to know, for example, that there are more patrol officers out there and that their risk of arrest is higher than normal. They have to know that a new law imposes a mandatory jail term for a first-offense drunk driving conviction, or that a new law requires a mandatory 10-year prison term for a drug possession conviction.

Second, potential offenders have to *perceive* the consequences of lawbreaking as *unpleasant* and therefore something to be avoided. They have to believe that arrest, prosecution, conviction, imprisonment, and having a criminal record would be bad for them.

Third, they have to *believe* that a real *risk* of arrest, conviction, and punishment exists. If they don't believe that they will be caught, they are not deterred. If they don't believe that they will be convicted, they will not be deterred. As Scott Decker and his colleagues point out, "Deterrence is essentially a psychological process that involves the balancing of personally held beliefs about possible punishment and anticipated gain."[5] Certainty and swiftness of punishment are regarded as essential to this process in order to reinforce the connection between a crime and its consequences.

Finally, and perhaps most important, deterrence theory assumes that people are *rational actors* who weigh the relative costs and benefits of their actions and make conscious decisions about the best course. Many economists who do research on criminal justice like deterrence theory because it involves a favorite economic theory, *rational choice,* which holds that changing the costs or benefits can influence human behavior. Thus, if we raise the costs by making punishment more certain and/or more severe, we will influence people not to commit crime. Or, if we educate kids about the personal costs of doing drugs, they will choose not to use illegal drugs. A major problem with deterrence, of course, is that some people do not act rationally.

Deterrence operates in two ways, depending on the target audience. *Specific* deterrence is directed at the individual offender. The punishment is intended to teach that person right and wrong, that criminal activity leads to unpleasant consequences. *General* deterrence is directed at the society as a whole. Punishing a few criminals is designed to communicate a message to the larger audience.[6]

An alternative approach to deterrence conceptualizes it in terms of *structural deterrence,* as opposed to perceptual deterrence. Structural deterrence looks at macro-level changes in public policy, such as increases in the number of police officers or different police strategies that are designed to increase the risk of apprehension. Perceptual deterrence, by contrast, focuses on the perceptions of deterrable offenders and whether they get the message. (In our view, frankly, there is little practical difference between the two ways of thinking about deterrence. If you increase the number of police officers, you are still thinking about whether many potential offenders will perceive that change and change their behavior.)[7]

With respect to our objectives, there is an important distinction between *absolute* and *marginal* deterrence. No one really expects absolute deterrence: that a particular threat will completely deter crime, or a particular crime. Instead, we think in terms of marginal deterrence: a relative improvement over what we are currently achieving.[8] We discussed this in Chapter 1 with regard to realistic goals. A 10 percent reduction related to one policy is not to be ignored. Our broader goal should be to think in terms of the aggregate impact of several policies.

Deterrence theory was out of favor among criminologists for decades, but then enjoyed a tremendous revival in the 1980s. The revival was not confined to criminal justice policy. Ronald L. Akers points out that the idea of rational choice became a "hot topic" in many of the social sciences in the 1980s.[9] It was especially influential in economic theory and many aspects of social policy. Recent welfare reform, for example, rests on the assumption that traditional welfare programs provided too few incentives for finding employment. Cutting welfare benefits and putting a cap on the number of years of eligibility, conservatives argue, encourages people to find employment and get off welfare.[10]

As we explained in Chapter 1, there has been a lot of political shifting of sides with regard to crime policy. Deterrence theory is generally favored by conservatives. On certain issues, however, many liberals also believe in deterrence. Some believe that the exclusionary rule will deter illegal searches and seizures by police officers, or that citizen review of complaints against the police will deter police misconduct. Many liberals also support mandatory arrest for domestic violence in the belief that it will deter that crime.[11]

From Theory to Practice: Four Problems

There are several reasons for questioning how effectively deterrence-oriented policies work in practice.[12] First, we know little about the long-term effects of policies on potential criminals. Part of the "cost" of crime is the social stigma of arrest and punishment. But if arrest and imprisonment are common experiences for a particular social group, the stigma begins to lose its negative effect. Many observers believe that this is precisely what has happened with young and poor African American males as a result of the war on crime. So many people in their neighborhoods are arrested and convicted that it is simply a "normal" life experience, with little deterrent effect. Obviously, the career criminals we discussed in Chapter 4 are not deterred by their frequent arrests and convictions.

Second, Nagin points out that we know relatively little about the process of how perceptions of risk are formed. How do people develop their understanding of the risk of a drunk driving arrest or an arrest for drug possession? Is the message communicated at all? How do people process that message, and understand both the risk and the potential negative consequences? One of the crucial elements of some innovative programs we will examine involves new ways of communicating the message to potential offenders.

Third, the impact of particular policies depends upon how they are implemented. One of the most important principles for understanding criminal justice is that policies are not always implemented as intended. Many factors get in the way. As we learned in Chapter 5, for example, two police departments may add the same number of new police officers, but one may use them far more efficiently and effectively in terms of crime fighting. In an inefficiently run department, the potential deterrent effect of more officers is lost. With respect to domestic violence, we are not absolutely certain that police officers faithfully carry out mandatory arrest laws or policies As we learned in Chapter 3, the courtroom work group has a tremendous ability to undermine new laws or policies that disrupt the established going rate. California's "three strikes" law has been used extensively in Los Angeles but only to a very limited extent in San Francisco. Historically, many "mandatory" sentencing provisions were undermined by the refusal of prosecutors to use them, or more often to trade them away in a plea bargain (we will examine this in Chapter 8 on "loopholes" in the system). There can be little if any deterrent effect where a policy is not used.

SCARE THE *%!#@ OUT OF THEM!

A Famous but Failed Program

A popular deterrence-based program for potential offenders is Scared Straight, which originally involved exposing juveniles to the terrible experience of going to prison as a way of scaring them out of criminal behavior. Scared Straight gained national prominence as the title and subject of a 1978 television documentary that was loosely based on an actual program in the Rahway, New Jersey, penitentiary. (There is also a more recent version available on DVD, following up on the story 30 years later.) The program was begun by inmates serving life sentences. On the surface it seemed like a great idea. Who better to give kids a realistic idea of where crime leads than a group of lifers?[13]

Scared Straight is a simple deterrence-based program: Give juveniles direct and frightening evidence about the unpleasant consequences of criminal behavior. Many other programs are based on the same theory. Some drug awareness programs, for example, try to convince people that drug use will cause permanent damage. One of the most famous, of course, was the old "This is your brain on drugs" advertisement (we will discuss this in Chapter 13). Many antismoking advertisements warn about the hazards of smoking. The original Marlboro Man, for example, who eventually died of lung cancer, starred in an antismoking ad. Anti–drunk driving programs try to scare kids by showing them pictures of cars that have been totaled in drunk driving accidents.

The evidence on Scared Straight, however, is not good. One review examined all the evaluations of Scared Straight–type programs that met evidence-based standards (independent evaluation, randomized or quasi-randomized assignment to treatment and control groups, etc.). They found a total of nine studies over 25 years that involved over 1,000 participants.[14]

None of the programs effectively reduced crime, and some even had adverse outcomes. A Michigan program in the 1960s resulted in a 43 percent recidivism rate for those who were "scared" compared with only 17 percent for the control group. Several studies had results that were statistically insignificant, but with more negative than positive results. Finckenauer's evaluation of the highly publicized New Jersey Scared Straight program found recidivism rates of 41 percent for those in the program and only 11 percent for the controls. Only one of the nine evaluations found positive results, but they were not statistically significant.

Despite these depressing findings, Scared Straight programs continue to be popular. This represents another triumph of faith over facts. Because it has a common sense appeal, people don't want to consider the evidence. In fact, when the negative results of the Squires program in California were released, officials abolished the evaluation and kept the program.

Why did some of these programs have criminogenic effects, and produce higher rates among the treatment group compared with the control group? What is it about these programs that is harmful? Some people argue that fear-based campaigns only heighten the allure of the product and lead to higher usage. In some cases, the claims are so exaggerated that they become jokes among the intended audience. The "this is your brain on drugs" ads, for example, were often laughed at. This leads us to conclude:

PROPOSITION 14
Fear-based deterrence programs do not reduce crime.

The Risk of Arrest: Some Preliminary Evidence

Because deterrence theory rests on the actual and perceived risk of crime, it is useful to review what we learned in Chapters 2 and 3 about the administration of justice. While the criminal law and the justice system may have some general deterrent effect, the fact is that the risk of apprehension and punishment for most crimes is very low. According to the NCVS, only 37 percent of all Index crimes are reported to the police. The police then clear only 20 percent of these crimes. Thus, only about 8 percent of all Index crimes result in arrest. And since about half of all felony arrests are dismissed, only 4 percent of all crimes are prosecuted. In short, a rational person can reasonable conclude that the overall risk of punishment for crime in general is extremely low.

The risks are somewhat higher for particular crimes. Virtually all murders are reported, and the police clear about 68 percent of them. A Justice Department report found that 87 percent of all husbands tried for murdering their wives were convicted, and 81 percent of them were sentenced to prison.[15] Only about 54 percent of all robberies are reported, however, and the police clear only about 26 percent of them. This yields an overall apprehension risk of 14 percent.

Looking at the risks of crime from the perspective of individual offenders, particularly career criminals, creates some additional problems for deterrence theory. The Rand Inmate Survey (RIS) found that offenders were extremely fatalistic about being arrested and punished. Unfortunately, neither the perceived risk nor the actual experience of imprisonment seemed to deter them from criminal activity. James Q. Wilson and Allan Abrahamse concluded that the RIS offenders did not act rationally, as deterrence theory requires.[16] And in a study of 1,000 Nebraska prisoners, Julie Horney and Ineke Marshall found that offenders with higher arrest rates relative to self-reported crime also reported higher perceptions of the risk of arrest and punishment.[17]

IS THE DETERRENT MESSAGE COMMUNICATED?

The crucial question in deterrence is whether the message is communicated to potential offenders to the point where they change their behavior. Do they get it? Do they hear the message about their greater risk of arrest or harsher punishments? Do they understand that their lives will be significantly worse if they commit a serious crime, or, in the case of active offenders, continue to commit crimes?

The Rand Inmate Survey interviewed prisoners in three states (California, Michigan, and Texas), asking them to estimate the probable results of doing crime. Well over 80 percent of the prisoners believed that they had an "even chance" of being arrested, imprisoned, injured, or killed. Over 60 percent believed that they had a "high chance" of arrest and imprisonment, or that it was "certain." In short, the prisoners were extremely fatalistic about the consequences of criminal activity. Significantly, they were only half as likely to expect a high chance or certainty of enjoying the benefits of crime, such as "high living," having "expensive things," or "being own man".[18]

Analyzing these responses, James Q. Wilson and Allan Abrahamse asked the obvious question: If their estimate of bad consequences is so high and their estimate of good consequences is so low, why do they commit crime? (These were imprisoned offenders, many of whom were repeat offenders who had considerable experience with crime, the justice system, and prison.) The answer is that they do not act on the basis of a rational calculation of costs and benefits. Wilson and Abrahamse, for example, found that they consistently overestimated the financial rewards of crime. They acted impulsively, overestimating the immediate, short-term gains of crime and underestimating unpleasant consequences, such as imprisonment, which lay in the future.[19] At the same time, they also may have felt that they had no meaningful alternatives in terms of legitimate work—in other words, they perceived no positive rewards for a law-abiding lifestyle. In short, the RIS evidence provides little support for traditional deterrence theory. The message about unpleasant consequences is simply not communicated effectively to offenders. This leads us to the following conclusion:

PROPOSITION 15
General deterrence policies, based on the risk of arrest and punishment, are not effective.

"PULLING LEVERS": COMMUNICATING THE MESSAGE

Perhaps all is not lost, however, with respect to deterrence. Some exciting recent innovations in policing suggest that it may be possible to get the message across to known offenders and to cause them to change their behavior and stop (or at least reduce their offending). These innovations included some problem-oriented policing (POP) and gun reduction programs. The most promising were pioneered by the Boston Gun Project in the 1990s and have been employed in other cities. We reviewed some in Chapter 5 and will look at them again in Chapter 10, which addresses gun crimes.[20]

The most promising strategies involve "pulling levers." One "lever" is the fact that repeat offenders are frequently on probation or parole, and can be ordered to appear at a meeting. The "lever" is that failure to comply, or violating a condition of probation or parole can send them back to prison. Another "lever" is that, if the program is run properly, members of the target audience are actively engaged in crime and are vulnerable to arrest. The crucial element of the pulling levers strategy is that it is focused on a short list of specific individuals: people the police know, and believe are involved in crime, or are associated with other people who are. This factor distinguishes pulling levers from most deterrent-oriented programs that are directed toward the general population, and thus are too diffuse.

The Cincinnati Initiative to Reduce Violence (CIRV) "pulls levers" through a carefully coordinated partnership among the police (including federal agencies), the courts, correctional agencies, social service agencies, and community leaders. CIRV describes itself as a "focused deterrence" approach. "Key actors," known to be associated with crime, are ordered to come to "call-in" meetings where they are given "a specific message of deterrence," and equally important, "are told to "relay this message to others in their group." At the call-in meetings, law enforcement officials tell them that if there is another murder they will be subject to "swift targeted enforcement" of any and all possible violations. Then, social service providers describe the opportunities available to them if they want to seek help. Finally, community representatives lecture them about the damage they are doing to their neighborhoods.[21]

CIRV is a data-driven effort. In collaboration with criminologists from the University of Cincinnati, data are collected on major gangs, their members, and their relationships with each other. Additional information is obtained from beat officers in the Cincinnati who, it turned out, have detailed information about the bad characters in their areas. All of the data allows the call-in sessions to cast a somewhat wider, although still focused, net. At the first session, for example, only 19 percent were currently on probation or parole. The data allowed CIRV officials to communicate the message that the police know who gang members are. Anecdotally, officials had learned that, gang members did not really believe this beforehand. Thus, the message was a shock to many people at the call in meetings.

Crucial to the effectiveness if CIRV is delivering on the message to a small and carefully selected audience. Law enforcement officials had to carry out "swift and certain" responses as they threatened to do. (Remember, swift and certain consequences are a cornerstone of deterrence theory.) Also, the social services personnel had to be able to provide the services they had promised to provide (no waiting lists, no waiting for a program to be funded, etc.).

Does CIRV work? While admittedly "not definitive," an initial evaluation found a 61 percent drop in "group member involved" homicides following the first two call-in meetings. Experience from other programs suggested that one meeting is not sufficient to get the message across. There was also a sharp drop in nonfatal shootings.[22]

The Cincinnati findings are reinforced by the results from similar programs in other cities. In Lowell, Massachusetts, the problem was more aggravated assaults involving guns than homicides. Following an episode of gang-related violence, police officers, probation officers, and youth service workers "flooded" the affected area, actually walking the streets, communicating the message (as in Cincinnati) of both targeted law enforcement and the availability of services. Special attention was given to "impact players," people regarded as particularly dangerous. The result was a 43 percent reduction in aggravated assaults involving guns. Comparisons with other Massachusetts cities indicated, moreover, that Lowell had far greater success than the others in controlling gun-related violence.[23]

The evaluation pointed out that the pulling levers strategy was a "focused application of deterrence principles." The key elements of the programs we have examined here are: (1) a data-driven effort that (2) focuses on a select group of targets, (3) delivers a very specific message with both deterrent and rehabilitative components, and (4) delivers on its threats and promises. The failure of most deterrent-oriented programs has always been that they are addressed to a diffuse general audience and have no credible capacity for delivering the threat. The very promising evidence leads us to the following:

PROPOSITION 16
Carefully designed and narrowly targeted deterrence programs
have demonstrated a capacity to reduce crime.

THE DEATH PENALTY

The death penalty provides additional perspective on deterrence theory. Not only do many people believe that capital punishment deters crime; but there is considerable research on the subject.

Sorting Out the Issues

We can debate the merits of the death penalty in terms of three separate issues.[24] First is the moral question of whether it is a just form of punishment. Some people firmly believe that the death penalty is a morally justifiable form of punishment for murder, whereas others believe that it is morally wrong. This debate involves basic conceptions of morality and justice and is not subject to empirical proof one way or the other.

The question of whether the death penalty is constitutional is the second issue. Constitutional challenges began in the 1960s and eventually led to the 1972 *Furman v. Georgia* decision, in which the U.S. Supreme Court ruled that the death penalty had been applied in an unconstitutionally arbitrary and capricious fashion.[25] It rejected the argument that capital punishment was inherently cruel and unusual. Four years later, in *Gregg v. Georgia,* the Court upheld the constitutionality of the death penalty where there were guidelines to control its application.[26]

The third issue is whether the death penalty deters crime. This is the focus of our discussion here. The moral and constitutional questions are extremely important, but as we explained in Chapter 1, this book focuses on issues of crime policy.

Executions and Crime: The Debate Continues

The deterrent effect of capital punishment has been hotly debated and intensively researched for several decades. The research has been marked by dramatically increasing research methodologies. One of the earliest studies, by the noted criminologist Thorsten Sellin, compared neighboring states, two with and one without the death penalty. He found that Ohio and Indiana, two death penalty states, did not have lower crime rates than Michigan, which did not have the death penalty. Murder rates in all three states changed in roughly the same direction during the period studies, decreasing from the 1930s to the early 1960s and then rising sharply. This suggests that broad social factors common to all states, rather than executions, were the primary causal factors in homicide rates.[27] Sellin's method would not be acceptable by today's standards.

Isaac Ehrlich raised the debate to a new level in 1975 with a methodologically sophisticated study of executions and crime trends between 1930 and 1969. He concluded that the death penalty had a powerful deterrent effect, with each execution preventing seven or eight murders.[28] An economist, he embraced the rational choice theory of human behavior, popular in that discipline, explaining that the "propensity" to commit crimes "is influenced by the prospective gains and losses associated with their commission."[29] Critics, however, found serious flaws in his analysis. As is the case with studies using many variables and large data sets, his approach is highly sensitive to problems with the reliability of the data and the time frame studied. In their respective analyses, Brian Forst, Peter Passell, and William Bowers and Glenn Pierce all argue that when you exclude the years from 1962 to 1969, Ehrlich's deterrent effect vanishes.[30] His formula does not explain the trends between the 1930s and the early 1960s, when executions declined while the crime rate either declined or remained stable.

Ehrlich's use of FBI Uniform Crime Report data is also problematic. We have good reason to believe, however, that because of the lack of professionalism in most police departments, these data seriously undercount the amount of crime. In New York City alone, for example, at least two well-documented episodes (in 1955 and 1965) occurred in which administrative changes in the police department produced huge increases in officially reported crime. In Chicago, meanwhile, reporters in 1983 caught the Chicago police unfounding a substantial number of crimes. In other words, the apparent risk of apprehension was higher in the pre–1960 years because police record keeping kept the number of reported crimes artificially low.[31] Consequently, the real risk of apprehension had not declined as much between 1930 and 1969 as Ehrlich asserted.

The most recent and most comprehensive review of death penalty studies found a lack of consensus of opinion. Some studies found a deterrent effect, while others did not. How do we explain such conflicting evidence? A central problem is that each study is guided by assumptions about the "appropriate data, control variables, model specification," and other factors that have "major effects" on the resulting findings. In the end, the review concludes "that there is little empirical evidence in favor of the deterrence hypothesis." We agree, and offer the following:

PROPOSITION 17
The death penalty does not deter crime.

Delays and Deterrence

The conflicting studies of the impact of the death penalty provide a useful glimpse into how the justice system works, and how problems in the administration of justice affect deterrence and other criminal justice policies.

One issue involves the long delays in carrying out executions. In fact, the average time between conviction and execution is over eight years. Appeals in some cases take 15 years or more. Also, many death sentences are vacated, through appeal, executive clemency, or death by natural causes. In 2003, 65 offenders were executed while four times as many (265) were removed from death row by other causes.[32] Death penalty advocates argue that these factors undermine both the certainty and the swiftness of the death penalty. If we would eliminate these obstacles, the argument continues, the deterrent effect would work.

Long delays in death penalty cases are to be expected. Someone sentenced to die is going to explore every possible avenue of appeal. The process of appeal is an essential part of the criminal justice system, designed to protect against errors in the process.

And mistakes do happen. Hugo Bedau and Michael Radelet identified a total of 350 miscarriages of justice in potentially capital cases since 1900. They define *miscarriage of justice* as a case in which "the defendant was erroneously convicted of a capital crime." Of the 350 cases they identified, 139 were given death sentences, and 23 were actually executed.[33] In January 2000, the governor of Illinois suspended all executions after 13 people were released from death row because they had been wrongly convicted. The Innocence Project, established by Barry Scheck and Peter Neufeld, had won exoneration for 245 convicted offenders by late 2009 through the use of DNA technology.[34]

Research on the effect of the death penalty on crime is extremely mixed. Because so many different factors influence criminal behavior, it may never be possible to determine the extent of any deterrent effect. For the moment, then, we can say that the advocates of capital punishment have not persuasively established the existence of a deterrent effect.

DETERRING THE DRUNK DRIVER

In the 1980s, a crusade against drunk driving arose and swept the country. Spurred by a wave of public outrage, virtually every state enacted new laws and policies, most of which were designed to deter drunk driving through tougher punishment.[35] Leading the national crusade was an organization called MADD (Mothers Against Drunk Driving), founded by Candi Lightner, whose 13-year-old daughter, Cari, was killed in a crash involving Clarence Busch, who had two previous drunk driving convictions and was out on bail on a third drunk driving charge. Cari Lightner's death confirmed the belief of many people that repeat drunk drivers beat the system.

The "Killer Drunk" and Other Myths

Like so many aspects of criminal justice, the subject of drunk driving is dominated by myths that inhibit the development of sound and effective policies. It is widely believed, for example, that drunk drivers are responsible for half of all traffic fatalities. One Justice Department report repeated the widely publicized claim that drunk driving kills 50,000 people every two years—"almost as many American lives as were lost in the entire ten years of the Vietnam war."[36] This grossly exaggerated estimate originated in a 1968 report by the U.S. Department of Transportation (DOT) and has been widely repeated ever since.

Current data indicate that 32 percent of all traffic fatalities in 2008 involved "alcohol impaired driving."[37] This involved 11,773 deaths that year. Alcohol was not necessarily the *cause* of each of those accidents, however, but only that the driver was impaired by alcohol. There is an important distinction between drivers who have been drinking and those whose driving is *impaired* by drinking.[38]

Another myth is that many "killer drunks," people with a serious drinking problem and many arrests, frequently beat the system.[39] The myth of the killer drunk has several aspects. First, it places the blame on a small number of dangerous people. Second, it emphasizes the killing of innocent people. Third, it puts much of the blame on the criminal justice system for not punishing these offenders and keeping them off the road. Fourth, it makes criminal punishment the primary focus of efforts to reduce traffic fatalities.

Ross argues that each of these aspects distorts the reality of alcohol-related fatalities. First, the general problem of drunk driving is not confined to a few dangerous people. Driving after drinking is fairly common. Ross estimates that every year about 20 percent of all drivers, or 33 million people, drive after drinking. That is a lot of people. Moreover, because about 20 to 30 percent of the population does not drink at all, the percentage of drinkers who drive after drinking is higher than 20 percent. Ross's point is that drinking and driving is a routine part of a society where driving is nearly universal (and practically necessary in terms of work) and drinking is an acceptable social custom.[40]

This is not to say that there is not a small number of people who are chronic drunk drivers. There is. These people are repeatedly caught, punished, but drive drunk again. At some point, their arrests make the news. Keeping in mind what we learned in Chapter 2, we need to see them as classic "celebrated cases." They are indeed a problem, but they distort our perception of the broader drunk driving problem and how we might control it.

Second, innocent drivers or bystanders are not the typical victims of alcohol-related crashes. Two-thirds (68 percent) of all the people killed in 2008 were the drivers themselves, and another 16 percent passengers in other cars, 10 percent the drivers in other cars, and only 6 percent pedestrians. In some of these cases, they were themselves impaired by alcohol.[41]

Third, the argument that the criminal justice system is "soft" on drunk drivers is one part of a general view of the criminal justice system which we have already discussed in Chapters 2 and 3. We will take a close look at the alleged loopholes in the criminal justice system in Chapter 8. Later in this chapter we will look specifically at the handling of drunk driving cases.

In fact, most of the drivers killed in alcohol-related crashes do not have a history of drunk driving. It is not possible, therefore, to spot them in advance on the basis of their driving records. Once again, we are up against the prediction problem we discussed in Chapter 4. The crash that killed Cari Lightner, involving an innocent victim and a driver with a long record, is the classic "celebrated case" at the top of our criminal justice wedding cake.

Fourth, and perhaps most important in terms of reducing drinking and driving, both H. Laurence Ross and James B. Jacobs argue that many different kinds of policies can contribute to reducing alcohol-related traffic fatalities.[42] Most do not involve deterrence-oriented enforcement. We will examine some of these policies in the "Alternative Strategies for Dealing with Traffic Fatalities" section below.

Deterrence and Drunk Driving

Deterrence-oriented efforts to reduce drunk driving involve both short-term enforcement crackdowns and long-term changes in sentencing policy.[43] There are several reasons for thinking that tougher punishment is more likely to work with drunk driving than, for example, with robbery or burglary. Because people who drink and drive are more representative of the general population, more of them will have a stake in society and therefore feel threatened by the stigma of arrest and the impact on their jobs and families. Reasons also abound for thinking that the probability of arrest is higher for drunk driving: It is a public crime, occurring in plain view and readily observable to the police, over an extended period of time. The evidence, however, suggests that these assumptions do not work in practice and that deterring the drunk driver is extremely difficult.

One of the most famous drunk driving crackdowns involved the 1967 Road Safety Act in England. The law empowered the police to require a breath test of any driver and specified that refusal to submit to the test was punishable as an actual failure. It attempted to increase the certainty of apprehension, without changing the severity of punishment.[44]

As Figure 6.1 indicates, weekend traffic fatalities and serious injuries dropped to one-third of their previous levels after the law went into effect. Some observers saw this as evidence of a deterrent effect. But it is also obvious that the effect gradually wore off. Within three years, fatalities returned to their previous level. This decay appears to be a general phenomenon in enforcement crackdowns. A 1984 Justice Department evaluation of four anti–drunk driving campaigns found similar results and concluded that the deterrent effects of an enforcement effort, even when it exists, "appear to diminish over time."[45]

Lawrence Sherman characterizes the decline in deterrent effect as "initial deterrence decay." Some deterrent effect does remain, and he calls this "residual deterrence."[46] The challenge for policymakers is to increase the amount of residual deterrence over the long term. Unfortunately, the evidence indicates that short-term crackdowns do not achieve this effect.

The British crackdown illustrates a phenomenon known as the *announcement effect*. The publicity surrounding a crackdown causes people to alter their behavior: People decide not to have another drink, or they ask someone else to drive them home; a bartender refuses to serve a drink, or friends tell someone that he or she has had enough to drink. In short, people do perceive the threat of punishment and make rational decisions to alter their behavior. In some instances,

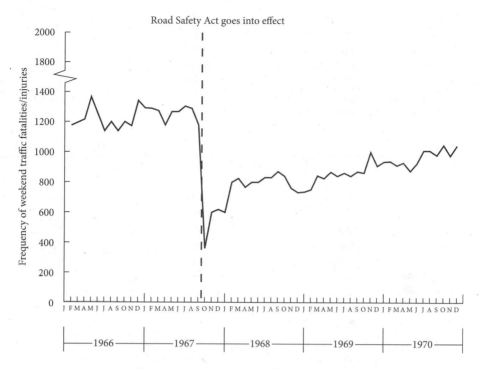

FIGURE 6.1 The effect on traffic fatalities and serious injuries of a crackdown on drunk driving, United Kingdom, 1966–1970.

SOURCE: Reprinted by permission of the publisher, from *Deterring the Drinking Driver: Legal Policy and Social Control*, by H. Laurence Ross (Lexington, MA: Lexington Books, D. C. Heath and Company). Originally appeared in Ross, 1973, *Journal of Legal Studies*, University of Chicago Press.

these changes occur before the law actually goes into effect, as people's awareness of the potential penalty rises.

The announcement effect may also change the behavior of police officers, causing them to become more active in stopping drunk drivers in the early months of a new law. A Justice Department evaluation of four anti–drunk driving campaigns, for example, found that arrests went up in three of them but not in the one in which "relatively little publicity" was made about the mandatory imprisonment law.[47]

As the publicity surrounding an enforcement effort diminishes, however, the effect wears off. Drinkers become less conscious of the risks and revert to their normal behavior. Police officers return to their normal levels of enforcement activity.

One of the main problems with drunk driving crackdowns is that the risk of arrest is extremely low. In his evaluation of the British experiments, H. Laurence Ross estimated that the probability of being asked to submit to a breath test was 1 per million vehicle miles driven. (Consider this figure in terms of the mileage on your odometer.) The risk was higher for drinking drivers because their behavior attracted the attention of the police, but it was still "low by any reasonable criterion." The U.S. Department of Transportation estimates that someone would have to drive drunk between 200 and 2,000 times to be apprehended—and even then would face only a 50 percent chance of being punished.[48]

Most people, moreover, believe that the risk is low. A survey of Minneapolis and St. Paul residents found that 75 percent thought that their chances of being arrested if they drove drunk were "unlikely" or "very unlikely."[49] And according to deterrence theory, the deterrent effect is weak or nonexistent if the perceived risk is low.

Looking at enforcement from the perspective of the police officer helps explain why the risk is low. Both regular patrol officers and traffic unit officers are theoretically on the lookout for drunk drivers. Regular patrol officers, however, have many responsibilities—law enforcement, order maintenance, and service—and are concerned primarily with answering calls for service. Moreover, as we learned in the previous chapter, they are spread very thin and are responsible for patrolling streets that are not prime "hunting grounds" for drunk drivers. Traffic unit officers, meanwhile, represent no more than about 10 percent of the sworn officers in a department. They also have other responsibilities, such as watching for speeders. Drunk driving is heaviest at those hours when the police are busiest with other assignments. In short, not that many police officers are concentrating exclusively on drunk driving.

Certain disincentives affect aggressive traffic enforcement. Traffic stops are unpleasant and occasionally dangerous experiences for police officers. Citizens resent them and sometimes let the officer know it. Traffic situations are the fourth most hazardous situation for police officers in terms of officers killed on duty (and these situations include accidents resulting from pursuits).[50] In the absence of any strong incentives, such as ticket quotas, most cops prefer to avoid traffic stops except in the most serious cases.

When officers do make arrests, the law of diminishing returns comes into play. Processing an arrest may take up to two hours (or more, depending on local procedures). Thus, each arrest removes the police officer from the street and lowers the level of enforcement. While there may be some gain in specific deterrence related to the person arrested, there is an offsetting loss in general deterrence.

If the hunters are few, the hunted are many and well hidden among law-abiding drivers. Experts estimate that even during the peak drunk driving hours (Friday and Saturday nights), only about 3 to 4 percent of all drivers are legally drunk.[51] Perhaps another 5 percent have some detectable level of alcohol in their blood. But some drivers who are legally drunk may not be impaired, and their driving may not attract the attention of the police. The drive home from a neighborhood bar may be very short, leaving a small window of opportunity for detection.

Drunk Drivers in Court

Another factor undermining the deterrent effect of a crackdown is the fate of drunk driving cases in court. James B. Jacobs estimates that about 90 percent of all arrested drunk drivers are convicted through guilty pleas.[52] In this respect, the prosecution of drunk driving offenses closely resembles the handling of other criminal cases. Those data, however, reflect only convictions. The main purpose of crackdowns is to deter drunk driving by increasing the severity of punishment, usually through a mandatory jail or prison sentence.

Mandatory sentencing provisions can be evaded through dismissal, plea bargaining, or blatant disregard for the law. H. Laurence Ross and James P. Foley examined the implementation of new mandatory sentencing laws enacted in New Mexico and Indiana in the 1980s. The New Mexico law required a jail term of not less than 48 hours for offenders with a prior drunk driving conviction, and prohibited suspended sentences. Ross and Foley found that in 238 cases the mandated sentence was imposed and served in only 106, or 45 percent of the total. In another 60 cases (25 percent) the mandatory sentences were imposed but there was no documented proof that the offenders served them. In 10 percent of the cases, the judge suspended the sentence, and in another 20 percent the offender served no jail sentence. The Indiana law mandated five days in jail, with at least 48 consecutive hours, or a minimum of 80 hours of community service for offenders with a prior drunk driving conviction. Yet 30 percent of the convicted offenders did not serve the mandated sentence. Of 753 cases, 64 percent served the 48 consecutive hours, and another 6 percent did the required 80 hours of community service.[53]

Ross and Foley offer several possible explanations for this evasion of mandatory sentences. In some cases, the judges may have been ignorant of the offender's prior record. We might ask whether they chose not to find out as a deliberate strategy for evading the mandatory sentencing provision. It is possible that some jurisdictions do not have data systems that accurately record all prior convictions. Or, it is possible that prosecutors do not file evidence of prior convictions (This is one of the methods prosecutors use to evade "three strikes" laws). In others, judges may have chosen to interpret the law as covering only certain kinds of prior convictions (for example, felonies and not misdemeanors). Judges may have simply ignored the law in some cases. For some sentenced offenders, the term "48 hours" may not have been interpreted literally. Correctional officials may have counted a few hours a day as representing the entire day; if the offender spent a few hours in jail spanning midnight, he might have been credited with having served both days. Similar evasions of mandatory sentencing have been found in studies of other crackdowns.

Evasion of the law by justice officials is not universal by any means. The Justice Department's evaluation of enforcement efforts in Seattle found that the incarceration rate for convicted drunk drivers went from 9 to 97 percent as a result of new procedures. In Memphis, it went from 29 to almost 100 percent.[54] A 1982 California law increased the statewide jail incarceration rate for second-time offenders from 83 percent in 1980 to 97.5 percent in 1984. In Sacramento County, the percentage of first-time drunk drivers sent to jail went from 10 percent to more than 50 percent. These data make it clear that second-offense drunk drivers were not getting off easy before passage of the new law. The most significant effect of the California law was on first-time offenders; the percentage going to jail increased from about 10 percent to over 50 percent.[55]

Nonetheless, as the Ross and Foley study suggests, a certain amount of evasion of mandatory sentencing persists in some jurisdictions that undermines both the certainty and the severity of punishment. This compounds the low perceived and actual risk of arrest. In the end, most experts believe that enforcement crackdowns are not likely to deter drunk driving. After reviewing all the evidence, Ross concludes that "deterrence-based policies are questionable in the long run. No such policies have been scientifically demonstrated to work over time."[56] Jacobs agrees but adds that deterrence-based laws play a symbolic role in expressing society's moral condemnation of drunk driving.[57] Our conclusion can be stated as follows:

PROPOSITION 18
Enforcement crackdowns do not deter drunk driving over the long term.

Crackdown Costs

When a drunk driving crackdown does result in more punishment, it imposes significant costs on the criminal justice system. The most direct impact is on local jails and courts. Additional judges were needed in Seattle to handle the increase in cases. Cincinnati had to add an additional daily traffic court. In Sacramento County, California, more defendants insisted on going to trial, with the result that convictions at trial decreased. In Seattle, the county had to open a new jail facility just to handle the drunk drivers. In Memphis, some offenders had to wait six or seven months to serve their jail sentences. In two California counties, the jails became so overcrowded that courts found jail conditions unconstitutional.[58]

Illustration by Frank Irwin, © Wadsworth, Cengage Learning.

In short, as with other "get tough" policies, drunk driving crackdowns not only may fail to achieve their intended goals but may also impose unintended costs on the justice system.

EFFECTIVE STRATEGIES FOR DEALING
WITH TRAFFIC FATALITIES

Actually, there is considerable good news about traffic fatality trends. As Table 6.1 indicates, the motor vehicle death rate per 100,000 vehicle miles dropped from 16.33 in 1927 to 3.35 in 1977 to 1.27 in 2008 (this includes all fatalities and not just alcohol-related).[59] The long-term decline since 1930 is substantial, and the 20 to 50 percent reduction between 1998 and 2008 alone (1.58 to 1.27) is remarkable.

Interestingly, the number of motorcycle-related deaths doubled between 1998 and 2008, mainly because the number of motorcycles on the road doubled. Moreover, the fatality rate increased (per 100,000 registered vehicles and also per 100 million vehicle miles traveled). The increase in the rates suggests that many of the new motorcycle owners were inexperienced and/or careless about how to operate a bike. These increases offset the gains that were made with regard to cars and trucks, indicating that the gains there were even greater than the aggregate data suggest.[60]

How do we explain this success, especially in light of our conclusion that enforcement crackdowns do not work? The answer is that *some things do work.* Tougher enforcement by the criminal justice system may have contributed to this decline, but both Ross and Jacobs argue that at best it was only one factor. Other social policies also played important roles.

T A B L E 6.1   Motor vehicle deaths per 100,000 vehicle miles

Year	Death rate
1927	16.33
1937	14.68
1947	8.82
1957	5.98
1967	5.50
1977	3.35
1987	2.51
1997	1.71
2003	1.75
2008	1.27

SOURCE: *U.S. Department of Transportation Facts 2003* (Washington, DC: U.S. Department of Transportation, 2004).

First, cars have become safer. Steering wheels, for example, are less likely to impale a driver than they were in the 1950s. Dashboards and door handles have been redesigned over the years to reduce potential harm in accidents.

Second, seat belts are required on all new cars, and their use is mandatory in every state except New Hampshire. The National Highway Traffic Safety Administration estimates that seat belts saved 13,250 lives in 2008, and a total of 255,115 between 1975 and 2008. That is a lot of lives. The total number of people killed in 2008 would have been 35 percent higher if seat belts did not exist. Child restraints, meanwhile, saved 244 lives in 2008 and 8,959 between 1975 and 2008. Finally, the NHTSA estimated that air bags saved 2,546 lives in 2008. Motorcycle helmets saved another 1,829 lives. Table 6.2 presents the estimated life-saving totals for all safety devices and laws.[61]

Third, federal law has forced states to raise the legal age for drinking to 21 (by withholding federal highway funds if they do not). Although this law has not necessarily curbed teenage drinking, it may have helped reduce drunk driving by teenagers: the DOT estimates that it saved 714 lives in 2008.[62]

Fourth, the policy of administrative license revocation (ALR) has resulted in speedier loss of driver's licenses. In this procedure, a police officer can revoke a license on the spot if the driver fails a breath test. Forty-one states have ALR laws. It is important to point out that this is a *civil* law rather than a criminal law approach. It rests on the theory that a driver's license is essentially a privilege that can be withdrawn without resort to the full criminal process. Ross argues that it is both swift and certain, resulting in the immediate incapacitation of the offender (in the sense that the person cannot drive legally, although obviously some people drive without a license). He cites studies indicating that this approach has been effective in reducing alcohol-related accidents and fatalities.[63]

Fifth, socialization may have contributed to some of the long-term reduction in traffic fatalities. The national anti–drunk driving crusade, with all of the attendant publicity, may have helped change attitudes and behavior about drinking and driving. Public opinion surveys have found that the percentage of people saying that they "sometimes" drove after drinking fell from 25 percent in 1983 to 16 percent in 1995. The percentage indicating that they "never" did rose correspondingly.[64] We have good reason to assume that these attitudes reflect real changes in behavior. Not only has the number of traffic fatalities fallen, but the

T A B L E 6.2   Lives saved in 2008 by restraints and minimum drinking age laws

Age 4 and younger	Age 5 and older	Age 13 and older	All ages	Age 18–20
Child restraints	Seat belts	Frontal air bags	Motorcycle helmets	Minimum drinking age laws
244	13,250	2,546	1,829	714

SOURCE: National Highway Traffic Safety Administration, Traffic Safety Facts, *Lives Saved in 2008 by Restrain Use and Minimum Drinking Age Laws* (Washington, DC: NHTSA, 2009).

percentage that are alcohol related fell from 57.3 in 1982 to 40.9 in 1996 and remained at that level in 2003.[65]

Sixth, the National Safety Council's policy of Graduated Driver Licensing (GDL) allows limited driving privileges to teenagers and then gradually expands them. (For additional information, go to the National Safety Council website.) It is well known that teenagers, and young men in particular, engage in the riskiest driving behavior. Reducing their driving, and/or introducing them to driving gradually, is likely to reduce traffic accidents and fatalities. Although almost all states always had provisions for temporary licenses, the idea of a comprehensive system emerged only in the 1980s, first in New Zealand and then in Canada. It finally began to spread in the United States in the 1990s. Evaluations have found reductions in the number of crashes ranging from a high of 60 percent to a low of 4 percent among teenage drivers.[66]

Seventh, ignition "interlock" systems are in-car breathalyzers that prevent an alcohol-impaired driver from starting the car. Interlocks are increasingly popular. By 2009, 10 states mandated their use for convicted drunk drivers. The Insurance Institute for Highway Safety estimated that about 180,000 interlock systems were in use in 2009, and that if they were used in all vehicles, they could save 8,000 lives a year.[67]

In terms of deterrence, interlock systems are unique. They target a small group of people believed to be at risk for drunk driving. (Think in terms of the "pulling levers" programs we discussed earlier.) Harsh sentencing laws are diffuse, targeting the entire population, and as experience has taught us, leave a lot of room for judicial discretion to not impose the "mandated" sentences. And interlock systems keep the targeted person from even *driving the car*. True, there are ways of circumventing the system, but technological advances are reportedly making that more difficult. And even if the law mandates their use for first-time convicted drunk drivers, a judge may not order the system installed. Nonetheless, interlock systems appear to be a very effective way to reduce drunk driving related accidents and fatalities.

PROPOSITION 19
Multipronged strategies that do not rely completely on the criminal law can effectively reduce drunk driving and traffic fatalities.

Summary

There are some important lessons in our success in substantially reducing traffic fatalities. Most important, it is clear that relying solely on criminal law enforcement is *not* likely to produce significant results. In Chapter 13 we will discuss the limits of the criminal law with regard to drugs and other types of behavior (e.g., drinking). Second, it appears that *a variety of policies* operating in combination is likely to get results. Third, some of these policies do not impose costs on the justice system (e.g., interlock systems do not involve jail or prison terms). These points are at the heart of the community-focused crime prevention strategies that we will examine in Chapter 14.

CONCLUSION

The commonsense notion that people will avoid unpleasant things and that we can influence their decisions by increasing the unpleasantness does not necessarily work in the real world of criminal justice. Let us be careful about exactly what we are saying. As in so many other areas, it is not true that "nothing works." The criminal law does have some deterrent effect. Most of us, after all, do not become career criminals. The threat of punishment, however, probably plays a relatively minor role in influencing the behavior of law-abiding people. The threat works, but it just is not the major factor. In terms of controlling behavior, the broader processes of socialization are the primary factors. As Leslie Wilkins put it, there are "those of us who have never needed a deterrent."[68] When these processes have broken down, we should not expect the criminal justice system—and deterrence-oriented policies in particular—to fix the problem. We will return to this issue in Chapter 12 when we discuss procedural justice. Experts in this field argue that we need to put more emphasis on building voluntary compliance with the law and less effort on trying to scare people into being law abiding.

NOTES

1. The best treatment of the subject is still Franklin E. Zimring and Gordon J. Hawkins, *Deterrence: The Legal Threat in Crime Control* (Chicago: University of Chicago Press, 1973).

2. Tom R. Tyler, *Why People Obey the Law* (New Haven: Yale University Press, 1990).

3. Daniel S. Nagin, "Criminal Deterrence Research at the Outset of the Twenty-First Century," in Michael Tonry, ed., *Crime and Justice: A Review of Research*, vol. 23 (Chicago: University of Chicago Press, 1998), p. 3.

4. Ibid.

5. Scott Decker, Richard Wright, and Robert Logie, "Perceptual Deterrence among Active Residential Burglars: A Research Note," *Criminology* 31 (February 1993): 135.

6. Zimring and Hawkins, *Deterrence*, pp. 92–248.

7. Robert J. Kane, "On the Limits of Social Control: Structural Deterrence and the Policing of 'Suppressible' Crimes," *Justice Quarterly* 23 (June 2006): pp. 186–213.

8. Ibid., pp. 13–14.

9. Ronald L. Akers, "Rational Choice, Deterrence, and Social Learning Theory in Criminology: The Path Not Taken," *Journal of Criminal Law and Criminology* 81 (Fall 1990): 653–676.

10. See, for example, the extremely influential conservative argument in Charles Murray, *Losing Ground: American Social Policy, 1950–1980* (New York: Basic Books, 1984).

11. Dallin Oaks, "Studying the Exclusionary Rule in Search and Seizure," *University of Chicago Law Review* 37 (Summer 1970): 665–757.

12. Nagin, "Criminal Deterrence Research," pp. 4–6.

13. James O. Finckenauer, *Scared Straight and the Panacea Phenomenon* (Englewood Cliffs, NJ: Prentice-Hall, 1982).

14. Anthony Petrosino, Carolyn Turpin-Petrosino, and John Buehler, "Scared Straight and Other Juvenile Awareness Programs for Preventing Juvenile Delinquency: A Systematic Review of the Randomized Experimental Evidence," *The Annals of the American Academy of Political and Social Science* 589 (September 2003): 41–62.

15. Bureau of Justice Statistics, *Spouse Murder Defendants in Large Urban Counties* (Washington, DC: Department of Justice, 1995). NCJ 156831.

16. James Q. Wilson and Allan Abrahamse, "Does Crime Pay?" *Justice Quarterly* 9 (September 1992): 359–377.

17. Julie Horney and Incke Haen Marshall, "Risk Perception among Serious Offenders: The Role of Crime and Punishment," *Criminology* 30 (1992): 575–594. Nagin, "Criminal Deterrence Research," p. 16.

18. Wilson and Abrahamse, "Does Crime Pay?" p. 373.

19. Ibid., pp. 372–373.

20. David M. Kennedy, Anthony A. Braga, and Anne M. Piehl, *Reducing Gun Violence: The Boston Gun Project's Operation Cease Fire* (Washington, DC: Department of Justice, 2001).

21. Robin S. Engel, S. Gregory Baker, Marie Skubak Tillyer, John Eck, Jessica Dunham, *Implementation of the Cincinnati Initiative to Reduce Violence (CIRV): Year 1 Report* (Cincinnati: University of Cincinnati: April 14, 2008).

22. Ibid., pp. 29–32.

23. Anthony A. Braga, Glenn L. Pierce, Jack McDevitt, Brenda J. Bond, and Shea Cronin, "The Strategic Prevention of Gun Violence Among Gang-Involved Offenders," *Justice Quarterly* 25 (March 2008): 132–162.

24. Raymond Paternoster, *Capital Punishment in America* (Lexington, MA: Lexington Books, 1991), part IV, "Arguments for and against the Death Penalty," pp. 185–270.

25. *Furman v. Georgia*, 408 U.S. 238 (1972).

26. *Gregg v. Georgia*, 428 U.S. 153 (1976).

27. Thorsten Sellin, *The Penalty of Death* (Beverly Hills, CA: Sage, 1980).

28. Isaac Ehrlich, "The Deterrent Effect of Capital Punishment: A Question of Life and Death," *American Economic Review* 65 (1975): 397–417.

29. Ibid.

30. Brian Forst, "Capital Punishment and Deterrence: Conflicting Evidence," *Journal of Criminal Law and Criminology* 74 (Fall 1983): 927–942. Peter Passell, "The Deterrent Effect of the Death Penalty: A Statistical Test," *Stanford Law Review* 28 (November 1975): 61–80. William J. Bowers and Glenn Pierce, "The Illusion of Deterrence in Isaac Ehrlich's Research on Capital Punishment," *Yale Law Review* 85 (1975): 187–208.

31. Robert Hood and Richard Sparks, *Key Issues in Criminology* (New York: McGraw-Hill, 1980), pp. 40–41. Zimring and Hawkins, *Deterrence*, p. 334. Philip Wattley, "City Hit on Crime Data," *Chicago Tribune*, 28 April 1983: 1–2.

32. Bureau of Justice Statistics, *Capital Punishment, 2008* (Washington, DC: Department of Justice, 2009). NCJ 220219.

33. Hugo Adam Bedau and Michael L. Radelet, "Miscarriages of Justice in Potentially Capital Cases," *Stanford Law Review* 40 (November 1987): 21–179.

34. Recent data and facts on individual cases can be found at the Innocence Project's website. www.innocenceproject.org.

35. The two best surveys of the subject are H. Laurence Ross, *Confronting Drunk Driving: Social Policy for Saving Lives* (New Haven, CT: Yale University Press, 1992), and James B. Jacobs, *Drunk Driving: An American Dilemma* (Chicago: University of Chicago Press, 1989).

36. Bureau of Justice Statistics, *Jailing Drunk Drivers: Impact on the Criminal Justice System—Statistical Tables* (Washington, DC: Government Printing Office, 1984).

37. National Highway Traffic Safety Administration, *Traffic Safety Facts, 2008 Data: Overview* (Washington, DC: NHTSA, 2009). National Highway Traffic Safety Administration, *Traffic Safety Facts, 2008 Data: Alcohol-Impaired Data* (Washington, DC: NHTSA, 2009).

38. Jacobs, *Drunk Driving*, pp. 27–28; Ross, *Confronting Drunk Driving*.

39. Ross, *Confronting Drunk Driving*, pp. 21–22, 168–170.

40. Ross, *Confronting Drunk Driving*.

41. National Highway Traffic Safety Administration, *Traffic Safety Facts, 2008 Data: Alcohol-Impaired Driving*, Table 1.

42. Jacobs, *Drunk Driving;* Ross, *Confronting Drunk Driving*.

43. Lawrence W. Sherman, "Police Crackdowns: Initial and Residual Deterrence," in Michael W. Tonry and Norval Morris, eds., *Crime and Justice: An Annual Review of Research*, vol. 12 (Chicago: University of Chicago Press, 1990), pp. 1–48.

44. H. Laurence Ross, *Deterring the Drinking Driver: Legal Policy and Social Control*, rev. ed. (Lexington, MA: Lexington Books, 1984), pp. 24–34.

45. Bureau of Justice Statistics, *Jailing Drunk Drivers*, p. 2.

46. Sherman, "Police Crackdowns: Initial and Residual Deterrence."

47. Ibid.

48. Ross, *Deterring the Drinking Driver*, pp. 33, 105.

49. Donald E. Green, "Past Behavior as a Measure of Actual Future Behavior: An Unresolved Issue in Perceptual Deterrence Research," *Journal of Criminal Law and Criminology* 80 (1989): 781–804.

50. Federal Bureau of Investigation, *Law Enforcement Officers Killed and Assaulted, 2003*. Report issued annually.

51. Jacobs, *Drunk Driving*, p. 47.

52. Jacobs, *Drunk Driving*, pp. 98–100.

53. H. Laurence Ross and James P. Foley, "Judicial Disobedience of the Mandate to Imprison Drunk Drivers," *Law and Society Review* 21:2 (1987): 315–323.

54. Bureau of Justice Statistics, *Jailing Drunk Drivers*, p. 2.

55. Rodney Kingsworth and Michael Jungsten, "Driving under the Influence: The Impact of Legislative Reform on Court Sentencing Practices in Drunk Driving Cases," *Crime and Delinquency* 34 (January 1988): 3–28.

56. Ross, *Deterring the Drinking Driver*, p. 111.

57. Jacobs, *Drunk Driving*, p. 126.

58. Bureau of Justice Statistics, *Jailing Drunk Drivers;* Kingsworth and Jungsten, "Driving under the Influence."

59. National Safety Council, *Injury Facts* (Washington, DC: National Safety Council, 2003). National Highway Traffic Safety Administration, *Traffic Safety Facts 2008 Data: Overview*, Table 2.

60. National Highway Traffic Safety Administration, *Traffic Safety Facts, 2008 Data: Motorcycles* (Washington, DC: NHTSA, 2009).

61. National Highway Traffic Safety Administration, *Traffic Safety Facts: Lives Saved in 2008 by Restraint Use and Minimum Drinking Age Laws* (Washington, DC: NHTSA, 2009), Table 1.

62. Ibid.; "15,000 saved by air bags in past 20 years," *USA Today*, 12 July 2004.

63. U. S. Department of Transportation, *Reducing Highway Crashes Through Administrative License Revocation* (Washington, DC: Government Printing Office, 1986); Ross, *Confronting Drunk Driving*, pp. 63–67.

64. Bureau of Justice Statistics, *Sourcebook of Criminal Justice Statistics Online*.

65. National Safety Council, *Injury Facts*, 2003.

66. Herb M. Simpson, "The Evolution and Effectiveness of Graduated Licensing," *Journal of Safety Research* 34 (2003): 25–34.

67. "Alcohol Interlocks Are Gaining Traction," *The New York Times*, September 29, 2009. Insurance Institute for Highway Safety, *Alcohol Ignition Interlocks and the Prevention of Alcohol Impaired Driving*. Presentation, NHTSA Meeting, August 22, 2007, Washington, DC.

68. Quoted in Zimring and Hawkins, *Deterrence*, p. 97.

Lock 'Em Up

GETTING CRIMINALS OFF THE STREET

October 7, 2009, was a historic day in New York State. A new law on sentencing convicted drug offenders took effect, eliminating or scaling back some of the most severe features of the state's famous Rockefeller Drug Law. More than any other single event, the Rockefeller Drug Law—passed in 1973—had been the model for harsh sentencing practices that dominated American criminal sentencing over the next 36 years.

The American policy of locking up a lot of offenders is a matter of enormous controversy. The U.S. incarceration rate far exceeds that of other developed countries, including our closest counterpart, Canada. Conservatives argue that it has effectively reduced crime. Liberals argue that it has failed in its fundamental goal and has instead inflicted serious damage on American society: huge costs; diversion of money from other social needs; unjustifiable racial and ethnic disparities in punishment; and serious prison overcrowding, with all of its adverse consequences. Where does the truth lie?

The debate over locking up offenders is not a narrow criminal justice issue. It is central to a cluster of the most urgent issues in American society: crime, race, education, and communities.

Locking up offenders, and keeping them locked up and off the streets, is one of the main conservative crime control strategies. In this chapter we will take a look at the major "lock 'em up" programs: preventive detention, which is designed to keep defendants in jail before trial; the strategy of incapacitation; mandatory prison sentences; and long prison sentences (including "three strikes" laws). We end with a look at sex offender registration and notification laws designed to protect the community from sex offenders.

Lock 'em up strategies seek to limit the discretion of judges.[1] The underlying assumption is that judges have too much discretion to release dangerous criminals on bail, grant them probation, or sentence them to inappropriately short prison terms. Conservatives believe that the misuse of judicial discretion is the result of two factors. First, too many judges are "bleeding hearts" who are overly lenient with convicted offenders. Second, many of our policies encourage not locking people up. American law has traditionally embodied the principle of a right to bail. The philosophy of rehabilitation, meanwhile, encourages alternatives to prison for convicted felons. Conservative proposals attack these laws and policies as soft on crime.

Preventive Detention

Conservatives believe that people released on bail commit a large number of crimes. President Ronald Reagan's Task Force on Victims of Crime declared in 1982, "A substantial proportion of the crimes committed in this country are committed by defendants who have been released on bail or on their own recognizance."[2] Preventive detention, a policy that allows judges to deny bail to high-risk criminal defendants, is the conservative policy on this issue.

Preventive detention raises both *constitutional* and *empirical* questions. The constitutional question is whether the Eighth Amendment to the U.S. Constitution prohibits detaining someone solely for the purpose of preventing crime. The Eighth Amendment guarantees that "excessive bail shall not be required." As with many other parts of the Bill of Rights, the exact meaning of the Eighth Amendment is ambiguous. Traditionally, it has meant that all criminal defendants have a right to bail, with the exception of persons accused of "capital" crimes, or those crimes punishable by the death penalty. The original purpose of bail in Anglo-American law was to ensure the defendant's appearance at trial. Preventive detention, then, represents a fundamental change in the purpose of bail.[3]

The Supreme Court answered the constitutional question in 1987, when it upheld the preventive detention provision of the 1984 federal Bail Reform Act. In *United States v. Salerno,* the Court ruled that there is no absolute right to bail and that preventive detention is a legitimate "regulatory" measure.[4] In this context, *regulatory measure* refers to a crime control policy.

The empirical question we are interested in is whether preventive detention reduces serious crime. How much crime do offenders commit while on bail? Does keeping criminal defendants in jail before trial significantly reduce the crime rate?

A Short History of Bail Reform

The demand for preventive detention is a backlash against the first bail reform movement of the 1960s. The civil rights movement focused public attention on the plight of the poor in the criminal justice system. In 1967, the President's Crime Commission found that 52 percent of all people in jail were awaiting trial (in 2002 it was only 28.2 percent). Critics labeled America's jails the "new poorhouses." Wealthy organized crime figures easily raised large bail amounts, while poor people stayed in jail.[5] Caleb Foote's pioneering studies of bail in the 1950s found that defendants not released on bail were more likely to be convicted and imprisoned, thereby compounding the injustice of denying them a constitutional right.[6] In addition, the money bail system raises the cost of operating the jails and often contributes to jail overcrowding.

Current data support Foote's earlier finding about the impact of pretrial detention. A 2007 Justice Department report found that 78 percent of those detained before trial were convicted, compared with 60 percent who were released. The gap was particularly wide for felony cases. Among those convicted of a felony, 69 percent had been detained, compared with only 46 percent of those released.[7]

The bail reform movement sought to correct these problems by facilitating pretrial release. The major innovation was *release on recognizance* (ROR), which allowed a defendant to be released without any financial considerations. Evidence of a job, family ties, or other roots in the community was used to evaluate whether the defendant was likely to appear for scheduled court dates. The 1966 federal Bail Reform Act directed federal courts to develop ROR procedures. Many states, meanwhile, developed their own ROR programs and/or adopted 10 percent plans that allowed defendants to post 10 percent of the dollar bail amount.[8]

The bail reform movement achieved many of its goals, although there has been a noticeable slippage backward in recent years. The percentage of people in jail who were being held for trial dropped from 52 percent in 1967 to 33 percent in 1971 and then to 28.2 percent in 2002, before rising to 43 percent in 2004.[9] The reversal is a result of both a more punitive public mood and probably the impact of worsening economic conditions, as many defendants cannot meet even minimal money bail conditions. In 2004, 26 percent of all felony defendants in large urban counties were released on nonfinancial conditions, and 32 percent were released on financial conditions (the remaining 43 percent were detained).

Because employment status is a major criterion for ROR, it discriminates against the unemployed and the marginally employed. Nearly three-quarters (72 percent) of employed defendants were released in 1990 compared with 46 percent of those who were unemployed. (Data on this factor are not included in later reports.) Nor has bail reform eliminated the practice of keeping defendants in jail simply by setting a high amount for bail. In 2004, 86 percent of those who remained in jail before trial were not able to post bail; only 14 percent (or 6 percent of all defendants) were denied bail altogether. We will return to this point shortly.[10]

Seriousness of the offense and prior record, which we discussed in Chapter 2, have a major influence on pretrial release decisions. Only 12 percent of defendants charged with murder in 2004 obtained pretrial release. Only 42 percent of robbers were released, compared with 58 charged with larceny/theft. Importantly, this is down from 68 percent in 2004. And since larceny/theft accounts for half of all felony arrests, the rise in that detention rate has a huge impact on jail crowding and the cost to tax payers. Also, as we learned in Chapter 2, prior record has an enormous impact on bail decisions: 71 percent of those with no previous convictions obtained their release. This was down from 77 percent in 2000—another indicator of increased punitiveness in recent years—compared with 61 percent of those with one conviction and only 41 percent of those with five or more.[11]

The first bail reform movement coincided with the great rise in serious crime. Between 1963 and 1973, the robbery rate tripled, while the burglary rate went up two and a half times. Conservatives argue that bail reform contributed to this by releasing many dangerous offenders. This section examines the evidence on that argument.

The focus of the backlash was Washington, DC. Because of rising crime rates, Congress passed a preventive detention law for the District of Columbia in 1970. By the 1980s, public support for preventive detention was widespread, and nearly all states had adopted it. Some states amended their state constitutions to limit the right to bail. The Michigan constitution allows preventive detention in four kinds of crimes when the judge finds a possibility of danger were the defendant to be released.[12] Let us take a look at how preventive detention works in practice.

An Early Test: Preventive Detention in Washington, DC

The 1970 District of Columbia law offered the first evidence of how preventive detention might work. The law allowed a judge to hold without bail for 60 days a defendant charged with a crime of violence or a dangerous crime. Several procedures were designed to protect defendants' rights. A formal hearing was required to determine that substantial probability of guilt existed and that no other release procedure could guarantee public safety. The defendant must have been convicted of a crime in the preceding 10 years; been a narcotics addict; or been on pretrial release, probation, or parole. Finally, if the trial were not held within 60 days, the defendant had a right to release on bail.

Something funny happened in Washington, however: The law was hardly ever used. (As we will see later in this chapter, the same thing happened with "three strikes" laws.) Judges detained very few defendants without bail. A study by Georgetown University and the Vera Institute found that in the first six months, prosecutors filed detention motions against only 20 of 6,000 felony defendants (or less than one-third of 1 percent!). These motions resulted in nine formal hearings and eight actual detentions. Another two defendants were detained through judicial initiative. Thus, only 10 defendants were detained in six months.[13]

This is not the end of the story, however. Five of the ten detentions were reversed on appeal or reconsideration. Another was dismissed when the grand jury refused to indict the suspect. Thus, a grand total of four people were fully detained during the entire 10-month period.

What happened? The answer to this question reveals some important aspects of how the criminal justice system works in practice. Federal prosecutors in the District of Columbia had full discretion to use or not use the law. (As we will see later in this chapter, prosecutors' decisions not to use recent "three strikes" laws have nullified those laws in a similar fashion.) It is easy to explain why they chose not to. They could detain someone simply by setting bail at a level beyond his or her financial means. Because most robbers are poor, unemployed, or marginally employed, setting a higher bail amount than a defendant can afford is easy to do.

This is the courtroom work group's traditional method of covertly undermining the nominal right to bail. In effect, it says, "Sure you have a right to bail—how much *can't* you afford?" And remember from our discussion of the courtroom work group in Chapter 3 that disagreements rarely erupt over bail.[14]

This practice continues today. In 2004, 42 percent of all robbery defendants faced bail amounts of $50,000 or more, and 56 percent faced $25,000 or more. Obviously, most robbers do not have sufficient resources, even under a 10 percent bail program. Keep in mind the profile of the typical robber: little education, unemployed and/or with a weak employment history, no stable family ties. Many would have trouble meeting a $10,000 bail. Meanwhile, 64 percent of accused rapists faced bail amounts of $50,000 or more. In short, judges can easily keep most robbery and rape defendants in jail by simply setting a high bail amount.[15]

The 1984 Federal Bail Reform Act

The 1984 Bail Reform Act allows federal judges to detain a defendant without bail if "no condition or combination of conditions ... will reasonably assure ... the safety of any other person and the community." The law has had a very different impact than the 1970 District of Columbia law. Federal judges have used it extensively, reflecting the "get tough" mood of the last twenty years. The number of defendants detained by federal judges increased from 2,733 in the first six months of 1987 (before the Supreme Court upheld the law) to 4,470 in the last six months of 1988. The war on drugs accounted for much of this increase: More people were arrested for drug offenses, and prosecutors requested detention for drug defendants far more often than for defendants of other crimes. Between 70 and 75 percent of the prosecutors' requests for detention were granted.[16]

A closer look, however, reveals that the *overall detention rate* did not increase that much. The percentage of all federal defendants detained before trial only increased from 24 to 29 percent (and to 34 percent by 1996). The major change was a shift in the *method* of detention. Before the 1984 law, virtually all of the detained defendants remained in jail because they could not raise bail. Of the 29 percent detained after the law went into effect, 19 percent were detained under the preventive detention law, and 10 percent were detained because they could not raise bail.[17] In short, the 1984 law gave judges legal authority to do openly what they had previously done covertly.

The important question, from our perspective, is whether preventive detention has helped reduce crime. Unfortunately, none of the studies of bail reform evaluates the impact on the overall crime rate. Evaluations have focused on crime by persons released on bail and have found no significant impact on pretrial crime. The percentage of federal defendants granted pretrial release who were rearrested for a felony increased from 1.2 percent in 1983 to 1.3 percent in 1985. The percentage arrested for misdemeanors went from 0.6 to 0.7 percent.[18] It is important to note how small a percentage of defendants were being rearrested before 1984. If anything, the percentage should have gone down, since judges were now able to detain suspected repeat offenders. These data force us to take a closer look at the whole question of crime by persons out on bail.

Crime on Bail: Myths and Reality

Contrary to popular belief, defendants out on bail do not commit that much crime. Let's take a look at the data on this issue. A defendant released on bail can "fail" in one of two ways: either by committing a crime or by failing to appear (FTA) at a scheduled court hearing. Let's first look at crime on bail. In 2004, 21 percent of all felony defendants in large urban counties released before trial were rearrested prior to the disposition of their case; 14 percent were rearrested for a felony and 7 percent for a misdemeanor (Table 7.1). These figures are all higher than they were in 2000, so we do need to face the fact that the behavior of defendants out on bail has worsened somewhat. Interestingly, persons originally charged with a violent crime were rearrested at a slightly lower rate (19 percent) than were persons charged with property (23 percent) or drug (21 percent) offenses. Contrary to public impression, defendants awaiting charge for rape had the lowest rearrest rate of all, only 6 percent. The rearrest rate for robbers, 21 percent, was slightly lower than for most property crime (23 percent for burglars, for example).[19]

Most "failures" on bail are actually failures to appear (FTA) at a scheduled court hearing. In 2004, 21 percent of all felony defendants failed to appear for a court date. Most FTAs are not intentional, however. Defendants forget their court date or are confused about the process (remember, felony defendants are not known for their self-discipline). Most FTAs are located and eventually appear in court. The ones we should be concerned about are the FTAs who flee and become fugitives from justice. In 2004, fugitives from justice represented only 6 percent of all felony defendants released before trial.[20]

The Prediction Problem Revisited

The relatively low rearrest and reconviction rates bring us back to the prediction problem we discussed in Chapter 4. A judge faces the problem of spotting

T A B L E   7.1   Pretrial misconduct by released felony defendants, 2004

	Not rearrested	Felony arrest	Misdemeanor arrest
All Felony Defendants	79%	14%	7%
Murder	69	29	10
Rape	94	3	2
Robbery	79	12	9
Burglary	75	18	7
Drug trafficking	79	14	7

SOURCE: Bureau of Justice Statistics, *Felony Defendants in Large Urban Counties, 2004–Statistical Table 17* (Washington, DC: Department of Justice, 2008). NCJ 2211502.

in advance the defendants likely to commit a crime on bail, especially those 14 percent who will be rearrested for a new felony. The point of preventive detention is to detain them and *only* them. Overpredicting dangerousness will result in many people needlessly being detained in jail. How successful are judges likely to be in this effort?

Predicting Dangerousness: Pretrial Drug Testing.   Many people believe that testing arrestees for drug use would be a reliable method of predicting whether a defendant is likely to commit a crime on bail. The assumption is that the combination of an arrest and illegal drug use indicates a lifestyle that includes crime.

A National Institute of Justice study of pretrial misconduct in six cities, however, found that "except for heroin use, pretrial drug testing did not appear to help predict rearrests." In fact, even those defendants who tested positive for more than one drug were not more likely to be rearrested than other defendants. Heroin use did predict rearrest, and was a particularly strong predictor in three of the six cities. Cocaine use was a predictor of only FTAs. In the end, the best predictor of rearrest was the number of prior arrests.[21] In short, testing for drug involvement does not help judges improve their decisions related to pretrial misconduct.

A Natural Experiment.   A 1984 Supreme Court case on preventive detention for juveniles produced a natural experiment in predicting dangerousness. (A natural experiment occurs when a change in policy or practice creates comparable experimental and treatment groups.) A New York law authorized preventive detention of juveniles who posed a "serious risk" of committing another crime if released. In 1981, however, a federal judge declared it unconstitutional and enjoined its operation. New York appealed, and in 1984 (*Schall v. Martin*) the U.S. Supreme Court ruled that preventive detention for juveniles was unconstitutional.[22]

The district court decision had a quirk, however; the judge enjoined the commissioner of corrections from detaining allegedly dangerous juveniles, but judges were not so enjoined. Thus, judges continued to order some juveniles detained. These kids were turned over to the commissioner of corrections, who was forced to release them. This arrangement produced a natural experiment that allowed an examination of how accurate the judges were in predicting the dangerousness of a small group of juvenile defendants who were ordered detained but promptly released.[23]

Jeffrey Fagan and Martin Guggenheim identified 69 "at risk" juveniles who were ordered detained by judges but then released. They were compared with a control group of 64 with similar backgrounds but who were not ordered detained. After 90 days, 40 percent of the at-risk group had been rearrested, compared with only 15.6 percent of the control group. In short, the judges were reasonably accurate in identifying juveniles who posed a higher risk than comparable offenders. This was achieved, however, at the cost of a high rate of false positives: 60 percent of the at-risk group were not rearrested. Moreover, only 19 percent were rearrested for a violent crime, meaning that the judges were not very successful in predicting violent behavior.

Fagan and Guggenheim argue, as others have, that the goal of policy reform is not to achieve perfection but to improve on current practice, to make some *marginal* improvement in predictive accuracy. (Economists refer to this as the marginal utility: How much do you gain through one investment strategy or tax policy compared with another?) If you used an actuarial method for making preventive detention decisions based on objective criteria and applied it to all the juveniles in their study, you would detain members of the control group. Remember that they were comparable to an at-risk group in terms of their background characteristics (about 90 percent of both groups had some prior criminal record, for example). Yet only 15.6 percent of the control group were arrested within 90 days (think of them as false negatives). Applying the same objective prediction formula to the control group would result in detaining the 84.4 percent of the control group who were not rearrested. This outcome translates into five false positives for every true positive. (Recall from Chapter 4 that the Wenk study produced eight false positives for every true positive.)

Fagan and Guggenheim concluded that "the accuracy of prediction of dangerousness during the pretrial period remains questionable." And because of the costs and limited marginal gains likely to be achieved, "preventive detention appears to be unjustified."[24] As we will see shortly, the Rand Corporation reached a similar conclusion regarding the prediction of high-rate criminal offenders.

Because the evidence clearly indicates that only a small percentage of people on bail are rearrested, and because we cannot predict which ones will commit more crime, we conclude:

PROPOSITION 20
Preventive detention will not reduce serious crime.

Speedy Trial: A Better Way

If we want to prevent both crime on bail and failure to appeal, speedy trial is a much better approach. Among the 1992 defendants who were rearrested prior to trial, 8 percent were rearrested in the first week and 37 percent within a month (more recent data on this point are not available).[25] Disposing of all cases within five to six weeks would prevent about half of the crime committed by persons out on bail (this assumes that most will be convicted and sentenced to some confinement). Speedy disposition would also reduce the FTA rate and preserve two constitutional rights: the right to bail and the right to a speedy trial. Therefore, we can draw the following conclusion:

PROPOSITION 21
Speedy trials can reduce crime while preserving constitutional rights.

Actually, we have tried to require speedy trials. Congress and many states have enacted speedy-trial laws. Yet, as Malcolm Feeley found in his research on court reform, these laws were often evaded by the courtroom work group.[26] Thus, we face another dilemma: how to achieve a desired reform in the face of resistance by the courtroom work group. One possibility might be to expedite trials for only those offenders who are high risks. This policy would preserve their constitutional rights to both bail and a speedy trial as well as protecting the public.

THE PHILOSOPHY OF INCAPACITATION

Incapacitation is a crime policy that seeks to reduce crime by imprisoning repeat offenders. It represents the same logic underlying preventive detention: Keep criminals off the street so that they cannot commit more crimes. Incapacitation further assumes that if we keep them in twice as long, we will prevent twice as many crimes. As a sentencing philosophy, incapacitation does not try to rehabilitate offenders; nor does it seek to deter them; it is intended only to get them off the street. With regard to deterrence, for example, it makes no difference whether the offender gets the message—or any message—or not. He is in prison and off the street.[27]

There is an important distinction between two kinds of incapacitation. *Selective incapacitation* is designed to lock up only the few high-rate offenders, or career criminals. Like preventive detention, it builds on Wolfgang's career criminal research, which we discussed in Chapter 4. *Gross incapacitation,* on the other hand, involves locking up large numbers of offenders regardless of their criminal histories. Three-strikes laws are the ultimate form of gross incapacitation.

Selective Incapacitation: The Rand Formula

Selective incapacitation was one of the hot ideas in criminal justice in the 1970s and 1980s. James Q. Wilson endorsed it in his influential 1975 book, *Thinking about Crime,* claiming that serious crime could be reduced by *one-third* if each person convicted of a serious crime received a mandatory three-year prison sentence. He cited an earlier study claiming that selective incapacitation could reduce crime by an amazing 80 percent.[28]

These extravagant claims generated much excitement, and some criminologists set out to develop sophisticated selective incapacitation formulas. The most notable was a 1982 study, *Selective Incapacitation,* by Peter Greenwood and his associates at the Rand Corporation.[29] We have already discussed this work in Chapter 4; let's take another look at it in terms of sentencing policy.

Selective Incapacitation estimated that a fine-tuned sentencing policy could reduce robbery by 15 percent while also reducing prison populations by 5 percent. This claim of a double benefit—better crime control *and* lower costs—seemed almost too good to be true. It turned out that it was. The reduction in the prison population (with the resulting cost savings) would be achieved because the longer prison terms for career criminals would be offset by reduced punishments for low risk offenders (i.e., shorter prison terms or probation).[30] And that is exactly where the idea of selective incapacitation went wrong.

The Rand sentencing proposal was based on the Rand Inmate Survey (RIS), discussed in Chapter 4. In the most important part of the RIS, interviews with 2,190 prison and jail inmates in California, Texas, and Michigan were used to develop estimates of the *average annual offending rates* for offenders.[31] These estimated offending rates were then used to estimate how much crime would be reduced by locking up particular types of offenders.

The estimated annual offending rates are the crucial linchpin in the idea of selective incapacitation, and they proved to be the subject of considerable controversy. Using the wrong estimate has a huge impact. If you estimate that the average career criminal commits more than a hundred crimes a year, incapacitation will achieve significant crime reduction. But if the average offending rate is only about five crimes a year, the payoff will be relatively small.[32]

Rand developed a prediction instrument by correlating inmates' background characteristics with their self-reported criminal behavior. The result is a seven-point scale of factors associated with high rates of criminal behavior (see Table 4.3, Chapter 4). Offenders were then classified as low risk (one point), medium risk (two to three points), and high risk (four to seven points).

Rand then correlated inmates' predicted offense category with their actual self-reported level of criminal activity (see Table 4.4). The prediction scale was correct 51 percent of the time. The 51 percent figure is calculated by adding the predicted low rate and actual low rate (14 percent), the predicted medium risk and actual medium risk (22 percent), and the predicted high risk and actual high risk (15 percent). The prediction device was grossly wrong 7 percent of the time (the 4 percent who were predicted high but actually low, and the 3 percent predicted low but actually high). In the remaining 42 percent of the cases, the prediction scale was only moderately accurate.[33]

Once again, the challenge is to improve on current practice (that is, to gain some marginal utility). When the Rand experts correlated their predictions with inmates' actual sentences, they found that the judges imposed a "correct" sentence (that is, a long sentence for a predicted high-rate offender) 42 percent of the time. In short, this figure is only a slight improvement over what judges are currently doing.[34]

Why such a small marginal improvement? The Rand formula has several problems. Most important is our old friend the prediction problem. As other studies have found, prior criminal records and other indicators such as drug use are relatively weak predictors of future behavior. We consistently get significant numbers of false positives and false negatives. In fact, in the face of widespread criticism, Rand itself reexamined its proposal five years later and admitted that its earlier estimates were "overly optimistic." It concluded that "there are no reliable methods for either measuring or predicting future offense rates." That is a major concession, and it calls into question the entire enterprise of estimating crime reduction.[35]

The estimated offending rates developed by Rand are *averages* that, like all averages, are inflated by the extremely high rates for the very worst offenders. The Rand report itself observes that "most offenders reported fairly low rates of crime." The median robbery rate was only 5 per year, but the worst 10 percent averaged 87 per year![36] Incapacitating a member of the 90th percentile will produce a significant crime reduction, but there will be very limited payoff for locking up any of the other offenders with low annual offending rates.

The most shocking aspect of the Rand prediction scale is the use of employment history as a criterion for sentencing. An offender acquires one point for having been unemployed for more than half of the two preceding years. It carries the same weight as a prior conviction for the same offense. Under the formula, an additional point might reclassify the offender from a low risk to a medium risk, and thus it would mean the difference between jail and prison.

When you take out any one of the seven factors in the prediction scale, the entire scheme begins to collapse. With only six factors, the success rate will fall below the 51 percent that Rand estimates. You would then be doing no better than judges currently do, using a combination of presentence investigations and pure hunch.

It is outrageous that imprisonment might be contingent on unemployment. The Rand formula takes us back 200 years to the days of imprisonment for debt. Even if such a policy were to become practice somewhere, it would immediately be challenged in court. The fact is that unemployment *is* highly correlated with criminal activity but that correlation is not something we should translate into crime policy. An alternative response to the problem would be not to punish people for being unemployed but to provide greater employment opportunities.

Finally, the Rand *Selective Incapacitation* proposal faces a major political obstacle. The idea of not imprisoning low-risk and medium-risk offenders is exactly what corrections experts advocated in the 1960s. The 1967 President's Crime Commission argued that we locked up too many people and for prison terms that were unnecessarily long, and recommended greater use of probation. In 1980 the American Bar Association's *Standards for Criminal Justice* stated that "in many instances prison sentences which are now authorized, and sometimes required, are significantly higher than are needed in a vast majority of cases."[37] Because of the public demands to "get tough," however, these recommendations have been consistently rejected in favor of a policy of gross incapacitation.

If selective incapacitation seems too good to be true, that is because it is. The evidence indicates that because of the prediction problem and the political obstacles related to adopting the lower sentences that would make the Rand policy cost-effective, we have to conclude as follows:

PROPOSITION 22
Selective incapacitation is not a realistic strategy for reducing serious crime.

Gross Incapacitation: Zedlewski's New Math

Selective incapacitation is a fine-tuned surgical instrument that involves making careful distinctions among criminal offenders. The political reality is that we have completely ignored this approach and adopted instead a policy of gross incapacitation: locking up a lot of people and sending them to prison for long terms. This is the main reason that the prison population has soared since the 1970s. Let us take a look at the impact of gross incapacitation on the crime rate.

One of the most extraordinary endorsements of incapacitation is Edwin J. Zedlewski's report *Making Confinement Decisions.*[38] He reached the startling conclusion that imprisonment actually *saves* money. Challenging the liberal conventional wisdom about the high cost of imprisonment, he calculated that for every dollar we spend imprisoning a criminal, we save $17 in total social costs. Although he focused on the dollar costs of crime, his formula has important implications for crime reduction.

How did Zedlewski reach such an amazing conclusion? Let us take a close look at his figures. First, he estimated that in 1983 crime cost American society a total of about $100 billion. This included $33.8 billion for criminal justice system expenditures, $35 billion in victim losses (medical care, lost wages, property damage, etc.), $26.1 billion for private security expenses, and so forth. The National Crime Victimization Survey (NCVS), meanwhile, estimated that 42.5 million crimes were committed in 1983. Thus, Zedlewski calculated that each felony costs society $2,300 ($100 billion ÷ 42.5 million).

Using the RIS, Zedlewski then estimated that each criminal commits an average of 187 crimes a year. Locking up each offender for one year, therefore, "saves" society $430,000 per year ($2,300 × 187 = $430,000). After you subtract the cost of imprisonment ($25,000 per year), you get a net social "savings" of $405,000 a year for each offender imprisoned (or about 17 times the $25,000 cost of incarceration).

If this seems too good to be true, it is. Franklin Zimring and Gordon Hawkins demolished the key assumptions underlying Zedlewski's computations.[39] The most serious problem is the estimate of 187 crimes a year. They point out that Zedlewski does not mention the great disagreement among career-criminal specialists over annual offending rates. Many put the figure at about 18 crimes a year, and some use an even lower estimate. If the average is only 18, then locking up one criminal saves only $43,000 a year, according to Zedlewski's formula.

It was professionally dishonest of Zedlewski not to mention the debate over annual offending rates and to use one of the highest possible estimates. As we mentioned in Chapter 1, faith often triumphs over facts in discussions of crime policy. Here we have a case of someone deliberately misrepresenting the facts to make a point.

Zedlewski also did not take into account the problem of diminishing returns. As we lock up more people, we quickly skim off the really high rate offenders and begin incarcerating more of the less serious offenders. Because they average far fewer crimes per year (perhaps as few as five, according to the RIS), we get progressively lower returns in crime reduction and dollar savings.

The estimate of the dollar savings is also flawed. A reduction in crime does not produce a direct reduction in criminal justice system costs. If the crime rate goes down by 25 percent, we are not going to cut police department budgets by 25 percent. Also, because 80 to 90 percent of all department budgets involve personnel costs, this would really mean laying off one-quarter of all the officers. In fact, police departments have not reduced their size as a result of the great crime drop. Police officers do a lot more than fight crime. About 70 to 80 percent of patrol work involves order maintenance and service activities.[40] These are important tasks that people want the police to perform. The same is true for other criminal justice system costs. If crime drops by 25 percent, the cost of running the criminal courts will not automatically decline by the same percentage.

In the most devastating attack on Zedlewski, Zimring and Hawkins show that his own formula leads to absurd estimates of crime reduction. We have been running a natural experiment in gross incapacitation. They point out that between 1977 and 1987 the prison population increased by 230,000. If each criminal did an average of 187 crimes a year, that should have "prevented" 43 million crimes (230,000 × 187 = 43 million). Yet this figure is more than the number of crimes that the NCVS reported as occurring in 1987. In short, Zedlewski's formula predicts the complete elimination of all crime by 1986!

Of course that did not happen. First, criminals do not average 187 crimes a year, as Zedlewski estimated (a very small percentage of them do, but most average only a few crimes). And second, he did not consider the replacement factor: As some drug dealers are arrested, others take their place. You can do your own update of Zimring and Hawkins's critique with more recent data. Compute the increase in the prison population from the mid-1980s to the present and, using the estimated annual rate of 187 crimes per offender, estimate the amount of expected crime reduction. In fact, as Frank Zimring points out in his sober discussion of the Great Crime Decline in the 1990s, when you look at imprisonment rates and crime rates for the entire period beginning with the early 1970s, you find that crime rates fluctuated like a roller coaster (up in the late 1980s, down in the 1990s), with no clear correlation between the two.[41]

Incapacitation: A Sober Estimate

Having demolished Zedlewski's fantastic estimates, Zimring and Hawkins undertook their own study of incapacitation, examining incarceration and crime trends in California. Using a variety of sophisticated models, they concluded that the incarceration of each offender in California in the 1980s prevented 3.5 crimes per year. We should note that this is *one-fiftieth* of the 187 figure used by Zedlewski and is even lower than the estimates of many experts on career criminals. The huge increase in the state prison population (115,000) reduced the crime rate by 15 percent.[42]

As Zimring and Hawkins pursued their analysis, however, some problems surfaced. For burglary, juvenile arrests declined significantly, but adult arrests increased. This is "exactly the opposite" of what the incapacitation model would predict, because most of those incarcerated were adults. A similar pattern appeared with larceny and rape, but not robbery. Consequently, Zimring and Hawkins concluded that it was not absolutely clear that incapacitation was the "primary cause" of the drop in crime.[43]

Zimring and Hawkins also did a cross-state comparison of changes in incarceration rates and crime rates in 17 states during the 1980s. California stood at

Illustration by Frank Irwin, © Wadsworth, Cengage Learning.

one extreme, with the greatest increase in imprisonment and the greatest reduction in crime. Yet Georgia had a very high increase in imprisonment and one of the highest rises in crime. Minnesota, meanwhile, had almost no increase in incarceration and virtually no change in the crime rate. In short, Zimring and Hawkins could detect "no clear patterned relationship" between incarceration rates and crime rates.[44]

Serious crime declined in the 1990s, but we should be skeptical of claims that incapacitation was the sole or even the primary cause. Remember that we have been on an imprisonment binge for 35 years. Imagine going to a doctor, getting a prescription, taking the medicine (two pills a day), but not getting any better. You go back to the doctor, who increases the dosage (four pills a day). But you still do not get any better. The doctor then raises the dosage again (six a day). You repeat this process for 20 years. Finally, in about the nineteenth year, you begin to get better. Was it the medicine? Probably not. You cannot claim success for a prescription (pills/prisons) that failed for 19 years and then suddenly appeared to work in the twentieth year. In his more recent book on the Great Crime Decline, Zimring points out that the greatest proportional increase in imprisonment occurred in the five years after 1982, but that was a period of increasing crime. And recall that unlike deterrence, where it may take some time for the message to take effect, incapacitation operates immediately: the robber is in jail and then prison beginning with his arrest. Finally, as we discussed in Chapter 1, Zimring points out that Canada enjoyed a reduction in crime almost identical to the United States while the imprisonment rate actually declined by 6 percent. Clearly, incapacitation was not a factor in Canada's success.[45]

The evidence indicates no clear link between incarceration and crime rates. Moreover, gross incapacitation locks up many low-rate offenders at a great dollar cost to society. Consequently, the evidence leads us to the following conclusion:

PROPOSITION 23
Gross incapacitation does not reduce serious crime.

Collateral Damage: The Cost of Overimprisonment

Liberals argue that America's sentencing policies not only do not reduce crime, but have led to a serious problem of overincarceration. Imprisoning 2.3 million people by 2008 (both prisons and jails) also inflicts major collateral damage on our society. The specific damages include:

Prison Overcrowding.   Mandatory sentencing is responsible for much of the serious California prison overcrowding problem. Across the country, high imprisonment rates contribute directly to the resource crisis which we discussed in Chapter 1. California's practice of revoking parole accounts for about three-quarters of the people entering its prison, but revocation is simply another manifestation of the "lock 'em up" mentality.[46]

Inability to Provide Treatment Alternatives.   The huge cost of imprisonment has diverted money away from nonprison alternatives. Many policy experts argue that drug courts and other treatment alternatives are both more effective in helping offenders and much cheaper. The Urban Institute report, *To Treat or Not to Treat,* estimates that every dollar spent on drug court treatment programs saves $2.21.[47] We will take a closer look at drug courts in Chapters 11 and 13.

High Prison Medical Expenses.   The expanding use of life sentences results in high and unnecessary prison medical expenses. Providing basic health care to prisoners is not an option. The Supreme Court has ruled (*Estelle v. Gamble* [1976]) that states are required to provide a level of care that meets a "community standard." In addition to elderly prisoners, inmates who are HIV positive create additional costs. In the crowded environment of a prison, communicable diseases are a particular problem. Risky behavior includes tattooing, unprotected sex, fighting that results in cuts, and even intravenous drug use. (Overcrowding, of course, makes it even more difficult for prison officials to control these risky behaviors.) The Pew Center report argues that hepatitis C, a blood-borne and life threatening disease, is the greatest threat. Half of the 3,200 inmates at the Vacaville prison are believed to be infected with hepatitis C. It costs $30,000 a year to care for an infected person. Elderly inmates, a consequence of the growth of life sentences, are also very costly. Normal health problems associated with aging; vulnerable to attack by younger inmates; many require hospital beds.[48]

Crowding Out Other Social Needs.   The cost of imprisoning 2.3 million people has diverted scarce public funds from other critical society needs, including education. The Pew Center on the States found that in the 20 years between 1987 and 2007, state spending on prisons increased 127 percent, while education spending increased only 21 percent. In 2007, five states spent as much or more on corrections as on education. Minnesota, which consistently has had the lowest or next to lowest incarceration rate in the country, spends only 17 cents on corrections for every dollar spent on education. Many social commentators ask, Which is the best crime prevention measure, prison or good schools?[49]

Racial and Ethnic Discrimination.   Some of the greatest disparities, however, are found in felony sentencing. People of color represent two-thirds of the prisoners currently serving life sentences around the country, and 90 percent of the inmates in New York State convicted under the harsh Rockefeller Drug laws (see our later discussion of this).[50]

Destructive Social Effects.   Finally there is the impact of gross incarceration on families, communities and democracy itself. Massachusetts estimated that two-thirds of its inmates had not paid any of their child support payments; two-thirds of the state's parolees, meanwhile, had paid at least some. State felony disenfranchisement laws deny an estimated 5.3 people the right to vote. Voting is the cornerstone of democracy, and felony disenfranchisement sends a strong message of exclusion to the very people we want to integrate into American society. In Chapter 12 we will examine the impact of a high level of imprisonment—especially among African Americans and Latinos—on the legitimacy of the criminal justice system. As Todd Clear puts it in the title of his book, *Imprisoning Communities,* our policy of locking up so many people has destroyed entire communities.[51]

Summary

We can criticize America's over-incarceration on human rights grounds: over-crowded prisons, lack of medical care, lack of drug treatment programs, denial of the right to vote, and so on. But let's keep focused on the central purpose of this book: effective crime control. Over-incarceration also blocks the implementation of meaningful alternatives that would help to reduce crime.

MANDATORY SENTENCING

October 7, 2009 was a historic day in New York State, as revisions to the state's Rockefeller Drug laws took effect. As we indicated at the beginning of this chapter, the 1973 Rockefeller Drug Laws became the model for harsh sentencing laws across the country over the next 36 years, putting a special emphasis on mandatory prison sentences. A Justice Department report on sentencing policies found that all 50 states had some form of mandatory sentencing by 1994. Most of these laws apply to specific offenses. Forty-one states have it for repeat offenders, 31 for certain drunk driving offenses, 32 for certain drug offenses, and 42 for some weapons offenses.[52] Meanwhile, by 1996, about 22 states had adopted three-strikes laws, which represent the most extreme form of mandatory sentencing.[53]

Imposing mandatory prison sentences is a leading conservative crime control strategy. Actually, mandatory sentences are a *means* to an end: incapacitating or deterring offenders. Mandatory sentencing is operationalized in two ways: mandatory imprisonment for a certain crime and/or mandatory minimum prison terms.

The popularity of mandatory sentencing can be explained in part by the Celebrated Case syndrome we discussed in Chapter 2. Public opinion is heavily influenced by a few highly publicized cases. The Polly Klaas case in California was responsible for "three strikes" sentencing laws. Twelve-year-old Polly was brutally murdered by Richard Allen Davis, who was out on parole and had been twice convicted of kidnapping.

"THE NATION'S TOUGHEST DRUG LAW"

Because of its influence on sentencing laws across the country, it is worth taking a close look at the 1973 New York Rockefeller Drug law, often referred to as the "nation's toughest drug law."[54] The law contained three major provisions designed to incapacitate drug offenders and deter future drug use: mandatory and long prison terms for heroin dealers, restrictions on plea bargaining for heroin dealers, and mandatory prison terms for certain categories of repeat offenders.

The prescribed prison terms were considered awesome at the time, but they are very common today. The law established three categories of heroin dealers. Class A-I offenders (major dealers, defined as people who either sold one ounce of heroin or possessed two ounces) would serve minimum prison terms of 15 or 25 years and a maximum of life imprisonment. Class A-II (middle-level dealers, defined as those who sold one-eighth of an ounce of heroin or possessed one to two ounces) would serve prison terms of at least six to eight and one-third years and a maximum of life. Class A-III offenders (minor street dealers, defined as anyone who sold less than one-eighth of an ounce of heroin or possessed up to one ounce) would serve a minimum prison term of at least one to eight and one-third years and a maximum term of life. In short, anyone caught selling heroin would definitely go to prison and would face the possibility of life imprisonment.

The law attempted to prevent abuse of plea bargaining. Anyone arrested for either an A-I or A-II offense could plead guilty to an A-III charge, but people originally charged with an A-III offense could not plead to anything lower. The result was a floor that meant at least some prison time and a potential life term. The law also included a habitual-criminal provision, imposing mandatory prison terms on anyone with a prior felony conviction. To cope with the anticipated increase in the criminal courts' workload as a result of the law, New York added 49 new judges, 31 of them in New York City.

In practice, the law was a paper tiger in some important respects (but, not all). An evaluation concluded that "the threat embodied in the words of the law proved to have teeth for relatively few offenders."[55] An enormous amount of slippage or leakage occurred between arrest and conviction. Between 1972 and 1976, the percentage of drug arrests leading to indictment declined from 39 to 25 percent. Meanwhile, the percentage of indictments resulting in a conviction fell from 86 to 80 percent. Thus, the overall percentage of arrests leading to conviction fell from 33.5 to 20 percent.

The law did not completely fail to achieve its objectives. For those who *were convicted,* the rate of incarceration went up from 33 to 55 percent. Nonetheless, if only 55 percent were going to prison, about half the defendants were evading the supposedly mandatory sentencing provisions. In this respect, little changed. The percentage of people arrested for sale of heroin who went to prison was 11 percent in 1972–1973, and it was 11 percent in 1976. The big change involved the longer prison terms. Although there was obvious slippage in the number of offenders convicted, the percentage of those who were convicted receiving a sentence of three years or longer rose from 3 percent of all those convicted to 22 percent. This was the most important effect of the law, and we will look at it more closely in a moment.

The slippage that occurred in the application of the New York law is consistent with the long history of mandatory sentencing laws. The process can be explained in terms of the thermodynamics of the criminal justice process, which we discussed in Chapter 3. An increase in the severity of the potential punishment creates pressure to avoid its actual application. In this case, the controls over plea bargaining did not prevent a rise in dismissals. The enormous increase in the potential prison terms, meanwhile, encouraged defense attorneys to go to trial. The percentage of defendants demanding a trial increased from 6 to 15 percent. Because a tried case takes 15 times as long to process as a case that is not tried, the addition of even a few trials significantly disrupts the process. Disposition time for all drug cases doubled under the new law despite the addition of the new judgeships (and for some unexplained reason, the new courts were noticeably less efficient than previously established courts were).

Much of the slippage involved criminal justice officials adapting to the harsh terms of the law. As early as 1976, the chief prosecutor of drug cases in New York City quietly announced that he would no longer enforce the law's prohibitions on plea bargaining. Three years later, the legislature formally eliminated these same prohibitions and permitted more flexibility in sentencing. It also allowed resentencing of some offenders given extremely long sentences under the original law.[56]

An important part of the slippage occurs after sentencing. As states have sent more offenders to prison and for longer terms, many prisons have become seriously overcrowded. The California prison crisis by 2008–2009 was simply the worst in the country. States deal with overcrowding by releasing prisoners early through a variety of schemes. One avenue is a state law providing for emergency release when prisons reach a certain level of overcrowding. Other avenues, however, are covert backdoor schemes embedded in changes in correctional practices. Pamala Griset's study of correctional trends in New York, which we discussed in Chapter 3, illustrates the extent to which this strategy involves both a hidden form of sentencing and a device for undermining the intent of mandatory sentencing laws.[57]

Finally, and most important, the law had no significant effect on crime or drug use. An evaluation found that heroin use in New York City was as widespread in 1976 as it had been in 1973. Serious property crime, the kind generally associated with heroin users, increased 15 percent between 1973 and 1975, but neighboring states had similar increases. Even more important, the law did not stop the crack cocaine epidemic, which hit New York City very hard in the late 1980s. The epidemic eventually subsided, but for a variety of reasons. The sentencing law was not one of them (see our discussion in Chapter 10). According to the National Household Survey, drug use did begin to decline in the late 1980s, but this trend was nationwide, and we cannot say that the New York law had any special impact in that state.[58]

The Long-Term Impact—and the 2009 Reforms

Even with all the slippage, the Rockefeller Drug Law led to a dramatic increase in the number of people sent to prison on drug charges. Critics, however, charge that in another example of the "bait and switch" syndrome, it mainly hit minor targets rather than major ones. Many if not most prison sentences were disproportionate to the harm of the crime involved. Although supposedly directed toward drug "kingpins," most of those people imprisoned under the law were convicted of low-level, nonviolent crimes, and many had no prior criminal records. The law resulted in serious prison overcrowding, with all the associated costs. In 2009, the 12,000 offenders then in prison under the law represented 21 percent of all state prisoners, at a cost of an estimated $525 million a year (at $45,000 per year per inmate in New York). Two-thirds had never been imprisoned before, and 80 percent had never been convicted of a violent felony. No evidence that the offender will recidivate. African Americans and Latinos represent 90 percent of those in prison under the law. And as we will argue in Chapter 15, this disproportionate impact has a devastating effect on families and communities.[59]

The 2009 reforms reduced the penalties in several different ways. They eliminated mandatory sentencing for first time Class B, C, D, and E drug related felonies. Eliminated mandatory sentences for second time C, D, and E drug related felonies. In both cases, judges can sentence convicted offenders to probation, treatment alternatives, or prison. Prison is still mandatory for second time Class B drug felonies if the defendant was convicted of or had pending a violent felony in the past 10 years. Additionally, the reforms expanded drug treatment and alternatives to incarceration, with an appropriation of almost $71 million. Finally, it allowed resentencing for about 1,500 currently imprisoned offenders in certain categories. The new law did keep mandatory prison sentences for the most serious offenses: Class A-I and A-II felonies.

Did the 2009 reforms of the Rockefeller Drug laws make a difference? It is still too early to tell, but we should keep an eye on the state prison population, the percentage of prisoners sentenced for drug crimes, and the number of life terms. Also important, did the New York reforms have any influence on sentencing laws in other states?

THE FEDERAL SENTENCING GUIDELINES

The 1987 federal sentencing guidelines also included a number of mandatory sentencing provisions. Intended to achieve "truth in sentencing," the guidelines reduced the range of possible sentences and abolished discretionary parole release. The percentage of convicted federal offenders sentenced to prison increased from 51 percent in 1982 to 78 percent by 2004. Also, the average prison term increased 27 percent, from an average of 48 to 60 months.[60]

A basic question is whether prosecutors and judges are complying with the federal sentencing guidelines. There is mixed evidence on this issue. A study by the Federal Judicial Center found that slightly less than half of the offenders who were eligible under a mandatory minimum provision actually received it. This is a fairly high rate of slippage and leakage.[61]

Another problem is plea bargaining—specifically, charge bargaining that allows defendants to plea to a lesser offense and avoid a long mandatory minimum. Section 5K1.1 of the federal sentencing guidelines allows a departure from the presumptive sentence where the defendant "has provided substantial assistance in the investigation or prosecution of another person who has committed an offense."[62] In other words, a defendant can reduce his or her potential sentence by cooperating and naming other criminals.

Ilene H. Nagel and Stephen J. Schulhofer examined plea bargaining in three federal district courts and found that departures from the guidelines occurred in between 15 and 25 percent of all cases, with the national average about 17 percent. They concluded that circumvention of the guidelines was not the norm and that it was not necessarily unfair. They did, however, find some cases in which defendants won substantial sentence reductions: in one case, from 168 to 21 months; in another, from 69 months to nine.[63] These reductions may be excessive compared with what most defendants receive.

The point is that through prosecutorial discretion, "mandatory" sentences are not necessarily mandatory in practice.

The Growth of Life Sentences

A particularly popular aspect of mandatory sentencing has been the growth of life sentences, many of which are specifically life without parole. By 2008, 1 in 11 American prisoners was serving a life term. This involved a total of 140,610 prisoners (up from 34,000 in 1984), 41,095 of whom have no possibility of parole. In five states, the ratio is one in six prisoners. In California, because of its "three strikes" law, 20 percent of the prisoners are serving life terms. Finally, there are 6,807 juveniles serving life terms. (In the fall of 2009, the U.S. Supreme Court heard a case challenging the constitutionality life sentences for juveniles.)[64]

The situation in California illustrates how very harsh sentences encourage some prosecutors to use their discretion to avoid them. The California prison overcrowding would be much higher if San Francisco prosecutors used the life sentences of the state's three strike law very often. As of September, 2008, there were 3,140 "three strikes" lifers from Los Angeles but only 39 from San Francisco.

Public pressure for getting tough on crime has also affected pardon and commutations for lifers. Pennsylvania averaged 12 commutations a year between 1971 and 1994. But after a sensational double murder by an offender who had a previous sentence commuted, there were only three between 1994 and 2009.

Life terms are often disproportionate to the risk of reoffending, particularly when you compare a life sentence to a 15 or 25 year prison term. Criminologists established long ago that the likelihood of recidivism goes down sharply with age. Experience confirms this. Of 21 people over the age of 50 released in Ohio in 2000, none was rearrested in the next three years. In Pennsylvania, there was a recidivism rate of 1.4 percent in 10 to 22 months after release in this same age group. Finally, life terms aggravate the costs of dealing with elderly inmates, which we discussed earlier. Old inmates have increasing health problems, just like people on the "outside." California estimates that it costs the state $98,000 to $138,000 a year for elderly prisoners, which includes the construction of needed hospital beds for seriously ill inmates.[65]

Mandatory Sentencing and Crime

The basic question, of course, is whether mandatory sentences effectively reduce crime. As early as 1982, a Justice Department report concluded that "it is difficult, perhaps fundamentally impossible, to substantiate the popular claim that mandatory sentencing is an effective tool for reducing crime."[66] Years later, we had much more experience with mandatory sentencing. A 1996 report on structured sentencing in a variety of states found no correlation between incarceration rates and crime rates.[67] Zimring and Hawkins's multistate comparison of incapacitation, which we cited earlier, also did not find any clear correlation between incarceration rates and crime rates.[68]

After reviewing all of the evidence on mandatory sentencing, Michael Tonry, one of the leading experts on sentencing, declared, "Mandatory penalties do not work."[69] In his view, they are widely circumvented, tend to shift discretion from justices to prosecutors, and often result in punishments that are "unduly harsh." We agree. Our position is as follows:

PROPOSITION 24

Mandatory sentencing is not an effective means of reducing serious crime.

THREE STRIKES—WE ARE ALL OUT

The most radical approach to mandatory sentencing involves the so-called "three strikes and you're out" laws. The idea of three strikes emerged very suddenly in the early 1990s. State laws vary, but the basic concept is a mandatory life prison sentence for anyone convicted of a third felony. The state of Washington passed the first law, the Persistent Offender Accountability Act, in November 1993. The idea really caught fire after the brutal murder of Polly Klaas in California by Richard Allen Davis, a man with a long criminal record who had been paroled only three months earlier. California passed its three-strikes law in March 1994.[70]

States' three-strikes laws vary considerably. The Washington law mandates life without parole for conviction of a "most serious offense" if the person had two prior convictions of "most serious offenses," which includes a wide range of felonies. The California law has separate two-strikes and three-strikes provisions. The second-strike provision doubles the sentence for a person convicted of a felony who has a prior felony conviction to a designated "strikeable" offense. The third-strike provision mandates life imprisonment, with no parole eligibility before 25 years, to someone convicted of a felony who has two prior convictions for designated strikeable offenses. The 1994 Georgia law mandates life without parole for a second conviction to a "serious violent felony."[71]

Three-strikes laws were almost universally condemned by criminologists and experts on sentencing. Franklin Zimring called it "the voodoo economics of California crime." Jerome Skolnick denounced it as representing the values of "the dark ages." John J. DiIulio, a defender of the idea, argued that "society has a right not only to protect itself from convicted criminals but to express its moral outrage at their acts by, among other things, keeping them behind bars."[72]

One of the major criticisms has been that three-strikes laws are crude instruments and do not focus on serious repeat offenders. The first California case, in fact, involved Jerry Williams, who stole a slice of pepperoni pizza. The first woman prosecuted under the law was arrested for a $20 cocaine purchase that occurred 14 years after her second strike. One of the first people sentenced to life in prison in the state of Washington had stolen $151 from a sandwich shop; his two previous strikes involved robberies totaling $460. In short, they violate the basic principle of selective incapacitation by failing to focus on the few offenders with the most serious criminal records.

Actually, most states have had some kind of repeat offender law for many decades. The first such law in the United States was passed in 1797. A famous 1926 New York law mandated life in prison for conviction to a third felony. A national survey of repeat offender laws by William F. McDonald in the mid-1980s found that they were "rarely used" and widely regarded as a "dead letter."[73] Forty-one states had some kind of repeat offender or habitual offender law on the books in February 1994, before the three-strikes movement took off.[74] Three-strikes laws raise the same questions we have already considered in this book. First, will a law in fact be implemented or simply evaded by the courtroom work group? Second, assuming it is implemented, what impact will it have on the criminal justice system? Third, will it reduce serious crime?

Implementation

With the exception of California, and to a certain extent Georgia, states have not used their three-strikes laws. An early study found that Wisconsin used its law only once in the first year and a half, while Tennessee, New Mexico, and Colorado did not use theirs at all.[75] Local prosecutors simply do not file the necessary charges. In some instances, the law becomes a plea bargaining tool. Many cases can be filed either as felonies or misdemeanors (say, misdemeanor assault versus felonious assault). The law gives the prosecutor a powerful weapon to get a guilty plea to a misdemeanor; in Sacramento, California, there were charge reductions in 67 percent of all the eligible cases. Even in California, application of the law varied tremendously. Two-thirds of all cases under the law originated in Los Angeles County. Officials in San Francisco, meanwhile, have publicly stated that they will not use it in certain kinds of cases, including drug cases.[76]

Impact on Crime

The California law was far more punitive and more far-reaching than the laws in other states. While the laws in most other states applied only to serious or violent offenses, the California law doubled the sentence length for *any* felony conviction if the offender had one prior serious or violent felony conviction. Another provision mandated a 25-year-to-life sentence for any felony conviction if the offender had two prior serious or violent felony convictions. Finally, "strikers", people convicted under the law, are not eligible for parole until they have served 80 percent of their sentence.

What happened? Did the law reduce serious crime as its supporters promised? Did it cause huge backlogs in criminal courts as its opponents warned? What was the fiscal impact on the state? In 2004, to mark the tenth anniversary of the California law, the Justice Policy Institute (JPI) undertook an evaluation of the law's impact.[77]

First, the law did send a lot of people to prison for long terms. By 2004 over 42,000 strikers were serving terms in California prisons, between 20 and 25 percent of all prisoners. Second, the immediate impact of the law was not as great as initially expected. The California Department of Corrections had projected an additional 80,000 prisoners by 1999, but they did not arrive until years later. The reason was simple: only a few prosecutors in California used the law very heavily. Los Angeles prosecutors used it a lot, but San Francisco prosecutors hardly at all.

Third, consistent with the "bait and switch" problem we discussed in Chapter 1, the law weighed most heavily on the less serious offenders. The number of third strikers grew from 254 in 1994 to 7,234 in September 2003, but the number of second strikers soared from 4,154 in 1994 to 35,211 in September 2003. The JPI concluded that "[t]he Three Strikes law has a disproportionate effect on people convicted of non-violent offenses." Almost two-thirds (64.5 percent) of second and third strikers were in prison for a nonviolent offense.[78]

The law also compounded the racial disparities in the California justice system. The JPI found that the African American incarceration rate for third strikes

(143 per 100,000 African American residents) was 12 times higher than the third-strike incarceration rate for whites (12 per 100,000 white residents). Latinos were only moderately affected by the law.

Most important from our standpoint, the three-strikes law did not produce a reduction in crime. In *Punishment and Democracy: Three Strikes and You're Out in California,* Franklin Zimring and his colleagues argue that even if fully applied, the law would have only a modest impact on crime. They estimate that even if all the arrestees who were eligible under the law "were to disappear from the earth without a trace," the result would be only a 10.6 percent reduction in felonies.[79]

The failure of the law to reduce crime was also confirmed by cross-state comparisons. States without three-strikes laws experienced a greater average drop in violent crime in the 1990s than states with such laws.

Additionally, in 2000, California voters passed Proposition 36, the Substance Abuse and Crime Prevention Act, which required that drug possession offenders be eligible for drug treatment instead of prison. This included offenders who were three strikes–eligible and had been out of prison for five years.

Summary: Striking Out

Three-strikes laws represent all the worst aspects of the "get tough" approach to crime. First, they are a classic example of overreaction to celebrated cases. Second, they represent a crude, meat-ax policy that sweeps up many nondangerous criminals. Third, they are not consistently implemented and thus increase the arbitrariness of the administration of justice. Fourth, they upset the normal going rate and impose new costs on local criminal justice systems, including more trials, delays, and greater dollar costs. Finally, no clear evidence indicates that they will reduce serious crime (and some good evidence shows that they incarcerate a lot of people who will not commit any crimes at all).

Rereading today William F. McDonald's 1986 report on the old repeat offender laws is a sobering experience. In effect, McDonald predicted all of the problems associated with three-strikes laws. Surveying all of the states with such laws, he found: "Only a small fraction of eligible habitual offenders have been or are currently being sentenced as such." McDonald interviewed members of the courtroom work group (prosecutors, defense attorneys, judges) and found a general perception that "prior criminality is already being taken proper account of under the normal sentencing structure."[80] In short, as we argued in Chapter 3, the prevailing going rate did allow serious offenders to avoid significant punishment. For the most part, the old repeat offender laws were used as plea bargaining tools. Not surprisingly, prosecutors gave the laws generally favorable ratings, while defense attorneys and judges were highly critical.

McDonald's report also anticipated the conceptual confusion that surrounds three-strikes laws. The old repeat offender laws failed to distinguish among seriousness, repetitiveness, intensity, and dangerousness. *Seriousness* refers to gravity of the particular crimes, including both the immediate crime for which an offender is being prosecuted and past crimes. *Repetitiveness* refers to a defendant's prior record or criminal career. *Intensity* refers to the rate at which a defendant has committed crimes in the past, as in the annual offending rate. *Dangerousness,* meanwhile, represents a predictive assessment of the amount of harm an offender might do to the community. McDonald found that practitioners believed that the old laws often sentenced offenders who were "not truly dangerous predators but comparatively petty offenders."[81] As we have seen, three-strikes laws are blunt instruments that often result in the incarceration of persons convicted of relatively less serious offenses but whose records happen to fit a mechanical formula.

PROPOSITION 25
Three strikes and you're out laws are a terrible crime policy.

JUST KEEP THEM AWAY FROM US:
SEX REGISTRATION AND NOTIFICATION LAWS

The national panic over sex offenses, especially sexual abuse or rape of children, has led to a set of restrictive policies directed at sex offenders, including sex offender registration, notification requirements, and restrictions on where they may live. The underlying idea is that if we can't keep them in prison, then at least we can keep them away from our neighborhoods and our children.

The current national panic over sex offenders began with a classic celebrated case, the 1994 rape and murder of seven-year-old Megan Kanka in New Jersey. As a result, many laws are referred to as Megan's Law. Every state now has some kind of law; a 1996 federal law requires sex offenders who are released to the community to register with state officials. The law allows state and local officials some discretion in establishing procedures for notifying community residents about where convicted sex offenders are living. The 2006 federal Adam Walsh Act expanded the categories of offenders required to register for their entire lives. Also, for the first time, juveniles as young as 14 were required to register for 15 years.[82]

Advocates of registration and community notification believe that sex offenders pose a high risk of reoffending, that registration will assist law enforcement in surveilling and/or arresting them, that the knowledge of this surveillance will deter them from reoffending, and that notification will help residents take protective measures they feel are appropriate.

The New Jersey registration and notification law illustrates how many laws operate. It has three tiers based on an assessment of the offender's risk of reoffending. Tier one offenders, in the lowest risk category, are only required to notify local law enforcement officials and their victim after release from prison. Tier two offenders are also required to notify organizations such as schools, day care centers, and summer camps. Tier three offenders, in the highest risk category, are subject to public notification through posters, pamphlets, and the Internet.[83]

The New Jersey law and all other laws bring up our old friend the prediction problem (see Chapter 4). How accurate are the New Jersey risk classifications? Are they evidence-based? These questions, in turn, force us to take a look at the facts on sex offenders and their reoffending rates. As we have already seen in our discussion of bail, rapists have the lowest reoffending rate of all major felony categories.

The Center for Sex Offender Management (CSOM), summarizing that available data, estimates that sex offenders reoffend at a rate of between 10 and 24 percent. In short, fewer than one-third recidivate.[84] In one study, the rearrest rate for parolees who had been convicted of rape over three years was 46 percent within the next three years after parole. While this was higher than in other studies, it was still lower than the rearrest rate for all felons paroled (67 percent); it was far lower than the rearrest rate for robbers (70 percent) and burglars (74 percent). In short, the danger of sex offenders reoffending has been greatly exaggerated.[85]

The data on reoffending rates focuses our attention on the relevant question: Where does the real danger lie regarding sex offenders? How can we effectively protect society? In fact, reported sex offenses have been declining for years. Adult rape and sexual assault went down 69 percent between 1993 and 2005. This is just one part of the Great Crime Decline that unfolded during that period. In New Jersey, the decline in reported sex offenses began in 1985. The social and political panic over predatory sex offenders, therefore, is grossly exaggerated.

The data on who offends, moreover, suggest that registration and notification laws do not protect us from the real potential offenders. Among sexual assault victims under age 18, 90 percent knew their abusers; 34 percent of the offenders were family members, and 59 percent were acquaintances. In short, the image of the stranger predator lurking in the park to snatch a child does not reflect most sex offenders. Nor are most sex offenders repeaters: 87 percent of persons arrested for sex crimes had no previous criminal conviction. Politicians repeatedly cite recidivism rates of 40, 74, or even 90 percent (A public opinion survey found that the public believes it is about 75 percent). Yet the data do not support such claims. A Justice Department study of 15 states found that among 9,691 male offenders, only 5.3 percent had been arrested for a sex crime (and 3.5 percent had been convicted) after three years.[86]

The Celebrated Case Syndrome Again

For obvious reasons, child abduction and sexual assault cases generate enormous publicity. Yet, they are very rare. DOJ estimates that there are about 155 child abductions every year by nonfamily members. There are a number of problems with current sex offender and registration laws. They include the following:

Overbreadth. The laws cover many people who are not really dangerous offenders, and are certainly not likely to kidnap and rape or kill a child. The laws cover people who have been convicted of urinating in public (exposure is classified as a sex crime); people who have engaged in consensual sex, for example between an adult male and a teenage female; adults who buy and sell sex with each other; and even children who expose themselves as childish pranks (the old game of "playing 'Doctor'"). There is also overbreadth in the length of time people are required to register. Seventeen states now make people register for life.[87]

Residency Restrictions.   The Human Rights Watch report, *No Easy Answers,* concludes that the residency requirements in sex offender laws "may be the harshest as well as the most arbitrary" of all the new restrictions. About 20 states have laws that put restrictions on where sex offenders can live. Typically they forbid an offender from living less than 1,000 or 2,500 feet from schools, day care centers, and public parks and swimming pools. Some homeless shelters refuse to accept sex offenders. In some cases, there is almost no place an offender can live. In Orange City, Florida, only 5 percent of the city is outside a zone where sex offenders cannot live. Nearly half the sex offenders in Florida reported they could not live with their family members. Meanwhile, hundreds of cities have similar local ordinances. And in Miami, Florida, a group of offenders were living under a bridge because they could not find housing anywhere. One offender in Iowa could not live with and care for his sick grandmother because she lived near a child care center. Another Iowa registrant listed his address as "behind the Target [store] on Euclid [street]."[88]

Enforcement Problems

Because of overbreadth, local law enforcement officials have difficulty even keeping track of all the registered sex offenders they are responsible for. In Iowa, for example, the County Attorney's Association reported that local prosecutors had lost track of half of all registered offenders. Offenders move and don't report where they are going; they lie about their status in their new location. One county reported that before the law took effect, they knew where 90 percent of the offenders were; afterwards, they knew the residence of only about 50 to 55 percent. The laws make enforcement difficult because they drive offenders underground. The requirements often separate them from their families if, for example, family members live too close to a school.

Recall the notorious Garrido kidnapping and rape case we discussed in Chapter 2. Garrido was a registered sex offender, yet the law did not prevent him from holding his victim prisoner for 10½ years. If anything, the law might have hindered his detection. Neighbors avoided Garrido, and thus were less likely to notice that something very serious was going on.

An earlier evaluation of the Wisconsin community notification law found that it imposed more work on probation and parole officials, especially when intensive supervision was part of the requirement, and that community notification meetings left as many people attending those meetings feeling worried about being victimized as were reassured. Offenders almost unanimously reported that notification hindered their readjustment to society, making it difficult to find housing and jobs, generating threats or harassment, and creating a general atmosphere of social ostracism. (When we examine offender reentry programs in Chapter 14, we will examine the many obstacles facing offenders who return to the community.) The Wisconsin study did not, however, attempt to evaluate the law's effect on recidivism.[89]

Interfering with Effective Treatment.   Registration, notification, and residency restriction laws interfere with effective treatment for sex offenders. Family members are the very people who are likely to be supportive of and help them rehabilitate themselves (reminding them to attend their counseling sessions, keeping an eye on them, etc.). In many cases, the added financial stress of maintaining two residences disrupts offenders' lives and those of family members. Numerous laws, meanwhile, prevent them from finding employment. It is difficult to get and keep a job when you are living out behind a Target store or under a bridge. Some employers are required to check sex offender registries. Many employers refuse to hire offenders even though the law does not prohibit them from doing so. States do, however, have laws barring employment at schools and child care centers. Parolees unable to meet the employment conditions of their release, of course, are more likely to recidivate (as is the case with all ex-offenders, regardless of their crime).[90]

Failure to Protect Society

Perhaps most seriously, the laws do not really protect society. A Minnesota study found that offenders were more likely to recidivate if they traveled to a different city. The two offenders who did commit new sex crimes committed them miles from where they were living. A 2007 Minnesota study found that most repeat offenders found their victims through social networks and not as strangers on the street or in a park.[91]

An evaluation of the New Jersey Sex Offender Registration and Notification law found only "limited effects" on crime. It had "no demonstrable effect on the number of victims involved in sexual offenses." Sex crimes began declining in the state since 1985, a decade before the law was passed, and that downward trend continued. As is the case nationally, half of all sex offenses involve incest or child molestation, and in half of all cases the victim knows the offender. In 2006, counties across New Jersey spent an estimated $3.9 million implementing the law.[92]

Are there Effective Treatment Programs?

Do effective treatment programs exist? Early evaluations of programs in the 1970s and 1980s found little evidence that treatment programs were effective in reducing recidivism among sex offenders. In recent years, however, the development of cognitive-behavioral therapy (CBT) forms of treatment have found more promising results. CBT programs vary, but the key elements include getting the client in treatment to focus on specific thoughts and behaviors and helping them to recognize inappropriate patterns and to develop alternatives.

SUMMARY

So, after looking at all the evidence, what do we know? The best answer is reflected in the title of the Human Rights Watch report: there are *No Easy Answers*. Sex crimes are indeed a serious problem, with terrible, traumatic effects on their victims, particularly when they are children. A certain number of sex offenders do repeat. We should not minimize these unpleasant facts. The problem is that our current policies have swung too far in the direction of crime control, exaggerating the problem and imposing restrictions that are not only irrelevant for many offenders, but are ineffective for the real problem cases and often counterproductive. Human Rights Watch found that the United States is the only country in the world with such an array of restrictions on sex offenders. Other countries debated similar laws but rejected them. As is the case with over-incarceration of offenders, the U.S. is "alone in the world" on this issue.[93]

PROPOSITION 26

Sex offender registration, notification, and residency restriction laws are not effective in preventing repeat sex crimes, and in certain respects inhibit effective control and treatment of offenders.

CONCLUSION

From a commonsense standpoint, lock 'em up strategies appear to be a simple and effective way to reduce crime: Get repeat offenders off the street and they won't be able to prey on society. Unfortunately, it is not that simple in the real world of the criminal justice system. First, we cannot precisely identify the small group of high-rate offenders. Second, gross incapacitation policies create all sorts of problems in the justice system. Third, because of these problems, the courtroom work group often finds ways to evade extremely punitive laws. Fourth, no conclusive evidence indicates that locking up a lot of people actually produces the promised reductions in crime. Finally, even where some crime reduction does occur, it is not clear that it is worth the enormous dollar cost to society.

Where does that leave us? As we have already suggested, the best response is captured by the title of the Human Rights Watch Report: there are *No Easy Answers*. Dangerous criminals do exist, and they deserve to be punished. The problem is that it is difficult to spot them early in their criminal careers. The prediction problem gets in the way of many easy-sounding solutions. Unfortunately, we have ignored the prediction problem and embarked on a course of gross incapacitation. As we have argued, this not only does not effectively reduce crime, but imposes many other high costs on society. In Chapter 14, we will try to bring together some of the promising policies that have emerged and suggest some sensible answers to our very difficult crime problem.

NOTES

1. On the general subject of discretion, see Samuel Walker, *Taming the System: The Control of Discretion in Criminal Justice, 1950–1990* (New York: Oxford University Press, 1993).

2. President's Task Force on Victims of Crime, *Final Report* (Washington, DC: Government Printing Office, 1982), p. 22.

3. Caleb Foote, "The Coming Constitutional Crisis in Bail," *University of Pennsylvania Law Review* 113 (May 1965): 959–999 and (June 1965): 1125–185.

4. *United States v. Salerno*, 481 U.S. 739 (1987).

5. On the background of the bail issue, see Wayne Thomas, *Bail Reform in America* (Berkeley: University of California Press, 1976). Bureau of Justice Statistics, *Profile of Jail Inmates, 2002* (Washington, DC: Department of Justice, 2004). NCJ 201932.

6. Caleb Foote, "Compelling Appearance in Court: Administration of Bail in Philadelphia," *University of Pennsylvania Law Review* 102 (1954): 1031–1079.

7. Bureau of Justice Statistics, *Pretrial Release of Felony Defendants in State Courts, 2004* (Washington, DC: Department of Justice, 2007). NCJ 214994.

8. Thomas, *Bail Reform in America*.

9. Ibid., p. 37. Bureau of Justice Statistics, *Jail Inmates at Midyear 2008—Statistical Tables* (Washington, DC: Department of Justice, 2009). NCJ 225709.

10. Bureau of Justice Statistics, *Pretrial Release of Felony Defendants, 1992* (Washington, DC: Department of Justice, 1994). NCJ 148818. Bureau of Justice Statistics, *Felony Defendants in Large Urban Counties, 2004* (Washington, DC: Department of Justice, 2008). NCJ 221374.

11. Bureau of Justice Statistics, *Felony Defendants in Large Urban Counties, 2004: Statistical Tables, Table 14.*

12. John Goldkamp, "Danger and Detention: A Second Generation of Bail Reform," *Journal of Criminal Law and Criminology* 76 (Spring 1985): 1–74.

13. *Preventive Detention in the District of Columbia: The First Ten Months* (Washington, DC: Georgetown Institute of Criminal Law and Procedure, 1972); Thomas, *Bail Reform in America*, pp. 231–232.

14. Frederic Suffet, "Bail Setting: A Study of Courtroom Interaction," *Crime and Delinquency* 12 (1966): 318–331.

15. Bureau of Justice Statistics, *Felony Defendants in Large Urban Counties, 2004.*

16. General Accounting Office, *Criminal Bail: How Bail Reform Is Working in Selected District Courts* (Washington, DC: Department of Justice, 1987). Bureau of Justice Statistics, *Pretrial Release and Detention: The Bail Reform Act of 1984* (Washington, DC: Department of Justice, 1988).

17. Thomas E. Scott, "Pretrial Detention under the Bail Reform Act of 1984: An Empirical Analysis," *American Criminal Law Review* 27.1 (1989): 1–51. Bureau of Justice Statistics, *Federal Pretrial Release and Detention, 1996* (Washington, DC: Department of Justice, 1999). NCJ 168635.

18. Bureau of Justice Statistics, *Pretrial Release and Detention*, Table 9. Bureau of Justice Statistics, *Sourcebook of Criminal Justice Statistics—1998* (Washington, DC: Department of Justice, 1996), p. 401.

19. Bureau of Justice Statistics, *Felony Defendants in Large Urban Counties, 2004, Statistical Tables.*

20. Bureau of Justice Statistics, *Felony Defendants in Large Urban Counties, 2004, Table 16.*

21. William Rhodes, Raymond Hyatt, and Paul Scheiman, *Predicting Pretrial Misconduct with Drug Tests of Arrestees: Evidence from Six Sites* (Washington, DC: Department of Justice, 1996).

22. *Schall v. Martin,* 467 U.S. 253 (1984).

23. Jeffrey Fagan and Martin Guggenheim, "Preventive Detention and the Judicial Prediction of Dangerousness for Juveniles: A Natural Experiment," *Journal of Criminal Law and Criminology* 86.2 (1996): 415–448.

24. Ibid., pp. 445, 448.

25. Bureau of Justice Statistics, Pretrial Release of Felony Defendants, 1992.

26. Malcolm Feeley, *Court Reform on Trial* (New York: Basic Books, 1983).

27. Franklin E. Zimring and Gordon Hawkins, *Incapacitation: Penal Confinement and the Restraint of Crime* (New York: Oxford University Press, 1995).

28. James Q. Wilson, *Thinking about Crime* (New York: Basic Books, 1975), pp. 200–202.

29. Peter Greenwood, *Selective Incapacitation* (Santa Monica, CA: Rand, 1982).

30. Ibid., p. xix.

31. Jan M. Chaiken and Marcia R. Chaiken, *Varieties of Criminal Behavior: Summary and Policy Implications* (Santa Monica, CA: Rand, 1982).

32. Alfred Blumstein, Jacqueline Cohen, Jeffrey Roth, and Christy Visher, eds., *Criminal Careers and "Career Criminals"* (Washington, DC: National Academy of Sciences, 1988).

33. Ibid., p. 59.

34. Ibid., p. 60.

35. Peter W. Greenwood and Susan Turner, *Selective Incapacitation Revisited: Why the High-Rate Offenders Are Hard to Predict* (Santa Monica, CA: Rand, 1987).

36. Ibid., Table 4.3.

37. American Bar Association, *Standards for Criminal Justice,* "Sentencing Alternatives and Procedures," Standard 18–2.1 (Boston: Little, Brown, 1980), pp. 18–25. A good discussion of current developments is Ryan S. King, *The State of Sentencing 2008: Developments in Policy and Practice* (Washington, DC: The Sentencing Project, 2009). www.sentencingproject.org.

38. Edwin W. Zedlewski, *Making Confinement Decisions* (Washington, DC: Department of Justice, 1987).

39. Franklin E. Zimring and Gordon E. Hawkins, "The New Mathematics of Imprisonment," *Crime and Delinquency* 34 (October 1988): 425–436. See also Zimring and Hawkins, *Incapacit..tion.*

40. Eric J. Scott, *Calls for Service* (Washington, DC: Department of Justice, 1981).

41. Franklin E. Zimring, *The Great American Crime Decline* (New York: Oxford University Press, 2007), pp. 46–56.

42. Zimring and Hawkins, *Incapacitation.*

43. Ibid., p. 126.

44. Ibid., pp. 106–107.

45. Zimring, *The Great American Crime Decline*, pp. 51, 120–121.

46. Ryken Grattet, Joan Petersilia, and Jeffrey Lin, *Parole Violations and Revocations in California* (Washington, DC: Department of Justice, 2008).

47. Avinash Singh Bhati, John K. Roman, Aaon Chalfin, *To Treat or Not to Treat: Evidence on the Prospects of Expanding Treatment to Drug-Involved Offenders* (Washington, DC: The Urban Institute, 2008).

48. Pew Center on the States, *One in 100: Behind Bars in America 2008* (Washington, DC: Pew Center on the States, 2008), pp. 12–13.

49. Pew Center, *One in 100: Behind Bars in America 2008*, pp. 14–16.

50. The Sentencing Project, "Felony Disenfranchisement." www.sentencingproject.org. Walker, Spohn, and DeLone, *The Color of Justice: Race, Ethnicity, and Crime in America*, 4th ed. (Belmont, CA: Thomson, 2007).

51. Pew Center, *One in 100: Behind Bars in America 2008*. Marc Mauer, *Lessons of the "Get Tough" Movement in the United States* (Washington, DC: The Sentencing Project, 2004). Todd Clear, *Imprisoning Communities: How Mass Incarceration Makes Disadvantaged Neighborhoods Worse* (New York: Oxford University Press, 2007).

52. Bureau of Justice Assistance, *National Assessment of Structured Sentencing* (Washington, DC: Department of Justice, 1996), pp. 24–25.

53. Campaign for an Effective Crime Policy, *The Impact of "Three Strikes and You're Out" Laws: What Have We Learned?* (Washington, DC: Campaign for an Effective Crime Policy, 1996).

54. U.S. Department of Justice, *The Nation's Toughest Drug Law: Evaluating the New York Experience* (Washington, DC: Author, 1978).

55. Ibid., p. 18.

56. Malcolm M. Feeley and Sam Hakim, "The Effect of 'Three Strikes and You're Out' on the Courts," in David Shichor and Dale K. Sechrest, eds., *Three Strikes and You're Out: Vengeance as Social Policy* (Thousand Oaks, CA: Sage, 1996), p. 141.

57. Pamala Griset, "The Politics and Economics of Increased Correctional Discretion over Time Served: A New York Case Study," *Justice Quarterly* 12 (June 1995): 307–323.

58. Bureau of Justice Statistics, *Drugs, Crime, and the Justice System* (Washington, DC: Department of Justice, 1992), p. 30.

59. Drug Policy Alliance, *New York's Rockefeller Drug Laws: Explaining the Reforms of 2009* (New York: Drug Policy Alliance, 2009). www.drugpolicy.org. Partnership for Responsible Drug Information, *Rockefeller Drug Law Information Sheet* (New York: PRDI, 2009). www.prdi.org.

60. Bureau of Justice Statistics, *Compendium of Federal Justice Statistics, 2004* (Washington, DC: Department of Justice, 2006). NCJ 213476.

61. Barbara Meierhofer, *The General Effect of Mandatory Minimum Prison Terms* (Washington, DC: Department of Justice, 1992).

62. U.S. Sentencing Commission, *Federal Sentencing Guidelines Manual* (St. Paul, MN: West, 1990), p. 281.

63. Ilene H. Nagel and Stephen Schulhofer, "A Tale of Three Cities: An Empirical Study of Charging and Bargaining Practices Under the Federal Sentencing Guidelines," *Southern California Law Review* 66 (1992): 501–566.

64. Ashley Nellis and Ryan S. King, *No Exit: The Expanding Use of Life Sentences in America* (Washington, DC: The Sentencing Project, 2009).

65. Ibid.

66. U.S. Department of Justice, *Mandatory Sentencing: The Experience of Two States* (Washington, DC: Department of Justice, 1982).

67. Bureau of Justice Assistance, *National Assessment of Structured Sentencing*, p. 117.

68. Zimring and Hawkins, *Incapacitation*.

69. Michael Tonry, "Mandatory Penalties," in Michael Tonry, ed., *Crime and Justice: A Review of Research*, vol. 16 (Chicago: University of Chicago Press, 1992), p. 243.

70. Franklin E. Zimring, Gordon Hawkins, and Sam Hakim, *Punishment and Democracy: Three Strikes and You're Out in California* (New York: Oxford University Press, 2001). A good collection of material on three-strikes laws is Shichor and Sechrest, eds., *Three Strikes and You're Out: Vengeance as Social Policy*.

71. Michael G. Turner, Jody Sundt, Brandon K. Applegate, and Francis T. Cullen, "'Three Strikes and You're Out' Legislation: A National Assessment," *Federal Probation* 59 (September 1995): 16–35.

72. Jerome H. Skolnick, "Wild Pitch," *American Prospect* 17 (Spring 1994): 31–37. Shichor and Sechrest, *Three Strikes and You're Out*. John J. DiIulio, Jr., "Instant Replay," *American Prospect* 18 (Summer 1994): 12–18.

73. William F. McDonald, *Repeat Offender Laws in the United States: The Form, Use, and Perceived Value* (Washington, DC: Department of Justice, 1986), p. 5.

74. Bureau of Justice Assistance, *National Assessment of Structured Sentencing*, pp. 24–25. Turner et al., "'Three Strikes and You're Out' Legislation."

75. Zimring, Hawkins, and Hakim, *Punishment and Democracy: Three Strikes and You're Out in California*.

76. Ibid.

77. Scott Ehlers, Vincent Schiraldi, and Jason Ziedenberg, *Still Striking Out: Ten Years of California's Three Strikes* (Washington, DC: Justice Policy Institute, 2004). Available on the Justice Policy Institute website.

78. Ibid.

79. Zimring, Hawkins, and Hakim, *Punishment and Democracy: Three Strikes and You're Out in California*.

80. McDondald, Repeat Offender Laws in the United States, Abstract, np.

81. Ibid., pp. 7, 9.

82. Human Rights Watch, *No Easy Answers: Sex Offender Laws in the United States* (New York: Human Rights Watch, 2007). Peter Finn, *Sex Offender Community Notification* (Washington, DC: Department of Justice, 1997). NCJ 162364.

83. Kristen M. Zgoba, and Karen Bachar, *Sex Offender Resistration and Notification: Limited Effects in New Jersey* (Washington, DC: Department of Justice, April 2009).

84. Human Rights Watch, *No Easy Answers*, p. 33. Center for Sex Offender Management, "Information About Managing Sex Offenders." www.csom.org.

85. Bureau of Justice Statistics, *Recidivism of Prisoners Released in 1994* (Washington, DC: Department of Justice, 2002), Table 9. NCJ 193427.

86. Human Rights Watch, *No Easy Answers.*

87. Ibid., p. 5.

88. Ibid., p. 7.

89. Richard G. Zevitz and Mary Ann Farkas, *Sex Offender Community Notification: Assessing the Impact in Wisconsin* (Washington, DC: Department of Justice, 2001). NCJ 179992.

90. Human Rights Watch, *No Easy Answers*, pp. 81–86.

91. Ibid., pp. 115–116.

92. Kristen M. Zgoba, and Karen Bachar, *Sex Offender Resistration and Notification: Limited Effects in New Jersey.*

93. Human Rights Watch, *No Easy Answers*, p. 10.

8

Close the Loopholes

Do dangerous criminals "beat the system" and escape punishment because of loopholes in the system? Do their lawyers get their cases dismissed? Are they allowed to plead guilty to lesser offenses, so that they either don't go to prison, or only for short terms? Do they have their convictions overturned on appeal, so that they go free? Conservatives believe that loopholes allow many dangerous criminals to avoid conviction and punishment, and are a major part of our crime problem.

PROSECUTE THE CAREER CRIMINAL

To keep dangerous criminals from avoiding conviction and punishment, some prosecutor's offices have created *major-offender* or *career criminal programs*. The basic idea is to focus special attention on them to make sure they are prosecuted, convicted, and sentenced to an appropriately long prison term. Some programs focus on the career criminals we discussed in Chapter 4, offenders with long criminal records. Others focus on particularly serious crimes, such as sexual assaults or crimes where guns are used. Do they work? Do they close a loophole in the system? Does this loophole even exist? And if it does, how big is it?

Special prosecutor's units address the distinction between a "horizontal" approach to prosecution versus a "vertical" approach. Most large urban prosecutors' offices use a horizontal approach. One group of prosecutors handles the initial filing of charges and arraignment. Another group takes the case to trial and negotiates plea bargains (in some offices, a separate group handles the few trials that occur). In the vertical approach, one prosecutor (or more, if it is a complex case) handles the case from initial charge through to its end.

Advocates of vertical prosecution believe that it can yield many benefits. One prosecutor becomes intimately involved in each case. Relevant factors are not lost as a case is passed from one group of attorneys to another. Prosecutors are more likely to become involved in each case and with the victims, and less likely therefore to negotiate to a much lesser charge. An additional benefit is that the crime victims gain some comfort from dealing with only one attorney throughout the case. With regard to sex crimes or gun crimes, moreover, prosecutors develop expertise in handling those kinds of cases. Continuity can also help eliminate disparities disposition. Presumably, you don't have different prosecutors negotiating very different kinds of plea bargains.

Does a Special Prosecutorial Unit Make a Difference?

Comparing Two Cities   Spohn and Beichner sought to answer our questions by comparing the prosecutor's office in Kansas City, Missouri—which had a special prosecutorial unit for sex crimes—with the office in Miami, Florida, which did not have one. In Kansas City, special unit prosecutors handle cases from the initial charging decision through to the final disposition. In Miami, one set of attorneys handles the initial charging decision, and the case is then passed to a separate group who handles the case to its end. Most notably, charges were filed in nearly identical percentage of cases (both around 58 percent). Interviews, moreover, found that prosecutors in both offices reported that the same factors influenced decisions. Both charged or dismissed on whether there was proof beyond a reasonable doubt of the defendant's guilt. Both asked, Can we win this case? A statistical analysis of factors associated with charging decisions also found nearly identical patterns between the two offices. Of particular interest is the fact that neither prosecutor's office allowed a differential racial mix (especially black defendant, white victim) to affect its charging decisions.[1]

The main implications of the findings are that a special unit for sexual assault cases did not close a loophole that allowed offenders to slip through with no charge or significantly lower charges. Strength of the evidence and the likelihood of conviction shaped decisions in both offices. There was no loophole.

The San Diego Major Violator Unit   Does a special unit result in a higher rate of convictions and a higher percentage of prison sentences? An evaluation of the San Diego Major Violator Unit addressed these issues. The unit targeted robbery and robbery-related homicide cases in which the defendant was charged with three or more separate robbery-related offenses or had been convicted of one or more serious offenses in the preceding ten years.[2] Taking a vertical approach, the individual prosecutor was assigned a major-violator case and followed it through to final disposition.

Like many other special prosecutor programs, the Major Violator Unit included restrictions on plea bargaining.[3] Prosecutors could not "charge bargain," that is, accept a plea to a lesser offense; they could only accept a guilty plea only to the top felony count. Charge bargaining, as we will see when we discuss plea bargaining later in this chapter, is believed to be the main way in which offenders avoid prison, or a long mandatory prison term, by pleading to a misdemeanor or a lesser felony.

Despite these special procedures, however, the unit had only a modest impact on the prosecution of career criminals. True, it won conviction in an impressive 91.5 percent of its cases, but San Diego prosecutors normally convicted 89.5 percent of all career criminals. The unit did increase the percentage of convicted offenders sent to prison, from 77.1 percent to 92.5 percent. But this change was less significant than it might appear. Well over 90 percent convicted offenders were already being incarcerated. The difference is that some had gone to jail (and thus for short terms).[4] In short, as we indicated in Chapters 2 and 3, the system was already very tough on career criminals. There was no loophole to close.

The San Diego data illustrate another often misunderstood aspect of sentencing in America. The category of incarceration includes both sentences to prison and *split sentences,* in which the offender does some time in jail followed by release on probation. Split sentences are actually fairly common. In 2004, 72 percent of all defendants in large urban counties were sentenced to some form of incarceration. But the majority of those were sentenced to jail (41 percent of the total) rather than prison (31 percent).[5] The distinction between prison and jail sentences can have an enormous impact on public *perception* of how the system works. If you ask what percentage of convicted offenders went to prison (31 percent), the system looks somewhat weak. But when you include everyone who is incarcerated, meaning prison and jail (73 percent), it looks a lot tougher. True, going to jail is not as serious as going to prison, but it is still an unpleasant experience, and these offenders are not beating the system.

The Major Violator Unit *did* double the average length of incarceration. In this respect, it significantly increased the severity of punishment. But it is important to recall that the length of prison terms had begun rising all across the country in that time period, particularly for serious crimes and defendants with long criminal histories. It is likely that much of the increase in prison terms in San Diego probably would have occurred even without the Major Violator Unit.

Did the San Diego Major Violator Unit have any impact on the crime rate? The evaluation did not address this question. Common sense, however, suggests that it could not have had any significant effect, because the changes in the percentage of offenders convicted and the percentage incarcerated were so small. True, there was an increase in incapacitation as a result of the longer prison terms. But as we learned in Chapter 7, there is no evidence that increasing incapacitation actually reduces crime.

These data on the prosecution of so-called career criminals confirm the points made in Chapters 2 and 3. First, the criminal justice system is generally tough on repeat offenders who have committed a serious crime. Second, these patterns of prosecution and sentencing reflect the going rate agreed upon informally by the local courtroom work group. In short, local prosecutors and judges, without the benefit of a special program, are generally very tough on major offenders. Many people are surprised to find that the system is consistently tough on career criminals. In 2002, 67 percent of Americans felt that the criminal courts in their area were not harsh enough in dealing with criminals.[6] We can explain this misperception in terms of our criminal justice wedding cake (Chapter 2). Public perception is heavily influenced by a few celebrated cases in the top layer: the armed robber who got probation; the rapist who pled guilty to misdemeanor assault. Do such things happen? Of course, they do. But they are the exceptions rather than the rule, and the major lesson of this book is that we should not develop policies on the basis of exceptional cases.

The evidence leads to the following proposition:

PROPOSITION 27
Special prosecution units do not produce
either higher conviction rates or lower crime rates.

ABOLISH THE INSANITY DEFENSE

John W. Hinckley never succeeded at much in life, but he is singlehandedly responsible for some significant changes in American criminal justice. Hinckley's acquittal for the attempted assassination of President Ronald Reagan in 1981 sparked a national outcry over the insanity defense.[7] In the following years almost every state and the federal government changed its law on the insanity defense. Twelve states adopted a new "guilty but mentally ill" (GBMI) standard and five abolished the insanity defense altogether.[8]

Hinckley's acquittal touched one of the raw nerves of public opinion: the sight of a guilty person "beating the rap" and "getting off" because of a "technicality." There was no question that John Hinckley shot and wounded the president; the videotape was broadcast on television all across the country. People were outraged over the Hinckley verdict of not guilty by reason of insanity (NGRI), which appeared to let him off. The fact is that he was institutionalized—in a hospital rather than a prison. He remains there today, although in 1999 he was granted the right to leave the hospital to have supervised visits with his parents, and in 2000 gained longer unsupervised visits. Over the next ten years, he gained, lost, and then regained greater privileges through a series of court hearings. In 2009 he won the right to have a driver's license, for example. His notoriety has probably kept him in the hospital longer than if he had shot an ordinary person, pled guilty, and gone to prison.

For many people, the insanity defense is the classic loophole. It conjures up images of criminally insane persons roaming the streets in search of more victims. Insanity defense proceedings also anger many people. The parade of psychiatrists and expert witnesses on both sides of the case creates the impression that you can always find an expert somewhere to say what you want said. Like the O. J. Simpson trial, the Hinckley case supports the impression that the wealthy can buy lawyers and experts who will win them acquittal. In one public opinion survey, 87 percent of the respondents felt that the insanity defense was a loophole; about 40 percent called it the "rich person's defense."[9]

The conservative response is to try to close the loophole. Changes in the law over the past two decades fall into six categories: (1) abolishing the insanity defense altogether; (2) changing the test of insanity; (3) shifting the burden of proof to the defendant (instead of the state having to prove criminal intent, the defendant has to prove mental illness); (4) creating a new "guilty but mentally ill" verdict; (5) revising trial procedure for raising an insanity plea; and (6) changing procedures for committing a person found not guilty by reason of insanity.[10]

Sorting Out the Issues

To make sense of changes in the law on the insanity defense we need to sort out four separate issues. The first concerns the extent of the use of the defense. How many criminal defendants successfully win verdicts of not guilty by reason of insanity? A second issue involves the fate of those who do win acquittal. Do they return to the streets? How soon? Do they endanger the public? The third issue is predicting dangerousness. If some offenders are dangerous, how can we identify them? How can we tell when it is safe to release them? The fourth issue is the effect of abolishing the insanity defense. What is the impact on crime and the criminal justice system?

The Reality of the Insanity Defense

Despite all the attention it receives, the insanity defense is very rarely used successfully. Very few defendants even try to use it, and not many of them succeed. Studies have consistently found that the insanity defense is raised in less than 1 percent of all criminal indictments, and only between 15 and 25 percent of those efforts are successful.[11] Henry J. Steadman and his colleagues, for example, found that in four states (California, Georgia, Montana, New York), the insanity defense was *raised* in slightly less than 1 percent (0.90 percent) of all felony indictments, and only about 23 percent of these *succeeded* in getting an NGRI verdict.[12] The American Psychiatric Association Insanity Defense Work Group concluded, "While philosophically important for the criminal law, the insanity defense is *empirically unimportant* (involving a fraction of 1 percent of all felony cases)."[13]

Illustration by Frank Irwin, © Wadsworth, Cengage Learning.

The insanity defense is simply not used that often. The most recent study of its use examined cases in New York County (one of the five jurisdictions in New York City). In a sample of 172 defendants indicted for a felony who claimed a psychiatric defense between 1988 and 1997, only 10 percent (a total of 17) went before a jury where the insanity defense was argued, and only four resulted in an acquittal. That represents only 2 percent of those defendants who raised a claim of insanity, and 24 percent of the few cases that went to trial. In short, few offenders raise it, fewer still get to court with it, and most of those do not win with it.[14]

The extent of public misunderstanding about the frequency of the insanity defense is extraordinary. An Illinois poll found that people believed that nearly 40 percent of all criminal defendants used the insanity defense. This misunderstanding explains the fact that nearly half of the respondents wanted the insanity defense abolished.[15]

Given how infrequently the insanity defense is successfully used, closing this alleged loophole would have no noticeable impact on the crime rate. Additionally, there would be absolutely no impact on robbery and burglary cases, since the insanity defense is most often raised in murder cases. The few successful insanity defense cases are the classic celebrated cases in the top layer of the criminal justice wedding cake. They are completely unrepresentative and tell us nothing about how most serious crimes are routinely handled.

When the insanity defense is successfully used, it is usually the result of a plea bargain or a stipulated finding. That is, the prosecutor, defense attorney, medical experts, and judge all agree that the defendant is indeed mentally ill. This is another example of the courtroom work group in operation: settling cases through mutual agreement. A study of 60,432 felony indictments in Baltimore, Maryland, in 1991 found that the insanity defense was raised in only 190 cases; it was eventually dropped in 182 cases, and the remaining eight defendants were stipulated mentally ill by both prosecution and defense.[16] This is not a picture of innumerable dangerous criminals beating the system.

Another popular myth about the insanity defense is that the people who use it are violent and dangerous. Not all of the defendants committed to mental health institutions by way of an insanity verdict have committed a violent offense, however. Of the 500 men in the Bridgewater (Massachusetts) State Hospital for the Criminally Insane, more than 100 were charged with vagrancy.[17] These people are not dangerous sociopaths. Many are pathetic individuals who have serious mental health problems and cannot cope with their lives. Most sank through the various safety nets and ended up on skid row, where they finally were arrested.[18]

Aftermath of Acquittal

What happens to defendants who are committed to mental institutions after winning not guilty by reason of insanity verdicts is a matter of much controversy. Liberals generally contend that they are likely to spend more time in a mental hospital than if they had been found guilty of the crime and sent to prison. Conservatives argue that they get out too soon.

In the past, there was some truth to the liberal argument. Many allegedly mentally ill people were hospitalized for years, even decades, without any treatment or any evidence that they were really dangerous. Supreme Court decisions and new state laws, however, have led to greater protection of the rights of the confined.[19] One of the most important is a mental patient's right to periodic review of his or her condition to determine whether continued confinement is justified. The landmark case of *Baxstrom v. Herold* (1966) forced the release of persons held for long periods of time in the New York State Hospital for the Criminally Insane and necessitated the development of new procedures for continued confinement.[20]

Nonetheless, persons hospitalized after being found not guilty by reason of insanity still spend more time confined in hospitals than comparable offenders spend in prison after being found guilty of the crime. Henry Steadman and his associates found that in New York, 88 percent of all NGRIs were hospitalized; of the 12 percent immediately released, a disproportionate share were women. Those who were charged with murder but found not guilty by reason of insanity spent an average of 6.4 years in the hospital; those acquitted of other violent crimes were hospitalized for an average of 5.2 years; and for nonviolent crimes, hospital stays averaged 2.8 years. For all the crimes except murder, these terms of confinement were longer than for offenders found guilty of similar crimes.[21]

In an earlier study, Steadman studied a group of defendants found incompetent to stand trial to see whether they "beat the rap." A defendant who is too mentally ill to comprehend the nature of a criminal trial is committed to an institution until he or she is able to understand the proceedings, at which point the criminal process resumes. Steadman found that those defendants deemed "nondangerous" spent less than two years in mental institutions, whereas the "dangerous" were confined an average of two years and two months. If they were subsequently convicted at trial, they faced the possibility of additional prison time. Do you beat the rap by taking the mental health route? Steadman argues not: "Mental hospitals are simply an alternative place to do time."[22] In short, the system is not turning hordes of dangerous psychotics loose on society.

Danger to the Community

How dangerous are the criminally insane? We have had some natural experiments on this question as a result of court decisions that forced the release of criminal defendants. A 1971 decision forced the clinical reassessment of 586 inmates of Pennsylvania's Fairview State Hospital for the Criminally Insane. More than two-thirds were eventually released. Over the next four years, 27 percent were rearrested, but only 11 percent for a violent crime. Including some others who were rehospitalized for a violent act, a total of 14.5 percent of those released proved to be dangerous.[23] A recent review of the literature concluded that the recidivism rate for persons acquitted by reason of insanity was "no greater than that of felons."[24]

Once again we encounter our old friend the prediction problem from Chapter 4. A decision to release or confine a person alleged to be criminally insane involves a prediction about his or her future behavior. Does he or she pose a danger to the community? The success rate in predicting the dangerousness of the criminally insane is no better than in other areas of criminal justice. Because only 14.5 percent of the Fairview inmates committed another violent act, you could argue that the experts were wrong about the other 85.5 percent. This translates into six false positives (people unnecessarily locked up) for each true positive.

The Impact of Abolition

For many people, "abolishing" the insanity defense (like "abolishing" plea bargaining) is a slogan. As we have seen, changing the law on the insanity defense can be done in six different ways. Each of these changes involves complex legal and practical problems.

Abolishing or modifying the insanity defense raises fundamental issues about the criminal law. Our justice system rests on the principle that the accused is innocent until proven guilty and that the prosecution must prove guilt beyond a reasonable doubt. To prove guilt, the prosecution must establish three things: The accused committed the act (*actus reus*), the accused had criminal intent (*mens rea*), and a connection exists between the two (that is, the accused did it and intended to do it).[25]

The key issue with the insanity defense is the *mens rea* requirement. The criminal law has long recognized different degrees of intent. The law distinguishes between a planned murder (first degree) and one committed in the heat of passion (second degree). It further recognizes that some homicides occur without any criminal intent (manslaughter). Differences in the degree of intent are reflected in the severity of the punishment. First-degree murder carries a potential death sentence in many states.

The law has historically recognized that some people lack full criminal intent because they do not understand what they are doing. We readily accept the idea that the 5-year-old who picks up the loaded handgun and accidentally kills his brother does not have criminal intent. He simply does not understand the nature and consequences of firing the gun. Another example is the truly deranged person who kills because he or she hears voices from another planet. Like the child, this person does not appreciate the criminal nature of his or her act.[26]

Unfortunately, not all cases are as simple as these examples. The legal system has struggled for 150 years to develop a formula for resolving questions about the accused's mental state. The principle of insanity first entered English law in 1843 with the famous *M'Naughton* case, which established the "right-wrong test": Did the accused understand the difference between right and wrong? Because this test is somewhat crude, legal scholars have attempted to develop alternatives, such as the "irresistible impulse" test. Laypersons are often mystified by the arcane distinctions among those alternatives, none of which resolves the basic problem created by the intersection of medical diagnoses, with their inevitable shades of gray, and the legal system, with its requirement of an absolute verdict of guilt or innocence.[27]

Attempts to abolish the insanity defense run up against the *mens rea* requirement. Suppose a state adopted a law that said "mental condition shall not be a defense to any charge of criminal conduct." This might be interpreted as abolishing the *mens rea* requirement altogether. The prosecution would not have to prove anything about the accused's mental state, only that he or she did the crime. Among other things, it would wipe out the distinction between first-degree murder, second-degree murder, and manslaughter. It is doubtful that even the most ardent opponents of the insanity defense seriously want to take this approach, which would probably be found unconstitutional. Wisconsin (1909) and Mississippi (1928) abolished the insanity defense early in this century. In both cases, the new laws were declared unconstitutional under the due process clauses of their state constitutions.[28]

A more limited interpretation of the law that mental condition shall not be a defense to any charge of criminal conduct would be that an affirmative plea of not guilty by reason of insanity could not be raised. The crucial distinction here is between affirmative and ordinary defenses. An *ordinary defense* is simply an attempt to show that the prosecution has failed to connect the accused with the crime. An *affirmative defense* is that, yes, the accused did kill the victim and intended to, but he or she does not have criminal responsibility for the act (because of self-defense, duress, insanity).

What would happen if we abolished insanity as an affirmative defense? As a recent review of the literature pointed out, we have little empirical evidence on this question, because so few states (five) have actually abolished the insanity defense and also because there are so few cases. Put yourself in the shoes of a defense attorney, and the answer is obvious. You would directly attack the prosecution's case on the basic *mens rea* requirement and argue that your client lacked the necessary criminal intent. You would not win every time, of course, but you might win some of the time, with the net result that your client would be fully acquitted. The people who oppose the insanity defense would find this outcome even more outrageous than our current situation. Even if you did not win, you would force the prosecution to address your client's mental state. In short, the basic issues underlying the insanity defense would reappear in a different form. There is no getting around it; the *mens rea* requirement is a bedrock principle of our legal system.

The GBMI alternative has three serious flaws. First, it strikes indirectly at the *mens rea* requirement, introducing the slippery notion that the accused had partial, but not complete, criminal intent. Second, it creates a lesser and included offense that judges and juries may choose simply as a compromise verdict. They may decide that the accused probably did something wrong and deserves some punishment, but they are unwilling to bring in a verdict of guilty on the top charge. The GBMI option would allow them to split the difference and choose the lesser verdict. Finally, the GBMI verdict does not guarantee treatment for the person who has been declared mentally ill.

Prisons and jails, many of which are overcrowded, cannot handle their current inmates with mental problems. A 2000 Bureau of Justice Statistics survey found that 16 percent of state prison inmates were receiving some treatment for mental illness; 10 percent were receiving some medication (in five states 20 percent were on medication). State prison systems spend an average of only about 10 percent of their budgets on all forms of health care; obviously only a small part of those expenditures involve *mental* health care.[29]

For the GBMI offenders, we can imagine the sequence of events. The convicted offender is sentenced to prison, where his behavior becomes a problem. He is then transferred to the state mental hospital for treatment. After his behavior stabilizes, he is transferred back to prison, where, because of the brutal conditions, his behavior again deteriorates. The cycle then repeats itself. This is not to suggest that our mental hospitals are models of effective treatment and humane custody. They are not, and much of the "treatment" is meaningless. But sending an allegedly mentally ill person to prison is an even worse solution.

The GBMI option has already proved to be a bogus reform. A 1981 Illinois law added GBMI as an additional verdict, retaining the traditional insanity defense. In Cook County (Chicago), NGRI verdicts actually increased from 34 to 103 between 1981 and 1984. At the same time, GBMI verdicts went from 16 in 1982, the first year the option was available, to 87 in 1984. This represents a variation on the "bait and switch" problem that we discussed in Chapter 1, whereby a new law is advertised as affecting one category of crime but actually affects other less serious ones. GBMI verdicts appear to have involved people who would otherwise have been found guilty, not defendants who would have been found not guilty by reason of insanity.[30]

The Illinois GBMI law also failed to provide medical treatment for GBMI defendants. An evaluation found that "not a single GBMI offender has been transferred from the Department of Corrections to the Department of Mental Health" for treatment. The law only "complicated rather than resolved [the] fundamental issues surrounding the insanity defense."[31] A study of the GBMI verdict in another state reached similar conclusions: There was no reduction in the number of insanity pleas, jurors were more likely to be confused about the legal issues, many offenders receiving a GBMI verdict were placed on probation, and offenders had no assurance that they would receive any medical treatment.[32]

The real function of the guilty but mentally ill option is symbolic, to appease public opinion. The public has little concern for the details of what actually happens to a mentally ill criminal defendant. Basically, it wants a symbolic statement of guilty. In practice, as Richard Moran points out, the GBMI verdict has as much meaning as "guilty but brown eyes."[33]

In sum, the various proposals to abolish or modify the insanity defense fail on two counts. Not only do they fail to reduce crime, because the insanity defense is so rare, but they create new problems for the criminal justice system. The evidence is overwhelming that the insanity defense is not a loophole that allows thousands of dangerous offenders to beat the system. This leads us to conclude:

PROPOSITION 28
Abolishing or limiting the insanity defense will have no impact on serious crime.

Richard Moran offers the best verdict on this issue: "The insanity defense has been misinterpreted and abused"—not by criminal defendants but "by politicians and journalists who mistakenly attack it as a major loophole in the law."[34] A review of attempts to revise or abolish the insanity defense over the past 20 years concluded that all of these changes have had "little effect," in large part because "there is no real evidence that it is broken."[35]

ABOLISH OR REFORM PLEA BARGAINING?

Everyone seems to dislike plea bargaining. Conservatives believe that it is a major loophole through which criminals beat the system and avoid punishment. Liberals, meanwhile, believe that it is the source of grave injustices: with prosecutors offering better deals to some types of defendants than others; with defense attorneys making private deals with prosecutors rather than fighting for their clients; and with defendants being coerced into waiving their right to a trial.[36]

We should be concerned about plea bargaining. After all, it is how the overwhelming majority of criminal cases are resolved. In 2004, 97 percent of all convictions in large urban courts were obtained through a guilty plea. Additionally, our justice system is different from European countries. A comparative study of plea bargaining in the U.S., German, France, and Italy concluded that "Prosecutors' overly broad and essentially unchecked discretion remains perhaps the most distinctive feature of the American criminal justice system."[37] Uncontrolled discretion is usually an invitation to trouble.

In many instances, the process of plea bargaining makes a mockery of justice. In court the judge goes through the charade of asking the defendant whether any promises have been made in return for the guilty plea, and the defendant answers no. But, of course, a deal has been made.[38]

Efforts to eliminate the problems associated with plea bargaining fall into two categories. Some people want to abolish it altogether. Others want to keep it but reform it through rules and regulations.

Abolishing Plea Bargaining: Alaska Tries

For a few years in the 1970s, there were loud calls to abolish plea bargaining. Public outrage reached its peak in 1973, when Vice President Spiro Agnew, in perhaps the most famous plea bargain of all time, avoided going to prison on extortion charges by pleading no contest to a lesser charge of tax evasion. In 1973 the National Advisory Commission on Criminal Justice Standards and Goals recommended that plea bargaining be abolished within five years.[39] It didn't happen. When we take a closer look at plea bargaining, including Alaska's ban, we will begin to understand why.

The most celebrated attempt to abolish plea bargaining occurred in Alaska, when Attorney General Avrum Gross abolished plea bargaining in the entire state.[40] On July 3, 1975, he issued a memorandum that read, in part:

> I wish to have the following policy implemented with respect to all
> adult criminal offenses in which charges have been filed on or after
> August 15, 1975:

1) District Attorneys and Assistant District Attorneys will refrain from engaging in plea negotiations with defendants designed to arrive at an agreement for entry of a plea of guilty in return for a particular sentence.... (4) ... While there continues to be nothing wrong with reducing a charge, reductions should not occur simply to obtain a plea of guilty. (5) Like any general rule, there are going to be some exceptions to this policy [which must be approved by the attorney general's office].

The new policy attacked plea bargaining in three ways: forbidding "sentence bargaining" and "charge bargaining," and establishing procedures for supervising plea negotiations. Gross's action was possible in part because of the special structure of Alaska's criminal justice system. Local prosecutors are appointed by and work under the supervision of the state attorney general. In other states, local prosecutors are elected and enjoy almost complete political and administrative independence.

What happened when Alaska banned plea bargaining? Contrary to popular expectations, the criminal courts did not collapse. The traditional defense of plea bargaining is that it is necessary to handle the heavy load of cases and that the courts will grind to a halt if it is abolished. The Alaska courts, however, continued to function pretty much as they had before. Additionally, there was little change in the rate of guilty pleas. Trials increased, from 6.7 to only 9.6 percent of all cases.[41]

Other dire predictions also did not come true in Alaska. Many experts argue that discretion cannot be eliminated and that attempts to abolish it only serve to move it to other parts of the justice system. Restricting a prosecutor's discretion to accept guilty pleas, according to this argument, will shift discretion "upstream" to police officers or "downstream" to judges.[42] Specifically, some experts believe that banning plea bargaining will give judges more discretion and lead to more sentence bargaining.

No radical shift in discretion occurred as a result of the ban in Alaska. One way to measure this effect is to examine the pattern of rejections and dismissals of cases. Some experts believe that if a prosecutor cannot settle cases by accepting pleas to lesser offenses, more cases will be dismissed altogether. The rate of dismissals in Alaska, however, remained consistently high: about 52 percent before and after the ban. Dismissals in drug possession and morals cases increased, but this seemed to be a function of the low priority prosecutors gave these cases rather than anything related to the ban on plea bargaining.[43]

One surprising result of the ban was that cases actually moved through the courts faster than before. The expectation had been that there would be more delays because of more trials and a greater backlog of cases. In Anchorage, the mean disposition time for felony cases was cut in half, dropping from 192.1 months to 89.5 months. Case processing time also dropped in Fairbanks and Juneau. We can explain this unexpected outcome. Restrictions on plea bargaining eliminate certain alternatives and uncertainties about which one to choose. With less to negotiate, the prosecutor and defense attorney reach agreements more quickly. Or to put it another way, the courtroom work group has a smaller menu to choose from.[44]

For our purposes, the most significant result was that the ban on plea bargaining had no impact on cases involving defendants charged with serious crimes or those with substantial criminal records. An evaluation concluded that "the conviction and sentencing of persons charged with serious crimes of violence such as murder, rape, robbery, and felonious assault appeared completely unaffected by the change in policy." In short, dangerous offenders had not been beating the system beforehand through plea bargaining (any more than they had in San Diego), and the ban did not change that.

The ban did, however, have an unexpected effect on less serious cases, and resulted in more severe sentences. This is another variation of the "bait and switch" problem. Our wedding cake model helps explain this process. Policies directed toward second-layer cases actually have their greatest impact on third-layer cases. As Zimring and Hawkins argue, "bait and switch" occurs when a new policy promises to deal with serious crime but ends up affecting mainly less serious ones.[45] Under normal circumstances, third-layer cases—low-level assaults or burglaries where little of value is stolen—are often settled with pleas to even lesser offenses and sentences of probation. A "get tough" policy, such as a ban on plea bargaining, however, closes off this avenue of mitigation and produces both convictions on more serious charges and harsher sentences than would normally be the case. Third-layer cases are moved into the second layer, where they are treated more harshly. The problem, of course, is that these third-layer cases were not the original target of the policy change, and there is no impact on serious crime.

From the standpoint of our inquiry, the important question is whether the Alaska ban on plea bargaining affected the crime rate. The evaluation did not examine this issue. Nonetheless, the mere fact that the ban had no real effect on the disposition of cases involving serious crimes suggests that it probably had no impact on the crime rate.

Reforming Plea Bargaining in King County, Washington

No one today seriously believes that you can "abolish" plea bargaining—or that you should even try. Similarly, no one seriously proposes abolishing police discretion, or completely eliminating all judicial discretion in sentencing (as some people proposed in the 1970s, with something called "flat time" sentencing.) Discretion is inevitable, and most experts acknowledge that it can serve some good purposes. The realistic approach to the problems associated with discretion is to regulate it with formal policies and procedures.[46]

Deidre M. Bowen examined a reformed system of plea bargaining in King County, Washington (Seattle), which included a structured process for handling cases, with some clear rules on plea negotiations and higher levels of supervision for attorneys. The new process uses a horizontal approach to prosecution, in which cases are initially handled by the Charging Unit and then passed to the Early Plea Unit (EPU). Cases that are not settled through a guilty plea are then handled by the Trial Unit. The main rules for plea negotiations are that plea negotiations are not available to any case that bypasses the EPU, that no plea negotiations should occur at trial, and that plea offers must be in writing. These changes eliminate the traditional informality of plea negotiations and, through the EPU (which, in practice, consisted of a single prosecutor at the time of the study), centralize negotiations and presumably make them more consistent.[47]

The net result was a high level of consistency in case processing. Seventy percent of cases were settled by the EPU. The court room work group, consistent with our discussion in Chapter 3, operated with a high degree of collegiality, cooperation, an understanding of the rules of the game. "Overwhelmingly," Bowen found in her interviews, members of the work group "took the view that they should work together to settle on the appropriate charge and punishment." Significantly, the facts of a case were rarely in dispute, and the work group called most of them "no brainers." In part, this was the result of a very conservative charging policy, in which charges were filed only on charges the attorneys felt they could win at trial. Overcharging, adding additional charges to be traded away in plea negotiations, was explicitly discouraged.

In practice, there were some adaptations to work about the rules. Trial attorneys were willing to negotiate pleas in some cases because of their workload, despite the rule on no negotiations at that point. Defense attorneys admitted they monitored the calendars of trial prosecutors for this reason. There were some opportunities for negotiating pleas with the supervising prosecutor (rather than the EPU), and this was mainly because of what Bowen terms "history:" a long-standing personal relationship" among members of the court room work group.

The implementation of a more formal process, with some clear rules, did not in the end make any significant changes in the handling of cases. There may have been greater efficiency because the rules were clear to everyone, and there was greater openness and less chance of misunderstanding because of the rules of the game. Higher levels of supervision, moreover, enhanced consistency among cases. It is likely that, as is the case with rule on police discretion and sentencing guidelines, formal rules eliminated the exceptional cases that really did depart from the norm and discredited the system.[48]

In Search of Plea Bargains

Plea bargaining has proven to be a phantom loophole. Despite the criticisms, it is not a device by which large numbers of serious offenders are beating the system. Attempts to abolish it either have no effect whatsoever or produce changes that are contrary to the intended result.

Our discussions of the criminal justice wedding cake (Chapter 2) and the role of the courtroom work group (Chapter 3) help explain why plea bargaining survives. As Malcolm Feeley suggests, we should think of the criminal courts as *supermarkets,* handling a high volume of business with fixed prices.[49] Once the work group reaches a consensus about the proper "going rate" for different kinds of cases, not much actual bargaining is necessary. A National Center for State Courts report characterizes this consensus as a shared "norm of proportionality" about the seriousness and worth of different cases.[50]

Virtually all of the studies of plea bargaining have found a high degree of regularity and predictability in the disposition of cases. One of the most systematic studies concluded that you can predict the outcome if you know the seriousness of the top charge and the defendant's prior record.[51]

Courtroom work groups have accommodated themselves to sentencing guideline laws. Many observers have feared that by restricting the discretion of judges, these laws would radically shift power to prosecutors and result in more charge bargaining and/or more trials. Studies of the impact of sentencing guideline jurisdictions, however, have found that most courtroom work groups conduct their business pretty much as before, with relatively little change.[52] This is but another example of both the enduring strength of routine plea bargaining practices and the power of the courtroom work group to accommodate major change.

SUMMARY

The evidence is overwhelming: Plea bargaining is not a loophole that lets many dangerous offenders beat the system. Therefore, we can safely conclude:

PROPOSITION 29
Abolishing plea bargaining will not reduce serious crime.

RESTRICT APPEALS

Conservatives believe that postconviction appeals undermine the criminal justice system in several ways. First, some offenders win and thereby escape punishment altogether. Second, appeals delay final resolution of a case and undermine the deterrent effect of the law. Deterrence theorists believe that punishment must be swift and certain for the deterrent effect to work. Third, appeals transform the criminal process into a "sporting contest," a game rather than a search for truth. Liberals, on the other hand, see the absence of finality as a virtue. Protection of individual rights requires recognition of the possibility of error in the criminal justice process.[53]

Years ago, Judge Macklin Fleming argued that granting numerous postconviction appeals represented a quixotic search for "perfect justice."[54] He listed 26 possible challenges available in California on search-and-seizure grounds alone, including moving for dismissal of all charges at the preliminary examination; appealing a denial of that motion to the state supreme court; moving to have the case transferred to federal court on grounds that federal civil rights had been violated; objecting to admission of the evidence at trial; if convicted, appealing for postconviction relief in the state supreme court; and if that failed, appealing the conviction in federal court.

Nor is this all. Fleming points out that "in almost every one of the foregoing steps the losing defendant can petition for a rehearing or reconsideration by the court that ruled against him."[55] Thus, innumerable potential challenges to a criminal charge can be made just on Fourth Amendment search-and-seizure issues. If these fail, many postconviction appeals are possible—for example, on grounds of inadequate assistance of counsel in violation of the Sixth Amendment. For the imaginative and determined offender, the possibilities are seemingly endless. As we shall see, however, the key word here is *seemingly*.

Limiting Appeals

Conservatives believe that limiting appeals will close a loophole that undermines the criminal justice system. The 1981 Attorney General's Task Force on Violent Crime recommended a three-year statute of limitations on habeas corpus petitions and a prohibition on federal courts' holding evidentiary hearings "on facts which were fully expounded and found in the state court proceeding."[56]

Habeas corpus is one of the cornerstones of Anglo-American law. The British Parliament formalized it with the Habeas Corpus Act of 1679, and Americans wrote it into the U.S. Constitution. Article III, Section 9, of the Constitution reads, "The privilege of the writ of habeas corpus shall not be suspended, unless when in case of rebellion or invasion the public safety may require it." The writ of habeas corpus is a device to challenge the detention of a person taken into custody. A person under arrest or in prison may demand an evidentiary hearing before a judge to examine the legality of the detention. The writ of habeas corpus is purely procedural: It guarantees only a right to a hearing and says nothing about the substance of the issues in the case.

The Supreme Court greatly expanded the ability of an offender convicted in a state court to obtain a rehearing in federal court in the 1963 decision *Fay v. Noia*.[57] One of the underlying issues here is the role of the Supreme Court in a federal system. Conservatives have long argued that the Court, particularly under Chief Justice Earl Warren, intruded into matters that should be left to the states and to legislatures. Liberals, on the other hand, saw the Court as the principal guardian of individual rights.

The Reality of Postconviction Appeals

In actual practice, postconviction appeals play a very minor role in the administration of criminal justice. A national study of 10,000 habeas corpus petitions filed in federal district courts by offenders challenging their convictions found that only 1 percent succeeded. Federal judges dismissed 63 percent (usually for failing to exhaust state remedies) and ruled against the offender on the merits of the case in 35 percent. The typical habeas corpus petition was filed by someone convicted of a violent offense (23 percent had been convicted of murder) and sentenced to a long prison term. The most frequent claim raised was ineffective assistance of counsel.[58]

How many convicted offenders "abuse" the right to appeal? The study found a rate of 14 habeas corpus petitions for every 1,000 prisoners—or only 1.4 percent of all imprisoned offenders. This figure confirms what we have already learned: that most convictions are obtained through plea bargains in which the facts of the case are not seriously contested. The study also found that the impact of habeas corpus petitions on the workload of the courts has been greatly exaggerated. These appeals represented only 4 percent of the civil case filings in U.S. District Courts.

In short, Macklin Fleming's nightmare vision of convicted offenders endlessly filing appeals on all of the theoretically possible issues is pure fantasy. Appeal of felony convictions through habeas corpus petitions is very much like the insanity defense: a procedure that raises a lot of fascinating legal issues but is rarely used in practice and rarely successful even when tried. There are two important exceptions to this rule. People on death row do exhaust every possible appeal, and appeals may drag on for 15 years or longer. The fact is that mistakes do occur with the death penalty. In early 2000, the governor of Illinois ordered a halt to all executions in the state because 13 people sentenced to die had their convictions overturned—as many as had actually been executed since the death penalty was restored in that state. The possibility that innocent people might be wrongfully executed dramatizes the importance of keeping open all possible avenues of appeal.

A second exception involves the "writ writers," prisoners who file innumerable appeals in federal court challenging their conviction or prison conditions. These individuals represent a tiny proportion of all inmates. The few who succeed in winning their release make a negligible contribution to the crime rate, even in the worst circumstances.

The available facts about the use of appeals do not support the conservative argument that multiple appeals contribute to crime. Conservatives argue that appeals delay "finality" and thereby undermine the deterrent effect of the criminal process. Several things are wrong with this argument. First, appeals are filed in so few cases that they cannot have any broad impact on criminal justice. Second, as we have also learned, many factors affect the deterrent effect (low probability of arrest, a relatively high probability of the charges being rejected or dismissed, whether the threat of punishment even works for certain categories of offenders, and so forth). Appeals are at best a very minor factor.

Like the insanity defense, postconviction appeals are mainly a *symbolic* issue. On occasion, a convicted offender is released through a successful appeal. But these are the few celebrated cases that do not represent the general pattern in the criminal justice system. Therefore, our proposition is:

PROPOSITION 30
Limiting habeas corpus appeals of criminal convictions will have no effect on serious crime.

CONCLUSION

We will not reduce serious crime by trying to close alleged loopholes in the criminal justice system. The reason for this is simple: Those loopholes do not exist. The idea that thousands of criminals beat the system through the insanity defense, plea bargaining, or appeals is a perception based in a very small number of unrepresentative celebrated cases. The justice system is actually fairly harsh in dealing with those serious offenders who are arrested.

NOTES

1. Dawn Beichner and Cassia Spohn, "Prosecutorial Charging Decisions in Sexual Assault Cases: Examining the Impact of a Specialized Prosecution Unit," *Criminal Justice Policy Review* 16 (December 2005): 461–498.

2. U.S. Department of Justice, *An Exemplary Project: Major Violator Unit—San Diego, California* (Washington, DC: Department of Justice, 1980).

3. Some examples are described in William F. McDonald, *Plea Bargaining: Critical Issues and Current Practices* (Washington, DC: Department of Justice, 1985).

4. McDonald, *Plea Bargaining*.

5. Bureau of Justice Statistics, *Felony Defendants in Large Urban Counties, 2004: Statistical Tables* (Washington, DC: Department of Justice, 2003), Table 25. NCJ 221152.

6. National Opinion Research Center, *General Social Surveys, 1972–2002*, cited in Bureau of Justice Statistics, *Sourcebook of Criminal Justice Statistics*, online edition, Table 2.47.

7. Jack Hinckley, *Breaking Points* (Grand Rapids, MI: Chosen Books, 1985).

8. Randy Borum and Solomon M. Fulero, "Empirical Research on the Insanity Defense and Attempted Reforms: Evidence Toward Informed Policy," *Law and Human Behavior*, 23 (no 1, 1999): 117–135.

9. Reported in Rita J. Simon and David E. Aaronson, *The Insanity Defense: A Critical Assessment of Law and Policy in the Post-Hinckley Era* (New York: Praeger, 1988), p. 166.

10. Simon and Aaronson, *Insanity Defense*, Table 3.2, p. 40.

11. Borum and Fulero, "Empirical Research on the Insanity Defense," p. 120.

12. Ibid., pp. 27–28.

13. American Psychiatric Association, *American Journal of Psychiatry* 140 (1983): 681–688.

14. Stuart M. Krischner and Gary J. Galperin, "Psychiatric Defenses in New York County: Pleas and Results," *Journal of the American Academy of Psychiatry and the Law* 29 (No. 2, 2001): 194–2001.

15. Valerie Hans, "An Analysis of Public Attitudes toward the Insanity Defense," *Criminology* 24 (May 1986): 393–414.

16. Jeffrey S. Janofsky, Mitchell H. Dunn, and Erik J. Ruskes, "Insanity Defense Pleas in Baltimore County: An Analysis of Outcome," *American Journal of Psychiatry*, 153.11 (1996): 1464–1468.

17. *Newsweek*, 24 May 1982.

18. For a good study of this subject, see Egon Bittner, "Police on Skid Row: A Study in Peacekeeping," *American Sociological Review* 32 (October 1967): 694–715.

19. *Rights of the Mentally Disabled: Statements and Standards*, rev. ed. (Arlington: American Psychiatric Publishing, 2002).

20. *Baxstrom v. Herold,* 383 U.S. 107 (1966).

21. Henry J. Steadman et al., *Before and After Hinckley* (New York: Guilford, 1993), pp. 58–61, 97–99.

22. Henry J. Steadman, *Beating a Rap? Defendants Found Incompetent to Stand Trial* (Chicago: University of Chicago Press, 1979), p. 104.

23. Terence P. Thornberry and Joseph E. Jacoby, *The Criminally Insane: A Community Follow-up of Mentally Ill Offenders* (Chicago: University of Chicago Press, 1979). For another study with similar results, see Henry J. Steadman and James J. Cacozza, *Careers of the Criminally Insane* (Lexington, MA: Lexington Books, 1974).

24. Borum and Fulero, "Empirical Research on the Insanity Defense," p. 121.

25. Norval Morris, *Madness and the Criminal Law* (Chicago: University of Chicago Press, 1982).

26. Ibid.

27. Ibid.

28. Grant H. Morris, *The Insanity Defense: A Blueprint for Legislative Change* (Lexington, MA: Lexington Books, 1974).

29. Bureau of Justice Statistics, *Mental Health Treatment in State Prisons, 2000* (Washington, DC: Department of Justice, 2001). NCJ 188215. *Prisoners Receiving Mental Health Treatment in State Correctional, by Region and State, June 30, 2000,* Bureau of Justice Statistics, *Sourcebook of Criminal Justice Statistics, on-line edition,* Table 6.73.

30. John Klofus and Ralph Weisheit, "Guilty but Mentally Ill: Reform of the Insanity Defense in Illinois," *Justice Quarterly* 4 (March 1987): 39–50.

31. Ibid.

32. Kurt M. Bumby, "Reviewing the Guilty but Mentally Ill Alternative: A Case of the Blind 'Pleading' the Blind," *Journal of Psychiatry and the Law* 21.2 (1993): 191–220.

33. Moran, "Insanity Defense," p. 81.

34. Ibid., pp. 77–78.

35. Borum and Fulero, "Empirical Research on the Insanity Defense," p. 133.

36. The most critical view of plea bargaining is Abraham Blumberg, *Criminal Justice: Issues and Ironies,* 2nd ed. (New York: New Viewpoints, 1979). The best recent study is McDonald, *Plea Bargaining.*

37. Bureau of Justice Statistics, *Felony Defendants in Large Urban Counties,* 2004. Yue Ma, "Prosecutorial Discretion and Plea Bargaining in the United States, France, Germany, and Italy: A Comparative Perspective," *International Criminal Justice Review* 12 (2002): 22–52.

38. On the "copout" ceremony, see Jonathan D. Casper, *American Criminal Justice: The Defendant's Perspective* (Englewood Cliffs, NJ: Prentice Hall, 1972), pp. 81–86.

39. National Advisory Commission on Criminal Justice Standards and Goals, *Courts* (Washington, DC: Government Printing Office, 1973), p. 46.

40. Michael L. Rubinstein, Stevens H. Clarke, and Teresa J. White, *Alaska Bans Plea Bargaining* (Washington, DC: Department of Justice, 1980).

41. Rubinstein et al., *Alaska Bans Plea Bargaining.*

42. Norval Morris and Gordon Hawkins, *Letter to the President on Crime Control* (Chicago: University of Chicago Press, 1977), p. 61.

43. Rubinstein et al., *Alaska Bans Plea Bargaining*.

44. This point is argued in Samuel Walker, *Taming the System: The Control of Discretion in Criminal Justice, 1950–1990* (New York: Oxford University Press, 1993), pp. 95–96.

45. Franklin E. Zimring and Gordon Hawkins, *Crime Is Not the Problem, Lethal Violence in America* (New York: Oxford University Press, 1997), p. 19.

46. Samuel Walker, *Taming the System: The Control of Discretion in American Criminal Justice*.

47. Diedre M. Bowen, "Calling Your Bluff: How Prosecutors and Defense Attorneys Adapt Plea Bargaining Strategies to Increased Formalization," *Justice Quarterly* 26 (March 2009): 2–29.

48. This point is argued in Walker, *Taming the System*.

49. Malcolm W. Feeley, "Perspectives on Plea Bargaining," *Law and Society Review* 13 (Winter 1979): 199.

50. Brian J. Ostrom and Roger A. Hanson, *Efficiency, Timeliness, and Quality: A New Perspective from Nine State Criminal Courts* (Williamsburg, VA: National Center for State Courts, 1999). Available on the National Center for State Courts website.

51. Peter F. Nardulli, James Eisenstein, and Roy B. Flemming, *The Tenor of Justice: Criminal Courts and the Guilty Plea Process* (Urbana: University of Illinois, 1988).

52. Bureau of Justice Assistance, *National Assessment of Structured Sentencing* (Washington, DC: Government Printing Office, 1996), pp. 98–100. NCJ 153853. Jeffrey T. Ulmer, *Social Worlds of Sentencing* (Albany: State University of New York Press, 1997).

53. Herbert Packer, "Two Models of the Criminal Process," in Packer, *The Limits of the Criminal Sanction* (Stanford, CA: Stanford University Press, 1968), pp. 149–173.

54. Macklin Fleming, *The Price of Perfect Justice* (New York: Basic Books, 1974).

55. Ibid.

56. U.S. Department of Justice, *Attorney General's Task Force on Violent Crime* (Washington, DC: Government Printing Office, 1981), p. 58.

57. *Fay v. Noia,* 372 U.S. 391 (1963).

58. Bureau of Justice Statistics, *Federal Habeas Corpus Review: Challenging State Court Criminal Convictions* (Washington, DC: Department of Justice, 1995). NCJ 155504. See also Victor E. Flango, *Habeas Corpus in State and Federal Courts* (Williamsburg, VA: National Center for State Courts, 1994).

PART III

The Middle Ground:
Guns and Victims

On one thing, conservatives and liberals agree: Guns are a major part of the crime problem. They disagree, however, on the exact nature of the problem and the solution to it. Liberals focus on guns and want to limit their availability. Conservatives focus on criminals who use guns and want to get tough with them. The policies each side recommends reflect their fundamentally different assumptions about crime and criminals. There is also a certain amount of agreement with respect to crime victims. Both sides support certain programs designed to assist victims. In this section we will examine policies directed toward the victims of crime, guns, and gun-related violence.

Protect Crime Victims

For many decades, in fact for hundreds of years, the crime victim was the forgotten person in the criminal justice system. Unless required to testify in court (and we know how few cases actually go to trial), victims typically received little if any follow-up from the police or prosecutors. They had no input into plea bargains, which they often did not know about or have a voice in, and no right to express their views to the judge about the sentence. In 1982, the chair of the President's Task Force on Victims of Crime declared: "The neglect of crime victims is a national disgrace."[1]

All that began to change in the 1970s. A new victims' rights movement arose with powerful political support, advocating new policies that would give victims certain formal legal rights, or provide direct assistance to them, or make other changes in the justice system designed to protect them. The Justice Department established the Office for Victims of Crime (OVC) in 1983 to provide a broad range of services and information. Over thirty states have amended their constitutions to include provisions related to crime victims, and all states have passed victims' rights laws. The OVC estimates that there are 27,000 victims' rights laws across the country.[2]

This chapter takes a look at the goals, achievements, and limitations of the victims' rights movement. What reforms have been proposed? Which ones have been adopted? Do victims' rights laws work? If so, which ones, and why? Were they good ideas in the first place? We will look at some policies that are intended to help crime victims, but actually interfere with real protection for them. And we will also look at some reforms that really have benefitted crime victims.

THE VICTIMS' RIGHTS MOVEMENT

In modern Anglo-American law, the crime victim has had no formal role in the criminal process. The prosecutor represents the public interest, including that of the victim. This is why, in some states, cases are formally titled "The People versus...." As an American Civil Liberties Union (ACLU) handbook on *The Rights of Crime Victims* explains, "The victim is not a formal party to a criminal proceeding."[3] In fact, as we will see shortly, in some states with victims' rights laws today, it is not clear that victims have legal standing to bring suits when they are denied one of those rights!

It was not always this way. Until the mid-nineteenth century, crime victims represented themselves, bringing their own cases before magistrates and judges. The office of the modern prosecutor gradually emerged in the nineteenth century, assuming the role of representing the public in general and crime victims in particular.[4]

Having a professional public official handle criminal cases serves several important purposes. First, it establishes the idea that a crime is an offense against society as a whole and not just an individual. Second, it removes the element of vengeance from the handling of a case. A public official is more likely to be free of anger and personal animosity toward the offender. The desire to keep emotionalism out of the criminal justice process explains why in two early cases on victim' rights laws the U.S. Supreme Court has ruled that victim impact statements at sentencing in death penalty cases are unconstitutional.[5] Third, professionals bring training and experience to the job, which increases the likelihood that justice will be done.

The victims' rights movement found fault with all parts of the criminal justice system: police and prosecutors did not inform victims about important events related to their cases, such as bail hearings or even trials; victims had no say in plea bargain agreements, sentencing, or parole decisions. An early survey found that in Alameda County, California (Oakland), only about 12 percent of victims had ever been notified that an arrest had been made in their case.[6]

Although conservatives have dominated the victims' rights movement, groups with other political perspectives have also advocated change. Feminists have helped to secure new laws and policies to protect the victims of domestic violence and rape, such as mandatory arrest laws for domestic violence, shelters for victims, and counseling programs for offenders. Mothers Against Drunk Driving (MADD) led a national anti–drunk driving crusade to protect the victims of drunk driving (see Chapter 6). Advocates of protecting children against sexual predators have fought for sex offender registration and notification laws (see Chapter 7). Even the ACLU, which vigorously opposes many victims' rights proposals as unconstitutional, published a handbook on *The Rights of Crime Victims* in 1985.[7]

New Laws and Programs

The victims' rights movement has been successful in achieving some of its legislative goals. By the early 1990s, every state had passed some kind of victims' rights law, and over 30 had amended their constitution to include some victims' rights. The 1990 Victims' Rights Amendment to the Arizona State Constitution is fairly typical of the changes across the county (see Box 9.1). Meanwhile, a

---

B o x 9.1   State of Arizona Constitution, Article 2, Section 2.1

A) To preserve and protect victims' rights to justice and due process, a victim of crime has a right:

1. To be treated with fairness, respect, and dignity, and to be free from intimidation, harassment, or abuse throughout the criminal justice process.
2. To be informed, upon request, when the accused or convicted person is released from custody or has escaped.
3. To be present at and, upon request, to be informed of all criminal proceedings where the defendant has the right to be present.
4. To be heard at any proceeding involving a post arrest release decision, a negotiated plea, and sentencing.
5. To refuse an interview, deposition, or other discovery request by the defendant, the defendant's attorney, or other person acting on behalf of the defendant.
6. To confer with the prosecution, after the crime against the victim has been charged, before trial or before any disposition of the case and to be informed of the disposition.
7. To read presentence reports relating to the crime against the victim when they are available to the defendant.
8. To receive prompt restitution from the person or persons convicted of the criminal conduct that caused the victim's loss or injury.
9. To be heard at any proceeding when any post conviction release from confinement is being considered.
10. To a speedy trial or disposition and prompt and final conclusion of the case after the conviction and sentence.
11. To have all rules governing criminal procedure and the admissibility of evidence in all criminal proceedings protect victims' rights and to have these rules be subject to amendment or repeal by the legislature to ensure the protection of these rights.
12. To be informed of victims' constitutional rights.

---

series of federal laws included the 1970 Crime Insurance Act, the 1982 Victim Witness Protection Act, the 1984 Victims of Crime Act, the 1984 Justice Assistance Act, the 1990 Victims' Rights and Restitution Act, and the 1994 Violent Crime Control Act.[8]

Critics of the Movement

The victims' rights movement has many critics. Civil libertarians in particular have criticized proposals to limit individual rights in the name of helping crime victims. The most sweeping criticism has been made by Robert Elias. In a series of books, he has argued that victims have been manipulated to serve a conservative political agenda, that most of the new victims' rights laws and policies have not provided much in the way of tangible help, and that many serious forms of victimization (workplace injuries, environmental pollution, unsafe products, and false advertising, among others) have been ignored despite their enormous toll in terms of peoples' health and costs to communities. As Elias sees it, the victims' rights movement has been largely an exercise in "symbolic politics" that leaves crime victims "victims still."[9]

Sorting Out the Issues

The victims' rights movement does not have a single agenda. Programs and services represent a variety of approaches. It is useful to divide them into three general categories.

Victims' Services.   One set of programs involves services for crime victims. The most important are financial compensation and counseling. Women's groups have led the fight for rape and domestic violence hotlines, counseling programs, and shelters.

Victims' Voice Laws.   A second group includes laws to enhance the role of victims in the criminal justice system, in particular to allow them to make a formal statement in court about bail setting or plea bargain agreements, or at sentencing or parole hearings.

Legal Standing for Crime Victims.   Even though every state has passed either victims' rights laws or a constitutional amendment, it is not clear in every state that a victim has legal standing to enforce his or her rights. Let's say, for example, that a state's victim's voice law gives the victim the right to express an opinion on the sentence, but the judge does not allow the victim to participate. How does the victim enforce his or her legal right? This is not a hypothetical situation. As we will see shortly, many crime victims are not informed of their rights under their state law. Several states have remedied that by specifically giving them standing. Arizona passed a law to implement its constitutional amendment (Box 9.1) giving victims the right to be represented by private counsel when their rights are involved. Maryland gave victims standing by statute. In other states, standing is implied but not expressly stated.[10]

"Get Tough on Crime" Laws.   A third group includes "get tough" ideas similar to ones which we have considered in other chapters. These include proposals to deny bail to dangerous offenders, close loopholes in the criminal justice system, and give longer prison sentences. They usually do not mention crime victims directly, but the underlying assumption is that getting tough on criminals will reduce the number of crime victims.

The six recommendations of the Attorney General's Task Force on Violent Crime listed in Figure 9.1 include three in the area of victims' services, one related to victims' voices, and two designed to get tough on crime.

Criteria for Evaluation

Four different criteria can be used to evaluate the various crime victims' programs and services.

Implementation.   The first issue, of course, is whether a law or policy is in fact being implemented or is likely to be implemented. As we have learned with other laws and policies so far in this book, the courtroom work group has

VI. Respecting the victim in the criminal justice process

19. Provide for hearing and considering the victims' perspective at sentencing and at any early release proceedings.

20. Provide victim-witness coordinators.

21. Provide for victim restitution and for adequate compensation and assistance for victims and witnesses.

22. Adopt evidentiary rules to protect victim-witnesses from courtroom intimidation and harassment.

23. Permit victims to require HIV testing before trial of persons charged with sex offenses.

24. Notify the victim of the status of criminal justice proceedings and of the release status of the offender.

FIGURE 9.1   Recommendations related to crime victims.

SOURCE: U.S. Department of Justice, Combating Violent Crime (Washington, DC: Government Printing Office, 1992), p. xii.

tremendous power to block or frustrate new policies if it upsets the established going rate. A 2009 report found that many court officials accommodate certain victims' rights laws only "when it is convenient or when they coincide with the justice system."[11]

Impact on Crime Victims.   A second issue is the impact of a crime victims' law on crime victims themselves. Does a particular law help them deal with the trauma of victimization, return to their normal lifestyle, and improve their evaluation of the criminal justice system?

Impact on the Criminal Justice System.   A third issue is whether laws and policies designed to help crime victims have undesirable effects on the criminal justice system. Many, for example, call for radical changes in constitutional law. Even if they might reduce crime or help victims, the cost to the justice system may be too great. Remember that our goal in this book is to find policies that are effective, practical, and sound.

Crime Reduction.   The fourth issue is the primary concern of this book: Do victims' rights laws help reduce serious crime? Some of the proposals we will examine may be sound, humane ideas that will genuinely help victims deal with their suffering. They should be supported for that reason. But the relevant question for us is whether they will reduce crime.

Special Populations of Crime Victims

The emphasis of the victims' rights movement has shifted over the years. Initially, it took a general approach, proposing reforms to benefit all crime victims. More recently, the emphasis is on special populations of crime victims. People with disabilities, for example, experience violent crime at a higher rate rather than people without disabilities, according to the NCVS, and are less likely to call the police.[12] Native Americans experience violent crime at twice the rate of the rest of the American population. The difference is in rates of robbery, assault, and sexual assault. The aggravated assault rate is 25 per 1,000, compared with 13 among African Americans and 8 among whites. The murder rate among Native Americans is the same as for the general population.[13]

Many changes have focused on women as victims of mainly rape and domestic violence. Some of the most important changes include rape shield laws, to prevent defense attorneys in rape cases from bringing up the victim's past sexual history, shelters for the victims of domestic violence, and mandatory arrest laws or policies that require the police to arrest in cases of domestic violence where there is a felonious assault.[14]

Although there is a lot of concern about elderly people as crime victims, they actually have the lowest violent crime victimization rate among all age groups. The rate for the 65 and older group, in fact, is dramatically lower than for the 50- to 54-year-old group (3.5 per 1,000 vs. 13.5, and 43.7 for 20- to 24-year-olds). Elder abuse, however, encompasses emotional and psychological abuse and forms of neglect that may not always rise to the level of crime. A special category of elderly crime victims, however, involves people in residential long-term care facilities. There are no reliable data on the rate of criminal abuse among this very vulnerable population, but the best study found that about 40 percent of a sample of residents reported being abused or seeing other residents abused, while 36 percent of a sample of staff members reported seeing physical abuse.[15]

Victim Assistance Programs

Perhaps the most popular victims' rights idea has been victim/witness assistance programs. By the late 1980s an estimated 4,000 such programs existed around the country. The 1984 Victims of Crime Act provides federal funds to local programs; in fiscal year 2007, that amounted to over $1 billion.[16]

Table 9.1 presents the range of services required by law in 2,282 prosecutors' offices in 1994. Note that the survey asked prosecutors only what services they were required to provide. It is not clear that all of these services were, in fact, provided. The survey found, for example, that some information, although required, was provided only upon the request of a victim.[17]

Victim/witness programs vary widely. Many provide emergency services in the form of shelter, security repair, financial assistance, and on-the-scene comfort. One national survey found that most provide follow-up counseling. Nearly all have some form of advocacy and support services, such as intervening with the victim's employer or landlord. Many help with insurance claims or efforts to obtain restitution. Nearly all provide court-related services concerned with the victim's role as witness for the prosecution, such as orienting victims or witnesses to court procedures, notifying them of court dates, providing transportation to court, escorting them at the court, and providing child care.

How well do these programs work? A survey of 62 victim service programs in North Carolina found that the state's 1986 Fair Treatment for Victims and Witnesses Act was meeting the needs of victims "only minimally."[18] Almost all of the programs were providing referral to social, restitution, and compensation

TABLE 9.1   Victim services that jurisdictions require prosecutors' offices to provide, 1994

		Percentage of offices		
		Full-time office (population served)		
Type of service	All offices	500,000 or more	Less than 500,000	Part-time office
Notification/alert				
Notify victim	82	87	85	73
Notify witness	55	67	59	42
Orientation/education				
Victim restitution assistance	60	62	62	55
Victim compensation procedures	58	73	65	41
Victim impact statement assistance	55	78	60	40
Orientation to court procedures	41	57	48	24
Public education	15	20	17	9
Escort				
Escort victim	23	39	28	9
Escort witness	17	31	19	9
Counseling/assistance				
Property return	38	46	39	35
Referral	32	46	37	18
Personal advocacy	17	26	22	5
Counseling	10	21	12	5
Crisis intervention	10	19	14	0
Number of offices	2,282	119	1,480	683

SOURCE: Bureau of Justice Statistics, *Prosecutors in State Courts, 1994* (Washington, DC: Government Printing Office, 1996), p. 9.

services; notification about court cases; and allowances for victim impact statements. Nonetheless, 59 percent of crime victims surveyed in the state expressed dissatisfaction with the criminal justice system. Particularly significant was the fact that about one-third were not even aware of their right to make a victim impact statement. This suggests that a major provision of the law was not being fully implemented. An evaluation concluded that the programs provided primarily *witness* assistance rather than *victim* assistance.

A national evaluation of victims' rights laws found that in many cases the laws were not fully implemented. Even in states with "strong" victims' rights laws, for example, 60 percent of victims were not given advance notice about offenders' pretrial release hearings, as required by law. Over 90 percent received notification about the arrest and trial date of the offender in these states, but compliance was much lower for all other stages in the criminal process.[19]

Looking at victim services from the perspective of our three criteria, we find very mixed results. Some victim services are delivered to some victims, and probably provide them with some relief. The impact on the justice system is uncertain. To the extent that services make people feel better about the system and less alienated, then they benefit the system. With one or two exceptions, victim services do not reduce crime, however. The major exception involves domestic violence shelters, which may in fact prevent immediate revictimization. We will discuss this issue again near the end of this chapter. Overall, we are led to the following proposition:

PROPOSITION 31

With the possible exception of domestic violence shelters, social service programs benefit crime victims but will not reduce serious crime.

Police/Victim Recontact

A slightly different service for crime victims is to provide more contact between them and the police. The President's Task Force on Victims of Crime recommended that police departments establish procedures for informing victims of violent crime about the status of the investigation of crimes.[20] Known as victim recontact programs, they are designed to overcome the problem of victims feeling alienated from the system because they never hear from the police.

Victim recontact is a sound and humane idea that is long overdue. There is absolutely no reason that the police should not keep victims informed and many reasons that they should. Mainly it would help build positive police/community relations. By 1997, about one-third of all city police departments and county sheriffs' departments had some kind of victim assistance program.[21] Meanwhile, almost all state prosecutors (93 percent) reported in 1990 that they informed victims of the outcome of cases. This compares with only 35 percent in 1974.[22]

Victim recontact may not deliver what its advocates expect, however. In one component of the Houston "fear reduction" experiment, police officers contacted crime victims to express sympathy and ask whether they needed any further assistance or information. An evaluation found that the program achieved none of its goals. Victims who were contacted did not express any less fear of crime or greater confidence in the police, compared with victims who were not contacted. Victims with poor English skills were actually more fearful than those who were not recontacted. They did not understand why the police were contacting them and became more fearful as a result.[23]

The Houston data suggest that perhaps victims' rights advocates have misinterpreted the victims' feelings about the criminal justice system. Many people may prefer just to be left alone. We should remember that according to the National Crime Victimization Survey, victims do not report 61 percent of all crimes. Many regard the crime as a private matter or say that it just was not important enough. In other words, even though something bad has happened to them, these people do not want any involvement with the criminal justice system. In other words, some people want to hear from the police—and they are the most vocal ones—but many people do not. It is important to remember and respect the variations in how people respond to criminal victimization.[24]

Protection Orders

A variation on police recontact involves court-issued protection orders forbidding an offender from having any contact with the victim. They are especially important in domestic violence incidents, where victims are often fearful of further violence. Protection orders are designed to both prevent repeat assaults and provide assurance and security to victims. Many people believe that they provide immediate relief for victims, whereas the criminal process is often very lengthy and has an uncertain outcome.

How effective are protection orders? An experiment in South Carolina compared proactive and reactive styles of enforcement. The standard approach is reactive enforcement: the police intervene only after the victim has reported a violation of the order. The experiment compared the standard, reactive enforcement style with proactive enforcement, where officials contacted both victims and offenders before any violation occurred. Over 400 misdemeanor domestic violence cases were randomly assigned to the two styles of enforcement. Proactive contact with victims was designed to educate them about the protection order, including how to recognize and document any violations. Meanwhile, officers also conducted surveillance of offenders.[25]

The results were very interesting, and tell us a lot about the difficulties of enforcing a seemingly simple law (contact known victims and offenders), and the behavior of both victims and offenders. Officers made an effort to contact 68 percent of the victims in the proactive enforcement group, compared with only 8 percent in the reactive group. Some effort was made to contact almost all offenders, but officers made actual contact (at least one) with only about 40 percent of them. Proactive enforcement made no difference on reoffending. Offenders in both the proactive and reactive groups were rearrested at about the same rate (approximately 39 percent). Proactive group offenders, however, were less likely to be rearrested for domestic violence.

There were particularly interesting patterns with regard to the victims. Proactive enforcement group victims were more likely to perceive that they were stalked or threatened by their offender. This may have been a product of the treatment: that they better understood the nature of the protection order and patterns of domestic violence. This could be counted as a successful outcome of the program. Proactive enforcement group victims were also more likely to be divorced or separated. This may reflect their greater efforts to end the relationship, and could also be counted as a successful outcome. Most interestingly, rates of contact with victims were very low. Out of over 400 cases, 28 refused to participate, 48 scheduled an interview but did not show up, and 10 did not complete interviews because of language barriers. As a result, there were only 141 completed interviews in the study, and 210 victims were never contacted at all. The study concluded that proactive enforcement "is not an effective means of increasing victim safety or reducing offender recidivism."

Looking at this program from the perspective of our three criteria, it appears that it had some impact on some of the victims (those who were more likely to report violations and/or end their relationship); had no apparent significant effect on the justice system; and most important from our perspective, did not reduce crime. The evidence leads us to the following proposition:

PROPOSITION 32
Victim recontact programs do not reduce crime.

Victim Compensation

The most popular victims' rights program involves financial compensation. California passed the first crime victims' compensation law in 1965, and today they exist in every state. The 1984 Victims of Crime Act provides federal financial support for state and local programs. Federal funds are derived from fines, assessments, and forfeitures (mainly bond forfeitures from failure to appear in court) from federal offenders. In fiscal year 2007, the fund received a record-breaking $1 billion from these sources. The money is then distributed to various victims' services programs. States are awarded up to 60 percent of the state funds they commit to victim compensation. Each state receives a base amount of $500,000, while public and private victims' services programs compete for additional funds. There are also OVC discretionary grants for demonstration projects, training, and technical assistance.[26]

Federal victim compensation funds totaled $431 million in fiscal year 2007. The majority, $251 million, went to victims of assault, including about 1.8 million victims of domestic violence. What is all this money used for? Half of all the money, $239 million, went to compensate people for medical expenses resulting from their victimization; $52 million went for funeral expenses; and $38 million went for mental health services.

Evaluations of victim compensation programs have not been overly favorable. Many requests are denied. The New York State Crime Victims Board denied as many as 60 percent of all requests in the late 1980s. The most common reason for denying claims is the failure to provide sufficient documentation.[27] Even more disturbing, according to William Doerner's study of Florida crime victims, is that those who did receive compensation did not have more favorable attitudes toward the criminal justice system than did victims whose claims were denied.[28] This failure to affect the attitudes of crime victims is one of the reasons that Robert Elias feels that the victims' rights movement is largely an exercise in symbolic politics.[29]

Despite some implementation problems, victim compensation is a worthy idea that is long overdue. The heavy toll that crime takes on people gives the government good reason to maintain some kind of insurance or compensation program. To the extent that compensation improves victims' attitudes toward the justice system, it benefits the system. Compensation, however, does not reduce crime, and is not intended to.

PROPOSITION 33

Victim compensation programs provide help for crime victims, but they do not reduce serious crime.

EXPANDING THE VICTIM'S VOICE

One of the major goals of the victims' rights movement has been to expand the role of victims in the criminal justice process, giving them a greater voice in bail decisions, plea bargains, sentencing, and parole release decisions. The President's Task Force on Victims of Crime recommended amending the Sixth Amendment to read: "Likewise, the victim in every criminal prosecution shall have the right to be present and to be heard at all critical stages of judicial proceedings."[30] Item #4 in the Victims' Rights Amendment to the Arizona State Constitution (Box 9.1) gives victims the right "To be heard at any proceeding involving a post arrest release decision, a negotiated plea, and sentencing."

The idea of expanding victims' voices has several goals. One is to give crime victims a feeling of participating in the justice system and to end their feelings of isolation and alienation. We should see this as a victim service program. Another goal is to ensure that offenders are properly punished and not allowed to get off too easily. The assumption is that the victim will object to a too-lenient plea bargain or sentence. We should regard this as a "get tough" program. Finally, giving victims a voice is consistent with the goals of procedural justice, which we will discuss in Chapter 12. Tom Tyler and other experts on this subject argue that people are more likely to have positive feelings about a process if they feel they have an opportunity to participate in it, to express their views (having a "voice"), and thereby have some control over the outcome. Greater satisfaction with the criminal process, Tyler argues, is likely to lead to greater trust in the justice system and lower levels of law breaking.[31]

Several states have enacted victims' voice laws. Proposition 8, adopted by California voters in 1982, provided that "the victim of any crime, or the next of kin of the victim … has the right to attend all sentencing proceedings … [and] to reasonably express his or her views concerning the crime, the person responsible, and the need for restitution."[32] The judge is required to take the victim's views into account in imposing sentence. The Office for Victims of Crime publishes a bulletin on *The Crime Victim's Right to be Present,* with current information on laws and procedures. A second bulletin covers victim input into plea agreements.[33]

Victim Notification.   The first step in giving victims a voice in any proceeding, of course, is to notify them about the proceeding itself. Most victims' rights laws include some specific requirement that they be notified of bail hearings, plea negotiations, sentencing, and release from custody, or some of those proceedings. Not all of the laws are clear on this point, however. Take another look at the Arizona Victims Rights Constitutional Amendment (Box 9.1). Item #2 specifically guarantees only a right "To be informed, upon request, when the accused or convicted person is released from custody or has escaped." Item #12 guarantees a right to be informed of their rights, but does not specify a right to be notified about other stages in the process (e.g., bail hearings, sentencing). In this situation, is it absolutely clear that officials have to notify victims about the date of a hearing? Or can they simply give victims a list of their rights and let them find out about dates of hearings on their own? Ambiguities of this sort undoubtedly result in much of the nonimplementation of victims' rights laws that have occurred.

Victims' Voice Laws: The Return of Vengeance?   Opponents of victims' voice laws fear that it brings vengeance (as opposed to justice) into the criminal process. One of the functions of a professional criminal justice bureaucracy is to ensure fair and impartial treatment of all accused persons. A professional is someone who is not emotionally involved in a case and acts impersonally on the basis of the facts and circumstances. A lawyer, for example, has a professional obligation to prosecute or defend a criminal defendant regardless of his or her personal feelings about the person or what he is accused of doing.

The Supreme Court has shared some of these fears about the danger of vengeance and emotionalism distorting the criminal process. In *Booth v. Maryland* (1987) and *South Carolina v. Gathers* (1989), the Court reversed death sentences because of statements read to the jury about the victim. In *Gathers,* for example, the prosecutor read from religious material that had been in the possession of a murder victim and also mentioned that he was a registered voter.[34] The Court ruled that this information was not related to the circumstances of the crime. Two years later, however, in *Payne v. Tennessee* (1991), the Court ruled that victim impact statements were not unconstitutional.[35]

The Impact of Victims' Voice Laws

There is very mixed evidence about the impact of victims' voice laws. On the one hand, many victims do not take advantage of the opportunities to participate in the process. Also, those who do are not always seeking severe punishment. Nonetheless, some evidence exists of harsher punishment for offenders in cases in which victims do in fact participate.

A national study found that among those victims who were notified about hearings (and many were not, as we have seen), over 90 percent chose to make an impact statement at sentencing. Participation was much lower for other stages in the criminal process, however. Less than 40 percent of those who were notified made a statement at bail hearings, and less than 20 percent chose to attend parole hearings.[36]

Does victim participation make a difference in the outcome? A study of 500 Ohio felony cases between June 1985 and January 1989 found several notable effects. First, victim impact statements (VISs) were submitted in about half

(55 percent) of all cases. Under the program, VIS staff solicited information from victims at the time of grand jury hearings. Only 18 percent of victims appeared at trial or sentencing, and only 6 percent exercised their right to speak. Victim participation was heavily influenced by the seriousness of the crime. VISs were filed in 73 percent of "aggravated or special felony" cases, including 81 percent of sexual offenses, but only 49 percent of property crime cases, and only 13 percent of those that were handled as misdemeanors. Somewhat surprisingly, 61 percent of male victims filed a VIS, compared with only 28 percent of females.[37]

Of those who did submit a VIS, 60 percent requested that the offender be incarcerated. Convicted offenders were somewhat more likely to be incarcerated if a VIS was filed or if the victim appeared in court or requested incarceration (but, surprisingly, not if the victim only spoke in court). Also, filing a VIS statement, appearing in court, and requesting incarceration were associated with longer prison terms. The overall impact of the VIS law was somewhat limited, however. Case outcomes were affected primarily by offense severity and offenders' prior record.[38]

An earlier study of sexual assault cases in Ohio found that 60 percent of the victims made statements at sentencing. This study concluded that the statements had little effect on sentencing. A high level of agreement was noted between the sentence the victim recommended and the sentence the judge considered appropriate.[39]

In Pennsylvania, however, a study found that victim impact statements had a very significant effect on the chances of an offender being paroled. The Pennsylvania Board of Probation and Parole denied parole in 43 percent of 100 cases in which there was some victim input but in only 7 percent of a comparable set of 100 cases in which there was no input.[40] These findings lend support to concerns about the possible undesirable effects of victim impact statements. Whether a victim makes a statement may be a matter of chance, and it means that one offender will serve longer than another who committed the same crime because of an arbitrary factor unrelated to the crimes they committed.

In any event, apart from the satisfaction that VIS may give to the victims themselves, no evidence indicates that they have any effect on serious crime. Some offenders may serve longer prison terms, but, as we have already seen, there is no evidence that they are any less likely to eventually recidivate.

The Problem of Implementation

One of the greatest problems with all victims' rights law is that they are simply not implemented at all. A 2009 report pointed out that since the 1970s, "victims' rights advocates have been dismayed to that, too often, victims' rights were violated with impunity." Often, they were simply never even informed of their rights or notified about the dates of court proceedings.[41] This is not entirely surprising. Remember, one of the main arguments of this book is that many changes in the criminal justice system are never fully implemented. As we argued in Chapter 3, the courtroom work group has an enormous capacity to frustrate significant changes.

The problem is illustrated by a comparison of two states with "strong" victims' rights laws and two with "weak" laws. Overall, the strong law states did a better job of notifying victims than the weak law states did, but even they often failed to fully comply with their laws. In the strong states, for example, less than 40 percent of victims were notified of the offender's pretrial release. This was better than the less than 30 percent rate in the weak states, but it nonetheless meant that more than 60 percent of victims were not notified. Victims were notified of plea negotiations at almost the same rate in the strong and weak states, but nonetheless in the strong states almost 45 percent were not notified.[42]

One solution to the lack of implementation has been to create victims' rights law clinics as advocates for victims. Some are associated with law schools and others housed in state agencies. A study of these clinics found that they engage in three main activities: (1) informally advising victims of their rights; (2) litigating certain issues to establish formal recognition of victims' rights, and (3) handling complex cases on appeal to establish broadly applicable case law affirming a particular right. The effectiveness of such clinics remains to be evaluated. But the mere fact that they have been created in the first place dramatizes the point that merely passing a law—in this case on victims' rights—does not guarantee that change is actually going to happen.[43]

PROPOSITION 34
Victim impact statements do not reduce crime.

SPEEDY TRIALS

Holding speedy trials is another popular victims' rights proposal. The underlying assumption appears to be that justice delayed is justice denied for the victim as well as the defendant. The irony is that the speedy trial has traditionally been seen as a defendants' rights issue, since the Sixth Amendment guarantees a speedy trial for the accused.

As we argued in Chapter 7, there is some evidence that speedy trials—that is, trials that are speedier than usual—could be an effective crime reduction policy. The likelihood that a defendant released on bail will commit another crime increases the longer he or she is out on release. Holding trials earlier would mean that a number of them would be tried, convicted, and imprisoned before they had time to commit another crime. In Chapter 7 we offered this as a reasonable alternative to preventive detention.[44] Even in the best of circumstances, however, we should not expect too much crime reduction here. As we have also learned, crimes committed by persons out on bail are a small proportion of the total.

Congress passed a federal speedy trial law in 1974 and several states have enacted their own laws. As we have already learned, however (Chapter 3), these laws have not worked as intended. Courtroom work groups frequently subvert the laws, often because attorneys on both sides have reasons for wanting to delay the case.[45] In short, it is not true that everyone wants a speedy trial or that holding a speedy trial is in the best interest of crime victims.

GETTING TOUGH ON CRIME: HELPING VICTIMS
THE WRONG WAY AND THE RIGHT WAY

Many victims' rights proposals are essentially designed to "get tough on crime." The President's Task Force on Victims of Crime, for example, recommended legislation "to abolish the exclusionary rule," "to abolish parole," to permit hearsay evidence at preliminary hearings, and to authorize preventive detention.[46] Few of these proposals address crime victims directly. The underlying assumption is that locking up more offenders will reduce crime and therefore result in fewer crime victims.

We have considered many of these proposals in other chapters. Our conclusion has been that they will not reduce serious crime. In Chapter 5, we found that repealing the exclusionary rule or the *Miranda* warning will not reduce crime. In Chapter 7, we found that limiting the right to bail through preventive detention is not likely to reduce violent crime. If these policies do not reduce crime, then they do nothing to help crime victims. In Chapter 11, we will examine whether abolishing parole would have any effect on crime.

Equally dangerous is the President's Task Force recommendation that hearsay evidence should be admissible at preliminary hearings. The idea is that this will protect the victim from the trauma of testifying in person. Relaxing the established rules of evidence to permit hearsay testimony at any stage in the criminal justice process sets a dangerous precedent. Allowing it only at preliminary hearings, moreover, is silly and misleading. It will be of little help in convicting the offender if it is inadmissible at trial.[47]

In Chapter 7 we learned how one set of laws designed to protect the victims of child kidnapping and sexual assault—sex offender notification and registration and residency restrictions laws—not only do not actually protect potential victims but make it difficult for officials to supervise and control the few really dangerous offenders.

Sex offender registration and notification laws cover a wide range of criminal acts, many of them consensual, such as sex between a 19-year-old male and a 16-year-old girl. The result is that agencies in charge of registration are overloaded with cases. This leaves them with little time and resources for potential predators. Officials all across the country simply don't know where the registered sex offenders actually are. By trying to do too much, these laws result in too little being done. Residency restrictions in many cases force offenders to live away from their homes and families, separating them from the people who are most likely to help them establish law-abiding lives. The stigma of being a registered sex offender, moreover, inhibits social reintegration.[48]

All of these problems are related to the issues we discussed in Chapter 1. The resource crisis in criminal justice is only aggravated when we overload the system with many noncritical cases—in this case, the numerous registered sex offenders who are not really predators. And recall again the horrific Garrido case in California. He was a registered sex offender. How could the parole officers in charge of his case not notice that something was terribly wrong? Were they simply overloaded with cases? When we overload the system, it is less able to operate effectively to prevent crime and to monitor ex-offenders in the community, and thus increase the risk of new victimizations.

A far more effective approach to protecting victims and potential victims is to develop narrowly tailored, intelligence-driven programs that focus on the few potentially high-risk recidivists. A surgical instrument, not a shotgun, in other words. We have already seen evidence of how such programs can operate successfully. The problem-oriented policing (POP) programs directed toward high rate offenders which we discussed in Chapters 5 and 6 are good examples. As we concluded, because they deliver a deterrence message to a very specific and limited target audience, they are more effective than deterrence messages delivered to the general population. Identifying that limited target audience is part of an intelligence-driven effort: employing a sophisticated data base to identify the right people. Such programs target offenders with a high risk of reoffending, do not overload the system with low-risk cases, and as a result provide real protection for potential crime victims.

Sex offender registration and notification and residency restriction laws are all based on the belief that strangers are the major threat. Abundant data, however, indicate that most kidnappings and sexual abuses of children are perpetrated by family members or acquaintances. Go back to Chapter 7 and review our discussion on this. In short, these "get tough" laws are not only too powerful for the job, but are directed at the wrong target.

This leads us to the following conclusion:

PROPOSITION 35
Policies intended to get tough on crime will not reduce crime or help crime victims, and may instead damage the criminal justice system.

Improving the Response to Domestic Violence

The issue of domestic violence has undergone a revolution in public policy in the last 30 to 40 years. Our point here is that most of these changes provide genuine protection for victims of this crime.

The changes include police department mandatory arrest policies for domestic violence (about 91 percent of all local police departments have some written policy on arrest for domestic violence), special prosecutors' policies or programs to ensure full prosecution of domestic violence cases, and new sentencing laws that raise the penalties for domestic violence. Equally important are various services for the victims of domestic violence: protection orders (see our discussion above), temporary shelters for victims and their families, crisis hot lines, and counseling programs for both victims and abusers. The laws and availability of

Illustration by Frank Irwin, © Wadsworth, Cengage Learning.

programs vary from state to state and locality. To give one example, a 2008 report found that 22 states and the District of Columbia had mandatory arrest laws;
another 6 had arrest-preferred laws, and 11 had laws guiding officer arrest
discretion.[49]

Put all of these changes together, and even allowing for nonimplementation
or nonenforcement, we have a genuine revolution in public policy. The Office
for Victims of Crime, as we pointed out earlier, spends a considerable amount of
its funds on domestic violence programs, with services going to about 1.8 million
victims each year in fiscal years 2007 and 2008—the largest single category of
crime victims. Federal funds assisted shelters or safe houses for about 400,000
victims each year. The point is that these involve real services to real victims of
crime, not symbolic changes that have no real impact, or supposedly "get tough"
laws that may actually interfere with effective crime control.

CONCLUSION

The victims' rights movement is one of the more significant developments in
recent criminal justice history. Thirty-five years ago, there was little concern
about crime victims and few programs to assist them. Today new crime victim
laws and programs are found in every jurisdiction.

Some of these laws and programs are good ideas, providing valuable assistance to people who have been harmed by crime. Some have not been fully
implemented, however. Some of the others are positively dangerous, undermining important constitutional principles and likely to damage the justice system.
Most important for our purposes, none of the programs we have discussed is
likely to have any impact on serious crime.

NOTES

1. President's Task Force on Victims of Crime, *Final Report* (Washington, DC: Government Printing Office, 1982), p. vii.

2. Office for Victims of Crime, *Putting Victims First: 2009 OVC Report to the Nation* (Washington, DC: Department of Justice, 2009). Available on the website of the Office for Victims of Crime. www.ojp.usdoj.gov/ovc/.

3. James H. Stark and Howard Goldstein, *The Rights of Crime Victims* (New York: Bantam, 1985), p. 19.

4. Allen Steinberg, *The Transformation of Criminal Justice: Philadelphia, 1800–1880* (Chapel Hill: University of North Carolina Press, 1989).

5. *South Carolina v. Gathers,* 490 U.S. 805 (1989). *Payne v. Tennessee,* 501 U.S. 808 (1991).

6. R. Lynch, "Improving Treatment of Victims: Some Guides for Action," in William McDonald, ed., *Criminal Justice and the Victim* (Beverly Hills, CA: Sage, 1976), pp. 165–176.

7. Stark and Goldstein, *Rights of Crime Victims.*

8. Emilio C. Viano, "The Recognition and Implementation of Victims' Rights in the United States: Developments and Achievements," in E. C. Viano, ed., *The Victimology Handbook: Research Findings, Treatment, and Public Policy* (New York: Garland, 1990). Dean G. Kilpatrick, David Beatty, and Susan Smith Howley, *The Rights of Crime Victims—Does Legal Protection Make a Difference?* (Washington, DC: Department of Justice, 1998). NCJ 173839.

9. Robert Elias, *Victims Still: The Political Manipulation of Crime Victims* (Newbury Park, CA: Sage, 1993). *The Politics of Victimization: Victims, Victimology and Human Rights* (New York: Oxford University Press, 1990). *Victims of the System* (New Brunswick, NJ: Transaction, 1984).

10. Robert C. Davis, James Anderson, Julie Whitman, and Susan Howley, *Finally Getting Victims Their Due: A Process Evaluation of the NCVLI Victims' Rights Clinics* (Washington, DC: Department of Justice, 2009).

11. Ibid.

12. Bureau of Justice Statistics, *Crime Against People with Disabilities, 2007* (Washington, DC: Department of Justice, 2009). NCJ 227814.

13. Bureau of Justice Statistics, *American Indians and Crime* (Washington, DC: Department of Justice, 2004). NCJ 203097.

14. Cassia Spohn and Julie Horney, *Rape Law Reform: A Grassroots Revolution and its Impact* (New York: Plenum Press, 1992).

15. Bureau of Justice Statistics, *Criminal Victimization, 2008* (Washington, DC: Department of Justice, 2009), Table 4.NCJ 227777. Catherine Hawes, Testimony, U.S. Senate, Elder Abuse in Residential Long-Term Care Facilities, June 18, 2002. Available on the National Center on Elder Abuse website (under Reports and Studies). www.ncea.aoa.gov.

16. Bureau of Justice Statistics, *Law Enforcement Management and Administrative Statistics, 1997* (Washington, DC: Government Printing Office, 1999), p. xix.

17. Bureau of Justice Statistics, *Prosecutors in State Courts, 1994* (Washington, DC: Department of Justice, 1996), p. 9. NCJ 145319.

18. Jerin et al., "Victim Service or Self Service," p. 152.

19. Kilpatrick et al., *The Rights of Crime Victims*, p. 5.

20. President's Task Force on Victims of Crime, *Final Report*.

21. Bureau of Justice Statistics, *Law Enforcement Management and Administrative Statistics, 1997*, p. xix.

22. Bureau of Justice Statistics, *Prosecutors in State Courts, 2001* (Washington, DC: Department of Justice, 2002). NCJ 193441.

23. Lee P. Brown and Mary Ann Wycoff, "Policing Houston: Reducing Fear and Improving Service," *Crime and Delinquency* 33 (January 1986): 71–89.

24. Bureau of Justice Statistics, *Criminal Victimization, 2008*.

25. Robert Brame, Catherine Kaukinen, Angela R. Gover, and Pamela Lattimore, *Impact of Proactive Enforcement of No-Contact Orders on Victim Safety and Repeat Victimization* (Washington, DC: Department of Justice, 2009).

26. Office for Victims of Crime, *Putting Victims First: 2009 OVC Report to the Nation*.

27. Andrew Karmen, *Crime Victims: An Introduction to Victimology*, 2d ed. (Pacific Grove, CA: Brooks/Cole, 1990), p. 321.

28. William Doerner, "The Impact of Crime Compensation on Victim Attitudes toward the Criminal Justice System," *Victimology* 5.2 (1980): 61–77.

29. Elias, *Victims Still*, p. 42.

30. President's Task Force on Victims of Crime, *Final Report*, p. 114.

31. Tom R. Tyler, *Why People Obey the Law* (New Haven: Yale University Press, 1990).

32. Edwin Villmoare and Virginia V. Neto, *Victim Appearances at Sentencing under California's Victims' Bill of Rights* (Washington, DC: Government Printing Office, 1987); Candace McCoy, *Politics and Plea Bargaining: Victims' Rights in California* (Philadelphia: University of Pennsylvania Press, 1993).

33. These and other bulletins can be found on the Office for Victims of Crime website.

34. *South Carolina v. Gathers*, 490 U.S. 805 (1989); *Booth v. Maryland*, 482 U.S. 496 (1987).

35. *Payne v. Tennessee*.

36. Kilpatrick et al., *The Rights of Crime Victims*, p. 6.

37. Edna Erez and Pamela Tontodonato, "The Effect of Victim Participation in Sentencing on Sentence Outcome," *Criminology* 28.3 (1990): 451–474.

38. Ibid.

39. Anthony Walsh, "Placebo Justice: Victim Recommendations and Offender Sentences in Sexual Assault Cases," *Journal of Criminal Law and Criminology* 77 (Winter 1986): 1126–1141.

40. William H. Parsonage, Frances Bernat, and Jacquelin Helfgott, "Victim Impact Testimony and Pennsylvania's Parole Decision Making Process: A Pilot Study," *Criminal Justice Policy Review* 6.3 (1994): 187–206.

41. Davis, et al., *Finally Getting Victims Their Due*.

42. Ibid.

43. Ibid.

44. Bureau of Justice Statistics, *Pretrial Release of Felony Defendants, 1992* (Washington, DC: Department of Justice, 1994).

45. Malcolm Feeley, *Court Reform on Trial* (New York: Basic Books, 1982).

46. President's Task Force on Victims of Crime, *Final Report,* pp. 17–18.

47. Cassia Spohn and Julie Horney, *Rape Law Reform.*

48. Human Rights Watch, *No Easy Answers: Sex Offender Laws in the U.S.* (New York: Human Rights Watch, 2007).

49. David Hirschel, *Domestic Violence Arrest Cases: What Research Shows About Arrest and Dual Arrest Rates* (August 25, 2008). Bureau of Justice Statistics, *Local Police Departments 2000* (Washington, DC: Department of Justice, 2004), Table 58. NCJ 196002.

10

Control Gun Crimes

THE PROBLEM WITH GUNS—AND GUN POLICY

Illustration by Frank Irwin, © Wadsworth, Cengage Learning.

Firearms, especially handguns, are arguably the most serious part of America's crime problem, and certainly the most deeply divisive issue among Americans. Even after the Great Crime Decline, firearms are associated with about 30,000 annual gun deaths annually. This adds up to $2.3 billion a year in medical costs for Americans, of which taxpayers pay $1.1 billion. In 2008 there were 9,484 firearm homicides in the United States, 6,755 involving handguns. Additionally, handguns were used in 38 percent of all robberies, according to the FBI. In 2005 there were 17,002 firearms suicides, more than half of all suicides.[1] Guns take a special toll among African Americans. In 2005 homicide was the leading cause of death among African American men between the ages of 15 and 34, accounting for almost half of the deaths among teenagers (15 to 19 years old). Guns were the leading cause of those murders.[2]

Handguns are a special part of the unique American crime problem. As Franklin Zimring and Gordon Hawkins argue, our problem is not simply crime, but lethal violence. International victimization surveys have consistently found that many other countries have higher rates of property crime—theft and burglary. In America, it is deadly violence, with handguns at center stage.[3]

Americans are very deeply divided—polarized, you might say—over what to do about guns. One side wants fewer guns, or at least greater restrictions on who can buy and own a gun; the other side wants more guns in the hands of law-abiding people and believes that the Second Amendment guarantees "the right of the people to keep and bear Arms." When asked in 2007 which policy is more important, 55 percent said controlling gun ownership, while 42 percent said protecting the right to own a gun.[4]

The Supreme Court Weighs In

The U.S. Supreme Court ruled on the gun issue in 2008 with a landmark decision ruling a District of Columbia gun control law unconstitutional, affirming for the first time a right to own guns: "In sum, we hold that the District's ban on handgun possession in the home violates the Second Amendment, as does its prohibition against rendering any lawful firearm in the home operable for the purpose of immediate self-defense." The *District of Columbia v. Heller* decision threw the gun debate into disarray, introducing a whole new set of questions.[5]

What exactly does the *Heller* decision mean? Are all gun control laws unconstitutional? Does absolutely everyone have a constitutional right to own a gun, including ex-felons and people with a history of mental health problems? The Second Amendment protects the right to "keep and bear arms." What, exactly, does "arms" include? Machine guns? A military howitzer is an "arm." Can people own them, too?

It turns out that the *Heller* decision was a lot less radical than it might appear. The Supreme Court itself answered the more alarming questions. Justice Antonin Scalia's opinion for the Court explicitly stated that the Second Amendment right was "not unlimited." It does not include "any weapon," or prohibitions against ex-felons and mentally ill people owning guns, or restrictions on carrying concealed weapons in public, or in "sensitive" public places such as schools and government facilities, or other restrictions on the sale of firearms. The dominant theme of Scalia's opinion was the right to own guns for self-defense.

In short, most existing gun laws restricting the sale, purchase, ownership, and right to carry are undoubtedly still constitutional after *Heller*. Nonetheless, the full impact of the decision on a wide range of gun polices—and ultimately on gun violence—is still uncertain.

SORTING OUT THE ISSUES

Because the debate over guns is so emotional, with passionate feelings on both sides, and a lot of misunderstanding and incorrect information, it is important to begin by identifying the various issues involved.

Policy Options

The policy options regarding guns and gun violence can be conveniently divided into two broad categories: supply reduction and demand reduction. As we will discover in Chapter 13, the same categories reappear regarding drug policy.[6]

Supply reduction sees guns as the problem, and seeks to reduce their availability: by banning guns, or at least some kinds of guns, or restricting who can own them. Demand reduction focuses on gun offenders, and seeks to reduce the demand for guns through tough enforcement: e.g., mandatory prison terms, long prison terms, etc. This combines deterrence and incapacitation strategies that we discussed in Chapters 6 and 7. The two positions do share some common ground. Everyone wants to prohibit people with criminal records or mental health problems from legally purchasing and owning guns. Some policies do not fit conveniently into either category. Pro-gun advocates support "right to carry" laws which allow citizens to carry concealed weapons in public. This is really a deterrence-oriented self-protection approach to crime.

What Firearms Are We Talking About?

Because there is often much confusion about what weapons are involved, it is important to clarify our terminology. The data are often misleading because it is not clear whether particular figures refer to all weapons or just handguns. The basic categories are the following:

- Weapons. This includes firearms, knives, hands and fists, poisons, etc. In short, anything that can inflict injury or death.
- Firearms. This includes handguns, rifles, shotguns, automatic weapons, etc.
- Handguns. This includes only handguns, regardless of size or firepower, including automatic pistols with large capacity magazines. It excludes "long guns" such as rifles and shotguns. The so-called "Saturday night special" is one kind of handgun—small, easily concealed, and cheap. Assault weapons, meanwhile, are rifles or pistols that are capable of rapid-fire action.

The distinctions among weapons are extremely important because virtually everyone agrees that handguns are the problem. They represent 96 percent of the firearms used in robberies (note: firearms, not weapons). True, rifles and shotguns are used, including in some of the horrific mass murder incidents, but such events are really very rare. Shotguns accounted for 444 homicides in 2008, and rifles 375. As we have stated, handguns are the problem with regard to crime, and that will be our focus.[7]

RECENT TRENDS—AND THE POLICY DEBATE

There is bad news and good news about guns and crime in America. First, the bad news. As Table 10.1 indicates, the United States stands alone in terms of the number of people killed each year by handguns.

The good news is that gun violence declined dramatically in the 1990s as part of the Great Crime Drop. Firearms-related homicides, for example, fell from 17,035 in 1993 to 9,484 in 2008. The use of firearms in nonfatal crimes (e.g., robberies) also declined sharply from 1993 to 2004 and then turned upward again (see Figure 10.1). Most of this reduction involved handgun-related homicides among 18- to 24-year-old men. Still, gun violence is a major problem, and it sets the American crime problem apart from that of other countries.[8]

Two policy questions concern us. First, what accounts for the high level of gun-related violent crime in the United States? Too many guns, as liberals argue, or a system that fails to punish criminals who use guns, as conservatives allege? Does this sound familiar? It should, because the alternatives parallel debates we have already considered in this book, and will consider in the remaining chapters. Second, what policies are effective, or are likely to be effective, in reducing gun-related violence?[9]

Public Attitudes About Guns and Gun Violence

Americans are deeply and passionately divided on the "hot button" issue of guns. In 2007, 55 percent of Americans said controlling gun ownership was the most important issue, while 42 percent said it was protecting the right to have a gun. Interestingly, only 3 percent did not have an opinion; clearly, this is an issue American people care about.[10] Part of the reason for Americans' deep interest is that firearms ownership is fairly widespread, and therefore proposals to restrict gun ownership directly affect a large number of people.

It is often reported that a majority of Americans favor gun control. This statement is only partly true. When some people say they favor "gun control," they may mean only restrictions on the purchase of guns by certain people, such as ex-offenders or the mentally ill, and not a complete ban on gun ownership.

T A B L E   10.1   An international perspective: People murdered by guns, 2006

18	Austria
27	Australia
59	England and Wales
60	Spain
190	Canada
194	Germany
10,177	United States

SOURCE: Brady Campaign Against Gun Violence. www.bradycampaign.org.

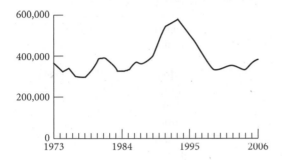

FIGURE 10.1 Trends in firearms-related crime, 1973–2006.

SOURCE: Bureau of Justice Statistics, National Crime Victimization Survey.

Or, they may mean tough penalties for criminals who use guns. It depends on which gun control policy you are referring to. In 2008, only 29 percent of Americans favored banning possession of handguns (and that was down from 43 percent in 1991). Half of Americans (50 percent) favored a ban on the manufacture, sale, and possession of assault weapons in 2004. The overwhelming majority (80 percent) favored requiring a police permit for purchasing a gun, and about the same percentage supported a five-day waiting period for a gun purchase. Similar majorities supported mandatory gun safety training and designing guns so they cannot be fired by children. Finally, large majorities favor tough criminal penalties: 78 percent support doubling prison terms for crimes committed with a gun.[11]

GUN OWNERSHIP AND GUN-RELATED VIOLENCE

Gun Ownership

The international Small Arms Survey estimates that there are 270 million firearms in circulation in the United States, or 90 for every 100 people. This includes about 97 million handguns. Additionally, about 1.5 to 2 million new handguns are manufactured or imported every year, replacing those that break or are lost or seized.[12] It is important to keep these 97 million handguns in mind throughout our discussion. They are out there, and they aren't going to disappear. Many are bought and sold on the black market every year. Any effective gun control policy has to take them into account.

Despite the tremendous increase in the total number of firearms, the percentage of households with some kind of firearm has declined significantly in recent years, falling from 52 percent in 1972 to 42 percent in 2008 (back up from an all-time low of 36 percent in 1999). People are most likely to own a rifle or shotgun; about 50 to 60 percent of those with a firearm have a handgun.[14] Men are more likely to own guns than are women, and whites are more likely than are African American. The most important variable is region:

B o x 10.1   Blowback: The Export Guns—Import Crime Problem

One new and alarming feature of the American gun problem is the "blowback" of violent crime by Mexican drug cartels. ("Blowback" is a term that originated with the CIA, and refers to unintended consequences of an action that are harmful to the country that took that action.) A 2007 Congressional Relations Service report identified six major cartels that have engaged in a radically escalating campaign of violence in Mexico. In addition to shooting each other in turf wars over control of drug trafficking, cartel enforcers have killed police officers and kidnapped individual citizens for ransom. Much of this violence is perpetrated with automatic weapons purchased in the U.S. One report found that 90 percent of the seized cartel guns that could be traced had originated in the U.S. The Mexican gun violence has spilled over the border into the U.S., with Mexican drug dealers using the deadly weapons they purchased in the U.S. on American soil. Gun control advocates argue that our lax controls over firearms first exported the problem to Mexico and have now brought it home to the U.S.[13]

People in the southeastern United States are the most likely to own a handgun, in large part because the region is predominantly rural and has a strong tradition of hunting. Handgun ownership is lowest in the urbanized Northeast. Data from the National Opinion Research Center's General Social Survey indicate that gun ownership is highly correlated with people "who are members of social groups where gun ownership is the norm."[15]

Handgun-Related Violence

The facts about handgun violence in the United States are grisly. In 2008, 20 percent of all violent crimes in the NCVS survey involved a weapon; about a third of those, or 7 percent of all violent crimes, involved firearms, most of which were handguns. According to the FBI UCR data, 38 percent of all robberies involved a firearm; the NCVS estimates it at 24 percent of all robberies in 2008. (As we pointed out in Chapter 1, the UCR and the NCVS use different methodologies and generally have different data on particular issues.)[16] The NCVS data do not include murder, so we need to add in the 6,755 murders committed with a handgun in 2008 (about half of the 14,160 murders). In addition, two-thirds of all police officers feloniously killed in the line of duty are slain by handguns. Finally, 413 of the 517 workplace homicides (80 percent) involved a shooting (including all firearms).

GUN-RELATED LAWS

It is a myth that the United States has no laws designed to control gun-related crime. In fact, we have numerous federal, state, and local laws on guns. They fall into the broad categories we have already mentioned. One group of laws seeks to limit the supply of guns, by banning them altogether, or outlawing their manufacture or importation, or banning certain kinds of weapons, or restricting who can purchase and own guns. Another group of laws is directed toward the criminal use of guns, but restricting purchase and ownership, or imposing harsh punishment for the illegal ownership or use of guns. The best source on this issue is BATF's annual compilation of *State Laws and Published Ordinances* (available on its website).[17] Our question, as it is in every chapter of this book, is whether particular laws are effective in accomplishing their purpose.

The federal system in the U.S. creates a special problem that other countries do not have. Each of the 50 states has its own laws, and some are far more restrictive than other states' laws. The result is that someone can easily buy a handgun in a state with weak laws governing sale and carry it to a state with very restrictive laws. There is considerable interstate trafficking in guns. A congressional report issued in 1997 found that many guns sold in Virginia, Florida, South Carolina, Georgia, and Texas—states with some of the weakest laws—ended up being seized in other states. In one report, the BATF identified 1,234 guns sold in Florida that were later used by criminals in other states, including 181 in New York.[18]

BAN HANDGUNS

The most extreme gun control proposal is to ban handguns. The idea of "banning" handguns actually consists of several different policies: outlawing possession, outlawing bullets, prohibiting the manufacture and sale of handguns, and banning only "Saturday night specials" or assault weapons.

Ban Possession

A few cities have actually banned the possession of handguns. Their experience gives us some idea of what this approach can and cannot accomplish. The District of Columbia banned the purchase, sale, transfer, and possession of all handguns in 1975. It exempted handguns and long guns previously registered under a 1968 gun registration law. In 2008, in a landmark decision, the Supreme Court held the law an unconstitutional violation of the Second Amendment.

Regardless of the Supreme Court decision, it is useful to examine the effectiveness of the DC law while it was in effect. The nation's capital represents a tough test of banning handguns because it is a major city with a lot of violent crime and a lot of guns on the streets. The U.S. Conference of Mayors, a leading gun control advocate, claimed that the law was responsible for a "significant reduction in both firearm and handgun crime." Other analysts, however, believe that the mayors' report was flawed and inconclusive. Edward Jones found that comparable cities experienced even greater reductions in gun-related crime during the same period, without the benefit of gun control. Jones conceded that the law may have made some contribution to reducing handgun crime, but it was impossible to argue that it was the only or even the most important cause.[19]

Murder trends in Washington over the last 35 years cast doubt on the effectiveness of the 1975 law. Murders declined significantly in the late 1970s and early 1980s, reaching a low of 147 in 1985. Then they skyrocketed to 482 by 1991, mainly as a result of the crack cocaine epidemic. Clearly, young men in Washington who wanted to obtain a handgun had little trouble getting one. Murders then declined again to 239 in 2000 and 169 in 2006, before rising slightly to 186 in 2008. These fluctuations reflected, in part, national patterns in violent crime. After an exhaustive review of all studies of the DC handgun ban, the National Academy of Sciences found "no conclusive evidence" regarding the impact of the law. In the Supreme Court case, briefs on each side presented evidence to support their case. (Find the briefs on the Web to see how each side used social science evidence to support its case.)[20]

The Limits of Banning Handguns

The Washington, DC, experience illustrates the limits of attempting to outlaw possession of handguns. The main problem is the 97 million handguns that already exist. No one has offered a realistic plan for how they might be removed from circulation. As law professor John Kaplan once pointed out, crusaders who seek to outlaw a product (alcohol, drugs, guns) always focus on the alleged dangers of the item and spend "little time and energy" estimating the costs of enforcement and the likelihood of effectiveness.[21]

A sizable black market in handguns and other weapons already exists. Surveys consistently indicate that criminals often obtain their guns through the illegal firearms market. Over half of arrestees in one study (55 percent) reported that guns were easy to obtain: More than a third (37 percent) said that they could obtain one in less than a week, and 20 percent said that they could get one in a day or less. Thirteen percent said that they had stolen a gun at some point in their life. A complete federal ban on handgun possession would probably foster the growth of the black market, just as the prohibition of alcohol (1920–1933) stimulated the growth of organized crime. We will discuss the consequences of attempting to outlaw certain products—alcohol, guns, drugs—in more detail in Chapter 13.

One problem with the DC law is our federal system, which we have mentioned earlier. The nation's capital is surrounded with states that have weak gun laws, particularly Virginia. Thus, it is easy to acquire guns—legally or illegally—and bring them into the District. As a result, many gun control advocates argue that any truly effective attempt to ban ownership of guns would require a federal law. No strong support for such a law exists at present, however. Also, it is safe to predict that millions of gun owners would refuse to turn in their weapons. Not only do about 20 percent of all American households currently have handguns, but many of those people fiercely believe that they have a constitutional right under the Second Amendment to own those weapons, and the Supreme Court has upheld that right. (Go to the National Rifle Association website for its views on this issue.) A federal ban would create a situation resembling Prohibition in the 1920s, when tens of millions of people drank alcoholic beverages despite a constitutional amendment prohibiting them. Any attempt to enforce such a ban would inevitably require highly intrusive measures by the police. Many right-wing groups already express intense hostility toward the BATF, and a federal ban would only inflame the situation further.

Ban the Manufacture and Importation of Handguns

Another way to reduce the availability of handguns in the United States is to outlaw their manufacture and importation. This approach is designed to dry up the supply of handguns over the long run. In practice, however, it would only stimulate an international black market like the one that already dominates the drug trade. Also, it has been estimated that the current supply of 97 million handguns is enough to last for the next hundred years.[22]

Buy Back Handguns

Another supply reduction strategy involves gun buy-back programs, where law enforcement agencies buy back handguns for cash or discount coupons. St. Louis conducted two buy-back programs, bringing in 7,500 guns in 1991 and another 1,200 in 1994. Richard Rosenfeld evaluated the program and found "little evidence" of any impact on gun assaults or homicides in the city. An evaluation of a buy-back program in Seattle also failed to find any reduction in crime.[23]

Trying to put a more optimistic interpretation on his findings, Rosenfeld argues that buy-back programs are more likely to be effective in achieving other goals such as strengthening community bonds and building support for community leadership and that they should be evaluated on those terms.

Buy-back programs have serious limitations. The available supply of guns is so huge that it is probably impossible to significantly reduce the number in any community. Many guns are turned in by people who are among the least likely to commit a gun crime (e.g., the elderly). Many simply want to dispose of an unwanted weapon. In St. Louis, 62 percent of those turning in a gun retained another weapon in the home. In short, there is no evidence that buy-back programs reduce crime.

The National Academy of Sciences has concluded that the theory underlying buy-back programs is flawed in three ways. First, the guns that are turned in are those least likely to be used in crime. Second, replacement guns can be easily obtained. Third, the likelihood of any one gun being used in a crime is very low (it based this conclusion on the estimates of 70 million guns; 6,500 handgun homicides in 1999).[24]

Ban "Saturday Night Specials"

A compromise strategy for banning handguns advocated by some liberals is to outlaw only the so-called "Saturday night specials."[25] The BATF defines the special as a gun of 0.32 caliber or less, with a barrel less than 3 inches in length and priced at $50 or less. In 1996, Los Angeles became the fourteenth city in the United States (along with the state of Maryland) to outlaw the sale of specials, specifically prohibiting 23 different weapons.[26] Advocates of outlawing the specials believe that these weapons are favored by criminals because of their price and concealability.

Outlawing only Saturday night specials probably will not accomplish what many people predict. The role of the specials in crime has been greatly exaggerated. Gary Kleck found that far from being the "preferred" weapon of criminals, they represent only between 10 and 27 percent of all handguns used in crime. Banning only the specials might produce a *substitution effect,* in which criminals simply move up to a larger weapon. Kleck further argues that specials are the primary self-defense weapon for low-income people. Banning them would deprive poor people, who are victimized by violent crimes more than middle-class people, of one of their principal means of self-protection.[27]

The proposal to ban only the Saturday night specials is essentially a political copout. It allows people to appear to be doing something about the gun problem without directly threatening most gun owners. The same can be said about the proposal to ban cop-killer bullets, which some people proposed in the past: It focuses on a small part of the problem, one that has high symbolic power, while avoiding the hard questions associated with the real problem.

Ban Assault Weapons

The rise of gang-related violence in the 1980s aroused public concern about so-called assault weapons. There was much publicity about gangs being heavily armed with Uzis, AK-47s, and similar weapons. The term *assault weapon* generally refers to "semiautomatic firearms with a large magazine of ammunition that [are] designed and configured for rapid fire and combat use."[28] They can be pistols, rifles, or shotguns. The BATF estimated in 1993 that about 1 percent of the 200 million guns in private hands were assault weapons. Many people want to ban them because they are not legitimate hunting weapons and have no purpose other than killing people. In the 1999 national opinion survey, 66.6 percent supported a ban on "all high capacity ammunition magazines."[29] The 1994 Violent Crime Control Act outlawed the manufacture and sale of 19 specific types of assault weapons for a period of 10 years. The ban expired in 2004.

Evaluations found that, at best, the ban had only a limited impact on gun crimes. One study estimated that assault weapons were used in only 2 to 8 percent of gun crimes before the ban, while large capacity magazines, which were also banned, were used in between 14 to 26 percent of gun crimes. The Brady Center, a leading gun control group, estimated that the ban produced a 66 percent drop in the use of assault weapons, reducing the usage rate to 1.1 percent. A study by Koper and Roth, however, concluded that the law may have contributed to the decline in gun violence, but that estimating the actual effect is extremely difficult because of a variety of methodological problems with this particular kind of crime.[30] In any event, the Violence Prevention Center argued that the gun industry undermined the law by producing weapons with only minor changes that technically complied with the law.

As with Saturday night specials, the importance of assault weapons has been greatly exaggerated. Kleck points out that the ordinary handgun remains the gun of choice among robbers. Virtually all of the police officers feloniously killed are killed with handguns. In short, although extremely deadly, assault weapons are not the real problem in gun-related crimes. The 1994 ban expired in 2004. Bills to reinstate it were introduced in Congress in 2007 and 2008, but were not acted on.

Summary

All of the policies designed to eliminate the possession of handguns or certain types of guns run up against the same basic problems: Millions of these weapons already are in circulation (including 70 million handguns), there is no practical plan for eliminating them, a black market already exists, and any kind of ban would only foster the growth of the black market. This leads us to the following conclusion:

PROPOSITION 36
Attempts to ban handguns, or certain kinds of guns, are not likely to reduce serious crime.

REGULATE THE SALE AND POSSESSION OF HANDGUNS

The basic American strategy for controlling handguns is to regulate their sale, purchase, and ownership. Innumerable federal, state, and local laws are designed to keep handguns out of the hands of convicted offenders, people with a history of mental illness, and juveniles. This is essentially a "bad person" strategy. The 1993 Brady Law requires a five-day waiting period so that a background check can be conducted on applicants. The 1994 Youth Handgun Safety Act outlaws possession of handguns by juveniles and the private sale or transfer of a handgun to a juvenile. The 1996 Lautenberg Amendment, meanwhile, outlaws gun ownership by anyone convicted of a domestic violence crime. The law has enormous implications for police officers and members of the military who must use weapons as part of their jobs.

Regulate Gun Dealers

Another strategy involves regulating gun dealers. Federal law requires all commercial gun dealers, including pawn shops, to obtain a federal license to sell guns. In 1992 there were about 284,000 federally licensed gun dealers (referred to as FFLs, for federal firearms licensees). Many of these were individuals, however, and one BATF survey found that 46 percent had sold no guns in the previous year. A series of reports found that many FFLs failed to comply with various federal regulations. Additionally, data indicated that a very small number of "problem" dealers were responsible for a very high percentage of guns used in crime. The BATF traced half of all seized guns back to less than 1 percent (0.4 percent) of all the licensed dealers.[31]

Beginning in 1993 a new set of laws and policies tightened up the regulation of FFLs (higher license fees; a requirement that they submit photographs and fingerprints of gun buyers; that they report gun thefts within 48 hours, etc.). As a result, the number of FFLs dropped to 109,000 by 2007. Many were people or businesses that had a license but did not really sell many guns. An evaluation by Christopher Koper found that the new regulations did eliminate a large number of problem FFLs, but it is not clear that this had a direct impact on gun-related crime. The changes occurred during the great crime drop (see Chapter 1) and may have contributed in some marginal way to that decline.[32]

Background Checks: The Brady Law

The 1994 Brady Handgun Violence Prevention Act requires background checks and a one-week waiting period for all handgun purchasers. The law forced 32 states to adopt new procedures; the others already had similar laws. The law specifically prohibits certain classes of people from purchasing handguns: convicted felons, people with mental disabilities, and known drug addicts. In 1996 the Lautenberg Amendment prohibited persons with domestic violence convictions, including even misdemeanors, from owning guns. This had serious potential implications for police officers and military personnel for whom carrying a gun is part of the job.

Did the law prevent crime by keeping guns out of the wrong hands? The administration of President Bill Clinton, which sponsored the law, cited that 2.2 percent of all gun purchase applicants were rejected under the law; this involved 66,000 would-be gun buyers in 2001. Between 1994 and 2008 a total of 1.8 million purchases were blocked by the law. Over half (56 percent) were rejected because of a felony conviction, and another 13 percent involved fugitives from justice. Cook and Ludwig compared violent crime trends in the 32 Brady states (the experimental "treatment" group) with those in the 18 states unaffected by the law (the "control" group). They found no significant differences in crime trends.[33]

The gun black market is a major issue affecting all current or proposed gun policies. Mark H. Moore estimates that between 500,000 and 750,000 gun transactions take place between private individuals every year.[34] Many of these do not involve active or potential criminals: They are sales or gifts between friends, family members, gun collectors, and hunters. But many do involve illegal sales among active criminals. James D. Wright found that only one-sixth of all gun-using felons acquired their guns through legal, retail transactions. Half had stolen a gun at one time or another. Additionally, almost 600,000 firearms are stolen from private homes every year, and as many as 300,000 are stolen from or lost by gun dealers. By definition, these guns go directly into the hands of people (thieves) who are barred from owning them.[35]

A Bureau of Justice Statistics report on gun use by criminals supports the idea that regulations on the commercial sales of guns can be easily evaded. It found that 14.2 percent of first-time offenders in prison purchased their weapon from a retail store, compared with only 6 percent of recidivists. Thirty-one percent of the first-time offenders got their weapon from an illegal source, while

42 percent of the recidivists did. Two points are important here. First, the number of offenders who obtained their weapon from a regulated retail outlet is extremely small. Second, people with criminal records readily shift to illegal sources.[36]

The Brady Law also stumbles over some serious problems with official criminal history data. Offenders whose records do not show up in the files will not be rejected. Some other people are incorrectly listed as having a criminal record (through mistaken identity, data that were entered inaccurately, mistakes that were not expunged, and so forth). There is also the problem of the "straw purchaser," someone who can legally purchase a firearm but then resells them to people who are ineligible under local law. In one Pennsylvania case, for example, one straw purchaser bought 26 guns in nine months, reselling them for money and drugs. He bought 15 of those guns at one store. This highlights a related problem: some gun dealers are known to be "easy," not carefully checking on whether purchasers are eligible.[37]

The mentally disturbed gun buyer represents an even more serious problem. A study by Congress estimated that the NCIS listed only 20 percent of the people who had been involuntarily committed to a hospital for mental health problems, or 402,000 people out of an estimated 2.7 million. Additionally, 18 states had not reported any mental health data at all to the NCIS. The most glaring and tragic example of this failure is the case of Cho Seung-Hui, the Virginia Tech student who shot and killed 32 students and faculty on campus (before killing himself) in 2007. A Virginia court had declared him a danger to himself, making him ineligible to own a gun, but the state did not forward his name to the NCIS.[38] There is no national data file of people with mental health problems—and some serious civil liberties questions exist about whether we would want such a file. What is meant by having a history of mental illness? Being hospitalized? That covers only a small number of people with problems. What about people who were treated by a private physician or counselor? Requiring these professionals to report all of their clients would be a serious invasion of privacy. And what level of seriousness would trigger the ban on gun ownership? Mild depression? That covers a lot of people. And of course millions of people with serious mental health problems never see a doctor or counselor.

Strong vs. Weak State Gun Regulations

As we pointed out in Chapter 1, the American criminal justice system is complicated by our federal system of government, with separate laws in each state. This factor has special relevance for gun violence, as some states have much less restrictive gun sale laws than do other states. A report by the group Mayors Against Illegal Guns used BATF trace data to identify the origin of guns seized in crimes, and then correlated that data with state gun laws. It found that 10 states supply interstate crime guns at a rate that is two and a half times the national average, and that these 10 states have comparatively weak gun laws. An effective national strategy is extremely difficult, if not impossible, given the patchwork quilt system of varying laws that result from our federal system.[39]

SUMMARY

For all of the same reasons that banning ownership of handguns seems futile, regulations designed to deny ownership to certain categories of "bad" people are not likely to succeed. Seventy million handguns are in existence, there is an active, thriving black market in guns, and criminals themselves say that they have or would have no trouble quickly obtaining a weapon. People intent on committing a crime are particularly motivated to obtain a gun. In short, it is not very efficient or sensible to try to control ownership of guns by the public at large when the real problem is the behavior of a very small part of the population—violent criminals.[40]

PROPOSITION 37
Attempts to deny ownership of handguns to certain categories of "bad" people are not likely to reduce serious crime.

GETTING GUNS OFF THE STREET: THE KANSAS CITY GUN EXPERIMENT

The most innovative recent approach to reducing gun crimes is the Kansas City Gun Experiment. The experiment involved intensive enforcement of existing laws on the illegal carrying of handguns. Funded by the federal Weed and Seed program, it represents a combination of two important innovations in policing: *problem-oriented policing,* in which the police focus on a specific problem, and *hot spots,* in which patrols focus on a particular area (see Chapter 5).[41]

The experiment was conducted in a particularly high crime precinct in Kansas City, Missouri, where the 1991 murder rate was 177 per 100,000, or about 20 times higher than the national average. Two two-officer patrol cars, working overtime, patrolled for six hours every night, concentrating exclusively on detecting and seizing illegally possessed guns. The officers would stop cars on legitimate legal grounds (for example, a traffic violation) but focus on weapons seizures. Almost half (45 percent) of all the guns eventually seized were found through a search incident to arrest, another 21 percent were found in plain view, and 34 percent were found in frisks as authorized by the Supreme Court in the 1968 *Terry* decision.

Over the course of 29 weeks, the gun unit officers seized a total of 29 guns. Meanwhile, regular patrol officers in the target beat seized another 47 guns, for a combined total of 76. The number of gun crimes in the target beat declined by 49 percent, but only by 4 percent in a control beat. The experiment controlled for a possible displacement effect and found that gun crimes went up in some of the neighboring beats and down in others. The reduction in gun crimes could have occurred as a direct result of removing guns from the area, or through deterrence, or through the incapacitation of potential offenders who were arrested and imprisoned.

The Kansas City Gun Experiment seems to suggest that a clearly focused program to remove guns from the streets can reduce gun-related crime. A number of questions about the program remain, however. It is extremely expensive when measured in terms of the cost per gun seized or crime prevented. It is not clear that a police department could afford to run such a program as a part of normal operations. Also, when Sherman replicated the program in Indianapolis, some serious questions were raised about the data and some of the claims made for its success. Other problem-oriented policing programs we discuss in this book seem very promising, but questions remain about the ones designed to get guns off the streets.[42]

Airports and Schools: Keeping Guns Away from Special Locations

Another approach to reducing gun violence in particularly sensitive locations is to ban guns from airports and schools. Airports are particularly important because of the danger of plane highjacking. Keeping guns out of schools, of course, is intended to protect children.

Airports. A federal law prohibits the carrying of a weapon onto an airplane, and all passengers are electronically screened at the gate. The electronic screening at airports makes enforcement fairly effective. In 2008 the Transportation Security Administration (TSA) seized 833 firearms at airports. This was only a small fraction of the over 13 million prohibited items seized, including a million and a half knives. This was about half the average seized in pre–9/11 years, so the publicity about the tighter security procedures did have some effect. Still, some people just didn't get it. On Thanksgiving weekend in 2002, for example, despite all the publicity about the new post–9/11 security procedures, airport personnel seized 15,982 pocket knives, 98 box cutters, six guns, and a brick.[43] Many of the people detained in these seizures apparently forgot that they had a gun with them. This testifies to the prevalence of guns in American society, the casualness with which they are carried around, and the limited deterrent effect of a well-known law. Nonetheless, the law has been effective in curbing airplane hijacking. The number of hijackings decreased from 40 in 1969 to only one attempted hijacking each in both 1990 and 1991, and none in either of the next two years. The 9/11 terrorist highjackings, of course, did not involve guns, but there was a failure to detect the box cutters used by the terrorists.[44]

The strategy of preventing airplane hijackings by prohibiting guns on planes is consistent with the place-oriented approach discussed by the University of Maryland *Preventing Crime* report.[45] The antihijacking effort appears to have been successful, but there are serious limits on its application to other areas of society. An airport is a special location: it is a confined space that involves a very small number of people, all of whom can be channeled through a metal detector. It is not clear how this strategy can be applied to society at large for the purpose of reducing ordinary robbery and burglary.

Schools.   Guns in schools are another special case. Because of a series of sensational crimes—the 1999 massacre in Littleton, Colorado, and several other highly publicized incidents—there has been great national concern about guns and violence in public schools. Several strategies have been adopted to keep guns out of schools. The 1994 Gun-Free Schools Act requires schools receiving federal education funds to have a policy mandating the expulsion of students who bring firearms to school. Some schools have instituted metal detectors similar to those used at airports.

The evidence, however, indicates that this is yet another example of the celebrated case phenomenon discussed in Chapter 2. In 2007 6 percent of American students in grades 9 through 12 reported bringing a weapon onto school property in the past 30 days (the survey does not identify the type of weapon, so we don't know what percentage were handguns). This was down by half (12 percent) in 1993. There were 19 homicides in schools in the academic year 2005–2006 and 27 in 2006–2007. This was a slight increase over the low of 13 in 1999–2000, but lower than the average of 30 or more through the 1990s. While guns in schools are indeed a problem, the data clearly indicate that there is no national epidemic of gun violence, and certainly no upsurge of school homicides.[46]

The reasons for the decline in gun incidents in schools are not clear, but one development is the adoption of a range of new school security measures. Between 1999 and 2006 the percentage of schools with one or more selected security measures more than doubled, from 19 to 43 percent. The five most widely used measures are controlled access to schools during school hours (in place in 85 percent of all schools), controlled access to the entire school grounds (41 percent), required IDs for all faculty and staff (48 percent), security cameras (43 percent), and random dog sniffs to detect drugs (23 percent).[47] The lesson seems to be that a range of reasonable and well-designed measures can make a significant difference. This parallels the lesson we discussed on traffic fatalities in Chapter 6. The fatality rate has gone down steadily since the 1920s not because of a single "get tough" measure, but because of a variety of changes, all of which make incremental contributions to the overall effect.

SUMMARY

The safest conclusion at this point is that the gun seizure approach may prove to be an effective strategy for reducing gun-related violence, but more research is needed.

PROPOSITION 38
Focused, proactive enforcement strategies related to special locations
can be effective in reducing gun-related crime in those areas.

MORE GUNS? RIGHT-TO-CARRY LAWS

Many gun owners believe that the best way to reduce crime and protect law-abiding citizens is to have more guns on the street. About 40 states have adopted "shall issue" laws, which require officials to issue permits to citizens who meet certain eligibility criteria allowing them to carry concealed handguns. These laws have replaced discretionary "may issue" laws, which give officials broad authority to deny permits. Advocates of these laws argue that they will deter crime by allowing potential victims to fend off assailants. Opponents counter by arguing that increasing the number of guns on the streets will only result in more gun violence, as carriers will be more likely to use them impulsively, especially in arguments that would not otherwise escalate to that point.[48]

In a highly controversial study, John R. Lott, Jr. and David B. Mustard estimated that if states without "shall issue" (i.e., right-to-carry) laws adopted them, it would prevent about 1,570 murders, 4,177 rapes, and over 60,000 aggravated assaults every year. Lott followed up with a book, *More Guns, Less Crime,* elaborating his argument that allowing people to carry concealed weapons would deter violent crime.[49]

Because of its direct implications for public policy, and the deep divide in public opinion over whether we should have fewer or more guns, Lott's work generated enormous controversy and further research. By 2005 there were an estimated 15 studies reanalyzing the original Lott and Mustard data. In addition, there have been studies using different data sets and methodologies. The result of this intensive research effort is inconclusive. About half (eight) of the reanalyses of Lott and Mustard generally confirmed their findings, while five found no effect on violent crime rates, and three found increases in violent crime. Other studies have also found conflicting results. The National Academy of Sciences undertook its own study and devoted an entire chapter of its report on guns to the issue, concluding that studies were highly sensitive to the model and to the control variables that were employed. This appears to be an inherent problem in all longitudinal studies that use many variables from different jurisdictions. Relevant variables that are often not included in such studies are local changes in the market for crack cocaine or other drugs, changes in the level of gang activity, and so on. Several studies have found that for some unknown reason, Florida has a powerful effect on studies that compare it with other states or in national studies. In some instances, including or excluding Florida reverses the findings. In the end, the National Academy concluded that it was not possible to determine a causal link between right-to-carry laws and the crime rate.[50]

PROPOSITION 39

The evidence is very mixed regarding the impact of right-to-carry laws on crime.

Handguns as Self-Protection

The underlying assumption in Lott's argument is that people will successfully use their guns to defend themselves against criminals. What is the evidence on this? The National Academy of Sciences found wildly varying estimates of the number of defensive gun use incidents per year. One survey estimated 116,000 incidents a year, while one gun owners' rights group currently claims that 2,375,349 lives were saved in 2009 alone because potential victims had guns to protect themselves.[51] The 2.3 million figure is certainly an exaggeration and a misuse of data.

Whatever the number of confrontations in which a potential victim had a gun, it is by no means certain that they all would have been killed. Think of a burglar who breaks in and is chased off by a gun-wielding home owner. Few burglaries involve murders. Analyzing data from the *National Crime Victimization Survey* from 1979 to 1985, Gary Kleck and Miriam DeLone found that robbery victims used a gun to resist the offender in only 1.2 percent of all robberies (this figure included both completed and attempted robberies). Very few of these incidents involved a shootout between victim and offender. Nonetheless, Kleck and DeLone argued that when victims did use guns, they were frequently successful in preventing a completed robbery. In short, victims use them in the same way that armed criminals do: to intimidate the other person.[52]

Most of those arrestees who carry a weapon say they do so for protection or self-defense. The result is a self-perpetuating gun culture. As more juveniles carry guns, their peers feel the need to carry one also for self-protection. As James D. Wright explains, these individuals "live in a very hostile and violent environment, and many of them have come to believe, no doubt correctly, that their ability to survive in that environment depends critically on being adequately armed."[53] They are "highly motivated gun owners who are not easily persuaded that they should not have one."

GET TOUGH ON WEAPONS OFFENSES

The primary conservative policy on gun-related crimes is to get tough on offenders convicted of using guns. This approach reflects two basic conservative assumptions about crime and the criminal justice system: first, that criminals and not guns commit crimes; and second, that the criminal justice system is soft on crime and criminals. The basic policy recommendation calls for mandatory prison terms for gun-related crimes and longer prison terms. Such laws are extremely popular. In 1994, 41 states had mandatory minimum sentencing laws for illegal weapons possession.[54] A 1975 Florida law is typical of those in other states. It imposed a mandatory minimum sentence of three years in prison for use of a weapon in the commission of certain crimes and prohibited the granting of certain types of good-time credit during the mandatory minimum period.

National data indicate that, contrary to widespread belief, the criminal justice system is not soft on gun-related crimes. In 2004, 84 percent of all persons convicted of a weapons offense in state courts were incarcerated—the same figure as for robbery. For those sentenced to prison, the average sentence was 43 months (about three and a half years). These data again confirm the point we have emphasized throughout this book, that the criminal justice system is fairly harsh on serious crimes.[55]

Getting Tough in Detroit: An Early Experiment

In 1977 Michigan passed a law mandating two years in prison for any gun-related crime. The law precluded either probation or parole and was advertised as "One with a gun gets you two." At the same time, the Wayne County (Detroit) prosecutor announced a new policy prohibiting plea bargaining of gun charges under the new law.

An evaluation by Colin Loftin and David McDowall focused on two questions: Did the law increase the certainty and severity of punishment? Did it lower the crime rate? The key issue in regard to the severity of sentences concerned the effective minimum prison terms, that is, how much time could a convicted offender reasonably expect to serve before becoming eligible for release, when reductions for both good time and parole were taken into account? They found "no statistically significant change in the expected minimum sentence" for gun-related murders and armed robberies, but a significant increase in the expected minimum sentences for gun-related assaults.[56]

Two factors—the going rate and the trickle-up phenomenon—explain what happened in Detroit. The expected minimum sentences for murder and robbery did not increase, because the going rate for these crimes was already high. Armed robbers in Detroit had been serving prison terms averaging six years before the new law, and few convicted robbers ever got probation. The system was not soft on crime beforehand, and the supposed get tough law did not change things.

Sentences for assaults increased because the going rate for those offenses had been rather low. Probation and suspended sentences were common, and incarcerated offenders got an average of six months. Much of this seeming leniency stemmed from the ambiguity of the crime of assault. The nature of the act is often difficult to specify with precision; it may also be difficult to determine who initiated the altercation. Moreover, as we argued in Chapter 3, criminal justice officials routinely treat assaults between people who know each other as essentially private disputes and frequently dismiss the charges or settle the case with a plea to a lesser offense. The new law raised the severity of sentences by eliminating this opportunity for mitigating punishment.

Loftin and McDowall also found that "the gun law did not significantly alter the number or type of violent offenses committed in Detroit." Murder, robbery, and assault did decline, but the decrease in the rate had begun five months before the law went into effect—long enough in advance to rule out the possibility of the announcement effect that has appeared with other laws toughening criminal penalties.[57]

The impact of mandatory sentences for gun crimes is extremely complex. When McDowall and Loftin (in collaboration with Brian Wiersma) pooled the results from six different studies, they reached somewhat different conclusions.[58] Mandatory sentencing appeared to reduce homicides in all six cities. In Detroit, there was a 14 percent reduction, with an average of 5.5 lives saved each month. On the other hand, there were no significant reductions in gun assaults or robberies in any of the sites. The authors characterized the results as a "logical puzzle," conceding that they did not know which features of the sentencing policy were "responsible for the preventive effects." More research is clearly needed, so we should be cautious about simplistic assertions on either side of the debate: that mandatory sentencing deters crime or that it does not work at all.

> ## PROPOSITION 40
> Trying to "get tough" on gun crimes, especially through mandatory prison sentences, will not reduce gun-related crime.

A PROMISING ALTERNATIVE: A COMPREHENSIVE, PROBLEM-SOLVING APPROACH TO GUN VIOLENCE

The Boston Gun Project: A National Model

The Boston Gun Project is possibly the most celebrated—and influential—criminal justice project of the last 15 years. It serves as a model of problem-oriented policing by focusing on a specific crime problem, making extensive use of partnerships, and combining traditional enforcement efforts with innovative nontraditional methods. It involved academic experts in the project's planning and development, drew upon the research literature about what works and what doesn't, utilized sophisticated data analysis, and allowed itself to be evaluated by top criminologists. It is the model for the Lowell, Massachusetts, gun initiative and the Cincinnati Initiative to Reduce Violence (CIRV) (see Chapters 5 and 6).

Boston suffered from a very serious upsurge in gun violence in the late 1980s, particularly involving young males. Community leaders finally took bold action, bringing together all of the relevant stakeholders to develop Operation Cease Fire. Analysis of the problem determined that much of the gun violence was associated with particular gangs. Consequently, a major part of Operation Cease Fire focused on the leaders of those gangs. The focus on a small group of individuals departed from traditional police "crackdowns" which have been unfocused and result in arrests of many people who are not really serious repeat offenders. (See our discussion of this in Chapters 5 and 6.) The partnerships involved collaboration among the Boston Police Department and other law enforcement agencies, state and county probation and parole agencies, other public and private social service agencies, and finally community groups.[59]

So, what exactly did Operation Cease Fire do? The basic strategy involved what has become known as "pulling levers": factors that give law enforcement and correctional officials leverage over people involved in gun violence. The levers were entirely legal: seeking out and arresting people with outstanding warrants; seizing the unregistered vehicles of people whose driver's licenses had been suspended; vigorously enforcing probation and parole conditions, for example, prohibitions on using drugs and alcohol or possessing guns. One advantage of this lever is that many of the suspected gang members have prior convictions and are out on probation or parole. One phase of the enforcement involved Operation Night Light, which were evening visits to suspects' residences by teams of police and correctional officers (note the partnerships), who have a legal right to make such visits of probationers and parolees (note the lever). The ex-offenders were told the reason for the enforcement, and what it would take to end it.

Operation Cease Fire was multiphased. Another part involved a coordinated effort (partnerships again) to track illegal guns and prosecute traffickers on federal charges. In addition, meetings were held with gang members to send a clear message of tough enforcement: if there were gun violence in their neighborhoods, authorities would pull every available "lever" until it ceased. There would be no "deal"; gang members would not get any favor for refraining from violence; they would be expected to be law-abiding.

Did it work? An evaluation found a 63 percent reduction in monthly youth homicides, and smaller reductions in youth gun assaults and calls to the police regarding gunshots. You might properly question these findings on the grounds that the entire country was experiencing a great reduction in violent crime during those years. The evaluation, however, found a greater reduction in Boston than across the country and in other New England Cities.

Implications.   It is important to note that the Boston Gun Project is different from most of the other gun violence reduction ideas discussed in this chapter. Banning guns or restricting the purchase of guns by ex-offenders fails because it tries to do too much. An overall ban on guns keeps them out of the hands of many people who are not criminals or gang members. Restrictions on the purchase of guns simply drive gang members into the black market, which readily serves their need for guns. Tough prosecution and enforcement supposedly only operates after there has been a crime committed and an arrest made. We know that clearance rates are low, especially for stranger crimes; one of the main themes of this book is how much can happen between an arrest and punishment to undermine the intent of a "tough" sentencing law. The virtues of the Boston Gun Project are that it is narrowly focused, with a specific target audience, and that it is proactive, operating before further gun violence occurs.

Going National: Project Safe Neighborhoods

The most comprehensive national approach to reducing gun violence is Project Safe Neighborhoods (PSN), a federal program launched in 2001 and implemented in all 94 U.S. attorneys' offices. It has spent $3 billion through 2008. This is a huge investment. What exactly does PSN do? And is it effective?[60]

PSN focuses primarily on increased federal prosecution of gun-related crimes. Sentences under the federal sentencing guidelines are generally tougher than state gun laws (with restrictions on plea bargaining, longer sentences, and no parole), and making a crime a federal crime presumably communicates a strong deterrent message. PSN, however, is much more than an old-fashioned "get tough" approach. It incorporates all the elements of the best contemporary thinking about crime fighting, including the Boston Gun Project: specific problem-oriented focus, strategic planning and utilization of research, partnerships with other criminal justice agencies and community groups, extensive training, community outreach, and accountability in the form of independent evaluation.

A national evaluation of PSN found some very promising results, but also some troubling findings. The good news is that in those jurisdictions where PSN was most fully implemented (a problem we discuss below), gun crimes and other violent crimes decreased substantially. All of the cities that most closely followed the Boston Gun Project model experienced reductions in gun crimes. Chicago implemented PSN in selected areas, and those areas experienced "very significant declines in gun crime compared with other Chicago neighborhoods." The results in some jurisdictions were either ambiguous or unable to be evaluated. A comparison of PSN and non-PSN cities found that violent crime fell more in the PSN than in the non-PSN cities.

Some troubling factors were also evident, however. Violent crime rose in all cities in 2004–2006, reversing the great decline that began around 1993. But the rebound was greater in non-PSN areas, or in those areas where the PSN effort was weakest. One of the main problems identified by the evaluation is sustainability, or the capacity to sustain a special crime-fighting effort over time. This has been a significant problem with all innovative criminal justice programs, such as community policing. Once the initial excitement wears off, officials often tend to fall back into their traditional ways, and the special effort loses its focus.

A number of implementation problems also troubled PSN in many areas. Strong leadership by the local U.S. attorney was critical, but at the same time successful programs involved "distributed leadership" where officials from participating agencies (the local police department, local prosecutor, etc.) also played important roles. At least a quarter of the PSN projects did not have partnerships with community leaders and groups. Data problems were a major obstacle to both planning and evaluation. Many jurisdictions did not have available timely crime data in a convenient electronic form. Some areas also lacked prosecution data in a useful form. There was also considerable fall-off of active participation over time. Even at its peak in 2002, only 60 percent of projects submitted data, and only a third were considered to be of good or very good quality. By 2005, moreover, data reports had fallen off to 10 percent.

Despite these problems, PSN offers hope for the effective control of gun violence. When a comprehensive problem-oriented approach is fully implemented, it appears to have a significant effect. The major problem is implementation.

PROPOSITION 41
Sustained, coordinated Problem-oriented approaches
can be an effective approach to gun violence.

CONCLUSION

Gun-related violence is a serious problem in American society. Many different solutions have been proposed. Most have been found to be ineffective. Banning guns is an empty gesture (and now unconstitutional), given the number of handguns already in circulation. Trying to keep guns out of the hands of "bad" people also appears to be futile. Nor does it appear that threats of severe punishment will deter or incapacitate offenders in a way that will significantly reduce crime. There is persuasive evidence, however, from Boston, Cincinnati, Project Safe Neighborhoods, and other examples, that carefully designed, research-based, coordinated problem-oriented approaches can help reduce gun violence.

NOTES

1. Centers for Disease Control and Prevention, *National Vital Statistics Reports,* vol. 52, no. 3, Sept. 18, 2003. Available on the Center for Disease Control website. The best overview of the problem of guns and violence is National Academy of Sciences, *Firearms and Violence: A Critical Review* (Washington: National Academy Press, 2005). IACP, *Taking a Stand.* Philip J. Cook and Jens Ludwig, *Gun Violence: The Real Costs* (New York: Oxford University Press, 2000).

2. "Deaths: Leading Causes 2005," National Vital Statistics Reports, 58:8 (December 23, 2009), Table 1.

3. Franklin Zimring and Gordon Hawkins, *Crime is Not the Problem: Lethal Violence in America* (New York: Oxford, 1997).

4. Data from the Pew Research Center for the People & the Press, 2008, cited in Bureau of Justice Statistics, *Sourcebook of Criminal Justice Statistics,* online edition, Table 2.0018.2007.

5. *District of Columbia v. Heller,* 554 U.S. ___ (2008).

6. Mark H. Moore, "Controlling Criminogenic Commodities: Drugs, Guns, and Alcohol," in James Q. Wilson, ed., *Crime and Public Policy* (San Francisco: ICS Press, 1983).

7. Federal Bureau of Investigation, *Crime in the United States 2008* (Washington, DC: Department of Justice, 2009), Expanded Homicide Data, Table 8.

8. Bureau of Justice Statistics, *Weapon Use and Violent Crime* (Washington, DC: Department of Justice, 2003). NCJ 194820.

9. The most comprehensive treatment of gun violence and gun control policies is Gary Kleck, *Point Blank: Guns and Violence in America* (New York: Aldine de Gruyter, 1991).

10. Data from the Pew Research Center for the People & the Press, 2008, cited in Bureau of Justice Statistics, *Sourcebook of Criminal Justice Statistics,* online edition, Table 2.0018.2007.

11. Bureau of Justice Statistics, *Sourcebook of Criminal Justice Statistics,* 2008, Tables 2.63–2.66. Check the current *Sourcebook* online for the most recent data. Older data: Tom W. Smith, *1999 National Gun Policy Survey of the National Opinion Research Center: Research Findings* (Chicago: NORC, 2000).

12. National Academy of Sciences, *Firearms and Violence: A Critical Review,* "Defensive Gun Use," pp. 103–108.

13. Brady Center, *Exporting Gun Violence: How Our Weak Gun Laws Arm Criminals in Mexico and America* (Washington, DC: The Brady Center, 2009). www. bradycampaign.org. Congressional Relations Service, *Mexico's Drug Cartels,* CRS RL 34215 (Washington, DC: Congressional Relations Service, October 16, 2007).

14. Bureau of Justice Statistics, *Sourcebook of Criminal Justice Statistics 2008,* Tables 2.59–2.62.

15. Edward L. Glaeser and Spencer Glendon, "Who Owns Guns? Criminals, Victims, and the Culture of Violence," *American Economic Review* 88 (May 1998): 458–462. Gary Kleck, "Crime, Culture Conflict and the Sources of Support for Gun Control, *American Behavioral Scientist* 39 (February 1996): 387–404.

16. Bureau of Justice Statistics, *Weapon Use and Violent Crime* (Washington, DC: Department of Justice, 2003). NCJ 194820.

17. Bureau of Alcohol, Firearms and Tobacco, *State Laws and Published Ordinances* (annual). www.atf.gov/.

18. Mayors Against Illegal Guns, *The Movement of Illegal Guns in America: The Link Between Gun Laws and Interstate Gun Trafficking* (Washington, DC: Mayors Against Illegal Guns, 2008). www.mayorsagainstillegalguns.org. "Report Links Crimes to States with Weak Gun Controls," *New York Times,* 9 April 1997.

19. Edward D. Jones, "The District of Columbia's 'Firearms Control Regulations Act of 1975': The Toughest Handgun Control Law in the United States—Or Is It?" *The Annals* 455 (May 1981): 138–149.

20. National Academy of Sciences, *Firearms and Violence: A Critical Review,* pp. 97–98.

21. John Kaplan, "The Wisdom of Gun Prohibition," *The Annals* 455 (May 1981): 11–23.

22. James D. Wright, Peter H. Rossi, and Kathleen Daly, *Under the Gun: Weapons, Crime, and Violence in America* (New York: Aldine de Gruyter, 1983), p. 320.

23. The St. Louis and Seattle evaluations, along with other articles, are in Martha Plotkin, ed., *Under Fire: Gun Buy-Backs, Exchanges, and Amnesty Programs* (Washington, DC: Police Executive Research Forum, 1996).

24. National Academy of Sciences, *Firearms and Violence: A Critical Review,* p. 95.

25. Robert Sherrill, *The Saturday Night Special* (New York: Charterhouse, 1973).

26. "Los Angeles Bans the Sale of Inexpensive, Small Guns," *New York Times,* 8 September 1996.

27. Kleck, *Point Blank,* pp. 85–86.

28. Bureau of Justice Statistics, *Guns Used in Crime,* p. 6.

29. Smith, *1999 National Gun Policy Survey of the National Opinion Research Center: Research Findings.*

30. Jeffrey A. Roth and Christopher S. Koper, *Impacts of the 1994 Assault Weapons Ban: 1994–96* (Washington, DC: Department of Justice, 1999). Christopher S. Koper, *An Updated Assessment of the Federal Assault Weapons Ban: Impacts on Gun Markets and Gun Violence, 1994–2003.* Research report to the National Institute of Justice (Philadelphia: Jerry Lee Center of Criminology, University of Pennsylvania, 2004).

31. National Academy of Sciences, *Firearms and Violence: A Critical Review,* "Regulating Gun Dealers," pp. 89–90.

32. Christopher Koper, "Federal Legislation and Gun Markets: How Much Have Recent Reforms of the Federal Firearms Licensing System Reduced Criminal Gun Suppliers?" *Criminology and Public Policy* 1 (2002): 151–178. And see also the comments by Deborah S. Azrael and James B. Jacobs.

33. Cook and Ludwig J. *Gun Violence: The Real Costs.*

34. Mark H. Moore, "Keeping Handguns from Criminal Offenders," *Annals* 455 (May 1981): 92–109.

35. Recent data from www.mayorsagainstillegalguns.org, citing surveys of gun owners. Wright et al., *Under the Gun.* Bureau of Justice Statistics, *Guns Used in Crime,* p. 4.

36. Bureau of Justice Statistics, *Firearm Use by Offenders* (Washington, DC: Department of Justice, 2001). NCJ 189369. More recent data can be found in Bureau of Justice Statistics, Criminal Victimization 2008.

37. *Inside Straw Purchasing: How Criminals Get Guns Illegally* (Washington, DC: Mayors Against Illegal Guns, 2008), p. 7.

38. Information from mayorsagainstillegalguns.org.

39. Mayors Against Illegal Guns, *The Movement of Illegal Guns in America: The Link Between Gun Laws and Interstate Gun Trafficking* (Washington, DC: Mayors Against Illegal Guns, 2008). www.mayorsagainstillegalguns.org.

40. Bureau of Justice Statistics, *Guns Used in Crime.*

41. Lawrence W. Sherman, James W. Shaw, and Dennis P. Rogan, *The Kansas City Gun Experiment* (Washington, DC: Department of Justice, 1995). NCJ 150855.

42. Ibid.

43. "More Than 800 Guns Seized at U.S. Airport Checkpoints Last Year," February 24, 2009. www.ticklethewire.org. The Transportation Security Administration posts very incomplete data on its web site. www.tsa.gov/. "Airports' Thanksgiving Seizures: 15,982 Knives and a Brick," *USA Today,* 3 December 2002.

44. Bureau of the Census, *Statistical Abstract of the United States, 1995.*

45. University of Maryland, *Preventing Crime: What Works, What Doesn't, What's Promising?* (Washington, DC: Department of Justice, 1997), chap. 7 (airports are covered on pp. 7–29 to 7–30). NCJ 165366.

46. National Center for Education Statistics and Bureau of Justice Statistics, *Indicators of School Crime and Safety: 2008* (Washington, DC: Department of Justice, 2009). NCJ 226343.

47. Ibid., Indicator 20, Figure 20.1.

48. Pro-right to carry information is available from the National Rifle Association. www.nra.org. Opposition material is available from the Brady Campaign. www.bradycampaign.org.

49. John R. Lott, *More Guns, Less Crime: Understanding Crime and Gun-control Laws* (Chicago: University of Chicago Press, 1998).

50. Tomislav V. Kovandzic, Thomas B. Marvell, and Lynn M. Vieratitis, "The Impact of 'Shall-Issue" Concealed Handgun Laws on Violence Crime Rates, *Homicide Studies* 9 (November 2005): 292–323. National Academy of Sciences, *Firearms and Violence.*

51. National Academy of Sciences, *Firearms and Violence*. Estimate of 2.3 million lives saved. www.learnaboutguns.com.

52. Gary Kleck and Miriam A. DeLone, "Victim Resistance and Offender Weapon Effects in Robbery," *Journal of Quantitative Criminology* 9 (1993): 55–81.

53. James D. Wright, "Ten Essential Observations on Guns in America," *Society* (March/April 1995): 66.

54. Bureau of Justice Statistics, *National Assessment of Structured Sentencing* (Washington, DC: Department of Justice, 1996), pp. 24–25. NCJ 153853.

55. Bureau of Justice Statistics, *Felony Defendants in Large Urban Counties 2004,* (Washington, DC: Department of Justice, 2008).

56. Colin Loftin and David McDowall, ' "One with a Gun Gets You Two": Mandatory Sentencing and Firearms Violence in Detroit,' *The Annals* 455 (May 1981): 150–167.

57. Ibid.

58. David McDowall, Colin Loftin, and Brian Wiersma, "A Comparative Study of the Preventive Effects of Mandatory Sentencing Laws for Gun Crimes," *Journal of Criminal Law and Criminology* 83.2 (1992): 378–394.

59. David M. Kennedy, Anthony A. Braga, and Anne M Piehl, *Reducing Gun Violence: The Boston Gun Project's Operation Ceasefire* (Washington, DC: Department of Justice, 2001). NCJ 188741.

60. Edward F. McGarrall, et al., *Project Safe Neighborhoods: A National Program to Reduce Gun Crime: Final Project Report* (Washington, DC: Department of Justice, 2009).

PART IV

Reform: The Liberal Prescription

Liberals take a very different approach to crime policy than do conservatives. As we indicated in Chapter 1, liberals are much more optimistic about our capacity to reduce crime by changing either people or society. In the two chapters that follow, we will take a close look at the two most important components of liberal crime policy. Chapter 11 examines both the concept of rehabilitation and specific programs designed to change criminal offenders into law-abiding citizens. Chapter 12 looks at potential reforms by increasing public confidence in the criminal justice system and as a consequence increasing commitment to lawful behavior.

11

Treat 'Em!

REHABILITATING CRIMINALS

The concept of *rehabilitation* is the cornerstone of traditional liberal crime control policy. Although the rhetoric has changed over the years, the basic idea remains the same: reduce crime by treating criminals, "correcting" their behavior, and rehabilitating them as law-abiding citizens. The terminology used by state agencies reflects the continued commitment to rehabilitation. We have departments of "corrections" but no departments of "punishment." Why do we use this terminology? The term *corrections* carries the aura of healing and helping people, placing corrections officials on the same professional status as medical doctors and social workers.[1]

The Philosophy of Rehabilitation

What exactly is rehabilitation? The National Academy of Sciences defines it as "any planned intervention that reduces an offender's further criminal activity."[2] The key words here are *planned* and *intervention*. As Wolfgang's career criminal research suggests (see Chapter 4), most lawbreakers stop sooner or later. It is well established that criminal activity peaks between the ages of 14 and 24 and then declines sharply. Aging is the best crime reduction policy we know about.[3] The goal of rehabilitation is to make offenders stop sooner rather than later through a planned intervention program, that might include counseling, education, job training, or some other program. As we explained in Chapter 1, rehabilitation is a crime prevention strategy; it simply takes a different approach than punishment-oriented strategies.

Old and New Programs

A variety of different programs have existed to rehabilitate offenders and reintegrate them into the community. Probation and parole have been the most important programs for over 100 years. During this time, both have tried a variety of

"Unfortunately, corrections is a field in which quackery is pervasive."
What Criminologist Francis T. Cullen and his colleagues call quackery, we call nonsense.
What they say about corrections is also true of almost every aspect of the criminal justice system.

FIGURE 11.1   Faith, Fads, and Quackery

SOURCE: Francis T. Cullen, Kristie R. Blevins, Jennifer S. Trager, and Paul Gendreau, "The Rise and Fall of Boot Camps: A Case Study in Common Sense Corrections," *Journal of Offender Rehabilitation* 40 (nos. 3–4, 2005): 55.

different approaches to enhance effectiveness. Intensive supervision is one good example. As we will see, the entire subject of rehabilitation has been afflicted with fads—new ideas that generate a lot of excitement and new programs, only to fade away when the evidence begins coming in that they don't really work or make much difference. Criminologist Francis Cullen and his colleagues put it bluntly (Figure 11.1): "Unfortunately, corrections is a field in which quackery is pervasive."[4] They call it quackery, we call it nonsense; but it is the same thing: ideas based on faith rather than facts.

Currently, there are two ideas generating a lot of excitement. One is the focus on *reentry*—what to do with the estimated 600,000 adult prisoners who reenter society every year. The federal government has made offender reentry programs a top priority and is supporting reentry programs across the country. (Reentry is really just a new term for the old one, reintegration.) Because of its special relevance to the community context, we will examine reentry in Chapter 14 along with other new community-focused crime policies. The other new program involves drug courts. As we will see, drug courts embody many elements of traditional rehabilitation programs. In this chapter we will take a close look at what is new and what is old in drug courts. Our main question will be this: Do drug courts put together many traditional elements in a new way that really does make a difference? And because, obviously, drug courts relate to drug offenders, we will look at them again in Chapter 12.

Prisons offer programs designed to reintegrate offenders into the community: academic and vocational education programs, drug and alcohol counseling, anger management and other forms of individual counseling, and work experience. Community-based correctional programs—probation and parole—place offenders in the community under some kind of supervision, on the assumption that offenders will respond more effectively to this more normal setting than the very abnormal setting of a prison.

Since the 1990s, a new set of *intermediate punishments* have appeared, designed to place offenders in the community but under much closer surveillance than traditional probation and parole.[5] These programs include boot camps, electronic monitoring, home confinement, and intensive supervision on probation or parole. Some observers believe that these measures represent a revival of rehabilitation as criminal justice policy. Others, however, are not so sure. This chapter examines first traditional rehabilitation-oriented programs and then looks at the new intermediate punishments to see if they are more effective. Our goal is to identify correctional treatment programs that are relatively more effective than others and that, if adopted, would help reduce crime.

THE "NOTHING WORKS" CONTROVERSY

Over 35 years ago criminologist Robert Martinson threw down the gauntlet over rehabilitation, framing the terms of a debate that continues today. In a 1974 article (and later a book), he concluded that "with few and isolated exceptions, the rehabilitative efforts that have been reported so far have had no appreciable effect on rehabilitation."[6]

Even though the Martinson report itself is several decades old, the debate continues to rage: Do rehabilitation programs work? Or are they ineffective? The question has direct relevance, for example, to drug courts. Do they work? What is the evidence? Or do they, as critics charge, allow many offenders to avoid the punishment of going to prison, undermine the deterrent effect of punishment, and allow these offenders to go free and prey on society?

Martinson's conclusions were a bombshell, although the report as a whole was widely misinterpreted. The title of his original article was "What Works?" Many people, however, interpreted it to mean that "nothing works." He did not actually say that. In fact, he found positive outcomes in 48 percent of the program evaluations he reviewed. That's almost half, which is a long way from "nothing." And a few years later, he unequivocally stated that "some treatment programs do have an appreciable effect on recidivism," adding, "The critical fact seems to be the conditions under which the program is delivered."[7]

The Martinson report is a classic example of how social science research is often misinterpreted (and misused) in the political arena. Many people wanted to believe that "nothing worked" because they were disillusioned with rehabilitation. They were angry over (by then) 10 years of soaring crime rates. Conservatives blamed rehabilitation programs for being soft on crime, whereas liberals attacked the same programs for violating standards of due process. The disillusionment with rehabilitation was part of a more general conservative mood that arose in the mid-1970s and continues today.[8]

The story of Martinson's report is fascinating in itself. His team reviewed all evaluations of correctional programs published in English between 1945 and 1967. In important respects, his report was a precursor to the current evidence-based policy movement, which we discussed in Chapter 1. They were able to find only 231 that met scientific standards. Most evaluations they rejected because these tests used unreliable measures, failed to specify the "treatment," did not use proper control groups, or drew questionable conclusions from the data.[9] Martinson exposed a scandalous case of professional irresponsibility: the correctional community's failure to develop a systematic process of evaluation. Programs routinely claimed "success" without any legitimate basis for doing so. The academic community shared much of the responsibility, as formal evaluations were done either by researchers under contract or by in-house professionals with academic training. Because his findings were so threatening, the state of

New York did not release the report and even denied Martinson permission to publish it. He sued and eventually forced the report's release.

Was Martinson Right?

Was Martinson's assessment of correctional programs accurate? The National Academy of Sciences' Panel on Research on Rehabilitative Techniques reviewed his work and concluded that he was "essentially correct."[10] It supported Martinson's view that there was little evidence "to allay the current pessimism about the effectiveness of institutional rehabilitation programs as they now exist."

The Prediction Problem Revisited

Criminologist Daniel Glaser replied to the Martinson Report by arguing that "certain sentencing and correctional policies, which differ according to the criminalization of the offender, are more likely than their alternatives to reduce recidivism rates."[11] His defense of rehabilitation highlights the central problem facing all treatment-oriented programs: the need for a good match between offender and treatment program. It is certainly true that *some* programs are effective for *some* offenders. Achieving the proper match, however, brings us back to our old friend the prediction problem (Chapter 4). Sentencing a convicted offender to a community-based drug treatment program represents a prediction that he or she (1) is not a serious danger to the community, and therefore does not need to go to prison, and (2) will respond positively to the drug treatment. Drawing on the work of John Hagan, Glaser argues that some individuals are more deeply "embedded in crime" than others.[12] Those who are less deeply embedded are more "amenable" to community-based treatment. So far, so good.

The crucial question is whether judges and correctional officials can correctly identify the more "amenable" offenders and sentence them to the right treatment program. Can we accurately pick, for example, those offenders who are likely to respond to a drug court program? We have already criticized conservative programs because of their inability to accurately predict which offenders are the really high risk ones who should be sentenced to long prison terms (Chapters 4, 7). Choosing which offenders to place on probation is simply the other side of the same sentencing coin. The criticisms we made of conservative punishment-oriented programs apply with equal force to liberal rehabilitation-oriented programs.

TRADITIONAL REHABILITATION PROGRAMS

Let us now examine the traditional rehabilitation-oriented programs—probation, parole, and diversion—to see what evidence there is regarding their effectiveness.

Probation

Probation is the most widely used rehabilitation program in the criminal justice system. In 2006, 4.2 million adults were on probation in the United States, almost four times the 1.1 million in 1980. Twenty-eight percent of all convicted felons were sentenced to "straight probation" in 2004, and others were placed on probation as part of split sentences (a jail term followed by probation).[13]

Probation embodies the traditional philosophy of rehabilitation by keeping convicted offenders in the community rather than sending them to prison. Probation "treatment" generally consists of supervision by a probation officer and some restrictions on a probationer's behavior: reporting regularly to a probation officer, not leaving the area without permission, not taking drug or alcohol counseling, furnishing employment verification or evidence of seeking a job, not possessing a weapon, and so on. Traditionally, probation was designed to help rehabilitate offenders by having probation officers help them find a job and deal with other personal problems.

Probation serves a number of different purposes. It is often an appropriate sentence for someone convicted of a less serious offense or for a first-time offender. In this respect it serves the goal of proportionality in sentencing. It is also far cheaper than imprisonment. The Pew Center for the States estimated in 2009 that regular probation costs $1,248 a year, compared with $28,835 for prison. Costs vary by the type of program and region. Intensive probation, for example, costs as much as $4,000 nationally, and in California it costs $43,000 a year for one inmate.[14] In effect, we use probation as a matter of necessity. We simply could not afford to imprison all convicted felons even if we wanted to.

The Effectiveness of Probation

Does probation work? Is it effective in rehabilitating offenders and reducing crime? Actually, there are two separate questions related to effectiveness. First, is probation more effective than incarceration? Second, are some kinds of probation programs more effective than others? There is much debate over the effectiveness of probation. Evaluations have found failure rates that range from 65 to 12 percent.[15] Where does the truth lie?

The Rand study of felons on probation in California is arguably the best data available. The findings are very depressing. After 40 months on probation, 65 percent of the probationers had been rearrested, and 51 percent had been reconvicted of a new offense. Moreover, one-third of those reconvicted (18 percent of the original sample) were reconvicted of a serious violent crime. Nor did they wait very long to fail. Probationers reconvicted of a violent crime took an average of only eight months to recidivate, while those reconvicted of property offenses took an average of only five months (see Figure 11.2).

In short, most felons placed on probation fail; they do not become law-abiding citizens. Why? Many experts argue that traditional probation programs do not provide any kind of meaningful supervision or treatment. The level of supervision has always been very minimal, involving a meeting with a probation officer (PO) perhaps once a month. The PO fills out the required reports, and that is that. Joan

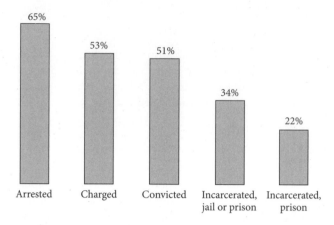

FIGURE 11.2 Probation outcomes after three years, California
SOURCE: Joan Petersilia, Granting Felons Probation (Santa Monica: Rand Corporation, 1985).

Petersilia found that offenders on regular probation in Los Angeles County met with their POs only once a month. Another report indicated that because some PO caseloads exceeded a thousand probationers, POs in Los Angeles spent an average of one hour and 47 minutes *per year* with each offender.[16] The level of supervision has gotten even worse in recent years because of the increase in caseloads. The total number of people on probation quadrupled between 1979 and 2006, from 1 to 4.2 million. The "war on crime" has resulted not just in a soaring prison population but also in a huge increase in the probation population.[17]

A third issue involved the quality content of treatment services. Even assuming that a probationer is officially enrolled in a drug treatment or anger management program, it is not clear that this particular program is well run or that any kind of service—in and of itself—can overcome the problems that led the probationer to commit crime in the first place. As we will see in Chapter 13, the evidence on the effectiveness of drug treatment programs is very weak.

In the long run, most probationers eventually rehabilitate themselves, through maturation, finding a job, getting married, and so on. John Hagan argues that whether a person becomes law abiding or continues in a life of criminal activity depends on the extent to which he or she is "socially embedded" in either legitimate or criminal opportunities. Some individuals have more contacts —with family members or friends in the neighborhood—that lead to jobs. These contacts, moreover, tend to multiply: One job results in additional contacts that lead to other and often better job opportunities. Individuals who are embedded in these kinds of networks are far more likely to establish law-abiding lives than those who are not—regardless of the kind of probation or parole services they receive. Generally, white youths are more embedded in positive networks than African American or Hispanic youths. Whites are simply more likely to have a family member, friend, or acquaintance who can refer them to a job opening than is the case with young men of color, who are more likely to live in economically devastated neighborhoods.[18]

Research related to offender reentry programs provides a valuable glimpse into the lives of criminal offenders. Although the research is specifically related to parole, it applies just as well to probation. Interviews with 400 recently released offenders who returned to Chicago found that they suffered from major problems that made readjustment to a normal life very difficult: 30 percent had "significant" health problems, but 81 percent had no health care; about half (48 percent) had no close friends, and among those with friends, 40 percent had a friend who had also been in prison. Convicted felons face restrictions on employment, housing, welfare, and voting. In short, they are embedded in social experiences that impose many hurdles but offer few supports.[19]

The evidence leads us to the following conclusion:

PROPOSITION 42

Probation is an appropriate sentence for many offenders,
but there is no evidence that one kind of probation treatment is more effective
in reducing crime than other kinds.

Parole

Parole is the second most prevalent rehabilitation program. Most offenders sent to prison are released early under some form of supervision. Parole is seen as a rehabilitation program because, like probation, it seeks to reintegrate the offender into the community. In 2006, 798,202 adults were on parole in the United States, more than three times the number in 1980.[20] The use of discretionary release parole has been declining as a result of the growth of sentencing guidelines. Sixteen states have abolished discretionary parole. One study found that more offenders left prison in 2006 through supervised mandatory release (51 percent) than discretionary parole release (39 percent).[21]

When it was first developed, experts believed that parole would facilitate rehabilitation by placing a prisoner's future in his own hands. The possibility of gaining an earlier release would, they believed, encourage good behavior. Despite these promises, parole has always been the unloved child of the criminal justice system. Ever since it became widespread in the U.S. in the 1920s, it has been criticized from all directions. Conservatives argue that it allows dangerous offenders to get out of prison early, while liberals argue that parole release decisions are made without any scientific foundation, and are thus arbitrary and often discriminatory.[22] Despite persistent criticisms, however, parole survives because it serves a number of purposes unrelated to rehabilitation: It offers prisoners an incentive to behave in prison, gives prison officials some power to control them, and serves as a safety valve for prison overcrowding.

Does Parole Work?

Do prisoners who are released on parole have lower recidivism rates than those who serve longer prison terms? Does parole supervision facilitate rehabilitation? Do some forms of parole supervision work more effectively than others? It is

T A B L E   11.1   Parole-outcome recidivism rates of prisoners released in 1994 from prisons in 15 states

	Cumulative Percent of Released Prisoners Who Were—		
	Returned to prison[a,b]	Rearrested	Reconvicted[a,c]
Time after release			
6 months	29.9%	10.6%	5.0%
1 year	44.1	21.5	10.4
2 years	59.2	36.4	18.8
3 years	67.5	46.9	25.4

[a]With a new sentence, including to state or federal prisons but not to local jails.

[b]Because of missing data, prisoners released in Ohio and Virginia were excluded from the calculation of those returned to prison with a new prison sentence.

[c]Because of missing data, prisoners released in Ohio were excluded from the calculation of percent reconvicted.

SOURCE: Bureau of Justice Statistics, *Recidivism of Prisoners Released in 1994* (Washington, DC: Department of Justice, 2002).

important to recognize that parole consists of two elements: *discretionary release* and *postrelease supervision,* which is supposed to deliver treatment services and ensure that the parolee does not engage in wrongdoing.

The effectiveness of parole has traditionally been measured in terms of the recidivism rate.[23] As with probation, an offender can fail either by being arrested for a new crime or through a technical violation of parole conditions. In terms of a new crime, it depends on whether we measure failure in terms of being rearrested, reconvicted, or reincarcerated (see Table 11.1).

The data on parole outcomes are as discouraging as for probation. The most recent and most thorough study of parole outcomes found that within three years 62.3 percent were rearrested for either a felony or a serious misdemeanor. This was little different from the 64.8 rearrest rate for offenders released unconditionally. About 47 percent were convicted of a new offense, and 41 percent were imprisoned for a conviction or a technical violation of their conditions of release.[24] These figures lend a great deal of support to the widespread belief that neither prison nor parole is successful in rehabilitating offenders. The policy question is whether parole can be made to work more effectively.

Failure rates of parolees have hardly changed over time. A 1994 Justice Department study found that the percentage of parolees originally convicted of a violent offense who were convicted of a new offense within three years was 41.9 percent in 1983 and 39.9 percent in 1994. Among property offenders, the reconviction rate over three years hardly changed at all: from 53 percent in 1983 to 53.4 percent in 1995. The reconviction rate of drug offenders did rise, however, from 35.3 to 47 percent. This was undoubtedly due to changes related to drug usage and drug markets.[25]

The problems with parole are similar to the problems with probation. First, parole supervision is generally pretty minimal. Petersilia reports that in California, 85 percent of parolees are on regular supervision, with each parole officer carrying an average caseload of 66 parolees and an average of 1.7 contacts per month.

The remaining parolees are on intensive supervision with an average of 5.6 contacts per month and parole officer caseloads of 25 per officer.[26]

Second, there are serious questions about the availability and content of treatment services. A California study estimated that 10,000 parolees were homeless but only 200 shelter beds were available to them. Similarly, only four mental health clinics were available for an estimated 18,000 parolees with psychiatric problems. And there were only 750 beds in treatment programs for 85,000 parolees with alcohol or drug problems.[27] Even if there were more of these services available, there is no strong evidence that we successfully match offenders to the specific treatment they need. This leads us again to our old friend the prediction problem.

Research on offender reentry confirms the inadequacy of treatment services. The Urban Institute interviewed 400 released offenders who returned to Chicago. Although 87 percent had participated in prerelease programs related to such practical matters as finding a job, obtaining a photo ID, and finding a place to live, once they were home only 25 percent received an actual referral to a job, only 15 percent received a referral to a substance abuse treatment program, and only 22 percent contacted a community program based on a referral from the prerelease program.[28]

The Prediction Problem Again. Parole is where criminal justice officials first encountered the prediction problem, beginning in the 1920s. For about 90 years, parole officials and criminologists have tried to develop formulas for predicting success on parole and to ensure that parole is granted only to those offenders who are rehabilitated and ready for release into the community. The sad fact, however, is that criminologists have been searching for better parole release criteria since the 1920s. They are no closer to a successful formula today than they were then.[29]

Repeatedly, research has confirmed the basic finding reported by Martinson: that some programs work for some offenders. The problem, of course, is in matching offenders to the right programs. Petersilia reports that California uses risk prediction instruments, but there is no evidence that they are any more effective in predicting success than the tools used in earlier decades.[30]

Does More Make It Better?

Intensive Supervision for Probation and Parole

Intensive probation supervision or intensive parole supervision (IPS) was one of the new intermediate punishments designed to improve both probation and parole. It is frequently combined with other intermediate sanctions (boot camps, home confinement, and electronic monitoring) and applied to high-risk offenders.[31]

The basic idea of intensive supervision was nothing new. California developed a pioneering Special Intensive Parole Unit (SIPU) program in the mid-1950s and maintained it for 10 years. Martinson reviewed the SIPU evaluations and found that three of the four phases produced no meaningful improvement in parolees' behavior. The phase involving smaller caseloads yielded some positive results. Parolees in this phase were returned to prison more often for technical violations. Martinson concluded that this was a deterrent rather than a rehabilitative effect. Parolees behaved themselves a little better when they knew that they faced a real prospect of being sent back to prison.[32]

The federal probation system, meanwhile, developed the San Francisco Project in the 1960s. Two IPS groups had caseloads of only 20 probationers, while two other groups had caseloads of 40, and another group had caseloads of several hundred clients. All other offenders were assigned to groups with normal levels of supervision, meaning that probation officers had between 70 and 130 clients.[33] An evaluation found no significant difference in the recidivism rates of offenders in the various groups. IPS did not consistently reduce the failure rate. And in fact, anticipating a problem that would affect the intermediate sanction programs of the 1980s and 1990s, intensive supervision resulted in a higher rate of technical violations of the conditions of probation.

The original IPS programs rested on a flawed assumption that increasing the intensity of supervision simply by lowering case loads and increasing the frequency of contact would enhance effectiveness.[34] Mere contact with a probation or parole officer, however, has little impact on an offender's behavior, and increasing the number of contacts makes no difference. The new IPS programs attempt to overcome some of this problem by incorporating other intermediate sanctions such as home confinement, mandatory drug and alcohol tests, and electronic monitoring.[35] One important aspect of this approach is that intensive supervision has become primarily enforcement oriented rather than treatment oriented. The basic goal is to control the offender.

Are the new IPS programs effective? That is, are they more effective than traditional probation? Joan Petersilia found the results in three California programs "particularly discouraging." After one year, about 35 percent of the IPS probationers had been rearrested, another 40 percent committed technical violations of probation conditions, and only 25 percent had no violations of any sort. Admittedly, the offenders assigned to these IPS programs were labeled high risk, but a 75 percent failure rate after only one year is a very poor showing. Perhaps even more significant, their rearrest rates were no different from those of other probationers. This outcome suggests that the intense supervision did not stop them from committing crime. Once again, more intensive supervision resulted in much higher rates of technical violations. This result is hardly surprising, because that is what frequent contacts and drug tests are designed to detect.[36]

Why are IPS programs no more successful than regular probation in reducing recidivism? The answer may be that no form of probation supervision—intensive or minimal—has any real impact on the lives of people who are embedded in environments with few positive opportunities, weak or nonexistent family supports, and many dysfunctional peer influences such as friends involved in drugs and crime. The "treatment" of intense supervision may not be able to overcome the real problems that offenders have.

This leads us to the following conclusion:

PROPOSITION 43
Intensive supervision, with either probation or parole, will not reduce crime.

Abolish Discretionary Parole?

Disillusionment with parole reached such a point in the 1970s that several jurisdictions simply abolished discretionary parole release (although some kept post-release supervision). The 1976 California Determinate Sentencing Law abolished discretionary parole release. Release dates are mandatory once a prisoner has served the sentence imposed by the judge and good time has been deducted. A one-year period of parole supervision remains, however. The federal sentencing guidelines that took effect in 1987 also abolished discretionary parole release and replaced it with a system of presumptive sentences. Sixteen states have now abolished discretionary parole release. As a result, the percentage of all prisoners released through discretionary parole declined to 33 percent by 2006, a sharp decline over the previous 20 years, while 48 percent were released through mandatory parole.[37]

Abolishing parole may not be an effective crime reduction policy. Bureau of Justice Statistics data indicate that in 1999 54 percent of the prisoners released through discretionary parole were successful (that is, not rearrested), compared with 33 percent who left prison through mandatory release. The Bureau of Justice Statistics uncovered the astonishing fact that when the state of California is excluded, the national success rate for mandatory release *doubles,* from 33 to 66 percent. This is due to both the enormous size of the California parole population, and its consequent impact on national data, but also to the extremely high parole revocation rate in California.[38] Joan Petersilia calls for a return to discretionary parole release, but the evidence on whether it is indeed more effective than mandatory release is still very inconclusive.[39]

For the moment, however, the evidence leads us to conclude that:

PROPOSITION 44
Abolishing parole will not reduce crime; and in fact it appears to lead to higher recidivism rates.

Perverting Parole: Crisis in California

Parole has been completely perverted in California, to the point where it undermines the original purpose of parole and also contributes directly to the prison overcrowding crisis in the state. Every year, more people enter prison because their parole was revoked than because of a sentence by a judge: 6 out of every 10 people entering prison. That involved 78,721 parolees in 2006. To put this in context, New York had the second highest total of revocations to prison with 11,548. The California prisons were so overcrowded by 2009 that a federal judge ordered a cap on prison populations, with the result that as many as 55,000 prisoners might have to be released.[40]

What caused this situation? California adopted a form of sentencing guidelines in 1978, which included an end to discretionary parole release. At the end of a sentence, a prisoner is automatically released. There is no discretion to hold someone in prison because he or she appears not ready for release. Then there is a period of one year of supervised parole. This system has transferred discretion to parole officers who were increasingly using parole revocation as a form of control: Violations of parole conditions or a new crime resulted in revocation. The emphasis on control diverted parole away from its original purpose of rehabilitation and offender reintegration. The process made a mockery of both parole supervision and revocation itself. Because parole officers had so many clients, they had almost no time for many of their clients. Some categories of parolees could even report to their parolees by mail. We can properly ask, What was the point of even pretending there was any supervision? Additionally, many of the revocations were for extremely short periods of time: one month, in some cases. The revolving door of revokees entering and then quickly leaving prison only overburdened and disrupted prison administration—which was already suffering from severe overcrowding. Could anyone reasonably expect this process to be successful in rehabilitating offenders, or even to send them any kind of positive message?

DIVERSION

Diversion was one of the great reforms of the 1960s. The President's Crime Commission gave it a strong endorsement in 1967, and in the 1970s an estimated 1,200 diversion programs were established.[41] A diversion program is a planned intervention with a treatment component and the goal of getting offenders out of the criminal justice system as early as possible.

Actually, diversion was nothing new in the 1960s. Historically, many offenders were diverted from the criminal justice system at an early stage. Police officers routinely chose not to arrest someone even though there was probable cause, and prosecutors dismissed cases when prosecution would not serve the "interests of justice." We call these practices the *old* diversion. The *new* diversion programs were different because they were formal programs, with official goals, a professional staff, and treatment services.[42] (As we will see, today's drug courts are essentially another form of diversion—although with important differences that we will discuss.)

Diversion programs are designed to rehabilitate offenders (and thereby reduce crime) in two ways. First, they keep people accused of relatively minor offenses out of jails and prisons. This reflects labeling theory in criminology, which holds that formal processing in the criminal justice system (and imprisonment in particular) only accentuates a person's tendency toward criminal behavior. The President's Crime Commission argued: "Institutions tend to isolate offenders from society, both physically and psychologically, cutting them off from schools, jobs, families, and other supportive influences and increasing the probability that the label criminal will be indelibly impressed upon them."[43] The Wolfgang cohort data we examined in Chapter 4, moreover, suggest that most juveniles "mature out" in relation to criminal behavior. Diversion programs assume that the best approach is to intervene in people's lives as little as possible.

Second, diversion programs are designed to provide treatment services that address the offender's real problems: drug or alcohol treatment, employment counseling, anger management, and so forth. Advocates of diversion believe that arrest, prosecution, and punishment aggravate rather than treat those problems (while at the same time overloading the criminal justice system).

Finally, diversion programs are intended to reduce the costs of the criminal justice system by avoiding the expenses of full criminal prosecution and imprisonment.

In short, diversion promised the best of all possible worlds—an approach that was more effective, more humane, and cheaper. An old adage says that if something seems too good to be true, it probably is. Let us take a look at diversion in practice.

Inspiration: The Manhattan Court Employment Project

The earliest and most influential diversion program was the Manhattan Court Employment Project. Sponsored by the Vera Institute, the project provided employment services to arrested persons. The basic assumption was that because unemployment is a major cause of crime, facilitating employment will reduce subsequent criminal activity. Even though the Court Employment Project occurred many years ago, its story highlights a number of enduring problems that affect more recent programs.

Each day staff members of the Court Employment Project reviewed the arrest docket and identified defendants who met the program's criteria: resident of New York City; between the ages of 16 and 45; unemployed or earning less than $125 a week; and charged with a felony other than homicide, rape, kidnapping, or arson. In addition, the defendant must have not had prior jail or prison experience of one year or longer. With the prosecutor's consent, the case was suspended for 90 days while the defendant received counseling, assistance in obtaining any short-term public assistance for which he or she might have been eligible, and referral to a job opening with one of the 400 cooperating employers. Charges were dropped completely if the defendant "succeeded" by keeping a job. If the person "failed" to secure employment, the case was prosecuted.

An early evaluation declared the Manhattan Court Employment Project a huge success. In its first three years, the project accepted 1,300 clients, about half of whom (48.2 percent) succeeded. About 70 percent of these 626 people had been unemployed at the time of arrest. Fourteen months later, about 80 percent of those who could be located were still employed. Only 15.8 percent of these successful clients committed another crime in the 12 months following their release from the program. This recidivism rate was half of that for both offenders who failed in the program and a control group. The program cost only $731 per client, or $1,518 per success.[44]

A subsequent evaluation, however, reached very different conclusions. It found that the project did not reduce recidivism and had no discernible effect on the employment record or the behavior of its clients. Moreover, it did not reduce pretrial detention time or lower the number of convictions. A major problem was that about half of the clients served by the program would not have been prosecuted at all if there had been no court employment project.[45] This is a classic example of "net widening." Because this phenomenon affects so many well-intentioned reforms, we need to discuss it in detail.

The Net-Widening Problem

Net widening is the process by which more people are brought under some form of social control through the criminal justice system. The unwritten law of net widening is that less punitive alternatives tend to be applied to people who would otherwise not be under any social control at all—that is, they would be truly diverted and not arrested, prosecuted, or incarcerated.

Evaluations of early diversion programs found that they led to substantial net widening. More than half of the juveniles referred to 15 diversion projects in California would not have been committed to any kind of program under traditional practice. Thomas G. Blomberg found that juvenile diversion programs produced a 32 percent increase in the total number of juveniles under some form of control. Other evaluations have found varying degrees of net widening.[46] And as we shall see, net widening has plagued many of the new intermediate punishments such as boot camps.

A study of reforms in the San Francisco juvenile justice system in the mid-1990s that included new prevention and intervention systems and cost $20 million found a significant increase in the detention of juvenile arrestees, even though juvenile arrests declined by about half. And in fact, the average length of detentions increased despite the original goal of diverting juveniles from the system.[47]

The dynamics of net widening are easy to understand. Officials continue to use severe sanctions (e.g., prison) for offenders they regard as dangerous and use new and less punitive programs for less serious offenders whose cases they might have dismissed altogether. Thus, instead of dismissing cases and keeping less serious offenders completely out of the system, they "divert" them into a treatment program. As a result, more people are under control of the criminal justice system. The problem, of course, is that most of those low-risk offenders probably would have succeeded without the benefit of the program. The "treatment," whatever it is, added no additional crime reduction.

The net-widening phenomenon suggests that the old diversion did a better job of achieving the basic goal of keeping people out of the system. When a police officer does not make an arrest, that person is truly diverted; when a prosecutor dismisses all charges, that defendant is genuinely diverted. New diversion programs, however, keep people under some form of control, thereby maintaining or even increasing the total costs to the system.[48]

Do Diversion Programs Rehabilitate?

The most important question for us is whether diversion programs effectively rehabilitate offenders. More precisely, the question is: Do diversion programs provide a treatment or intervention that reduces future criminal behavior more effectively than normal prosecution, or even dismissal? A number of evaluations have found that they do not. The Justice Department touted the Des Moines (Iowa) Adult Diversion Project as an "exemplary project" that other communities should adopt. An evaluation, however, found that it had "little impact in reducing recidivism among diverted, compared to non-diverted offenders." In another program, diverted offenders had lower recidivism rates than did juveniles sent to juvenile court but, alas, had higher recidivism rates than did kids released outright without the benefit of any "treatment."[49] More recent reviews have found similarly disappointing results.

The failure of diversion programs is the result of a number of problems— and these are issues that we should keep in mind when we look at drug courts, reentry programs, or other innovations. First, many do not actually deliver the treatment services they claim to deliver. Some intensive probation supervision programs, for example, promised a high rate of contact between probationers and probation officers but did not achieve that goal.[50] Second, even when treatments are delivered, there are questions about the content of those treatment services. Do drug and alcohol treatment programs effectively reduce substance abuse? How many of the successful clients would have done so on their own, without the benefit of the treatment?

Additionally, if net widening occurs, the promised cost savings will not necessarily come about because there are now more rather than fewer people under the control of the criminal justice system.

Finally, diversion programs introduce serious due process considerations. A person who agrees to enter a treatment program in the expectation of having criminal charges dropped is, in effect, admitting guilt. Rather than contest the charge, the person is saying, "Yes, I have done something wrong, and you have a right to force me to undergo treatment." By offering a seemingly more attractive alternative to prosecution and possible incarceration, the program coerces this tacit admission of guilt in a subtle but powerful way. In addition, the selection of the program's clients may be unfair.[51]

In the end, diversion offers a false promise. It fails to achieve its own goals, may in fact contradict them, and does not offer a realistic solution to the problem of serious crime. Diversion is not really used for persons charged with robbery or burglary. Nor is there persuasive evidence that it rehabilitates lesser offenders in a way that keeps them from becoming serious offenders.

An evidence-based crime policy approach leads us to the following proposition:

PROPOSITION 45
Traditional diversion programs do not reduce serious crime.

THE NEW INTERMEDIATE PUNISHMENTS

In their 1990 book *Between Prison and Probation,* Norval Morris and Michael Tonry leveled a major criticism at criminal sentencing in America. They argued that at sentencing, judges faced a stark choice between two extremes: probation or prison. In many cases, however, prison is too harsh a punishment, while probation is too lenient. Their argument exposed the problem that probation involves neither meaningful treatment nor effective control of offenders in the community. Consequently, they called for the development of a range of intermediate punishments that would be less extreme than prison but with more content than traditional probation.[52]

Correctional officials and politicians across the country responded to Morris and Tonry by developing a set of new programs called *intermediate punishments.* They include boot camps, shock incarceration, intensive probation/parole supervision, home confinement, and electronic monitoring. These programs often overlap, and sentences typically include two or more different programs. Boot camps are often defined as a form of shock incarceration and frequently include a period of intensive parole supervision following release. Intensive probation/parole

Illustration by Frank Irwin, © Wadsworth, Cengage Learning.

supervision might include home confinement, which may be enforced through electronic monitoring.[53] All of these programs may include frequent random drug tests. In examining a particular intermediate punishment, therefore, it is important to look beyond the label and determine exactly what program elements it contains.

Ted Palmer and some others regard the new intermediate punishments as a revival of rehabilitation. Is this true? Palmer's own choice of words raises some doubts. He refers to *correctional intervention* instead of *rehabilitation*. The difference is more than a matter of semantics. As we shall see, the new intermediate punishments emphasize surveillance and control of offenders, often with little emphasis on traditional treatment components. Joan Petersilia argues, as have other critics, that parole has become largely devoted to the surveillance and control of parolees and that services designed to help them adjust to society have decreased and in many instances vanished altogether. What kind of services or control exists, for example, for the California parolees who report to the parole officers by mail?[54]

We now have 20 years of experience with the new intermediate punishments. What is the evidence for their effectiveness? We will start with a discussion of boot camps, a classic example of a new idea that generated a lot of excitement, and then quickly faded away.

The Rise and Fall of Boot Camps

Does anyone remember boot camps? Most students reading this book will not. Most faculty will remember them, but even some of the younger faculty may not. Boot camps burst on the scene in the mid-1980s as an exciting innovation, generating publicity as an effective alternative to prison sentences. By 2000, there were 95 boot camps in the country, enrolling 12,751 prisoners.[55] Gradually, however, the excitement faded. The evidence began to mount that they were not an effective alternative—or at least no more effective than other sanctions. The title of the article by criminologist Francis Cullen and his colleagues in a special 2005 issue of the *Journal of Offender Rehabilitation* said it all: "The Rise and Fall of Boot Camps."[56]

Boot camps are a classic example of the fad syndrome in criminal justice: an exciting new idea today is gone tomorrow. If you do a Web search for "boot camps," you find mostly commercial camps for special interests: boot camps for fitness, for teens, for computer skills—just about something for everyone, except for criminals.

What Is a Boot Camp?.   A boot camp usually involves (1) a short period of incarceration (typically three to six months); (2) in a facility separate from a regular prison; (3) for young first-time offenders (many exclude offenders convicted of violent crimes); (4) with a program of rigorous physical, educational, and substance-abuse-prevention programs; followed by (5) a period of intensive supervision in the community.

Many of the first boot camps emphasized their purely military aspects: "military drill and ceremony, hard labor, physical training, and strict rules and discipline."[57] As time passed, correctional officials gave more emphasis to the treatment elements, such as drug counseling. As is the case with other intermediate punishments, boot camps have multiple and conflicting goals. They are simultaneously intended to rehabilitate, punish, control, and reduce prison overcrowding.

The basic idea underlying boot camps is nothing new. Judges have routinely given split sentences: short periods of incarceration followed by probation. Boot camps are different primarily by virtue of the military rhetoric that surrounds them and the intensive probation supervision that usually follows release.

Boot camp programs vary considerably in terms of how participants are selected, the content of the boot camp program, and the nature of the postrelease supervision. In some states, judges sentence offenders directly to boot camp (these are sometimes referred to as *front-end* intermediate punishments). In others, correctional officials select participants (referred to as *back-end* programs). In some states, boot camp participation is voluntary, meaning that an offender must choose it. In others, it is mandatory for those sentenced to it. Offenders in some states can voluntarily drop out of the boot camp and return to prison.[58]

In terms of content, Doris Mackenzie and her colleagues found that one of the greatest differences among the boot camps in the eight states they evaluated was "the amount of time in the daily schedule that is devoted to work, drill, and physical training versus such treatment-type activities as counseling, drug treatment, or academic education."[59] Some boot camps are almost entirely military-style programs, whereas others put much more emphasis on traditional rehabilitation efforts.

Do boot camps work? Are they more effective than other forms of correctional treatment in reducing recidivism? The good news is that boot camps have been subject to rigorous evaluations. The bad news is that they do not reduce recidivism rates. In an assessment of 10 years of experience with boot camps, a Department of Justice report found that they generally produced "positive short-term changes in attitudes and behaviors" among their participants but that "with few exceptions, these positive changes did not lead to reduced recidivism." The graduates of some boot camps did have lower recidivism rates, but they participated in camps with more treatment services, more intensive sessions, and more intensive postrelease supervision. In short, there is today no consistent evidence that boot camps are more effective in reducing recidivism than are other types of correctional programs.[60]

A number of problems affect boot camp programs. The Department of Justice report concluded that "the length of stay in boot camps—usually from 90 to 120 days—was too brief to realistically affect recidivism." In short, as with many other correctional programs, there was not much "treatment." The report also found that there was "little or no postrelease programming to prepare [boot camp] graduates to lead productive lives."[61] Increasing recognition of this problem has heightened interest in reentry programs which we will examine in Chapter 14. One-third to half of offenders fail to complete the program. There also appears to be significant net widening, as judges or correctional officials place low-risk offenders in boot camp programs. As a result, overall system costs often increase rather than decrease. One problem that has affected all new intermediate punishment programs is that the intensified surveillance (e.g., more contacts with parole officers, frequent drug tests) identifies more technical violations of the conditions of release. This increases the failure rate and results in sending more offenders back to prison, a development that eliminates the potential cost savings.

Some critics argue that the emphasis on military drill may be fundamentally misguided. Yelling at inmates, treating them with disrespect, and forcing them to undergo painful physical exercises may be counterproductive, teaching inmates that disrespect and verbal abuse are the keys to success in life. Such programs also value the most aggressive definition of masculinity. Finally, the legendary rigors of Marine boot camp at least offer a reward at the end: entry into the proud fellowship of the Corps. If prison boot camps offer nothing of comparable positive value at the end but only a return to the same neighborhood with the same bleak prospects (what Hagan refers to as a life socially embedded in crime), they are not likely to have a long-term positive impact on the people who pass through them.[62]

The evidence leads us to the following conclusion:

PROPOSITION 46
Boot camps do not reduce crime.

HOME CONFINEMENT AND ELECTRONIC MONITORING

Home confinement (HC) and electronic monitoring (EM) are designed to keep the offender under fairly strict surveillance and control. HC is essentially a curfew. In some cases, it is enforced through EM; in others, it is not. Both HC and EM have the same mixture of goals as does IPS. They are designed to simultaneously reduce prison overcrowding and both control and rehabilitate the offender.

Electronic monitoring emerged in 1983 when Judge Jack Love of Albuquerque adopted the Gosslink system for a convicted offender. The idea quickly caught on. By 1996, there were 13,868 probationers and 8,491 parolees in EM programs.[63] An early report found EM to be far cheaper than imprisonment: it cost as little as $1,350 per year, versus $20,000 for prison. Basically two different EM technologies are available. *Passive monitoring radio frequency systems* place a transmitter on the offender (a tamper-proof bracelet or anklet) and a dialer on the telephone. If the probationer leaves the premises, the signal is interrupted, and the dialer automatically calls the probation office. *Active monitoring programmed contact systems* involve periodic, usually random telephone calls to the probationer's home. The calling may be done automatically by machine or by the PO's personal phone call.

Initially, the largest group of offenders in EM programs were traffic violation offenders. By 1989, property offenders and drug offenders had become the two largest categories. Sentences generally ran from 60 to 120 days. A Justice Department survey found that most failures occurred within the first two months. About 4 percent of the total sample committed a new offense, and half of those occurred in the first 60 days. About 22 percent of the sample committed a technical violation of the terms of their confinement.[64]

Many people initially opposed EM because it conjured up images of George Orwell's famous novel *1984,* with Big Brother continuously monitoring everyone's private behavior. In actual practice, EM may not deliver on its promises. Although advertised as a technological "fix" for the crime problem, EM systems often have serious technical and administrative problems. The signal can be disrupted by certain kinds of housing construction, and random calls in the middle of the night disrupt the probationer's sleep (not such a good idea if we want that person to hold a steady job) and require that a staff person be on duty to respond to a violation. The cost savings are also relatively small. The 12,000 offenders in EM programs in 1992 (probation and parole combined) represented a minuscule fraction of the 4.8 million under correctional supervision that year.[65]

The intensive surveillance that EM (and IPS) provides creates a special problem for the criminal justice system. It does succeed in detecting violations of probation or parole conditions, and many of the offenders are returned to prison. As the report *Performance Measures for the Criminal Justice System* points out, there is serious disagreement over whether a high rate of technical violations indicates success or failure. If the purpose of EM is to control offenders and detect misbehavior, then EM is a success. But if the purpose is to control costs and reintegrate the offender into the community, then it is a failure.[66]

Most important for our purposes, evaluations indicate that IPS, HC, and EM are no more effective in reducing crime than conventional prison or probation programs. Offenders in these programs have the same rearrest rate as those on conventional probation or parole.

This leads us to conclude:

PROPOSITION 47
Home confinement and electronic monitoring do not reduce crime.

Lessons of the Intermediate Punishment Movement

Reviewing the first 10 to 15 years of the intermediate punishment movement, Joan Petersilia reached some sobering conclusions. Most of the programs were "more symbolic . . . than substantive."[67]

Most seriously, there was no evidence that intermediate sanctions were more effective than traditional programs in reducing recidivism. In many cases, this was the result of implementation problems: lack of adequate funding and program resources, selection of inappropriate offenders, and so on. The one "tantalizing" positive finding, Petersilia concludes, is the evidence that offenders who participated in a range of programs—substance abuse treatment, community service, employment programs—had lower recidivism rates than comparable offenders who did not.[68] This finding is a central element of many of the drug courts we discuss shortly.

Confused Goals

IPS suffers from both confused goals and exaggerated promises. Its advocates claim it will rehabilitate offenders, keep them under control, reduce prison overcrowding, and save money—all at the same time. As some critics point out, if all this were true, IPS would be "the wonderchild of the criminal justice system."[69] Yet, as many observers have pointed out, current IPS programs emphasize surveillance and control rather than rehabilitation. A Justice Department report on *Performance Measures for the Criminal Justice System* argues that if the goal is surveillance and control, then a high failure rate is a positive indicator of the program's performance: Offenders who violate the terms of probation or commit another crime are taken off the streets and sent to prison.[70]

Many IPS programs do not necessarily serve the clients for whom they were designed. Although generally intended for those designated high-risk offenders, only 20 percent of the clients in the Georgia and New Jersey programs fit that definition. Georgia officials privately conceded that 25 percent of the IPS clients were not "true" diversions from prison. There were also rumors that New Jersey judges sentenced some offenders to prison only to make them eligible for "diversion" through IPS.[71]

The very intensity of the supervision in IPS programs has introduced an entirely new problem. Joan Petersilia reports that one-third of those offenders eligible for intensive probation in Marion County, Oregon, chose to go to prison. In New Jersey, 15 percent of those who applied for IPS withdrew their applications when they found out what IPS would be like.[72]

It is easy to see why offenders choose prison. The Oregon IPS program included home visits two or three times a week, with telephone checks on other days, unannounced searches for drugs, and periodic urine tests for drug use. Offenders were required to perform community service work and were forbidden to associate with certain people. This regime would last for two *years*. The alternative was a two- to four-year prison sentence that usually resulted in three to six *months* of actual time served, followed by two years of routine parole supervision, which meant only one visit per month and none of the other IPS requirements. The IPS program was far more intrusive and punitive than prison and parole.[73]

SPECIAL TREATMENT PROGRAMS

Treatment for Domestic Violence Batterers

A variety of treatment programs have been used for offenders with a record of violence. Sentencing offenders to anger management programs is an increasingly popular alternative. For about 30 years, batterer treatment programs have been used for men guilty of domestic violence. The most famous of these is the so-called Duluth Model, originally developed in Duluth, Minnesota. It is based on the assumption that men who commit domestic assault basically want to control their partners. The program's curriculum uses a "power and control wheel" to outline the various tactics used by assailants and to help them understand and ultimately control their behavior. (You can find the wheel and other information about the program through a Web search for the "Duluth Model.")[74]

A National Institute of Justice evaluation of two batterer programs based on the Duluth Model, however, found that they were not effective. The Broward County, Florida, program had "little or no effect" on its clients. The program was evaluated in terms of several measures, including clients' attitudes toward the role of women and subsequent violations of probation or rearrest. Twenty-four percent of the members of the treatment group and a control group were rearrested in the following 12 months while on probation. The evaluation did find lower levels of violence among those who were employed, married, and owned their own homes. But these understandable factors were unrelated to participation in the treatment program.

The second program, in Brooklyn, New York, resulted in "only minor improvements in some subjects." An interesting natural experiment occurred after the local prosecutor objected to the length and cost of the original 26-week treatment program. The program was shortened to eight weeks, resulting in two treatment groups. The clients participating in the 26-week program were less likely to be arrested than either the 8-week participants or the control group. This finding did provide some glimmer of hope, suggesting that perhaps a longer period of treatment might be effective.

A meta-analysis of 22 batterer programs concluded: "Overall, effects due to treatment were in the small range, meaning that the current interventions have a minimal impact on reducing recidivism beyond the effect of being arrested."[75]

A CONSERVATIVE VARIATION:
FAITH-BASED TREATMENT

While treatment for offenders has always been the preferred policy for liberals, the idea now has support among conservatives. They believe that faith-based treatment services will be effective in reducing criminal behavior among adults and juveniles. President George W. Bush created the Office of Faith-Based and Community Initiatives in January 2001 and spent several billion dollars on programs such as "abstinence only" education ($31 million in grants in 2004, for example). The program continues, with a slight change in emphasis, as the Office of Faith-Based and Neighborhood Partnerships under President Barack Obama. Across the country there are now many treatment programs—drug abuse treatment, alcohol treatment, employment counseling, etc.—that have some kind of religious component.

What exactly is faith-based treatment? Like most of the programs considered in this book, it is surrounded by a lot of myths and misunderstandings. Let's begin by sorting out the issues so we can focus our attention on the effectiveness of faith-based correctional treatment.

Sorting Out the Issues

Faith-based treatment involves several different kinds of programs incorporating religious belief. The most general kind of faith-based program is derived from *organic religion*. This means that religion is an integral part of a person's life, independent of any deviant or criminal behavior. Byron Johnson reviewed 669 studies of the impact of organic religion and found a consistent positive impact on a wide range of conditions. People who indicated religious faith and/or activity were less likely to experience hypertension, depression, suicidal thoughts, or alcohol or drug use or be involved in delinquent or criminal behavior. This finding is consistent with criminological theories associating criminal activity with anomie, a lack of positive attachment to family, differential association with offenders, and so on.[76]

The second general category of faith-based program is *intentional religion*. This is defined as "exposure to religion . . . at a particular time in life for a particular purpose."[77] An example would be a religiously centered drug treatment program in a prison setting. The religious component is introduced to the participants in the program with the specific intent of helping them overcome their drug abuse problem.

Actually, there are two kinds of intentional religion programs. One would be a social service program provided by a faith-based organization that has no religious content. A good example would be a homeless shelter or soup kitchen run by a church where people can get a bed for the night and a meal without having to participate in any religious activity. Many advocates of faith-based programs argue that religious organizations can deliver these services more efficiently and effectively than government-based programs.

A different form of intentional religion program is one in which the program includes religious content. A good example would be the drug treatment program that includes religious services, in which the underlying assumption is that developing religious commitment will help the clients overcome their drug dependency. (In the case of old-fashioned homeless shelters, this is referred to as "soup, soap, and salvation." To get the food and the bed you have to participate in religious services.)

Are Faith-Based Programs Effective?

Our focus here is on the latter category: intentional religion programs with religious content. Is there any evidence that they are effective in treating criminal offenders? And are they more effective than secular programs? Byron R. Johnson conducted a thorough review of the literature for the Center for Research on Religion and Urban Civil Society. His 2002 report is consistent with the standards of evidence-based crime policy, and we should take a close look at his findings.[78]

Johnson's most notable finding was that the impact of intentional religion has not been extensively studied by social scientists. While there were 669 studies of organic religion, he could find only 97 studies of intentional religion, and only 25 of those examined program effectiveness. These 25 studies also suffered from a number of weaknesses. Some did not describe their methodologies. Only a few were published in refereed journals. Many used qualitative methods and case studies, as opposed to quantitative studies with random assignment to treatment and control groups. Also, the studies were not rigorous in defining and measuring the "faith" component of faith-based programs. It is not always clear exactly what the religious part of a particular program was. Nor is it always clear how significant the religious component was compared with other aspects of the program.

Of the 11 studies that did involve a multivariate analysis, 10 found the faith-based program to be effective in terms of lower recidivism rates. For example, the participants in a Bible study group run by the group Prison Fellowship were less likely to be rearrested during the one-year follow-up period. A study of Teen Challenge, a faith-based alcohol abuse treatment program, found that its clients were more likely to remain sober and maintain employment than a comparison group who participated in a secular treatment program.

PROPOSITION 48

There is no evidence that faith-based treatment programs are any more or any less effective in reducing crime than are secular treatment programs.

DRUG COURTS: A NEW APPROACH

Drug courts are the most important development related to the treatment of offenders—or at least some of them. They are really a form of diversion, offering treatment rather than full prosecution. They don't use the term "diversion," however. This is another example of an old idea reappearing in a new form and with a new label. We will discuss drug courts again in Chapter 13, when we get to drugs and crime, but it is important to cover them here with regard to rehabilitation.

The advocates of drug courts make extravagant claims for their effectiveness. As Figure 11.3 indicates, they claim that drug courts reduce crime, save money, help preserve families, and more. These claims should immediately put us on alert. Over the years many other programs have made similar claims. Ordinary probation was going to achieve all these things when it first appeared. More recently, diversion and boot camps were going to accomplish the same things. But rather than be cynical and immediately dismiss drug courts, we need to be fair and look at the evidence about their effectiveness. And by the same token, we should insist that the advocates of drug courts provide credible evidence that meets the standards of evidence-based policy making.

The Verdict Is In . . . [italics added]

Drug Courts Reduce Crime

FACT: Nationwide, 75 percent of drug court graduates remain arrest free at two years after leaving the program.

Drug Courts Save Money

FACT: Nationwide, for every $1.00 invested in drug court, taxpayers save as much as $4.36 in avoided criminal justice courts alone.

Drug Courts Ensure Compliance

FACT: Drug courts provide much more comprehensive and closer supervision than other community-based supervision programs.

Drug Courts Restore Families

FACT: Family reunification rates are 50 percent higher for family drug court participants.

FIGURE 11.3   The Claims for Drug Courts

SOURCE: National Drug Court Institute. www.ncdi.org/learn.drug-sourts-work/.

What Are Drug Courts?.   The drug court idea was born in 1989 in Miami. It spread rapidly and enjoyed significant financial support from the U.S. Department of Justice. By January 1, 2009 there were over 2,301 drug courts across the country. They included 459 juvenile drug courts, 328 family drug courts, 79 tribal drug courts, and 30 reentry drug courts.[79]

A drug court is a specialized criminal court that handles substance abuse cases through a comprehensive program of treatment, supervision, and alternative sanctions. If an offender successfully completes a treatment program, the drug court has the option of dismissing the original criminal charges, reducing or setting aside a sentence, providing a lesser penalty, or some combination of these alternatives.[80] This is the old idea of diversion: getting offenders out of the system early in return for participating in treatment.

Why, then, should we assume that drug courts will succeed where the old diversion programs generally failed? There are several reasons. One important difference is the role of judges in drug courts. They are much more heavily involved in overseeing the progress of cases. They cooperate closely with prosecutors, defense attorneys, and treatment personnel throughout the process. Item #7 of the key components of drug courts is that "Ongoing judicial interaction with each drug court participant is essential."[81]

This is a nontraditional role for judges. That, in fact, is one of the reasons why drug courts may be more effective than earlier diversion programs. The idea of officials playing non-traditional roles, moreover, is consistent with recent developments in other parts of the criminal justice system. Remember, the most promising new programs in policing are certain community-oriented policing (COP) and problem-oriented policing (POP) programs that involve innovative roles for the police: identifying specific neighborhood problems; developing clearly focused responses, some of which involve non–law enforcement approaches (e.g., helping clean up the appearance of neighborhoods); and establishing partnerships with community groups and other agencies (see our discussions in Chapters 5 and 6). It is also consistent with the new role for judges in Community Prosecution, which we will discuss in Chapter 14.

There are other components of properly managed drug courts that set them apart from many—perhaps even most—earlier diversion programs. They include careful "initial and ongoing planning"; "written criteria" to determine which offenders are eligible to participate; providing access to "a continuum of alcohol, drug, and other related treatment and rehabilitation services"; frequent drug and alcohol testing to ensure abstinence; "monitoring and evaluation [to] measure the achievement of program goals and [to] measure effectiveness"; and finally, "partnerships among drug courts, other agencies, and community groups.[82]

These elements represent a very high standard. Earlier correctional treatment programs were often ill-planned, lacking in written criteria for client selection; did not closely monitor clients' progress; and did not submit to rigorous independent evaluation. And because they represent such a high standard, it is difficult for some programs to maintain all the necessary components. This is a very important point. It would be unrealistic to assume that all drug courts do all the things they should do. (Remember that many community policing programs were not well planned or fully implemented.) But it is equally true that meeting these standards greatly increases the chances of success. An evaluation of 10 years' experience with drug courts in Portland, Oregon, for example, found that clients had more favorable outcomes when the judge was more heavily involved in the process, and that judges had better client outcomes the second time they participated in the drug court. Good management, full implementation, and experience are important keys to success.[83]

Are drug courts effective?.   The advocates of drug courts make extraordinary claims for the success of drug courts. A 2008 "National Report Card," citing a recent evaluation, reported that "no other intervention can rival the results produced by drug courts." A 2005 Government Accountability Office (GAO) report for Congress found that subsequent drug use and criminal activity remained low for drug court graduates.[84]

These are indeed impressive results, but we have learned enough at this point to be skeptical about such claims. Do drug courts really achieve all these things? Actually, a close reading of the GAO report reveals that it found mixed results on some outcomes. First, completion rates for drug court clients varied widely, from a low of 27 percent to a high of 66 percent. In short, we can say that in the poorest performing court, it "failed" for 73 percent of the clients. That is not a very good performance. On the other hand, of course, in the best-performing court a 66 percent completion rate is very good, given the standards of most treatment programs. Think about it: what percentage of people successfully complete weight loss or smoking cessation programs?[85]

Second, only 8 of 23 programs that were reviewed provided adequate data to permit an evaluation of the impact on clients remaining drug free. That is not a good management performance, but it is consistent with a long and not very worthy tradition of treatment programs in criminal justice. Drug testing data on clients did, however, show significant reductions in drug use during participation in the program.

Third, although many programs did not collect and report data on criminal activity following completion of the drug court program, of the 17 programs providing data, 13 reported that lower recidivism (measured in terms of rearrest) endured. That is good news, although more rigorous evaluations, with longer follow-up periods, are needed.

Finally, the evidence on cost saving benefits was very mixed—again because of poor data from so many programs. Only 7 out of 23 programs provided useful data. Nonetheless, they generally achieved overall criminal justice system savings.

The 2008 Urban Institute report *To Treat or Not to Treat* makes a strong argument about both the crime reduction and cost saving aspects of drug courts. The report estimated that nationally about 1.5 million arrestees who are probably guilty of their offenses are potential candidates for drug court treatment. Effectively treating them would prevent several million crimes. Presently, however, only 55,000 are being treated at any given time. The Urban Institute estimates that expanding treatment services nationally to include all the eligible candidates would cost $13.7 billion, but save $46 in total societal costs, which is a cost–benefit ratio of $3.36 in savings for every $1.00 spent.[86]

The Urban Institute report makes a strong recommendation for expanding treatment to all eligible offenders. A close reading of the report, however, raises some disturbing questions. Expanding treatment to all drug dependent or drug abusing offenders requires lowering the eligibility criteria. Many drug court programs, however, exclude offenders who are charged with violent crimes. Including them would be a huge leap. Violent offenders are very likely to be very different from those charged only with drug possession or drug sale or property crimes. Including them might very well undermine the effectiveness of drug courts.

> ## PROPOSITION 49
> Carefully designed and well-managed drug courts are
> a promising treatment program.

CONCLUSION: ANY FUTURE FOR
REHABILITATION?

In the end, the evidence on rehabilitation generally does not look very promising. It is true that most offenders eventually stop their lawbreaking behavior. But most simply mature out of crime. Unfortunately, with the exception of drug courts, there is precious little evidence of "planned interventions" (recall that this is our definition of correctional treatment) that consistently cause offenders to cease their criminal activity earlier than they otherwise might. None of the highly publicized innovations such as boot camps or intensive supervision seem to be more successful than traditional programs. It is indeed true that some programs do work for some offenders, but we do not have diagnostic tools to match individual offenders with the right programs. This is our old friend the prediction problem. In the end, liberals who advocate rehabilitation are no more effective in predicting future behavior than are the conservative advocates of incapacitation.

Drug courts, however, appear to be an exception to the generally depressing rule. Carefully designed and well-managed programs that include all the necessary elements have proven to be successful. Three things are required to build on this success. First, it is necessary to identify what it takes to create and maintain a successful drug court. Second, it is important to identify what it takes to ensure continuity of a drug court over time. Finally, we need to continually evaluate the effectiveness of drug courts to make sure that the apparent early successes are not an illusion.

NOTES

1. Charles H. Logan and Gerald G. Gaes, "Meta-Analysis and the Rehabilitation of Punishment," *Justice Quarterly* 10 (June 1993): 245–263.

2. Lee B. Sechrest, Susan O. White, and Elizabeth Brown, *The Rehabilitation of Criminal Offenders: Problems and Prospects* (Washington, DC: National Academy of Sciences, 1979), pp. 18–19.

3. Michael Gottfredson and Travis Hirschi, "The True Value of Lambda Would Appear to Be Zero: An Essay on Career Criminals, Criminal Careers, Selective Incapacitation, Cohort Studies, and Related Topics," *Criminology* 24 (1986): 213–234.

4. Francis T. Cullen, Kristie R. Blevins, Jennifer S. Trager, and Paul Gendreau, "The Rise and Fall of Boot Camps: A Case Study in Common Sense Corrections," *Journal of Offender Rehabilitation* 40:3–4 (2005): 55.

5. Michael Tonry and Mary Lynch, "Intermediate Sanctions," in Michael Tonry, ed., *Crime and Justice: A Review of Research*, vol. 20 (Chicago: University of Chicago Press, 1996), pp. 99–144.

6. Robert Martinson, "What Works? Questions and Answers about Prison Reform," *Public Interest* 35 (Spring 1974): 22–54.

7. Robert Martinson, "Symposium on Sentencing: Part II," *Hofstra Law Review* 7.2 (1979): 243–258. The full report is published as Douglas Lipton, Robert Martinson, and Judith Wilks, *The Effectiveness of Correctional Treatment* (New York: Praeger, 1975).

8. Samuel Walker, *Popular Justice: A History of American Criminal Justice*, 2nd rev. ed. (New York: Oxford University Press, 1998).

9. Lipton et al., *The Effectiveness of Correctional Treatment*.

10. Sechrest et al., *The Rehabilitation of Criminal Offenders*, pp. 14, 31, 102.

11. Daniel Glaser, "What Works, and Why It Is Important: A Response to Logan and Gaes," *Justice Quarterly* 11 (December 1994): 711–723; quote on p. 721.

12. Glaser, "What Works?" See also John Hagan, "The Social Embeddedness of Crime and Unemployment," *Criminology* 31 (November 1993): 465–491.

13. Bureau of Justice Statistics, Probation and Parole in the United States, 2006 (Washington, DC: Department of Justice, 2007). Bureau of Justice Statistics, *Felony Sentences in State Courts, 2000* (Washington, DC: Department of Justice, 2003). NCJ 198821.

14. Pew Center on the States, *One in 31: The Long Reach of American Corrections* (Washington, DC: Pew Center on the States, 2009).

15. Todd R. Clear and Anthony A. Braga, "Community Corrections," in James Q. Wilson and Joan Petersilia, eds., *Crime* (San Francisco: ICS Press, 1995), p. 431.

16. Petersilia and Turner, *Intensive Supervision Probation for High Risk Offenders,* p. 47.

17. Bureau of Justice Statistics, *Probation and Parole in the United States, 2006.*

18. Hagan, "The Social Embeddedness of Crime and Unemployment."

19. Nancy G. La Vigne, Christy Visher, and Jennifer Castro, *Chicago Prisoners' Experiences Returning Home* (Washington, DC: The Urban Institute, 2004). www.urban.org.

20. Bureau of Justice Statistics, Probation and Parole in the United States, 2006.

21. Ibid.

22. David J. Rothman, *Conscience and Convenience: The Asylum and Its Alternatives in Progressive America* (Boston: Little, Brown, 1980); Jonathan Simon, *Poor Discipline: Parole and the Social Control of the Underclass, 1890–1990* (Chicago: University of Chicago Press, 1993).

23. Joan Petersilia, "Measuring the Performance of Community Corrections."

24. Ibid., p. 512.

25. "Recidivism Rates of State Prisoners Released in 1983 and 1994," Bureau of Justice Statistics, *Sourcebook of Criminal Justice Statistics 2003*, Table 6.52.

26. Joan Petersilia, *When Prisoners Come Home* (New York: Oxford, 2003), p. 85.

27. Ibid., p. 81.

28. La Vigne et al., *Chicago Prisoners' Experiences Returning Home.*

29. Walker, *Popular Justice.*

30. Petersilia, *When Prisoners Come Home,* p. 71.

31. Bureau of Justice Statistics, *Correctional Populations in the United States, 1996* (Washington, DC: Department of Justice, 1999), p. 124.

32. Robert Martinson and Judith Wilks, "Save Parole Supervision," *Federal Probation* 41 (September 1977): 23–27.

33. J. Banks, A. A. Porter, R. L. Rardin, T. R. Silver, and V. E. Unger, *Evaluation of Intensive Special Probation Projects* (Washington, DC: Department of Justice, 1977).

34. Todd Clear and Patricia Hardyman, "The New Intensive Supervision Movement," *Crime and Delinquency* 36 (January 1990): 42–60.

35. Petersilia and Turner, *Intensive Supervision Probation for High Risk Offenders.*

36. Ibid.

37. Bureau of Justice Statistics, *Probation and Parole in the United States, 2006* (Washington, DC: Department of Justice, 2007).

38. Bureau of Justice Statistics, *Trends in State Parole, 1990–2000* (Washington, DC: Department of Justice, 2001). NCJ 184735.

39. Petersilia, *When Prisoners Come Home.*

40. Joan Petersilia, Ryken Grattet, and Jeffrey Lin, *Parole Violations and Revocations in California* (Washington, DC: Department of Justice, 2008). Bureau of Justice Statistics, Probation and Parole in the United States, 2006.

41. Raymond T. Nimmer, *Diversion: The Search for Alternative Forms of Prosecution* (Chicago: American Bar Foundation, 1974).

42. Nimmer, *Diversion*, pp. 11–18, 41–51.

43. President's Crime Commission, *The Challenge of Crime in a Free Society* (Washington, DC: Government Printing Office, 1967), p. 165.

44. Vera Institute of Justice, *The Manhattan Court Employment Project: Final Report* (New York: Vera Institute of Justice, 1972).

45. U.S. Department of Justice, *Diversion of Felony Arrests: An Experiment in Pretrial Intervention* (Washington, DC: Department of Justice, 1981).

46. Thomas G. Blomberg, "Widening the Net: An Anomaly in the Evaluation of Diversion Programs," in Malcolm W. Klein and K. S. Teilman, eds., *Handbook of Criminal Justice Evaluation* (Beverly Hills, CA: Sage, 1980), pp. 572–592.

47. Jacqueline Sullivan, *Widening the Net in Juvenile Justice and the Dangers of Prevention and Early Intervention* (San Francisco: Center of Juvenile and Criminal Justice, 2002). Available on the website of the Center of Juvenile and Criminal Justice.

48. Eugene Doleschal, "The Dangers of Criminal Justice Reform," *Criminal Justice Abstracts* 14 (March 1982): 133–152. A different perspective on criminal justice reform is in Samuel Walker, *Taming the System: The Control of Discretion in American Criminal Justice, 1950–1990* (New York: Oxford University Press, 1993).

49. Blomberg, "Widening the Net," p. 592.

50. Joan Petersilia and Susan Turner, *Intensive Supervision Probation for High Risk Offenders: Findings from Three California Experiments* (Santa Monica, CA: Rand, 1990).

51. Jamie Gorelick, "Pretrial Diversion: The Threat of Expanding Social Control," *Harvard Civil Rights—Civil Liberties Law Review* 10 (1975): 180–214.

52. Norval Morris and Michael Tonry, *Between Prison and Probation* (New York: Oxford University Press, 1990).

53. Richard A. Ball, C. Ronald Huff, and J. Robert Lilly, *House Arrest and Correctional Policy* (Beverly Hills, CA: Sage, 1988).

54. Petersilia, *When Prisoners Come Home,* p. 80.

55. Bureau of Justice Statistics, *Census of State and Federal Correctional Facilities, 2000* (Washington, DC: Department of Justice, 2003), Table 18. NCJ 198272.

56. Special Issue, "Rehabilitation Issues, Problems and Prospects in Boot Camps," *Journal of Offender Rehabilitation* 40 (nos. 3–4, 2005). Cullen et al., "The Rise and Fall of Boot Camps," 53–70.

57. Doris Layton MacKenzie, Robert Brame, David McDowall, and Claire Souryal, "Boot Camp Prisons and Recidivism in Eight States," *Criminology* 33 (August 1995): 351.

58. For a discussion of the distinction between front end and back end, see Tonry and Lynch, "Intermediate Sanctions," pp. 110–111.

59. MacKenzie et al., "Boot Camp Prisons and Recidivism in Eight States."

60. Dale G. Parent, *Correctional Boot Camps: Lessons from a Decade of Research* (Washington, DC: Department of Justice, 2003). NCJ 197018. Doris Layton MacKenzie, David B. Wilson, and Suzanne B. Kider, "Effects of Correctional Boot Camps on Offending," *The Annals* 578 (November 2001): 126–143.

61. Parent, *Correctional Boot Camps: Lessons from a Decade of Research.*

62. Merry Morash and Lila Rucker, "A Critical Look at the Idea of Boot Camp as a Correctional Reform," *Crime and Delinquency* 36 (April 1990): 204–222.

63. Bureau of Justice Statistics, *Correctional Populations in the United States, 1996*, p. 124.

64. Marc Renzema and David T. Skelton, *Use of Electronic Monitoring in the United States: 1989 Update* (Washington, DC: Department of Justice, 1990).

65. Bureau of Justice Statistics, *Correctional Populations in the United States, 1992.*

66. Bureau of Justice Statistics, *Performance Measures for the Criminal Justice System* (Washington, DC: Department of Justice, 1993), pp. 67–68.

67. Joan Petersilia, "A Decade of Experimenting with Intermediate Sanctions: What Have We Learned?" in National Institute of Justice, *Perspectives on Crime and Justice: 1997–1998* (Washington, DC: Department of Justice, 1998). p. 3. NCJ 172851.

68. Ibid., p. 6.

69. Todd Clear, S. Flynn, and C. Shapiro, "Intensive Supervision in Probation," in Belinda McCarthy, ed., *Intermediate Punishments* (Monsey, NY: Willow Tree Press, 1987), pp. 10–11.

70. Petersilia, "Measuring the Performance of Community Corrections," p. 67.

71. Clear and Hardyman, "The New Intensive Supervision Movement."

72. Joan Petersilia, "When Probation Becomes More Dreaded than Prison," *Federal Probation* 54 (March 1990): 23–27.

73. Ibid.

74. National Institute of Justice, *Do Batterer Intervention Programs Work? Two Studies* (Washington, DC: Department of Justice, 2003). NCJ 195079.

75. J. C. Babcock, C. E. Green, and C. Robie, "Does Batterers' Treatment Work? A Meta-analytic Review of Domestic Violence Treatment," *Clinical Psychology Review* 23 (January 2004): 1023–1053.

76. Byron R. Johnson, *Objective Hope: Assessing the Effectiveness of Faith-Based Organizations: A Review of the Literature* (Philadelphia: Center for Research on Religion and Urban Civil Society, 2002).

77. Ibid., p. 8.

78. Ibid.

79. The most recent data is on the website of the National Drug Court Institute. www.ndci.org.

80. Bureau of Justice Statistics, *Defining Drug Courts: The Key Components* (Washington, DC: Department of Justice, 1997), p. 7. NCJ 165478.

81. National Association of Drug Court Professionals, *Defining Drug Courts: The Key Components* (Washington, DC: Department of Justice, 1997).

82. Ibid.

83. Michael W. Finnegan, Shannon M. Carey, and Anton Cox, *The Impact of a Mature Drug Court Over Ten Years: of Operation: Recidivism and Costs* (Washington, DC: Department of Justice, 2007).

84. National Drug Court Institute, *Painting the Picture: A National Report Card on Drug Courts and Other Problem-Solving* (Washington, DC: Department of Justice, 2008), p. 2. Government Accountability Office, *Adult Drug Courts: Evidence Indicates Recidivism Reductions and Mixed Results for Other Outcomes,* Report to Congressional Committees (Washington, DC: Government Accountability Office, 2005).

85. Government Accountability Office, *Adult Drug Courts.*

86. The Urban Institute, *To Treat or Not to Treat: Evidence on the Prospects of Expanding Treatment to Drug-Involved Offenders* (Washington, DC: The Urban Institute, 2008).

12

Gain Compliance with the Law

THE BASIS OF AN ORDERLY SOCIETY

Compliance with the Law

The ultimate goal of the criminal justice system—and of all social institutions, including schools, fire departments, health systems, and all government agencies—is to create and maintain an orderly society in which people are free to go about their lives. This book has examined a number of strategies that rely on external coercion to get people to obey the law. Increasing the number of police or making sentences more punitive are designed to deter crime through fear. The evidence we have examined so far indicates that this approach does not really work – or at least does not make it work better than it already does. An important new direction in criminal justice policy broadens the focus to prevent crime by cultivating voluntary compliance with the law. It is a matter of achieving law-abiding behavior because people want to, because it is consistent with their own values.

How can this be achieved? How can we make people law abiding? The research by Wolfgang that we considered in Chapter 4 clearly suggests that most people do in fact obey the law—well, at least most of the laws most of the time. Furthermore, many of those who do break the law (or have a contact with the police, in Wolfgang's study) eventually stop and become law abiding. This chapter examines the recent research suggesting that the conduct of criminal justice agencies themselves can help instill law-abiding behavior.

Legitimacy and Compliance

The most important research on achieving voluntary compliance with the law is in the field of social psychology and specifically the subfield of procedural justice, with Tom Tyler as the major theoretician. Tyler argues that a critical factor in people's willingness to comply with the law is the *perceived legitimacy* of the law and the justice system.[1] If people believe the system is just and fair, they are more likely to obey the law. If they feel the police, the courts, and other criminal justice institutions are fair and effective, they will respect them, cooperate with them, regard them as legitimate, and as a result be more inclined to obey the law.

The National Academy of Sciences' report, *Fairness and Effectiveness in Policing,* makes an important distinction between *lawfulness* and *legitimacy.* Lawfulness refers to whether the police comply with the law (obeying statutes, department rules, and court decisions). Do they treat people equally? Do they not use excessive force? Do they comply with the *Miranda* decision? The same questions apply to prosecutors and judges. Do prosecutors handle plea bargains equally? Do judges sentence offenders fairly and in compliance with the law?

Legitimacy, on the other hand, refers to how people perceive the actions of police and other officials. Do they believe that the police treat people equally? Or do they believe, for example, that there is racial profiling? Do they believe that plea bargains and criminal sentences are fair? These perceptions are a matter of social psychology, and they may be consistent or inconsistent with what officials actually do. A police department, for example, may never engage in race discrimination, but if people believe it does, they will not regard the department as legitimate. Prosecutors may handle plea bargains fairly and consistently, but if people believe that the system is unfair they will distrust it.[2]

The concept of legitimacy originates with the founding of the field of sociology and the work of Max Weber. Weber argued that the social dynamics of authority in society involve not just the coercive power of social institutions to force people to do things, but the voluntary obligation that people feel to do those things—that is, to comply with the law.[3]

Sources of Legitimacy

With respect to criminal justice, the concept of procedural justice holds that people's satisfaction with the system depends heavily on how they feel they were treated by it. The important factor is the process, not just the outcome. Process involves procedural justice; outcomes involve distributive justice. People are more likely to feel that the system is fair if they have a chance to tell their side of the story, that someone in authority listens to them, and that they have some control over the process. The ability to tell your side of the story is referred to as having a "voice" in the process. Later, we will see how some criminal justice reforms are designed to give people a greater voice.

Think of this in terms of your grade in a course. The grade you receive represents distributive justice. You got a C+ and someone else got an A. Let's

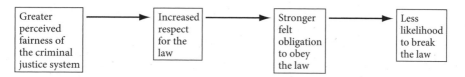

F I G U R E 12.1 Procedural justice model of crime prevention

say you appeal the grade. How the professor handles the appeal represents procedural justice. If he or she explains what you failed to include in your term paper, or how the paper was not well organized or clearly written, you are more likely to accept the grade. If you have an opportunity to tell your side of story (for example, to explain why you thought certain material was not relevant), you are more likely to feel that the process was fair. You are still unhappy about your grade, but you are satisfied with the process. As a result, you will have more trust in the teacher, the course, and the university. If, on the other hand, you do not get the chance to discuss your grade, or the professor treats you with disrespect, you will be angry about both your grade and the process. Your respect for and trust in the teacher and the university will suffer.

Now let's apply this scenario to criminal justice. Let's say that you are stopped for a traffic violation. You ask the officer, "What's the problem?" If the officer explains what you did, and speaks to you respectfully, you are likely to accept the legitimacy of the ticket. But if the officer refuses to answer your question, does not explain what you did, or is rude to you, you will be upset over the ticket and the officer's conduct. Sarah Stotland's research on trust and confidence in the police explored the extent to which people felt the police shared their priorities (e.g., effective crime control), were competent and dependable, and treated people with respect.[4] Many experts on racial profiling, for example, argue that officer behavior during the process of stops of African Americans leads to allegations of racial profiling. To correct this problem, the report on racial profiling by the Police Executive Research Forum offers a model policy for traffic stops that emphasizes respectful behavior on the part of officers. It recommends that officers introduce themselves, explain the basis for the stop, and offer an apology if the person has been mistakenly stopped.[5]

Does a sense of fairness and justice make a difference in terms of law-abiding behavior? Tyler investigates this question in his book *Why People Obey the Law.*[6] Tyler's study was based on interviews with 1,575 Chicago residents, 804 of whom were reinterviewed a year later. Respondents were asked about their own lawbreaking (e.g., speeding, littering, shoplifting) and their perceptions of and experience with the police and the courts. The latter questions were designed to determine respondents' sense of the legitimacy of the justice system. Tyler concluded: "Citizens who view legal authority as legitimate are generally more likely to comply with the law."[7]

In another study, Casper, Tyler, and Fisher found that among several hundred male felony defendants in three cities, procedural justice issues were associated with their evaluation of their experience in criminal court. Particularly important was how they felt they were treated by the police (e.g., did the officer "treat you in a businesslike manner?" or "use disrespectful language?") and the amount of time their lawyer spent with them. Interestingly, defendants' evaluations were not affected by whether they had a private attorney or a public defender, or whether they pled guilty or went to trial. In short, how they felt they were treated shaped their level of satisfaction with the system.[8]

Finally, a reanalysis of the Milwaukee Domestic Violence Experiment found that aspects of procedural justice were associated with lower recidivism rates.

Arrestees who felt they were treated in a procedurally fair manner had recidivism rates that were as low as the rates for those given a more favorable outcome (e.g., warned but not arrested).[9]

Does Justice Matter?

The major implication of procedural justice is that we have placed too much emphasis on fear and coercion as the basis for crime policy. We rely too much on increasing the fear of arrest, prosecution, and a long prison sentence to get people to obey the law. But as we have learned so far, increasing the risk of arrest is difficult if not impossible (Chapter 5), harsher sentences do not deter people for committing crime (Chapter 6), and so on. We have failed to invest the same amount of resources in making people feel positively about the law and the criminal justice system and gain their voluntary lawful behavior. The procedural justice perspective says that people are not motivated primarily by fear of punishment, but are more likely to be influenced by positive attachments and feelings of loyalty.

The Limitations of Procedural Justice Theory and Research

The procedural justice perspective, and its potential as a crime-reduction strategy, is a very important new direction for crime policy. The idea is still in its infancy and the research is limited, however, and we need to be as cautious and skeptical about as we are with other crime policies.

One major limitation with the research is a particularly important cause for concern. When we look at Tyler's research in *Why People Obey the Law* we find that the questions regarding law abiding behavior all involve minor offenses. The survey asked Chicago residents how frequently they "Drove over 55 miles per hour on the highways," "Parked [a] car in violation of the law," disturbed the neighbors with noise, or littered. The two most serious violations involved drunk driving ("Drove a car while intoxicated") or shoplifted ("Took inexpensive items from stores without paying for them.")[10] Needless to say, these violations are not the same as burglary, robbery or rape. They are the kind of things middle-class and generally law-abiding citizens do. Tyler correlated the responses with questions about how they perceived the justice system, including how they themselves were treated. If we are serious about reducing serious crime—burglary and robbery—we need to know how offenders who repeatedly engage in these crimes (the career criminals we discussed in Chapter 4) are affected by their perceptions of the justice system. Do better treatment and a resulting sense of fairness result in more law-abiding behavior? That is the real test of the procedural justice perspective.

This leads us to the following conclusion:

PROPOSITION 50
Creating a greater sense of the legitimacy of the criminal justice system may encourage law-abiding behavior and reduce crime.

BUILDING LEGITIMACY

Assuming that legitimacy may generate more positive attitudes toward the law and less lawbreaking, the question becomes, How can criminal justice agencies build and maintain legitimacy? One of the most important ways to build trust in the criminal justice system is to eliminate unlawful behavior injustice—and the perception of injustice—in the everyday operations of the system itself.

Reducing Unlawful Behavior by the Police

The most visible injustices occur in policing. Unlike other parts of the criminal justice system, the police work in the community—with patrol cars and uniformed officers out in the streets. The most inflammatory controversies involve police use of deadly force and excessive physical force. There has been considerable progress in reducing racial disparities in fatal shootings. For example, a recent Bureau of Justice Statistics report found that the racial disparity in persons shot and killed by the police is half what it was 25 years ago.[11] Nonetheless, fatal shootings of African Americans continue to provoke anger and accusations of racism in the African American community.

Racial profiling, defined as police making traffic stops based on race or ethnicity rather than genuine lawbreaking, is a major controversy. Public opinion surveys consistently indicate a widespread belief that racial profiling exists, even though the official data on stops have found it difficult to prove that belief conclusively.[12] Police departments have taken steps to reduce race discrimination in traffic stops and other activities through written policies, early intervention systems (EIS) to identify officers with performance problems, and improvements in the internal investigation of critical incidents. We do not, however, have comprehensive data on the overall impact of these accountability measures.[13]

Finally, there is evidence of significant disparity in drug enforcement. African Americans represent 38 percent of all drug arrests (in 2008) despite the fact that the National Household Survey of Drug Abuse (see Chapter 13) finds that African Americans are only somewhat more likely to use illegal drugs than whites (and Latinos less likely to use them than either of those two groups).[14] This disparity may be due to the fact that the police concentrate their drug enforcement efforts in minority communities while ignoring drug offenses in other communities. Jerome Miller characterizes the justice system's approach to young African American men as one of "search and destroy."[15] The perception of discrimination and injustice in this regard undermines the legitimacy of the criminal justice system.

The important but still unanswered question is whether reducing unlawful behavior would, by itself, have a significant impact on public attitudes, increase public trust in the justice system, and cause people to change their behavior. This is an extremely complex issue that would require a very elaborate research design. Let's assume, for example, that a police department succeeds in reducing the incidence of excessive force by its officers through a set of accountability measures. A research effort would have to investigate, first, whether citizens perceived the reduction in the use of force; second, attributed that change to the department's accountability efforts; then, developed greater confidence and trust in the department as a result; and finally, became more law abiding as a result. This would be an enormously difficult undertaking. But it is extremely important, because it lies at the heart of the procedural justice argument about developing more law-abiding behavior.

Improving Citizen Satisfaction with the Police

Another strategy for improving citizen satisfaction with the police is to engage in policing programs that people believe are consistent with their interests) or what Sarah Stoutland's defined as "priorities").[16] Community-oriented policing and problem-oriented policing are both designed to develop programs to fight crime and disorder that are tailored for specific neighborhoods and to engage community residents in that process. One way for the police to engage citizens is to conduct regular beat meetings where officers and citizens discuss neighborhood problems and monitor progress of initiatives. Beat meetings are consistent with the procedural justice concept of giving citizens a "voice" in matters that are important to them. The City of Chicago incorporated beat meetings into its community policing effort (CAPS, or Chicago Alternative Policing Strategy), and found reasonably good citizen participation in the meetings, and that CAPS had a generally positive impact on citizen attitudes. Its evaluation did not, however, investigate our question of whether more positive attitudes translated into more law-abiding behavior.[17] These findings are promising, but more research is needed on the impact of different community policing and problem-oriented policing programs on citizen participation in police programs, and the impact on citizen perceptions of the police.

Another strategy for increasing citizen satisfaction with the police is to improve citizen complaint procedures. Since the 1960s, one of the main complaints by African Americans has been that procedures for handling complaints about police misconduct do not investigate complaints thoroughly or fairly—and that the investigations are just "cover-ups" or "white washes," according to critics. Civil rights leaders have demanded independent citizen review of the police—civilian review boards, in many cases—to investigate complaints. Citizen review boards or other forms of citizen oversight exist in almost every big city today.[18]

Does citizen oversight of the police actually improve satisfaction with the complaint process and the police? And does that lead to more law-abiding behavior? There is no clear answers to the first question, and no evidence at all regarding the second. There has not been rigorous research on the impact of independent review boards, particular on citizen satisfaction.[19] One promising innovation regarding the handling of citizen complaints involves mediating complaints. Mediation is not designed to determine whether the officer did something wrong. Rather, it is a process by which the complainant and the officer meet to discuss the incident, with a trained mediator conducting the session. The goal is to allow each side to tell his or her story and listen to the other side. The process gives a "voice" to people on both sides, consistent with procedural justice theory. Research on complaint mediation programs has found that they result in much higher levels of satisfaction than traditional complaint investigation procedures—which in fact tend to alienate both officers and complainants.[20]

Perceived Injustice in Courts and Corrections

The perception of injustice also exists with regard to other parts of the criminal justice system. As we learned in Chapter 8, the traditional secrecy surrounding plea bargaining is the cause of much suspicion and distrust, particularly a feeling that some dangerous offenders get off easy with a plea to a lesser offense. Some recent reforms have attempted to open up the process and enhance public understanding. Victims' voice laws, which we examined in Chapter 9, are designed to give crime victims a "voice" in plea negotiations and in sentencing decisions.

Racial disparities in sentencing, particularly in drug cases and the death penalty, are the source of grievances among African Americans. Over half (53 percent) of African Americans in 2009 thought the death penalty was not applied fairly, compared with 32 percent of whites. Over the years, African Americans have been less supportive than whites of more law enforcement as a crime control strategy, and more supportive of strategies that address social problems.[21] Finally, innovative community prosecution programs seek to develop partnerships with neighborhood residents and businesses. We will examine community prosecution programs in Chapter 14.

This leads us to the following proposition:

> ### PROPOSITION 51
> Eliminating discrimination and the perception of injustice may reduce alienation from the criminal justice system. Whether it helps to increase law-abiding behavior is an unproven theory.

DECRIMINALIZATION

New Perspective on an Old Issue

For decades, decriminalizing certain offenses was a major liberal policy recommendation. Years ago, in their 1970 book *The Honest Politician's Guide to Crime Control,* Norval Morris and Gordon Hawkins called decriminalization a "first principle." Specifically, they proposed removing criminal penalties on (1) public drunkenness; (2) purchase, possession, and use of all drugs; (3) all forms of gambling; (4) disorderly conduct and vagrancy; (5) abortion; (6) private sexual activity between consenting adults; and (7) juvenile "status" offenses.[22]

We should clarify exactly what kinds of behavior are involved in the list offered by Morris and Hawkins. Public drunkenness is included, but not drunk driving. The person drunk on the street may be a nuisance but poses no real threat of harm to anyone else. The drunk driver does pose such a threat.

Sexual activity between consenting adults is included, but not sex between an adult and a child. Adults have the capacity to make choices; children are vulnerable and need the protection of the law. In short, the standard decriminalization proposal covers a limited range of activity and not a general repeal of all criminal laws governing drinking or sex.

While decriminalization has generally been a liberal policy recommendation, libertarian conservatives also support decriminalizing some offenses. A number of prominent conservatives now support the legalization of drugs, for example. In short, just as many liberals have adopted traditional conservative crime control ideas, so have some conservatives embraced some traditional liberal ideas. Decriminalization or legalization of drugs is a major policy alternative today. We will consider that issue in detail in Chapter 13, which deals with drugs and drug policy.

The issue of legitimacy puts the old idea of decriminalization in a new perspective. Many people are alienated from the law and the criminal justice system because they believe the criminalization of certain kinds of behavior interferes with their personal privacy, or has bad consequences for the justice system, or both. It is possible that decriminalization of certain offenses will remove that alienation and increase respect for the law. As a result, according to the idea of legitimacy, they may become more law-abiding with respect to other laws.

This chapter examines decriminalization from the standpoint of its potential impact on the tendency of people to commit more serious crimes, such as robbery and burglary.

The Rationale for Decriminalization

The basic assumption underlying decriminalization is the long-standing belief among liberals that the criminal law in the United States covers too much behavior. This is referred to as the *overreach* of the criminal law. In his classic work *The Limits of the Criminal Sanction,* Herbert L. Packer argues, "The criminal sanction is indispensable, [but] we resort to it in far too indiscriminate a way."[23] His point is that we should use it more sparingly and focus it on offenses that do genuine harm and about which there is a broad social consensus.

The overreach of the criminal law has several undesirable consequences.[24] First, it overburdens the justice system with relatively minor offenses, such as public drunkenness, leaving it with fewer resources for the really serious crimes of murder, rape, robbery, and burglary. Public drunkenness is a good example. A 1971 report by the American Bar Foundation defined the problem as *Two Million Unnecessary Arrests.*[25] Actually, the number of arrests for drunkenness has been declining steadily, from 1.2 million in 1975 to 713,000 in 1994 to 611,069 in 2008.[26] These arrests consume a large amount of police and court resources. We can legitimately ask whether this effort is worth the cost.

A second problem is that no strong public consensus prevails about whether some behavior should be criminalized. Packer argues that "the criminal sanction should ordinarily be limited to conduct that is viewed, *without significant social dissent,* as immoral" (emphasis added).[27] The problem, however, is that there is much dissent on many issues. Americans have very mixed attitudes about gambling, for example; they feel that something is immoral about it, but they love to bet on sports nonetheless.

This relates directly to the legitimacy issue as defined by Tyler. If people feel that the law is intruding on behavior that they believe is harmless and in which they want to engage, their respect for the law will suffer. One good example of this is the medical use of marijuana. Many people feel that the use of marijuana is a legitimate and effective treatment for relieving the pain of certain illnesses. They object to the fact that it is illegal.

One result of conflicting public attitudes is selective and often arbitrary law enforcement. This practice violates the principle of equal protection of the law and leads to cynicism about law enforcement among the public and police officers. Packer argues that "respect for law generally is likely to suffer."[28]

This issue is also at the heart of legitimacy as defined by Tyler. Racial and ethnic discrimination is the central controversy in the administration of justice. Public opinion polls consistently indicate that African Americans and Latinos have lower levels of confidence in the police and other parts of the justice system than do white Americans.[29]

A third problem is that making certain activities illegal leads to the development of criminal syndicates that provide the goods and services people want. Thirty years ago, the President's Crime Commission argued, "The core of organized crime activity is the supplying of illegal goods and services ... to countless numbers of citizen customers."[30] Gambling was historically the principal source of revenue for organized crime, and the United States' demand for illegal drugs sustains vast international networks and neighborhood drug gangs. In this sense, the law becomes criminogenic, creating forms of criminal behavior.

Fourth, the criminal syndicates that are created by making gambling and other activities illegal corrupt the justice system. The Knapp Commission's investigation into police corruption in New York City in the early 1970s found that police officers were receiving a weekly "pad" of between $300 and $1,500 a month for protecting illegal gambling.[31] Twenty years later, the Mollen Commission found that the worst forms of police corruption and brutality in New York City were associated with drug trafficking.[32] Finally, the huge corruption and brutality scandal that was discovered in the Los Angeles Police Department in 1999 was clearly associated with the war on drugs, which created a climate in which LAPD officers felt they could get away with anything.[33]

Fifth, many people believe that certain kinds of recreation—sex and the use of some substances—is a matter of private choice that should be protected by the law. The overwhelming majority of Americans believe that sex between two adults of the opposite sex should not be a crime. About half of all Americans today now believe that sex between two adults of the same sex should not be a crime. Over 80 percent of Americans believe that women have a right to terminate a pregnancy by abortion, although many believe that certain limited restrictions are also appropriate.[34] This can have a profound effect on the perceived legitimacy of the criminal justice system. If a lot of people feel that the law is intruding on their privacy, they will lose respect for the law and the system.

Sixth, many criminal justice and public health experts believe that the problems associated with drinking, gambling, and sex are really social, psychological, and medical problems that should not be addressed through the criminal law. The President's Crime Commission concluded that the criminal justice system "is not in a position to meet [the chronic alcoholic's] underlying medical and social problems."[35] Many drug policy reform experts have been arguing for decades that drug abuse is a medical problem that should be treated as such and not be made a crime. Arrest and prosecution do nothing to help the chronic alcoholic deal with his or her drinking problem, and in many cases they make matters worse. Medical and social services would be a far more effective response.[36]

The Terms of the Debate

Not everyone agrees with the traditional arguments in favor of decriminalization. The debate between advocates and opponents of decriminalization raises fundamental questions about the role of the criminal law, involving issues of moral standards and the practical effects of criminalization.

Everyone does agree with the principle that the criminal law expresses (or should express) the basic values of society and defines the boundaries of acceptable conduct. Robbery is a crime because we believe that taking something that

Illustration by Frank Irwin, © Wadsworth, Cengage Learning.

belongs to another person is wrong. Murder is a crime because taking another person's life is wrong. As Patrick Devlin puts it, "The criminal law as we know it is based upon moral principle."[37]

The question is not *whether* the law should express the values of society but *which values* it should express. As Packer says, "Whose morality are we talking about?"[38] Is gambling morally wrong or a legitimate form of entertainment? Is homosexual behavior morally wrong or a matter of private choice? Is abortion morally wrong (murder, in the eyes of anti-abortion activists) or a constitutionally protected private choice? Conservatives generally believe that these behaviors are morally wrong and therefore should be prohibited by the criminal law. Liberals generally believe that there is nothing immoral about these same behaviors and therefore they should not be made illegal. According to criminologist Gilbert Geis, certain forms of behavior are "not the law's business."[39]

Whether certain forms of behavior are wrong depends on how you define "harm." Advocates of decriminalization believe that gambling, for example, is a "victimless crime." Advocates of criminal prohibition believe that it produces real harms: people can become addicted to gambling, it can ruin their personal finances and harm their families, and it can lead to other crime as people try to pay off their gambling debts. Advocates of drug decriminalization believe that marijuana, for example, does not do the harm that it is alleged to do. Supporters of the current drug laws, on the other hand, believe that marijuana does real physical, psychological, and social harm. Devlin sums up the prohibitionist position by arguing that "society is entitled by means of its laws to protect itself from dangers, whether from within or without."[40]

Decriminalization is also debated in terms of the practical consequences of making certain behavior illegal. As we mentioned earlier, advocates of decriminalization believe that criminal prohibition overburdens the justice system, leads to arbitrary enforcement, encourages corruption, and does not help people who have a medical or psychological problem. The advocates of criminalization would reply that the moral issues at stake outweigh the bad consequences. Even if the law does not completely deter drug abuse, society should still condemn this behavior through the criminal law.

The Potential Impact of Decriminalization

Now let us take a look at some of the specific items on the traditional decriminalization agenda and discuss them in terms of both the potential direct impact on serious crime and the procedural justice perspective.

Public Disorder Crimes. Public drunkenness, disorderly conduct, and vagrancy are essentially public nuisances rather than predatory crimes. They may offend our sensibilities, but they do not inflict tangible harm on someone the way robbery and burglary do.[41]

The crime control strategy underlying decriminalization of these offenses assumes that it would give the police more time to concentrate on serious crimes. As we indicated, 611,069 arrests were made for drunkenness in 2008, representing slightly less than 5 percent of all arrests and almost as many arrests as for all violent Index crimes.[42]

The basic assumption is flawed. As we learned in Chapter 5, adding more patrol officers will not prevent more crime, and adding more detectives will not raise clearance rates. Insofar as decriminalization of public drunkenness saves police time and resources, it might be desirable as a cost-saving measure. We have no reason to assume, however, that it will help reduce serious crime.

Not everyone agrees with our analysis. Public-order offenses such as drunkenness and urinating in public are a central part of the zero-tolerance policy adopted by then New York City Police Commissioner William Bratton. He and others claim that aggressively enforcing the law on these minor crimes has contributed directly to the reduction of murder and other serious crimes.[43] Critics, however, point out that crime has also fallen in cities that do not have the zero-tolerance policy and that the decline began before Bratton became police commissioner.[44]

Arrest trends indicate that we have been de-emphasizing public order arrests for many years. The number of arrests for drunkenness are half what they used to be. Several factors account for this decline. First, some court decisions held that arresting someone because of a medical condition—as opposed to some behavior —was unconstitutional. In 1966, the U.S. Court of Appeals for the District of Columbia ruled in *Easter v. District of Columbia* that DeWitt Easter could not be convicted for public intoxication.[45] Second, states have decriminalized public intoxication (in part due to court rulings). Third, police departments informally de-emphasized public order offenses in order to concentrate on more serious crimes: robbery, burglary, drug offenses.

In the end, there may be good reasons for decriminalizing or de-emphasizing public disorder crimes, but doing so is unlikely to have any notable effect on serious crime.

Abortion.   Abortion was decriminalized by the famous 1973 Supreme Court decision *Roe v. Wade,* which declared existing criminal abortion laws unconstitutional.[46] We will not debate the morality of abortion here. It is important, however, to note that this issue dramatizes better than any other the moral basis of the criminal law and the conflict between different moral perspectives in our society. If you believe that the fetus is a human being, then it logically follows that abortion is murder. But if you believe that the fetus is not a human being, then it follows that the abortion decision is a private choice.[47]

In one of the most controversial pieces of criminological research in recent years, economists John J. Donohue, III, and Steven D. Levitt argued that the legalization of abortion did reduce crime. They conclude that the 1973 *Roe v. Wade* decision, which has resulted in about a million and a half abortions a year has reduced the number of unwanted children, and as a result reduced the size of the crime-prone age cohort (14–24 years old). They argue that legalized abortion accounts for as much as 50 percent of the crime drop of the 1990s. As we discussed in Chapter 1, however, Frank Zimring's analysis punches serious holes in the Donohue–Levitt argument.[48]

Sex Between Consenting Adults.   States traditionally outlawed different kinds of sexual behavior, including activity between consenting adults such as adultery, cohabitation, homosexuality, and sodomy (which in some states includes "unnatural" sexual acts as well as acts between people of the same sex). By the mid-1980s, 13 states still had laws making it illegal for unmarried people to live together, and 13 had laws against "fornication" (sexual intercourse between people who are not married).[49] The 1910 Mann Act makes it a federal crime to take someone of the opposite sex across state lines for "immoral purposes." These laws are another good example of how the criminal law is used to define the moral boundaries of society.

In actual practice, the laws on sexual activity were rarely enforced, and as public attitudes about sex began to change in the 1960s, enforcement dropped even further. Between the 1960s and 2003, 35 states abolished their sodomy laws. Then in 2003, the U.S. Supreme Court declared sodomy laws unconstitutional on the grounds that they violated the right to privacy *(Lawrence v. Texas)*.[50] And by early 2010, law reform had gone one step further, and people of the same sex are now allowed to legally marry in five states.

Whatever your views on adultery, cohabitation, or homosexuality, it is impossible to establish any connection between these activities and serious predatory crime. Legalizing or criminalizing cohabitation will have no effect on burglary or robbery.

One possible exception to this rule might be prostitution. In some instances, prostitution facilitates ancillary crimes: Customers are robbed; prostitutes are beaten by their pimps. It is possible that a system of legalized and regulated prostitution would remove streetwalkers from the streets and reduce some of these crimes.

Gambling.   The legal status of gambling in the United States has undergone a massive change in recent years. The old moralistic objections to gambling have collapsed as many states have created lotteries and authorized casino gambling.[51] Many Native American tribes have established betting casinos on tribal lands that are exempt from federal and state gambling laws. Despite the spread of legal gambling, however, many of the popular forms of illegal gambling—sports betting pools, the numbers game—continue to flourish.

Advocates of decriminalizing gambling see a number of possible benefits: saving scarce resources, ending arbitrary law enforcement, and undercutting the economic basis of organized crime, for instance. There is no expectation, however, that it would reduce predatory crime, which is the issue that concerns us.[52]

Some opponents of legalized gambling believe that it might actually lead to an increase in crime. They argue that gambling casinos attract a criminal subculture that involves more thefts, robberies, and other crimes. Several studies have examined this issue. The Illinois Criminal Justice Information Authority found that the advent of riverboat gambling had no impact on crime in Joliet,

Illinois.[53] David Giacopassi and B. Grant Stitt found that casino gambling had a mixed impact on crime in Biloxi, Mississippi. Auto theft and larceny did rise, but no significant changes were noted for other crimes.[54] Finally, crime did increase in Atlantic City, New Jersey, after gambling was legalized there in 1976, but it was primarily "in-house" crime inside the casinos themselves. No increase occurred in the community generally.[55] In short, no consistent evidence indicates that legalized gambling leads to higher crime rates.

Summary

Many arguments exist for and against criminalizing the different kinds of behavior that we have discussed. We can debate this issue on moral grounds, on grounds of the practical consequences of criminal penalties, or on both grounds. It seems very clear, however, that we have no reason to expect any direct reduction in serious crime. This leads us to the following conclusion:

PROPOSITION 52
With the possible exception of drugs, decriminalization will not reduce serious crime.

There is some possibility that decriminalizing certain offenses will decrease the alienation of some people from the legal system and, according to the theories of procedural justice, increase their perception of the legitimacy and their tendency to obey the law. The evidence on this is speculative at best, however.

CONCLUSION

The emerging procedural justice perspective suggests that reforming the criminal justice system may increase trust in the criminal justice system and as a consequence reduce crime. The theory is clear, but the research at this point is very limited. In particular, we do not have any evidence that it would make a difference with regard to serious crime. The decriminalization of offenses other than those related to drugs, meanwhile, is unlikely to make any difference with respect to serious crime.

NOTES

1. Tom R. Tyler, *Why People Obey the Law* (New Haven: Yale University Press, 1990). For a broader perspective, see Tom R. Tyler, ed., *Legitimacy and Criminal Justice: International Perspectives* (New York: Russell Sage Foundation, 2007).

2. National Academy of Sciences, *Fairness and Effectiveness in Policing: The Evidence* (Washington, DC: National Academy Press, 2004).

3. Ibid., p. 297.

4. Sara E. Stoutland, "The Multiple Dimensions of Trust in Resident/Police Relations in Boston," *Journal of Research in Crime and Delinquency* 38 (August 2001): 226–256.

5. Lorie Fridell et. al., *Racially Biased Policing: A Principled Response* (Washington, DC: Police Executive Research Forum, 2001), chapter 4.

6. Tyler, *Why People Obey the Law*.

7. Ibid., p. 62.

8. Jonathan D. Casper, Tom Tyler, and Bonnie Fisher, "Procedural Justice in Felony Cases," *Law and Society Review* 22.3 (1988): 484–507.

9. Raymond Paternoster, Robert Brame, Ronet Bachman, and Lawrence W. Sherman, "Do Fair Procedures Matter? The Effect of Procedural Justice on Spouse Assault," *Law and Society Review* 31 (1997): 163–204.

10. Tyler, *Why People Obey the Law*, Table 4.1, p. 41.

11. Bureau of Justice Statistics, *Policing and Homicide, 1976–1998: Justifiable Homicide by Police, Police Officers Murdered by Felons* (Washington, DC: Department of Justice, 2001). NCJ 180987.

12. Lorie Fridell, *By the Numbers* (Washington, DC: Police Executive Research Forum, 2005).

13. Samuel Walker, *The New World of Police Accountability* (Thousand Oaks, CA: Sage, 2005).

14. Department of Health and Human Services, 2003 *National Household Survey of Drug Abuse and Health* (Washington, DC: Author, 2004).

15. Jerome G. Miller, *Search and Destroy: African-American Males in the Criminal Justice System* (New York: Cambridge University Press, 1996).

16. Stoutland, "The Multiple Dimensions of Trust in Resident/Police Relations in Boston."

17. Wesley G. Skogan and Susan M. Hartnett, *Community Policing, Chicago Style* (New York: Oxford University Press, 1997).

18. Samuel Walker, *Police Accountability: The Role of Citizen Oversight* (Belmont, CA: Thomson, 1991).

19. Walker, *Police Accountability: The Role of Citizen Oversight*. The best discussion of the research issues is David Brereton, "Evaluating the Performance of External Oversight Bodies," in Andrew Goldsmith and Colleen Lewis, eds., *Civilian Oversight of Policing: Governance, Democracy and Human Rights* (Portland, OR: Hart Publishing, 2000), pp. 105–124.

20. Samuel Walker, Carol Archbold, Leigh Herbst, *Mediating Citizen Complaints Against Police Officers: A Guide for Police and Community Leaders* (Washington, DC: Department of Justice, 2002).

21. Bureau of Justice Statistics, *Sourcebook of Criminal Justice Statistics*, online edition, Tables 2.54.2009, 20013.2006. Cassia Spohn, *How Do Judges Decide?* (Thousand Oaks, CA: Pine Forge Press, 2002).

22. Norval Morris and Gordon Hawkins, *The Honest Politician's Guide to Crime Control* (Chicago: University of Chicago Press, 1970), p. 3.

23. Herbert L. Packer, *The Limits of the Criminal Sanction* (Stanford, CA: Stanford University Press, 1968), p. 364.

24. The best overview of this issue is still Packer, *The Limits of the Criminal Sanction*.

25. Raymond T. Nimmer, *Two Million Unnecessary Arrests* (Chicago: American Bar Foundation, 1971).

26. See the annual arrest data in Federal Bureau of Investigation, *Crime in the United States*.

27. Packer, *Limits of the Criminal Sanction*, p. 264.

28. Ibid., p. 287.

29. Timothy J. Flanagan and Dennis R. Longmire, eds., *Americans View Crime and Justice: A National Public Opinion Survey* (Thousand Oaks, CA: Sage, 1996). Until recently, most surveys did not investigate the attitudes of Latino/Hispanic Americans.

30. President's Commission on Law Enforcement and Administration of Justice, *The Challenge of Crime in a Free Society* (New York: Avon, 1968), p. 437.

31. Knapp Commission, *Report on Police Corruption* (New York: Braziller, 1973).

32. Commission to Investigate Allegations of Police Corruption and the Anti-Corruption Procedures of the Police Department, *Report* (New York: City of New York, 1994).

33. Los Angeles Police Department, Board of Inquiry, *Rampart Area Corruption Incident* (Los Angeles: Author, 2000).

34. Bureau of Justice Statistics, *Sourcebook of Criminal Justice Statistics—1995* (Washington, DC: Government Printing Office, 1996), p. 228.

35. President's Commission on Law Enforcement and Administration of Justice, *Task Force Report: Drunkenness* (Washington, DC: Government Printing Office, 1967), p. 3.

36. Nimmer, *Two Million Unnecessary Arrests*.

37. Patrick Devlin, *The Enforcement of Morals* (London: Oxford University Press, 1965), p. 7.

38. Packer, *Limits of the Criminal Sanction*, p. 263.

39. Gilbert Geis, *Not the Law's Business* (New York: Schocken, 1979).

40. Devlin, *Enforcement of Morals*, p. 13.

41. President's Commission, *Task Force Report: Drunkenness*.

42. Federal Bureau of Investigation, *Crime in the United States*, 2002 (Washington, DC: Department of Justice, 2002). Current data are available on the FBI website.

43. George L. Kelling and Catherine Coles, *Fixing Broken Windows* (New York: Kessler, 1996).

44. John E. Eck and Edward Maguire, "Have Changes in Policing Reduced Crime?," in Alfred Blumstein and Joel Wallman, *The Crime Drop in America* (New York: Cambridge University Press, 2000), pp. 207–265.

45. *Easter v. District of Columbia*, 361 F.2d 50 (D.C. Cir. 1966).

46. *Roe v. Wade*, 410 U.S. 113 (1973).

47. Lawrence H. Tribe, *Abortion: The Clash of Absolutes* (New York: Norton, 1990).

48. John J. Donohue, III, and Steven D. Levitt, "The Impact of Legalized Abortion on Crime," *Quarterly Journal of Economics*, 66 (no. 2, 2001): 379–420. Franklin Zimring, *The Great American Crime Decline* (New York: Oxford University Press, 2007).

49. Mitchell Bernard, Ellen Levine, Stefan Presser, and Marianne Stecich, *The Rights of Single People* (New York: Bantam, 1985), pp. 12–13.

50. *Lawrence v. Texas*, 539 U.S. 558 (2003). Vincent J. Samar, *The Right to Privacy: Gays, Lesbians, and the Constitution* (Philadelphia: Temple University Press, 1991). A Web search for the term "sodomy laws" will yield websites that provide current information.

51. John D. Rosecrance, *Gambling without Guilt: The Legitimation of an American Pasttime* (Pacific Grove, CA: Brooks/Cole, 1988).

52. Earl L. Grinois, *Gambling in America: Costs and Benefits* (New York: Cambridge University Press, 2004).

53. Illinois Criminal Justice Information Authority, *Riverboat Gambling and Crime in Illinois* (Springfield: Author, 1994).

54. David Giacopassi and B. Grant Stitt, "Assessing the Impact of Casino Gambling on Crime in Mississippi," *American Journal of Criminal Justice* 18 (1994): 117–131.

55. Daniel Curran and Frank Scarpitti, "Crime in Atlantic City: Do Casinos Make a Difference?" *Deviant Behavior* 12 (1991): 431–450.

The Drug Problem

O ne of the ground rules for this book is a focus on robbery and burglary. We are now going to violate that rule by examining drug policy. The drug crack was closely associated with the surge in gun violence in the 1980s. The Sentencing Project bluntly declares: "No issue has had more impact on the criminal justice system in the past two decades than national drug policy. The 'war on drugs' that was declared in the early 1980s has been a primary contributor to the enormous growth of the prison system in the United States since that time and has affected all aspects of the criminal justice system."[1]

Drug arrests tripled between 1975 and 2003, with the result that drug offenders went from 6 to 21 percent of all state prisoners; in the federal prisons they rose from 25 to 57 percent of prisoners. Prison terms also lengthened, from an average of 22 months for federal drug offenders in 1999 to 62 months today. Additionally, most of these prisoners are low-level dealers; only 11 percent of federal drug defendants are major dealers.[2] Let us take a look at the problem of drugs, the drug–crime connection, and the larger question of drug policy.

Sense and Nonsense
about Drugs and Crime

THE DRUG PROBLEM

In December 2009, Gil Kerlikowske, the new director of the Office of National Drug Control Policy (ONDCP), told an international audience about the need "to address drug control from a new perspective." His comment was a clear indication that long-standing policies had failed. What did he see wrong with those policies? Primarily, they "place disproportionate responsibilities on law enforcement in a negative way," and as a consequence, they "weaken the vitality and resolve of our communities." His critique is one that many criminologists and drug policy experts have been saying for decades (and which we say in Chapter 1 of this book).[3]

What new policies does the ONDCP director recommend? To begin, he wants a "new and balanced approach and broader and more holistic understanding" of the drug problem. What, exactly, does that involve? One specific "promising" initiative is Project Hope, a form of drug court that reportedly reduced relapse by meth abuses by 80 percent. He also recommended greater use of technology to provide more intensive supervision of probationers and parolees, along with online education systems, life skills training, and job placement. Aside from a general shift away from excessive emphasis on law enforcement, his speech was a little weak on details. Time will tell if new, "smarter" policies develop, and if they work.

Kerlikowske's remarks provide a useful starting point for this chapter. We agree that too much emphasis has been given to law enforcement and punishment. In this chapter we will look at those policies and examine why they are not only ineffective but in many respects destructive of communities. At the same time, however, we will take a hard look at alternatives. We have already examined drug courts in Chapter 11, and found them promising. But in the same chapter we found that intensive probation and parole were not effective. In Chapter 5 we looked at some innovative problem-oriented policing projects related to guns and gangs. Are they relevant to reducing drug trafficking? Let's look at these and other alternatives to existing drug policies.

To talk seriously about crime in America, we have to address the issue of drugs and drug policy. Drugs have been the focal point of the crime problem in the United States for years. Directly or indirectly, they were responsible for the dramatic rise in gun violence and the murder rate in the 1980s, gang violence, the soaring prison population, the worsening crisis in race relations, and the steady erosion of individual rights in the Supreme Court ruling.[4] Although the spike in gun violence has gone away, drugs are still closely associated with gangs and crime. Moreover, the drug problem appears to be taking a new and ominous turn with the growing power of Mexican drug cartels. The ONDCP estimates that the cartels now control 90 percent of all the cocaine imported into the U.S., and about 70 percent of all imported drugs. The cartels have brought unprecedented levels of violence to parts of Mexico, and some of that is spilling over into parts of the U.S. on the southwest border.

HYSTERIA OVER DRUGS

Public hysteria over drugs and drug-related crime prevents sensible discussion of policy. This has long been the case. In the 1930s, a wave of national hysteria arose over "reefer madness," with wild stories about the alleged dangers of marijuana. Rent the hilarious 1938 movie *Reefer Madness* (or find it on YouTube) and see for yourself. A similar scare erupted in the 1980s over "crack babies." Sensational news media stories appeared in 1988 about 375,000 crack babies born to addicted mothers. Reports claimed that these infants had severe physical and psychological damage, would never develop normally, and would be a permanent burden to society. One medical expert said, "It's as if the part of the brain that makes us human beings capable of discussion or reflection is wiped out."[5]

The truth turned out to be very different. The number of babies possibly affected by crack was grossly exaggerated. The original reports counted all babies who had been exposed to drugs during pregnancy, not just those who were genuinely addicted or even harmed. Some hospitals included mothers who had used marijuana. Later research found that the long-term damage even to addicted babies had been exaggerated. One study found no performance differences in crack and noncrack children by age four. Other studies found that the problems attributed to crack exposure were due primarily to inadequate prenatal care, a problem associated with low-income parents. Some studies suggest that alcohol does more harm to a fetus than cocaine. The Sentencing Project points out that there are far more alcohol-related deaths among adults every year (94,000) than drug-related deaths (21,000), but the criminal justice system is far harsher on drug offenses.[6]

Myths and Realities about Drugs and Crime

To help sort our way through the debate over drug policy, we need to establish some basic facts about drugs and crime. As with most criminal justice issues, many myths about drugs and crime inhibit the development of sound and effective policies on this problem. Let us begin by exploring some of the facts about the extent of illegal drug use, drug use trends, and the relationship between drugs and crime.

The Extent of Illegal Drug Use

The first question is: How extensive is illegal drug use? It is important to answer this question because of so much misinformation and public hysteria about an "epidemic" of drug use, with advocates of different policies claiming a dramatic rise or fall in drug use. There are four different surveys that measure the extent of illegal drug use, or at least part of it. (Table 13.1). Two are general social surveys, while two are surveys of specific subgroups of the population. There are concerns with the methodology of each survey, but they provide us with the best evidence on the extent of drug use in America.[7]

The broadest general survey is the National Survey on Drug Use and Health (formerly known as the National Household Survey), which collects self-report data on a sample of the general population. It is far from perfect, and shares some of the weaknesses that affect the National Crime Victimization Survey (NCVS). Respondents may not truthfully report their illegal drug use. More seriously, it surveys households and may miss many of the most serious drug abusers, who are transients or homeless, or former drug abusers who are now in prison (the survey asks about lifetime use of drugs).

The National Survey data indicate that illegal substance use is fairly widespread. In 2008 about 20 million Americans age 12 or older used an illicit drug in the past month. Marijuana was the most commonly used drug, with 15.2 million users in 2008. Meanwhile, 1.9 million used cocaine (down from 2.3 million in 2003, and 200,000 used heroin. Illicit drug use peaks among 18- to 20-year-olds and then declines steadily with each age group. In 2008, 21.5 percent of Americans reported using an illicit drug in the past month. About half of all adult Americans have used an illegal drug at least once in their lifetime, with 40 percent having used marijuana and 14.7 percent having used cocaine.[8]

The Monitoring the Future (MTF) survey provides self-report data from students in grades 8, 10, and 12. In 2008, 46,348 students in public and private schools participated. Students represent an important segment of the at-risk population, since they are among the most likely to use an illegal drug. The major weakness of the study is that it misses kids who have dropped out of school—precisely those who are likely to be the heaviest drug users. The MTF data indicate that illegal drug use has fluctuated over the years. It peaked in 1981 at 66 percent of all young people, declined to 41 percent in 1992, rose to 55 percent by 1999, and then fell to 47 percent in 2008.[9]

The Drug Abuse Warning Network (DAWN) focuses on a special aspect of drug use and provides an important perspective on the drug problem. DAWN collects data on hospital emergency department (ED) admissions related to alcohol

T A B L E 13.1   Sources of data on drug use

National Survey of Drug Use and Health

Monitoring the Future (MTF)

Drug Abuse Warning Network (DAWN)

Arrestee Drug Abuse Monitoring (ADAM) [terminated in 2003]

and drug-related problems. In 2006 it collected reports from over 250 hospitals across the country. The value of DAWN is that it measures the most serious consequences of drug abuse. An important limitation is that it reports *mentions* of drugs in a medical report, which does not necessarily mean that a drug *caused* the medical emergency. DAWN presents a very grim picture. In 2006 there were 536,544 million emergency department admissions that involved a single illicit drug. Now add 219,521 admissions involving an illegal drug in combination with alcohol, and another 142,535 involving an illegal drug in combination with a pharmaceutical. Cocaine was the most common drug reported, followed by marijuana. Some areas report high drug-related death rates. Albuquerque, New Mexico, had a drug-related death rate of 25.7 per 100,000 people in the general population in 2007. In St. Louis, the rate was only 11.1, and in the Washington, DC metropolitan area just 8.8 per 100,000. Variations in the death rate reflect differences in drug usage and the purity of drugs in the local market.[10]

Finally, the Arrestee Drug Abuse Monitoring (ADAM) program (originally known as DUF, or Drug Use Forecasting) collects urine specimens and self-report data on drug use from arrestees. The Justice Department terminated ADAM in 2003, but revived it as ADAM II in 2006. ADAM II involved only 10 sites, compared with 39 cities in the original ADAM. ADAM is limited to people who have been arrested, and is not a representative sample of the population; however, it is useful because it covers a particularly important group with regard to drugs and crime. In 2008 47.8 percent of the arrestees in Minneapolis tested positive for marijuana, and 22.5 tested positive for cocaine. In Atlanta, meanwhile, 31.8 tested positive for marijuana and 40.5 for cocaine.[11]

It is important to remember that ADAM only reports that the arrestee either tested positive for illicit drug use, or self-reported drug use, or both. It does not allow us to conclude that drugs *caused* the person to commit the crime for which he or she was arrested. In the next section we will discuss the relationship between drug use and crime.

One of the most important contributions of the ADAM data was to document the significant reduction in crack usage in many major cities in the 1990s. This reduction was closely associated with the significant drop in the crime rate, especially in certain cities, and some criminologists believe it was the principal cause of the crime decline.[12]

A Few Words about Using and Misusing Drug Use Data

The different measures of illegal drug use are very useful, but can also be misused—and often are misused. It is always important to look at long-term trends. The National Household Survey and Monitoring the Future both show short-term fluctuations. If you pick a short time slot within a longer period it is easy to show a dramatic rise or decline. In one of the strongest attacks on the misuse of drug data, *Lies, Damned Lies, and Drug War Statistics,* Matthew B. Robinson and Renee C. Scherlen accuse the Office of National Drug Control Policy of selecting particular time periods to demonstrate the effectiveness of ONCP policies. ONCB was not created until

1988. It cannot claim, therefore, that its policies were responsible for the decline in drug use that began around 1979. In other cases, ONDCP selected a certain period within the 1980s to make a point, when using a slightly earlier period easily led to a different conclusion.[13]

There is a very important lesson here if you want to make sense of crime policy: Have a keen eye regarding any claims about trends regarding drug use, crime, or both. What data are the author or agency using? Is it the best data? With respect to crime, is it UCR or NCVS data? With regard to drug use, is it arrest data (a select group of the population) or National Household or MTF data? This book is primarily a critique of nonsensical crime polices. A lot of that nonsense is supported by lies and damned lies about the data.

The Drug–Crime Connection

A second important question involves the relationship between drugs and crime. It is a popular myth that drugs *cause* crime, and that if we reduced illegal drug abuse we would reduce crime. The stereotype persists of the "drug-crazed criminal" who robs and murders while high on drugs. The old reefer madness stereotype, meanwhile, is that women become sexually promiscuous because of marijuana. Several years ago, the Office of National Drug Control Policy published a frightening graphic purporting to show the direct and harmful "Consequences of Drug Use" on "family, crime, violence, health, economic [circumstances, and] community." That report is no longer posted on the ONDCP website, but a new posting on *What Americans Need to Know About Marijuana* paints an equally frightening picture. Marijuana is not "harmless," it asserts, and heightens the risk of hospital emergency

Illustration by Frank Irwin, © Wadsworth, Cengage Learning.

room admission, schizophrenia, bronchitis and even cancer, heart and lung problems, loss of alertness and concentration, and possible suicide.[14] In short, drugs are the cause of serious personal and social problems.

The truth is much more complex than that. Scare messages, moreover, only get in the way of an intelligent discussion of the issue. (The "scared straight" programs we examined in Chapter 6 use this approach, and we found that it is not effective.) It is indeed true that drugs and crime *are* related, but in a very complicated way.[15] Crime associated with drugs falls into three categories. First, there are *drug-defined* crimes: the possession and sale of illegal substances. Second, there are *drug-related* crimes, including violent behavior caused by the pharmacological effects of a drug or robberies committed to get money to buy drugs. Third, there are crimes *associated with drug usage,* meaning that an offender was using drugs around the time he or she committed an offense, but the crime was not caused by drug use. This does not mean, however, that drugs caused the person to commit crime.[16]

The ADAM data confirm the fact that a large percentage of arrestees are involved with both drug and alcohol use. The majority of arrestees test positive for at least one drug. The rates vary tremendously: from 49 percent in Washington, DC, to 87 percent in Chicago in 2008. Many test positive for more than one drug (40 percent in Chicago). In most cities, marijuana is the most common drug, followed by cocaine. Merely testing positive for drugs, however, does not mean that the crime was *caused* by drugs. This is similar to the problem we discussed in Chapter 6: Just because a driver tests positive for alcohol does not mean that his or her driving was impaired by drinking. Most important, someone who has recently used marijuana is not "crazed," as the old *Reefer Madness* film tried to convince people. Interviews with prisoners provide a useful perspective: only 17 percent of prison inmates say they committed their offense to get money to buy drugs.[17]

A survey of offenders on probation, meanwhile, found that half admitted to being under the influence of drugs or alcohol at the time they committed the offense for which they were convicted. Two-thirds reported they had used drugs in the past and about one-third admitted they had used drugs in the month before they committed the offense for which they were convicted.[18] This involvement with drugs does not, however, mean that the crimes these individuals committed were caused by drugs. We encountered the same issue with regard to alcohol and traffic fatalities. The fact that a driver tested positive for alcohol does not mean that drinking caused the accident.

A Word About "Gateway" Drugs. One of the major arguments against legalizing marijuana is that it is a "gateway" to more serious drug abuse and then criminal behavior. The evidence does not support the gateway argument. Morgan and Zimmer, analyzing Center on Addiction and Substance Abuse (CASA) data, determined that 83 percent of reported marijuana users never go on to use cocaine.[19] Common sense supports this view. Consider the number of people reporting to the National Household Survey that they used marijuana in the last month. If any significant proportion of them went on to use cocaine or heroin, over time the accumulated number of users of those drugs would be huge. But it is not. And it isn't, for the simple reason that marijuana is the last stop for most people who use the drug.

A more realistic view, supported by good research on high-rate offenders, is that many began their criminal activity before they began using drugs. For some others, drug use preceded their criminal activity. Still others became involved in crime and drugs at about the same time. As a Justice Department report concludes, "For some individuals drugs use is independent of their involvement in crime. These people may continue to commit crimes even if drugs were unavailable."[20] David Farrington argues that "violent youth have many other 'co-occurring problems.'" These problems include truancy, early sexual initiation and sexual promiscuity, unstable employment records, bad relations with parents, and many other factors.[21] It is impossible to say that any one (e.g., drug use) *caused* subsequent violent criminal behavior.

The lack of a direct causal link between drugs and crime has important implications for crime policy. It means that even if we succeeded in substantially reducing illegal drug use—particularly marijuana—we would not necessarily reduce crime to the same degree. Crimes related to drug trafficking would certainly be reduced, but the impact on crimes associated with deviant lifestyles, which include the vast majority of robberies and burglaries, would be very limited. And by the same token, reducing crime would not necessarily reduce drug use. A causal relationship between the two behaviors simply does not exist. What we need to do is to reduce the circumstances that lead to deviant lifestyles that include both drugs and crime.

The Drug Policy Choices

What should we do about drugs and crime? Peter Reuter classifies policy advocates into three groups: hawks, doves, and owls (these categories are borrowed from the debate over the Vietnam War in the 1960s and 1970s). Hawks emphasize law enforcement to eradicate drug abuse, believing that we simply need to get tougher than we have been. Enforcement strategies include both supply reduction, designed to reduce the availability of drugs, and demand reduction, designed to decrease peoples' desire to use drugs.[22] American drug policy is dominated by the hawk approach, with most of the emphasis on supply reduction.

Owls prefer prevention and treatment of drug abuse, which are essentially demand-reduction strategies. Current drug policy includes prevention and treatment, but they have always received less emphasis than supply reduction–oriented law enforcement approaches.

Doves, meanwhile, believe that we should completely rethink our national drug policy. In general, they would prefer to define drug abuse as a public health problem. The National Council on Crime and Delinquency asserts that it "should be defined primarily as a health-related problem that should reside in the public health domain," rather than in the law enforcement arena.[23]

The radical dove approach is to legalize drugs. We discuss legalization later in this chapter. A more moderate approach is generally referred to as *harm reduction,* which means keeping the criminal penalties for drugs on the books, but not punishing drug users as harshly as we do now. Harm reduction is essentially the policy of many European countries with regard to drugs, particularly the Netherlands.[24]

To a certain extent, the drug policy debate is a discussion about what causes the greatest harm: drugs or drug policy. Hawks believe that drugs are the problem. Doves believe that drug policy is the problem, causing more harm than good.

The hawk/owl/dove categories do not conform to the conservative/liberal dichotomy we have used in this book. The Reagan and Bush administrations (1981–1993) put tremendous emphasis on tough law enforcement, but First Lady Nancy Reagan simultaneously led a highly publicized "Just say no" antidrug education campaign. The policies of the liberal Clinton administration included tough sentencing measures for drug offenders and postconviction restrictions on offenders' rights (see Chapter 14), but also more money for drug prevention programs. President George W. Bush reemphasized punishment as a basic policy, but with the appointment of Gil Kerlikowske as head of the Office of National Drug Control Policy, the Barak Obama administration appears to be moving away from that position.

THE WAR ON DRUGS:
POLICY AND CONSEQUENCES

Since passage of the 1914 Harrison Act, hawks have dominated American drug policy. We have defined certain substances as illegal and attempted to suppress their use though criminal law enforcement. Over the past 40 years, our policy has become increasingly hawkish, as a succession of presidents have declared "war" on drugs, and arrests and imprisonment for drug possession and sale have soared.[25]

The 2009 National Drug Control Strategy includes a mix of prevention, treatment, and law enforcement. Prevention efforts include a national antidrug media campaign (see our discussion later in this chapter), drug testing in schools, and supporting collaborative Drug Free Community efforts. Interestingly, the policy statement does not mention DARE, one of the most popular antidrug education programs, but which has been heavily criticized as being ineffective. Treatment efforts include drug courts, which we discussed in Chapter 11 and will discuss again in this chapter. Finally, law enforcement efforts emphasize disrupting drug markets, including the production of drugs here in the U.S. and the importation of drugs from other countries.[26]

The Impact of the War on Drugs

As we argued in Chapter 1, the war on drugs has had an enormous impact on U.S. society, on the criminal justice system, and on racial minorities in particular. The number of persons arrested for drug offenses almost tripled from 1975 to

2008, going from 601,000 to 1.7 million, and now represents 12 percent of all arrests. Persons convicted of drug offenses are the primary factor in the spectacular increase in the prison population. In 2009, 52 percent of all federal prisoners were incarcerated for drug offenses, compared with only 25 percent in 1980. About 20 percent of all state prisoners are in for drug offenses.[27]

Many critics argue that racial minorities are the primary victims of the war on drugs. The National Criminal Justice Commission argues that "we are on the verge of a social catastrophe because of the sheer number of African-Americans behind bars."[28] Some would argue that the catastrophe is already here. African Americans are treated more harshly at every stage of the criminal justice system, and the resulting cumulative disadvantage generates the enormous disparity between the percentage of African Americans in prison and their representation in the general population. Michael Tonry and Matthew Melewski point out that the facts of the racial disparities in the criminal justice system "have long been well known," but that little has changed. Outside of academics and liberal reformers, "few people ... much notice or care." We agree, but would only add that things have changed in recent years—they have gotten worse, particularly with regard to imprisonment.[29]

Data from both the National Survey on Drug Use and Health and Monitoring the Future puts a revealing perspective on the issue of drug use by different racial and ethnic groups. It is a popular stereotype that people of color use illegal drugs more heavily than white Americans. According to the National Household Survey, African Americans were more likely to use illegal drugs, but only somewhat more so. In 2008, 10.1 percent of African Americans reported using an illegal drug in the last month, compared with 8.2 percent whites, and 6.2 percent of Latinos (see Table 13.2). The low rate among Latinos surprises many people. These data do not justify the racial and ethnic disparities in persons arrested for drug offenses, and certainly not the overrepresentation of people of color for those offenses.[30]

Despite the data on drug use by race, the National Criminal Justice Commission argues that street-level drug enforcement "focus[es] almost exclusively on low-level dealers in minority neighborhoods."[31] At the federal level, the arrest disparities are amplified by the much-criticized federal sentencing guidelines, with their differential penalties for powder and crack cocaine. Possession of 5 grams of crack nets a mandatory minimum sentence of five years, whereas possession

T A B L E   13.2   **Illicit drug use,* by race and ethnicity, 2008**

	Past month
White (non-Hispanic)	8.2%
Hispanic or Latino	6.2
African American	10.1
Native American	9.5
Asian	3.6

SOURCE: Substance Abuse and Mental Health Services Administration, *National Survey on Drug Use and Health, 2008: National Findings* (Washington, DC: SAMHSA, 2009).

of the same amount of powdered cocaine carries a maximum sentence of only one year. This has a grossly disparate racial impact, as crack is favored by African Americans and powdered cocaine is preferred by whites.[32] In the face of widespread criticism, the Sentencing Commission has recommended revising the guidelines on this point, but Congress has refused.

Arrest and imprisonment have become extremely common experiences in underclass neighborhoods. As we pointed out in Chapter 6, some deterrence theorists argue that arrest loses its deterrent effect when it becomes a common experience for a group.[33] And as we argued in Chapter 12, the racial disparities associated with the war on drugs undermine the legitimacy of the criminal justice system in the eyes of many African Americans.

In short, the war on drugs has undoubtedly had a tremendous impact on U.S. society and on racial minorities in particular. Whether it has succeeded in reducing illegal drug use or serious crime associated with drug use is another question. Now let us take a look at some of the major components of the drug war.

Police Crackdowns

The principal police strategy for reducing drug abuse is aggressive law enforcement. One variation is the *crackdown,* an intensive, short-term, geographically focused campaign of arrests. As we discussed in Chapter 5, however, such efforts produce a high volume of arrests and much publicity, but little impact on crime, drugs, or gangs. A 1997 University of Maryland report concludes, "The evidence on drug crackdowns shows no consistent reductions in violent crime during or after the crackdown."[34] We agree.

In fact, local law enforcement efforts have not had any significant impact on the availability of drugs on the street. Monitoring the Future found that 84 percent of high school seniors in 2008 said they could get marijuana "fairly easily" or "very easily," and 42 percent said they could easily get cocaine. A 2002 survey asked undercover police officers in 25 cities how difficult it was to obtain various drugs. On a scale of 0 to 10, with 0 meaning not difficult at all, officers in Dallas, New York City, and Phoenix gave ratings of 0 for heroin, crack, and marijuana; no city gave a rating higher than 1.75 for marijuana; the overall rating for crack was 0.7 in the 25 cities.[35] In short, police officers themselves do not believe that their intensive antidrug efforts reduce the availability of drugs. This is a damning indictment of police crackdowns.

The situation is not completely hopeless. More recent problem-oriented policing projects, in Boston, Massachusetts; Cincinnati, Ohio; and Lowell, Massachusetts have produced promising results. As our discussions in Chapters 5 and 6 indicated, however, these programs are carefully planned and designed, involve considerable data collection and analysis, target specific offenders, and include prevention programs as well as enforcement. Such programs show evidence of effectiveness regarding gun violence, gangs, and drug-related crime. They appear to offer the best hope for effective law enforcement strategies regarding drugs.

PROPOSITION 53

Traditional police crackdowns will not reduce illegal drug use or serious crime associated with drugs.

Interdiction and Eradication

Two major supply-reduction efforts by the federal government include *interdiction,* stopping the flow of drugs entering the country, and *eradication,* reducing the production of drug plants in the field. The conservative policy advocates William J. Bennett, John J. DiIulio, and John P. Walters argue that interdiction of drugs should be a "top national security priority" for the United States.[36] In fact, the federal government has made a huge and steadily increasing effort at interdiction.

One of the centerpieces of U.S. international interdiction efforts has been Plan Colombia, a program to halt the production and export of cocaine from that country, including voluntary and forced eradication of plants by Colombian farmers. The Office of National Drug Control Policy in 2008 stated that Plan Colombia was a great success: seizing more cocaine, reducing drug-related violence, and strengthening the rule of law in Colombia.[37]

We should be very skeptical about such claims. Despite several decades of interdiction efforts, the problem of stopping the flow of drugs from other countries is today far worse than ever before. Mexico has emerged as the center of both drug imports into the U.S. and a wave of narcoterrorism that has begun spilling over into this country. This point is evident to anyone who pays attention to the news. A new and particularly deadly crisis has emerged on the U.S.–Mexican border, dominated by the emergence of powerful drug cartels in Mexico. The crisis consists of several interrelated aspects: the flow of drugs into the U.S. from Mexico; the virtual collapse of law and order in parts of Mexico, with rampant murder of police, other officials, and ordinary citizens; the flow of guns, particularly automatic and semi-automatic weapons, from the U.S. into Mexico; and the growing spread of drug-related violence into border areas of the U.S.[38]

The Mexican drug cartels now dominate the flow of drugs into the U.S. By 2009, the Office of National Drug Control Policy reports, they became responsible for 90 percent of the cocaine coming into this country. They are also the primary foreign source of marijuana and methamphetamine. The ONDCP estimates that the eight Mexican cartels "oversee" the distribution of major drugs in 230 American cities. Estimates place the wholesale value of drugs from Mexico anywhere between $13 and 43 billion a year. Moving south across the border are bulk quantities of cash derived from drug sales and illegal weapons.[39]

The impact of the cartels on crime and corruption has been particularly serious. Corruption of law enforcement and other officials is rampant. In late 2005 the Mexican attorney general estimated that as many as 20 percent of all Federal Investigations Agency officers were engaged in criminal activity and possibly working for one or more cartels. Murders have become so brazen that the cartels toss body parts into people's yards as warnings to them, broadcast executions on YouTube, and openly threaten police chiefs with death (at least one was actually executed). The most serious effects are felt only in certain regions of the country, but many experts worry that Mexico could become a "failed state," similar to Afghanistan and Sudan, where there is no effective government and criminal gangs or warlords hold the real power.

In response to this mounting crisis, the U.S government in 2008 appropriated $1.6 billion for a three-year partnership with the Mexican government. The goals of the program include enhancing intelligence gathering efforts; interdicting drugs, money, and weapons; prosecuting those involved in drug trafficking; disrupting and dismantling the cartel organizations; and developing new technologies to enhance the effectiveness of the entire effort.

If this interdiction program sounds familiar, it should. Interdiction of imported drugs has been a major U.S. program for decades. It has not only failed, but the problem along the U.S.–Mexican border is only getting worse. One of the troubling aspects of the rise to power of the Mexican cartels is that it has been partly a result of some successful antidrug efforts. One was the weakening of the Calí and Medellín cartels in Colombia; the other was the aggressive effort to control meth production in the U.S. In both cases, the process is a classic example of displacement and adaptation in response to increased enforcement efforts.

The failure of interdiction is easy to understand. The 20,000-mile border of the United States is too great, the possible methods of smuggling drugs too many, and the people engaged in the trade too numerous. Increased enforcement, moreover, produces a variety of adaptations: new points of entry, new methods of smuggling, shifts in drug use as prices change, and so on. Insofar as tougher enforcement raises the risks of drug trafficking, it drives the trade into the hands of those who are better organized, more heavily armed, and willing to take the risks—in short, the cartels that dominate the international cocaine market. Despite increased federal interdiction efforts, total worldwide production of drugs increased significantly between 1987 and 1991 alone. Production of marijuana rose from 13,000 to 23,000 metric tons, while coca leaf production increased from 291,000 to 337,000 metric tons.[40] A Rand report concludes, "Increased drug interdiction efforts are not likely to greatly affect the availability of cocaine in the United States."[41]

PROPOSITION 54
Drug interdiction and eradication efforts are doomed to fail.

Tougher Sentencing

Tough sentencing policies for persons convicted of drug offenses have been another major strategy of the war on drugs. This represents the incapacitation and deterrence strategies we examined in Chapters 6 and 7. It is not necessary to cover that ground again here. Our conclusion was that neither strategy is effective in reducing crime. In the case of drugs, incapacitation is often undermined by the *replacement effect*. Drug dealers who are imprisoned are replaced by others willing to take the risk of arrest and imprisonment. An important factor is the lack of legitimate job opportunities they see. In that context, the immediate gains to drug dealing are attractive, and the risk of punishment somewhat remote.

It is important to note that drug use and crime associated with drugs has remained highest among the underclass, the very group that has been the primary target of the war on drugs. Arrest and imprisonment have obviously not had deterrent or incapacitative effects on that group. Instead, as criminologist Todd Clear argues, our policy of massive incarceration has destroyed communities, particularly African American communities, undermining their capacity to sustain a healthy social environment that would control crime. In the title of his book, we have been *Imprisoning Communities*.[42]

PROPOSITION 55

Tougher sentencing is not likely to reduce illegal drug use or serious crime associated with drugs.

LIMITS OF THE CRIMINAL LAW:

THE LESSONS OF HISTORY

Many critics of current drug policy argue that a war-on-drugs approach is doomed to fail. History provides a valuable perspective on this issue, offering several examples of attempts to control products or services through the criminal law. Let us take a look at some of the more notable ones.

Prohibition.   Between 1920 and 1933, the manufacture and sale of alcoholic beverages were illegal under the Eighteenth Amendment to the U.S. Constitution. Stories from Prohibition have entered the national folklore: speakeasies, Al Capone, gangland shootouts, and so on. Prohibition did reduce drinking and probably contributed to the decline in deaths from cirrhosis of the liver (from 13.3 per 100,000 in 1910 to 7.2 per 100,000 in 1930). Citing these figures, some historians argue that Prohibition was a success.[43]

That is not the whole story, however. Other historians argue that Prohibition clearly did not end all drinking and inflicted enormous collateral damage on the country. By turning millions of casual drinkers into criminals, it undermined respect for the law. It created a vast illegal market that was filled by criminal syndicates, which corrupted police and politicians. Modern-day organized crime originated with Prohibition, as local crime syndicates consolidated into a few national syndicates with enormous power. Finally, Prohibition enforcement was accompanied by widespread abuses, particularly illegal searches and seizures by local police and federal prohibition enforcement agents. The lesson of Prohibition seems clear: people want to consume alcohol, and when the government tried to outlaw it, people were willing to take the risks to provide it for them.[44]

Social Gambling.   Gambling is big business in the United States. This was not always so. Gambling policy has undergone a revolution in recent years, with the spread of state lotteries and casinos. Until recently, it was heavily restricted, confined to a small number of racetracks, Las Vegas, and church-based bingo games. Nonetheless, millions of Americans routinely gambled illegally, betting on athletic events, the "numbers," and so on. The laws restricting gambling had many of the same collateral effects as Prohibition: turning otherwise law-abiding people into "law-breakers," creating disrespect for the law, fostering corruption, and providing a huge source of revenue for organized crime.[45]

Gun Control.   As we learned in Chapter 10, we have many laws barring certain people from owning guns, especially criminals. Yet active criminals have no trouble obtaining weapons through friends, the black market, or theft. Local ordinances to ban handguns, such as the one in Washington, DC, did not keep those weapons out of the hands of criminals. Before the Washington ban on guns was declared unconstitutional by the Supreme Court, crime in the city fluctuated over the years, with no evident relationship to the ban. Once again, we have a product—in this case, handguns—that some people want, and in the face of restrictive laws, some people are willing to take the risks to sell them guns.

The Old Criminal Abortion Laws.   Before the 1973 *Roe v. Wade* decision, abortion was a criminal offense in every state (several states did liberalize their laws between 1967 and 1973). But these laws did not eliminate abortions; experts estimate that as many as a million illegal abortions were performed every year. The potentially harmful consequences included death and permanent injury to women from unsanitary back-alley abortions, along with the risk of criminal prosecution for both the woman and the doctor.

Sodomy, Fornication, Adultery, and Prostitution Laws.   Various forms of sexual activity have traditionally been illegal in the United States: sex between members of the same sex (sodomy), sex between unmarried people of different sex (fornication), sex between a married person and someone other than his or her spouse (adultery), and sex for pay (prostitution). The law has been changing rapidly on some of these issues, however. The Supreme Court declared sodomy laws unconstitutional in 2003, and by early 2010 five states had legalized same-sex marriage. To put it mildly, none of these laws ever stopped people from engaging in these forms of sexual behavior. All of these behaviors have occurred since the beginning of recorded history.

The Lessons of History

These examples suggest the following four conclusions about the limits of the criminal law in controlling products or services that a large number of people want:

1. If a large number of people want a product or service, someone will take the risks to supply it.
2. Efforts to suppress the supply result in massive evasion and the creation of criminal syndicates to provide the product or service.

3. The enforcement effort itself will generate secondary crime (e.g., turf wars between gangs, corruption of law enforcement), abuse of individual rights (e.g., illegal searches and seizures), and loss of respect for the law.

4. Intensifying the enforcement effort encourages adaptations, either substitution of products (as in the case of some drugs) or transfer of the service to people more willing to take the increased risks.

In short, criminal law enforcement is inherently weak in the face of a strong public demand for a product or service. This point helps explain the failure of the war on drugs. Shortly, we will look at some policies designed to reduce the demand for drugs.

When Social Control Does Work

It is not true that *all* efforts to prevent undesirable behavior fail. In principle, prohibitions on certain kinds of behavior are good, even if they often fail. The criminal law expressed the basic values of any society. Killing people is wrong, and we should criminalize murder, even if many people break the law (14,180 murders in 2008). As children, we learn that stealing things and hitting people are wrong. The fact that we have high levels of theft, burglary and assault does not mean we should repeal those laws.

There is an important distinction between the laws against murder, assault, burglary, and other common crimes and laws against drinking alcohol, having an abortion, or engaging in private sexual behavior. The criminal laws against murder and other common crimes do not have the adverse consequences that we have seen with the other group of laws. That is the important point we have to keep in mind when discussing drug policies.

The case of smoking offers an interesting example of an apparently successful attempt at curbing harmful behavior. Smoking among adults has declined significantly in recent years. Between 1965 and 2008, the percentage of American men who smoked fell from 52 to 20.6 percent. Among women it declined from 34 to 18.3 percent.[46] These figures represent a substantial change in peoples' behavior. How was it achieved? The long-term decline in smoking is the result of a broad-based national effort involving both formal restrictions and a massive public education effort. The important point is that it has not involved an attempt to outlaw smoking. The new restrictions include prohibitions on smoking in certain places: government buildings, commercial businesses, and so on. You can still smoke, but you have to do it away from other people. The education effort includes warning messages on cigarette packages and organized antismoking public education campaigns. Increased taxes on cigarettes add an economic disincentive. Together, all these efforts represent a "soft" approach to controlling a harmful product. It is reasonable to speculate that a "hard" approach, similar to Prohibition or criminalizing drugs, would produce the adverse consequences we have seen with these other products.

It is also worth noting that the antismoking campaign has been least effective among young males (26.4 percent among males between the ages of 22 and 44).

Smoking is also much higher among poor people (31.5 among those below the poverty level) and with little education (35.7 among those with only 9 to 11 years of education).[47] In other words, the national antismoking effort has been least effective among those who are also most at risk for criminal behavior.

The decline in automobile fatalities that we discussed in Chapter 6 offers another useful example. This remarkable achievement in saving lives was the result not of traffic enforcement crackdowns, but of a number of social policies working in combination: improved roads, better-designed cars, seat belts, and so on. When we focus on alcohol-related fatalities, the use of the criminal law is now the most effective approach.

DEMAND REDUCTION: DRUG EDUCATION

The owl drug policy favored by most liberals includes demand reduction—getting people to not want to take drugs—through education and treatment. Let us take a look at drug education programs.

"Just Say No"

The most widely used drug prevention program, reflecting a demand reduction strategy, involves public education campaigns to persuade people not to use drugs. The most famous was Nancy Reagan's "Just say no" campaign in the 1980s. The Office of National Drug Control Policy continues this approach, and has made the Youth Anti-Drug Media Campaign one of its major efforts.[48]

Educational programs employ one or more of four different strategies.[49] The most common strategy is *information dissemination,* which seeks to change behavior simply by providing information. Sex education programs, for example, discuss the basic facts about reproduction, while health education programs explain the dangers of cholesterol. Like other deterrence-based programs, information dissemination assumes that people make rational choices and that information about the harmfulness of illegal drugs will cause people not to use them.

A second strategy is *fear arousal,* which attempts to change behavior by frightening people. Safe-sex education programs emphasize the danger of getting AIDS from unprotected sex. In the Scared Straight program we discussed in Chapter 6, adult prisoners told juvenile offenders about the horrors of imprisonment. The old "your brain on drugs" effort was a fear arousal approach.[50]

A third strategy is *moral appeal,* emphasizing the idea that certain behavior is wrong—that premarital sex is a sin, that gambling is immoral, and that taking drugs or any other illegal substance is wrong.

A fourth strategy is known as *affective education.* This approach attempts to develop personal and social skills that will help people resist certain behavior. Sex education programs, for instance, try to teach teenagers how to say no to someone who is pressuring them to have sex. Drug-related affective education programs try to teach teenagers techniques for saying no to people who try to get them to try drugs.

We have good reasons for questioning the effectiveness of antidrug educational programs. The problems are similar to the ones we discussed in Chapter 6 regarding deterrence theory. The message has to reach the intended audience, members of that audience have to perceive a real personal risk, and they have to make rational decisions to change their behavior. Messages delivered to the general population appear to be ineffective, but those delivered to a limited and carefully selected target audience are more likely to be effective.

There are questions about the impact of antidrug public education campaigns. The messages do reach their intended audiences. According to the National Household Survey, 78 percent of youths between the ages of 12 and 17 in 2008 reported they heard an antialcohol or antidrug message outside of school. And there was some impact. Illicit drug use was slightly lower among those who had heard a message (8.9 percent) than those who had not (10.2). The Household Survey further reports that a majority of students perceive a real risk in either taking drugs or binge drinking, and its data indicate lower rates of abuse among those who do perceive a risk than those who do not. The real question is the extent to which antidrug messages heighten the perceived risk and lower rates of abuse—independent of other influences. As our discussion of deterrence theory indicated, the risk has to be perceived in a cost–benefit context as being worse than the alternative (see Chapter 6). But many people trapped in very poor neighborhoods do not perceive any realistic long-term hopes for economic advancement. Consequently, the short-term benefits of immediate gratification weigh much more heavily for them.

Some of the education program messengers, meanwhile, are not credible. Was Nancy Reagan, for example, an influential role model for low-income teenagers in the 1980s? Another problem is that some fear arousal programs backfire by glamorizing the forbidden behavior. They may heighten the allure of drinking, smoking, sex, and drugs by portraying them as adult-only activities. In fact, the famous "This is your brain on drugs" concept became the subject of many parodies that undermined the purpose of the original campaign.[51]

Additionally, we cannot assume that the members of the target audience will make rational decisions even if they hear the message. Teenagers are notoriously focused on short-term gratification rather than long-term consequences. That's what growing up is all about: gaining a mature perspective that takes into account the consequences of one's actions. Antismoking campaigns have been least successful with this group. An education program is only one small factor influencing behavior and is likely to be very weak in the face of peer group influence.

Evaluation of a National Media Campaign.   The National Youth Anti-Drug Media Campaign in the late 1990s sponsored paid advertisements targeted at young people between ages of 9 to 18, with a special focus on 14- to 16-year-olds, along with parents of youth in these age groups. A major component of the campaign was a special Marijuana Initiative. An evaluation surveyed a representative sample of several thousand young people and adults.[52]

How effective was the campaign? Most parents (70 percent) and youth (80 percent) surveyed recalled having seen the ads at least once (consistent with the National Household data). Parents consistently had a favorable reaction to them. The impact on young people, however, was not positive. And among the primary target audience of 14- to 16-year-olds, marijuana use actually increased. With respect to attitudes, young people who were more exposed to the campaign were no more likely to express opposition to marijuana than were those who were less exposed.

DARE: Success or Failure?

Perhaps the most popular antidrug education program in the last 25 years has been DARE (Drug Abuse Resistance Education). Created by the Los Angeles Police Department and school system in 1983, the program consists of 17 45- to 60-minute classes, taught by sworn police officers, for fifth- and sixth-grade students. Over time, the DARE curriculum has expanded to other grades, and includes after-school programs. It relies primarily on affective education, attempting to provide the "skills for recognizing and resisting social pressures to experiment with tobacco, alcohol, and drugs" and "developing skills in risk assessment and decision making."[53]

DARE is extremely popular with parents, politicians, and the police. DARE bumper stickers can be seen everywhere. The 2008 Annual Report of DARE America (a private organization) claims that by 2009 it was operating in 75 percent of all U.S. school districts, with 14,000 active instructors, and in 43 other countries. At one point, the total cost of all programs was an estimated $750 million a year. The official DARE website estimated that 36 million students would participate in the program in the 2004–2005 school year. Eighty percent of all local law enforcement agencies reported having a special unit for in-school drug education.[54]

Evaluations of DARE have not found it effective, however. Evaluations have measured students' knowledge about drugs, attitudes toward drug use, social skills in resisting pressure to use drugs, and actual drug usage. A 2003 report by GAO Report reviewed six long-term evaluations of DARE and found "no significant differences in illicit drug use between students who received DARE in the fifth or sixth grades ... and the students who did not." A meta-analysis of 18 evaluations by the Research Triangle Institute of North Carolina, meanwhile, concludes that the program's effect on drug use is "slight, and except for tobacco use, not statistically significant."[55] Studies that have followed DARE and non-DARE students for up to five years after the program have consistently found that "DARE does not have long-term effects on drug use." A 10-year follow-up study of 1,002 people who had experienced the DARE program or an equivalent drug education program found that "in no case did the DARE group have a more successful outcome than the comparison group."[56]

There are several possible reasons why DARE does not affect drug use. The teaching method used, primarily classroom lectures, is inherently less effective than participative methods used in other kinds of programs. Some critics suggest that police officers may not be well trained for this activity and may not be effective role models. A more fundamental question is whether 17 hours of classroom lectures can overcome the other influences in a teenager's life—family (perhaps a dysfunctional family), peer group, neighborhood, and so on. It is likely that the program works only where it supplements existing positive influences such as a strong family and peer group environment. The evidence on DARE leads us to the following conclusion:

PROPOSITION 56

There is no evidence that DARE or other drug education programs reduce illegal drug use.

But *Some* Education Programs Do Work

Not all education programs are worthless. Some are effective, but it is important to examine why certain kinds of programs work for certain audiences.

AIDS education programs are a good example. Good evidence indicates that safe-sex education programs have changed behavior. In New York, the average number of unsafe sexual encounters per person dropped from 11 to only 1 per year between 1980 and 1991. As a result, the incidence of new AIDS cases among adult gay men also dropped. Nationally, the number of AIDS cases has dropped significantly since 1993.[57] Unfortunately, unsafe activity has continued among people in the underclass, including both unprotected sex and the use of unclean needles. As a result, AIDS has spread from male drug addicts to their female sexual partners and on to other men. Surveys of members of the underclass have found an incredible indifference to the known risks of using unclean needles and engaging in unprotected sex.[58]

Deaths related to AIDS rose sharply in the 1980s, peaked in 1994, and then began an equally dramatic decline which continues today. Education efforts have to be maintained and retooled for new generations, however. In early 2005 a new strain of drug-resistant HIV appeared, leading health officials to realize that members of a younger generation were engaging in risky sexual activities.

In 1990 50 percent of all AIDS diagnoses involved whites and 28 percent involved African Americans. By 2006 the distribution was reversed: about half involved African Americans.[59] Why the difference between the two groups? The adult gay community is a relatively successful group in U.S. society, with relatively high levels of education and professional careers. That segment of the gay community is also very cohesive, with a strong self-identity, networks of community institutions, and strong peer group support. Needle-drug users are at the other end of the social scale: They are unemployed, with little if any education, substantial criminal records, and no community identity or institutions. It is reasonable to conclude that successful, educated people are more likely to respond to information dissemination programs: to receive the information, process it, and make a rational decision to change their behavior. This process reflects a sense of empowerment and capacity to control one's own life. That sense of power and control is precisely what people at the bottom of society do not have.

Despite the early success of safe-sex education programs, disturbing recent evidence indicates that they are not having the same degree of success with a younger generation of gay men. The reasons are not yet clear, but the situation does highlight the fact that people's behavior is influenced by a complex mix of personal and social factors. We cannot assume that education programs, by themselves, will have a dominant influence on behavior.[60]

Another example is the antismoking crusade, which we have already discussed. As we mentioned earlier, smoking has increased among teenagers recently, despite a significant decline among adults. Why the difference? We can argue that adults, especially successful, middle-class, and professional adults, are more likely to make rational choices about their behavior. Teenagers are far more likely to make reckless decisions, to consider themselves invulnerable, and to fail to think about either the immediate or the long-term consequences of their actions.

The response of different groups to education programs is closely related to the problems associated with deterrence theory, which we have already considered. Just as some people are more likely to be deterred by the threat of criminal sanction than others, so educational programs will be more effective with some groups than others. People with a stake in society are likely to respond very differently than people at the very bottom who feel they have nothing to lose.

DRUG TREATMENT

Along with prevention-oriented education programs, drug treatment represents the approach most favored by liberals. Treatment raises all of the issues related to rehabilitation that we discussed in Chapter 11. It is a *planned intervention* designed to change behavior.

One of the major issues related to drug treatment is the availability of treatment programs. Critics of current drug policy argue that programs are not adequately funded and that many people who want treatment cannot receive it. Their proposal calls for funding to provide "treatment on demand." Slightly more than 900,000 people have been enrolled in alcohol and drug treatment programs per year since the early 1990s. About 30 percent of them are receiving drug treatment only. It has also been estimated, however, that about three or four times as many people need drug treatment as are currently receiving it. Prison-based treatment programs are seriously underfunded. It has been estimated that between 70 and 85 percent of state prisoners need drug treatment, but only 11 percent actually participate in treatment programs.[61]

Varieties of Treatment

As with drug education, several different kinds of drug treatment programs are available.[62]

Methadone Maintenance.   This treatment provides methadone as a substitute for heroin. A supervised medical treatment maintains the addiction at a steady level to prevent deeper dependency, eliminates the addict's need to turn to crime, and presumably reduces his or her association with drug addicts and criminals (and their peer influence). A supervised program of withdrawal can also be included. Because it involves providing an addictive drug, methadone maintenance is the most controversial of the three major forms of treatment.

Therapeutic Communities.   These are residential programs using intensive individual or group counseling techniques. Their primary goal is to temporarily remove the external influences that contribute to drug dependency and through counseling restructure the client's personality. Some of the more famous therapeutic communities include Synanon and Phoenix House. The therapeutic community is the most expensive of the three major types of programs.

Outpatient Drug-free Programs.   These programs provide counseling and other services to clients who remain in the community. Services include individual and group counseling on drug abuse and counseling or training for employment and family and other problems. Because they are the least expensive and least controversial type of program, outpatient programs are the most common.

Drug users can get into treatment in a variety of different ways. They can enter a program voluntarily. Many celebrities, for example, go to the Betty Ford Clinic, which is a therapeutic community. Others are compelled to enter treatment through the criminal justice system. Drug abuse counseling is often a condition of a diversion program, probation, or parole. Most of the new intensive probation supervision and boot camp programs (see Chapter 11) include drug and alcohol counseling. Opponents of drug legalization argue that the coercive aspect of the criminal law is necessary to get most people into treatment.

Faith-based Treatment.   A number of religious organizations operate faith-based drug treatment programs. As we learned in Chapter 11, however, there have been very few evaluations of any faith-based programs, and at this point there is no persuasive evidence that they are any more effective than secular programs.

Does Treatment Work?

The evidence on the effectiveness of treatment programs is very mixed. (We will discuss drug courts, the most successful program to date, below.) One review concludes that "all" the major types of programs "have been shown to be successful." Another survey concludes optimistically that "research provides convincing evidence for the effectiveness of treatment for drug abuse."[63]

Evaluations of drug treatment programs generally show that clients who successfully complete the programs are less likely to use illegal drugs and to commit crimes than before treatment. An evaluation of one Philadelphia methadone maintenance program found that clients averaged nine "crime days" per month before treatment but only three after treatment; their average number of days per month employed went from three to eleven. Of 202 men who completed the Phoenix House therapeutic community program, 72 percent were arrested in the three years before entering the program, whereas 41 percent were arrested in the three years afterward. Outpatient treatment in the Drug Abuse Reporting

Program reduced the arrest rate of clients from 87 percent beforehand to 22 percent after three years.[64]

Upon closer inspection, however, these claims are less impressive than they first appear to be. First, few if any programs claim to reduce completely illegal drug use or criminal activity. Especially disturbing are the high dropout rates in virtually all programs. Program evaluations that include only those who complete the program are artificially inflating their success rate because a dropout can legitimately be considered a failure.

Even more seriously, treatment programs report high rates of relapse into drug use. The report that says treatment is effective also states that "relapse to drug use is the rule."[65] That seems to undermine the claim of effectiveness. National data indicate that almost half of all heroin users in treatment have previously been in treatment three times or more. Almost 40 percent of cocaine users in treatment have previously been in treatment two or more times.[66] It is not exactly a ringing endorsement to say that failure is "the rule." Treatment programs seem to work for those clients who have made a personal commitment to get off drugs. Interviews with ex-addicts repeatedly reveal that they decided that the drug life was too much hassle, and that they could not put up with it anymore. In other words, treatment works for those who have decided to make it work. But treatment programs do not seem to be able to produce that change in personal commitment.[67]

The relapse problem arises with programs designed to treat alcoholism, smoking, weight problems, and criminal behavior. Millions of people try to give up smoking or lose weight every year. Most of them fail. In fact, most fail many times. We all know people who have made several efforts to quit smoking or lose weight. In some cases, however, they succeed. They finally quit smoking or lost the 20 pounds they always wanted to lose.

The challenge for effective treatment is to match the right program with the right client. To a great extent, the "right" client is the person who has already made a commitment to change his or her life. But as one treatment expert put it, "Little progress has been made in classifying drug users to identify what kinds of users will benefit most from particular kinds of programs."[68] If this sounds familiar, it is because it is another version of the prediction problem we have encountered several times before. As we have seen, bail decisions, selective incapacitation, probation, and parole all depend on identifying just the right people and only those people. Overpredicting produces false positives; underpredicting leads to false negatives. And as we have seen, the data and diagnostic tools are not available to us to make the precise predictions we want.

The Promise of Drug Courts

Drug courts are the most promising alternative for treating arrestees who are involved with drugs. As we explained in Chapter 11, drug courts represent a form of diversion: suspending prosecution or imprisonment pending successful completion of a drug treatment program. Several factors appear to make them more effective than traditional diversion programs and other forms of treatment. The most important is the heavy involvement of the judge in each case. This adds an important element of coordination and accountability for other officials involved in the program. Another key element is their selectivity with regard to offenders admitted to the program. Generally, people arrested for violent crimes are not eligible to participate.

The evidence on the success of drug courts is still a matter of debate, but it appears that well-planned and properly managed programs are effective in reducing both drug use and criminal behavior (see our discussion in Chapter 11).[69] Drug courts are also very cost-effective. The Urban Institute report, *To Treat or Not to Treat,* estimates that current programs save $2.21 for every $1 invested. It further estimates that expanding drug court treatment to the 1.5 million people arrested every year who are drug dependent or drug abusers would raise the cost–benefit ratio to $3.36 saved for every dollar invested. In Chapter 11 we questioned this proposal. Admitting offenders who are not currently eligible would likely bring in many who are not amenable to treatment and thus lower the effectiveness rate. This is still a matter for further debate and research.[70]

Nonetheless, the evidence suggests that drug courts are today the most promising drug treatment program. What to do about arrestees who have histories of violent crime and are not eligible for drug courts remains a difficult question. This leads us to the following proposition:

PROPOSITION 57
Drug treatment programs do not have a good record of effectiveness in either reducing drug use or criminal activity. Drug courts, however, are a very promising alternative.

But Something Positive *Did* Happen

It appears that our review of drug policies so far has not turned up many examples that have demonstrated consistent effectiveness, apart from some drug courts. But wait a minute: Something positive *did* happen in the 1990s. Use of crack declined substantially in many cities, and many criminologists believe that this is one of the factors—perhaps *the* factor—in the drop in the crime rate, particularly gun violence. In short, something worked.

The ADAM program gives us very good data on illegal drug use among persons arrested. Several points need to be emphasized. First, Manhattan is typical of many other cities in that the decline began first and was steepest among youthful (under age 18) offenders. This effect suggests that overall crack use in the city is likely to continue to drop as each cohort ages into adulthood.

Second, crack use declined in Washington, DC, despite the fact that its police department during these years was widely criticized for being disorganized and ineffective in dealing with crime.[71] This effect suggests that the decline in crack usage is unrelated to police enforcement patterns. Third, crack use remained stable in Phoenix. In some other cities it rose during this period (Indianapolis, for example). This effect suggests that patterns in crack usage are highly sensitive to local factors, with very different trends in different cities.

The ADAM data, however, do *not* tell us is *why* crack usage has declined so significantly in so many cities. As we suggested in Chapter 1, several explanations are possible. New York City officials claim that it is because of their zero-tolerance crime policy. But as we have already suggested, this does not account for similar trends in other cities with very different enforcement patterns. Many advocates of community policing claim that the new police officers hired under the COPS program are responsible for the decline in crack use. But the Government Accountability Office and other critics point out that most of those officers have been hired in cities and towns that never had a serious drug or crime problem in the first place, and as we learned in Chapter 5, there is very mixed evidence about the impact of community policing programs across the country. Still others claim that our sentencing policies have reduced both drug use and crime through a combination of deterrence and incapacitation. But as we found in Chapters 6 and 7, there is no strong evidence to support that argument.

Another possible explanation is that crack simply went out of style—that at some point it was no longer regarded as cool among those most likely to use it. An ethnographic study of young adults in New York City found that crack users had become negatively stereotyped as "crack heads" in their peer group and that they took pride in not using the drug. In particular, they defined "crack heads" as people who had lost control over their lives: They could not control their drug habit and often lost their apartments and custody of their children. In short, control of crack use was the result of peer pressure and a strong concern for self-image among one's peers, and not a result of law enforcement. A *New York Times* article suggested: "The crack epidemic behaved much like a fever: It came on strong, appearing to rise without hesitation, and then broke, just as the most dire warnings were being sounded."[72] Law enforcement undoubtedly played some role in changing attitudes toward crack as people saw the effect of arrest and incarceration on friends and other people they knew, but at best this was only one factor in their decision not to use crack.

LEGALIZE DRUGS?

By the 1980s, many thoughtful observers had concluded that the war on drugs was a disaster, particularly in terms of the impact on racial minority communities and the economic cost of the soaring prison population.[73]

These criticisms gave new life to the call to legalize drugs. Legalization is no longer something advocated by hippies left over from the 1960s. The advocates include prominent conservatives, such as the Nobel Prize–winning economist Milton Friedman and writer William F. Buckley. They are joined by civil libertarians, who agree with these conservatives on almost no other criminal justice issue. The American Civil Liberties Union adopted a policy in 1994 calling for the "full and complete decriminalization of the use, possession, manufacture and distribution of drugs." Public support for legalization has grown substantially, from 25 percent of the population in 1980 to 44 percent in 2009.[74]

The debate over legalization was sparked twenty years ago by Ethan Nadelmann's 1989 article in *Science* magazine, "Drug Prohibition in the United States." His case for legalization includes the following points: Criminal prohibition has not eliminated or even reduced drug use; we spend billions of dollars a year in this seemingly futile effort; the war on drugs produces numerous harmful side effects, including corruption and damage to poor and minority neighborhoods, prohibition of potentially beneficial medical uses of marijuana, and so on. The "logic of legalization," he argues, consists of two main points: that "most illegal drugs are not as dangerous as is commonly believed" and that abuse of the most dangerous drugs will not rise significantly under legalization.[75]

Varieties of Legalization

The debate over legalization has been confused because the term means different things to different people. It is often used interchangeably with *decriminalization*. Both terms embrace a variety of specific proposals. The basic point of both is the removal of criminal penalties for the possession and sale of at least some currently illegal drugs. Beyond that, however, much disagreement prevails over four issues: (1) Are all drugs to be legalized, or only some? (2) Are possession *and* sale to be legalized, or only possession? (3) Will legalization apply to adults *and* juveniles, or just adults? (4) Will some kind of regulation replace criminal penalties, and if so, what kind?[76] As Nadelmann points out, "There is no one legalization option."[77]

Legalization *maximalists* take the extreme position, advocating legalization of both sale and possession of all drugs for juveniles as well as adults. Legalization *moderates* want to remove criminal penalties for the possession of many drugs and the sale of some drugs, but for adults only. Legalization *minimalists,* meanwhile, would eliminate penalties only for adult possession of marijuana, particularly for prescribed medical use, and perhaps other less dangerous drugs. Finally, *agnostics* have not taken a final position on legalization but are convinced that current policy has failed and that we need a national debate on a new approach to drugs.[78]

Included within this general framework are a number of different policy options. One approach is to give states the right to set their own drug policy, allowing them to experiment as they see fit. Doing this would abandon a national policy. Under a proposal drafted by Daniel K. Benjamin and Roger Leroy Miller, any conflict between federal and state laws would be resolved in favor of state law.[79] Another alternative would be to legalize particular drugs for medical use only. California and Arizona took a step in this direction in 1996, and a total of fourteen states now legalize it for that purpose. A more comprehensive option would have the government-issue "user's licenses" to individuals who pass a required test.[80]

Except for radical libertarians, most legalization proposals would maintain some government regulation over drugs. The issue of regulation, however, is widely misunderstood. A wide range of legal products today are regulated (for example, tobacco and alcohol). Similarly, you cannot just buy a cow and sell milk from your front porch. These regulations are ultimately backed up by criminal penalties. It is illegal to sell cigarettes or beer to minors. Thus, legalization does not necessarily mean the complete elimination of all forms of government control or the threat of criminal punishment. But it does represent a shift in the basic direction of drug policy.

Medical Marijuana.   The one legalization proposal that has gained some ground is to legalize marijuana for medical purposes. In 1996 the voters in California passed Proposition 215, the Compassionate Use Act, by a margin of 56 to 44 percent. That same year, Arizona passed Proposition 2000 by a margin of 65 to 35 percent. By 2010, 14 states had legalized medical marijuana. Because these state laws contradict federal law, there has been considerable conflict with federal authorities over their legality.

The Impact of Legalization.   What would happen if we legalized drugs? And for the purposes of this book, would legalization reduce crime? Obviously, the answer depends on which form of legalization we are talking about. The effect of radical legalization would be very different from the moderate or conservative alternatives.

Whichever policy were adopted, these questions arise: (1) Would drug use increase or decrease? (2) Would predatory crime such as robbery and burglary increase or decrease? (3) How much money would in fact be saved? (4) What would happen to the drug-related criminal syndicates? (5) What would be the overall impact on the criminal justice system? (6) Would there be fewer violations of individual rights? (7) Finally, what would be the overall effect on the quality of life in the United States?

A Specific Proposal.   To focus our discussion of these questions, let us examine a specific legalization proposal drafted by Richard B. Karel that appears in a collection of essays on the legalization debate.[81]

Karel proposes legalizing drugs only for adults and making distinctions among various drugs based on their toxicity and potential harm. He would completely legalize coca leaves, which could be sold in supermarkets "as tea is now sold." Granular cocaine would be illegal, but people could obtain cocaine gum similar to the nicotine gum currently available. Access would be rationed through an Automated Teller Machine (ATM)–type system. You would have a card and you could "withdraw" so much per day or week. Crack cocaine would be completely illegal. Smokable and edible forms of opium would also be available through an ATM system. Heroin would be available to addicts, through either medical prescription or the ATM system, but PCP would remain illegal. Psychedelic drugs would be legally available to people who could demonstrate "knowledge as to their effects" through a written test and interview. The government would regulate the market by controlling distribution and ensuring product purity, much as the government now regulates alcohol and tobacco.

Karel's proposal falls somewhere in the moderate-to-conservative range of legalization alternatives. The most dangerous drugs—crack and PCP—would still be illegal. All drug use by and sale to juveniles would be illegal.

What would be the result? First, there would be an immediate and significant reduction in the number of arrests and persons sent to prison. This outcome would reduce the workload of the justice system and save a certain amount of money, particularly in terms of imprisonment costs. The dollar savings would be a lot less than many legalization advocates believe, however. With cocaine still illegal for adults and all drugs illegal for juveniles, we would still maintain most of the present law enforcement apparatus. And we should not forget that police do a lot of other things besides investigate drug crimes. Criminal syndicates would probably not disappear, because they would still try to serve the demand for cocaine and other drugs that were still illegal. In short, many of the gains promised by legalization advocates—the dollar savings, the disappearance of the drug profits and the criminal syndicates—would not materialize.

Karel's proposal also makes some assumptions about drug users that are debatable. His scenario assumes that they are basically rational people, deciding to go to the clinic to get their ration of gum cocaine or methadone, much the way middle-class yuppies decide whether to buy domestic or imported beer. This scenario does not come to grips with the irrational and self-destructive nature of drug abuse. Among teenagers, drug and alcohol abuse are acts of rebellion. Among the underclass, heroin and cocaine abuse is a way of retreating from a brutal world with no apparent opportunities.

Would Karel's proposal reduce crime? In one limited sense, yes. By definition, it eliminates certain drug-defined crimes involving possession and sale. It is not likely to reduce drug-associated crimes such as robbery and burglary, however. As we already noted, most of this criminal behavior is part of a deviant lifestyle that is the product of many different factors. Relatively little predatory crime is directly caused by drugs, and legalization will not end that criminal behavior. Because crack would still be illegal, drug gangs would still engage in the same violent struggle for control of the market.

Let us move beyond Karel's proposal and discuss the legalization of all drugs. Would drug use increase? Much controversy exists over this question. Even Ethan Nadelmann, one of the leading legalization advocates, concedes, "It is thus impossible to predict whether or not legalization would lead to much greater levels of drug abuse."[82]

Opponents of legalization argue that a tremendous increase in drug use would result. They believe that existing criminal penalties curb drug use, both by the threat of arrest and punishment and because the criminal law represents a statement about society's values.[83] Some evidence, however, suggests that drug use would not increase. The National Household Survey indicates that 20 million Americans use illegal drugs every month, with 15 million using marijuana. As we have already mentioned, 83 percent do not go on to use other drugs, and an even higher percentage do not become serious criminals. Marijuana is not the gateway drug some people claim it is. Why is that the case? The main reason is that marijuana use is purely recreational for most of the 15 million monthly users. For them, the process of socialization operates somewhat effectively. They may engage in some minor deviance—casual drug use, vandalism, even some petty theft—but they do not cross over the line into addiction or criminality. Moreover, drug abuse is not rampant in those European countries that have relatively tolerant drug policies. These countries do not have the same level of crime the United States has, and their example may not be relevant in this context.

The danger, however, is that the mechanisms of socialization might be overwhelmed by legalization. In a suburban high school, for example, drug use could become so prevalent that peer pressure encourages pervasive cocaine use. As drug use increases, academic performance could decline, leading to a complete change in the culture of the school.

To a great extent, this is exactly what has already happened in many schools and neighborhoods. Drug use is so pervasive that it is extremely difficult for young people to resist the pressures to join. Drug-related crime contributes to the dreadful quality of neighborhood life. This is one of the main reasons that African American leaders are some of the most vocal opponents of legalization. People such as Representative Charles Rangel, whose district includes Harlem, see a covert form of racism in the legalization idea.[84] They argue that it would abandon their communities to drugs and crime. In some respects that is already true. Poor and racial and ethnic minority communities are already ravaged by poverty, family breakdown, drugs and crime. The question is whether legalizing the least harmful drug, marijuana, would make things better or worse.

One of the strongest arguments against the war on drugs is that it converts many otherwise law-abiding people into criminals. The Rand Corporation interviewed people arrested for drug offenses in Washington, DC, and found that two-thirds held regular jobs. Drug dealing was essentially a part-time job. Their regular jobs paid an average of $11,000 to $14,000 a year, while they said they made an average of $24,000, tax free, from their drug dealing. The illegal drug markets represented a very tempting way to supplement their annual income. Looking at it another way, their $7-per-hour jobs were not adequate to support a decent lifestyle.[85] Legalizing drugs would eliminate this temptation to engage in criminal activity and save thousands of people from arrest and imprisonment and the subsequent problems associated with having a criminal record.

The full impact of legalization remains entirely a matter of speculation. It depends on which drugs would be legalized and whether they would be fully legalized or regulated. This leads us to the following conclusion:

PROPOSITION 58
The impact of legalizing drugs on serious crime is not known at this time.

CONCLUSION

In the end, what can we recommend in the way of a sensible drug policy? The first step should be to face squarely the fact that we do not have any convincing evidence of a program or policy that has consistently been proven effective in reducing drug abuse and crime associated with drugs. Some drug courts have had promising results, but much depends on how carefully planned and managed they are. Politicians and the public continually asked for more of the same old policies ("longer prison terms," "more treatment") without any evidence regarding their effectiveness.

Our discussion of drug control policies has brought back earlier discussions of various crime policies. What is absolutely clear is that the "war" on drugs is not only ineffective in controlling illegal drug use but is also destructive of entire communities. The impact of the war on drugs on the African American community has been particularly severe. Tougher law enforcement is no more effective with regard to drugs than it is with robbery or burglary. The threat of harsher prison terms also does not appear to have a deterrent effect. Similarly, antidrug education programs and traditional treatment programs are not supported by good evidence, as is the case with such programs related to other crimes.

Some promising alternatives have begun to emerge. Some drug courts appear to be successful. Some problem-oriented policing programs that we have studied in this and other chapters also appear to be effective in reducing gun violence and gang activity that are closely associated with drugs. Both of these two programs differ from the failed programs of the past because they are narrowly tailored and focused on particular problems and/or individuals.

NOTES

1. Sentencing Project, *Drug Policy and the Criminal Justice System* (Washington, DC: The Sentencing Project, 2001). Available on the Sentencing Project website.

2. United States Sentencing Commission, *Cocaine and Federal Sentencing Policy* (Washington, DC: Author, 1995), p. 172.

3. Gil Kerlikowske, Director, Office of National Drug Control Policy, *Statement*, Public Services Summit, December 10, 2009.

4. Sentencing Project, *Drug Policy and the Criminal Justice System* (Washington, DC: The Sentencing Project, 2001). Available on the Sentencing Project website. United States Sentencing Commission, *Cocaine and Federal Sentencing Policy* (Washington, DC: Author, 1995), p. 172. Elliott Currie, *Reckoning: Drugs, the Cities, and the American Future* (New York: Hill & Wang, 1992). Steven R. Donziger, ed., *The Real War on Crime: The Report of the National Criminal Justice Commission* (New York: HarperPerennial, 1996).

5. Dale Gieringer, "How Many Crack Babies?" in Arnold Trebach and Kevin B. Zeese, eds., *Drug Prohibition and the Conscience of Nations* (Washington, DC: Drug Policy Foundation, 1990), pp. 71–75.

6. The Sentencing Project, *Does the Punishment Fit the Crime? Drug Users and Drunk Drivers, Questions of Race and Class* (Washington, DC: The Sentencing Project, 1993). Available on the Sentencing Project website.

7. Peter Reuter, "Drug Use Measures: What Are They Really Telling Us?" *National Institute of Justice Journal* (April 1999): 13. An extended discussion of methodologies and findings is in Thomas Mieczkowski, "The Prevalence of Drug Use in the United States," in Michael Tonry, ed., *Crime and Justice: A Review of Research*, vol. 20 (Chicago: University of Chicago Press, 1996), pp. 349–414.

8. U.S. Department of Health and Human Services, *Results from the 2003 National Survey on Drug Use and Health: National Findings* (Washington, DC: Author, 2004).

9. Monitoring the Future, *Overview of Key Findings, 2008* (2009), Table 5. Monitoring the Future, *National Survey Results on Drug Use, 1975–2003* (Ann Arbor, MI: Author, 2004).

10. Health and Human Services, *Drug Abuse Warning Network, 2007: Area Profiles of Drug-Related Mortality* (Rockville, MD: HHS, 2009). Reuter, "Drug Use Measures: What Are They Really Telling Us?"

11. Office of National Drug Control Policy, *ADAM II: 2008 Annual Report* (Washington, DC: Office of National Drug Control Policy, 2009).

12. Andrew Lang Golub and Bruce D. Johnson, *Crack's Decline: Some Surprises Across U.S. Cities* (Washington, DC: Government Printing Office, 1997). NCJ 165707. Jeremy Travis and Michelle Waul, *Reflections on the Crime Decline* (Washington, DC: Urban Institute, 2002). Available on the Urban Institute website.

13. Matthew B. Robinson and Renee C. Scherlen, *Lies, Damned Lies, and Drug War Statistics* (Albany: State University of New York Press, 2007).

14. Office of National Drug Control Policy, *What Americans Need to Know About Marijuana* (Washington, DC: ONDCP, n.d.).

15. David N. Nurco, Timothy W. Kinlock, and Thomas E. Hanlon, "The Drugs–Crime Connection," in James A Inciardi, ed., *Handbook of Drug Control in the United States* (New York: Greenwood, 1990), pp. 71–90.

16. This typology is taken from the Office of National Drug Control Policy, *Fact Sheet: Drug-Related Crime* (Washington, DC: Author, 2000). NCJ 181056.

17. The data in this paragraph are summarized in ibid.

18. Bureau of Justice Statistics, *Substance Abuse and Treatment of Adults on Probation, 1995* (Washington, DC: Government Printing Office, 1998).

19. John P. Morgan, M.D. and Lynn Zimmer, Ph.D., *The Myth of Marijuana's Gateway Effect* (March 26, 2006), available at www.druglibrary.org, and other web sites. Andrew R. Morral, Daniel F. McCaffrey, and Susan M. Paddock, "Reassessing the Marijuana Gateway Effect," *Addiction* 97.12 (2002): 1493–504.

20. Bureau of Justice Statistics, *Drugs, Crime, and the Justice System* (Washington, DC: Government Printing Office, 1992), p. 2.

21. David P. Farrington, "Predictors, Causes, and Correlates of Male Youth Violence," in Michael Tonry and Mark H. Moore, eds., *Youth Violence* (Chicago: University of Chicago Press, 1998), p. 431.

22. A good discussion of the different positions on drug policy is Peter Reuter, "Hawks Ascendant: The Punitive Trend of American Drug Policy," *Daedalus* 121 (Summer 1992): 15–52. Mark H. Moore, "Controlling Criminogenic Commodities: Drugs, Guns, and Alcohol," in James Q. Wilson, ed., *Crime and Public Policy* (San Francisco: ICS Press, 1983), chapter 8.

23. Marsha Rosenbaum, *Just Say What? An Alternative View on Solving America's Drug Problem* (San Francisco: National Council on Crime and Delinquency, 1989), p. 17.

24. A good statement of the harm reduction position is Mark A. R. Kleiman, *Against Excess: Drug Policy for Results* (New York: Basic Books, 1992). Ed Leuw, "Drugs and

Drug Policy in the Netherlands," in Michael Tonry, ed., *Crime and Justice: A Review of Research*, vol. 14 (Chicago: University of Chicago Press, 1991), pp. 229–276.

25. Jerome G. Miller, *Search and Destroy: African American Males in the Criminal Justice System* (New York: Cambridge University Press, 1996); Donziger, ed., *The Real War on Crime*.

26. Office of National Drug Control Policy, *The President's National Drug Control Strategy January 2009*. Available on the website of the Office.

27. Office of National Drug Control Policy, *Drug Treatment in the Criminal Justice System* (Washington, DC: Department of Justice, 2001). NCJ 181857.

28. Stephen R. Donziger, ed., *The Real War on Crime*, p. 99.

29. Michael Tonry and Matthew Melewski, "The Malign Effects of Drug and Crime Control Policies on Black Americans," in Michael Tonry, ed., *Crime and Justice: A Review of Research*, vol. 37 (Chicago: University of Chicago Press, 2008), pp. 1–44. Samuel Walker, Cassia Spohn, and Miriam DeLone, *The Color of Justice: Race, Ethnicity, and Crime in America*, 4th ed. (Belmont, CA: Thomson, 2007).

30. Department of Health and Human Services, *Results from the 2008 National Survey of Drug Use and Health* (Washington, DC: Department of Health and Human Services, 2009), Figure 2.9. Available on the HHS website.

31. Donziger, *The Real War on Crime*, p. 115.

32. Michael Tonry, *Malign Neglect: Race, Crime, and Punishment in America* (New York: Oxford University Press, 1995), pp. 188–189; Bureau of Justice Statistics, *Sentencing in the Federal Courts: Does Race Matter?* (Washington, DC: Government Printing Office, 1993).

33. Daniel S. Nagin, "Criminal Deterrence Research at the Outset of the Twentieth Century," in Michael Tonry, ed., *Crime and Justice: A Review of Research,* vol. 23 (Chicago: University of Chicago Press, 1998), pp. 1–37.

34. Lawrence W. Sherman, "Police Crackdowns: Initial and Residual Deterrence," in Michael Tonry and Norval Morris, eds., *Crime and Justice: A Review of Research*, vol. 12 (Chicago: University of Chicago press, 1990), pp. 1–48. Lynn Zimmer, "Proactive Policing Against Street-Level Drug Trafficking," *American Journal of Police* 9 (1990): 43–74. University of Maryland, *Preventing Crime: What Works, What Doesn't, What's Promising* (Washington, DC: Government Printing Office, 1997), pp. 8–24.

35. Health and Human Services, *Monitoring the Future, Overview of Key Findings 2008* (2009). Office of National Drug Control Policy, *Pulse Check: Drug Markets and Chronic Users in 25 of America's Largest Cities* (Washington, DC: Author, 2004). NCJ 201398.

36. William J. Bennett, John J. DiIulio, and John P. Walters, *Body Count: Moral Poverty ... And How to Win America's War Against Crime* (New York: Simon & Schuster, 1996), p. 189.

37. Office of National Drug Control Policy, *Current State of Drug Policy: Successes and Challenges* (Washington, DC: ONCDP, March 2008), p. 21.

38. A vivid recent account is Howard Campbell, *Drug War Zone: Frontline Dispatches from the Streets of El Paso and Juarez* (Austin: University of Texas Press, 2009).

39. Office of National Drug Control Policy, *National Southwest Boarder Counternarcotics Strategy* (Washington, DC: Office of National Drug Control Policy, June 2009).

Congressional Research Service, *Mexico's Drug Cartels* (Washington, DC: Congressional Research Service, October 16, 2007).

40. Bureau of Justice Statistics, *Drugs, Crime, and the Justice System*, p. 36. For efforts by the U.S. Customs Bureau, go to its website.

41. Peter Reuter, Gordon Crawford, and Jonathan Cave, *Sealing the Borders: The Effects of Increased Military Participation in Drug Interdiction* (Santa Monica, CA: Rand, 1988), p. xi.

42. Todd R. Clear, Imprisoning Communities: How Mass Incarceration Makes Disadvantaged Communities Worse (New York: Oxford University Press, 2007).

43. Mark H. Moore, "Actually, Prohibition Was a Success," in Rod L. Evans and Irwin M. Berent, eds., *Drug Legalization* (LaSalle, IL: Open Court, 1992), pp. 95–97.

44. Samuel Walker, *Popular Justice: A History of American Criminal Justice*, 2nd ed. (New York: Oxford University Press, 1998), pp. 158–159.

45. The Knapp Commission, *The Knapp Commission Report on Police Corruption* (New York: Braziller, 1973).

46. Center for Disease Control, "Cigarette Smoking Among Adults and Trends in Smoking Cessation—United States, 2008," *MMWR Weekly* 58(44) (November 13, 2009): 1227–1232.

47. See the latest data on the Monitoring the Future website.

48. Reported in Office of National Drug Control Policy, *Current State of Drug Policy: Successes and Challenges* (Washington, DC: ONDCP, March 2008).

49. Gilbert J. Botvin, "Substance Abuse Prevention: Theory, Practice, and Effectiveness," in Michael Tonry and James Q. Wilson, eds., *Crime and Justice: An Annual Review of Research*, vol. 13 (Chicago: University of Chicago Press, 1990), pp. 474–477.

50. James O. Finckenauer, *Scared Straight and the Panacea Phenomenon* (Englewood Cliffs, NJ: Prentice Hall, 1982).

51. Jesse Greene, "Flirting with Suicide," *New York Times*, 15 September 1996: 41.

52. National Institute on Drug Abuse, *Evaluation of the National Youth Anti-Drug Media Campaign: 2003 Report of Findings Executive Summary* (Rockville, MD: Westat, 2003).

53. Bureau of Justice Assistance, *An Introduction to DARE*, 2nd ed. (Washington, DC: Government Printing Office, 1991). Information about the program is available on the official website of DARE, Inc.

54. Bureau of Justice Statistics, *Law Enforcement Management and Administrative Statistics, 1997* (Washington, DC: Government Printing Office, 1999), p. xix. Current data are on the official DARE website.

55. Susan T. Emmett, Nancy Tobler, Christopher Ringwalt, and Robert L. Flewelling, "How Effective Is Drug Abuse Resistance Education? A Meta-Analysis of Project DARE Outcome Evaluations," *American Journal of Public Health* 84 (September 1994): 1394–1401.

56. Five-year follow-up: Richard R. Clayton, Carl G. Leukefeld, Nancy Grant Harrington, and Anne Cattarello, "DARE (Drug Abuse Resistance Education): Very Popular but Not Very Effective," in Clyde B. McCoy, Lisa R. Metsch, and

James A. Inciardi, eds., *Intervening with Drug-Involved Youth* (Thousand Oaks, CA: Sage, 1996), p. 104. Ten-year follow-up: Donald R. Lyman, "Project DARE: No Effects at 10-years Follow-up," *Journal of Consulting and Clinical Psychology*, 67 (August 1999): 590–593.

57. Greene, "Flirting with Suicide"; Bureau of the Census, *Statistical Abstract of the United States, 1998*, pp. 146–147.

58. Currie, *Reckoning*, pp. 247–251.

59. Center for Disease Control and Prevention, HIV and AIDS in the United States: A Picture of Today's Epidemic (2009), www.cdc.gov/hiv/topics/surveillance/united_states.htm.

60. Greene, "Flirting with Suicide."

61. Office of National Drug Control Policy, *Data Snapshot: Drug Abuse in America, 1998*, plates 84, 86. Bureau of Justice Statistics, *Drugs, Crime, and the Justice System*, p. 109. Office of National Drug Control Policy, *Drug Treatment in the CJ System*.

62. George De Leon, "Treatment Strategies," in James A. Inciardi, ed., *Handbook of Drug Control in the United States*, pp. 115–138; Bureau of Justice Statistics, *Drugs, Crime, and the Justice System*, pp. 107–111.

63. M. Douglas Anglin and Yih-Ing Hser, "Treatment of Drug Abuse," in Tonry and Wilson, eds., *Drugs and Crime* (Chicago: University of Chicago Press, 1990), p. 393. De Leon, "Treatment Strategies," p. 120.

64. De Leon, "Treatment Strategies."

65. Ibid., p. 127.

66. Office of National Drug Control Policy, *Data Snapshot: Drug Abuse in America, 1998*, panels 89, 90.

67. Currie, *Reckoning*, pp. 154–155.

68. Ibid., pp. 132–133. Anglin and Hser, "Treatment of Drug Abuse," p. 395.

69. National Drug Court Institute, *Quality Improvement for Drug Courts: Evidence-Based Practices* (Washington, DC: National Drug Court Institute, 2008).

70. Avinash Singh Bhati, John K. Roman, and Aaron Chalfin, *To Treat or Not to Treat: Evidence on the Prospects of Expanding Treatment to Drug-Involved Offenders* (Washington, DC: Urban Institute, 2008).

71. Samuel Walker, *The New World of Police Accountability* (Thousand Oaks: Sage Publications, 2005), pp. 184–85.

72. R. Terry Furst, Bruce D. Johnson, Eloise Dunlap, and Richard Curtis, "The Stigmatized Image of the 'Crack Head:' A Sociocultural Exploration of a Barrier to Cocaine Smoking among a Cohort of Youth in New York City," *Deviant Behavior*, 20 (1999): 153–181. Timothy Egan, "A Drug Ran Its Course, Then Hid with Its Users," *The New York Times*, September 19, 1999: I.

73. Jerome G. Miller, *Search and Destroy: African American Males in the Criminal Justice System* (New York: Cambridge University Press, 1996).

74. A history of the debate over decriminalization/legalization of drugs is in Ronald Bayer, "Introduction: The Great Drug Policy Debate—What Means This Thing Called Decriminalization?" in Ronald Bayer and Gerald M. Oppenheimer, eds., *Confronting Drug Policy: Illicit Drugs in a Free Society* (New York: Cambridge University Press, 1993), pp. 1–23. American Civil Liberties Union, Board of

Directors, "Minutes, April 9, 1994," *ACLU Briefing Paper 19, Against Drug Prohibition* (New York: Author, n.d.). Gallup Poll data in Sourcebook of Criminal Justice Statistics, Table 2.67.2009.

75. Ethan A. Nadelmann, "Drug Prohibition in the United States: Costs, Consequences, and Alternatives," *Science* 245 (September 1, 1989): 939–947; quote on p. 943.

76. See the questions posed by James A. Inciardi, "The Case against Legalization," in Inciardi, ed., *The Drug Legalization Debate* (Newbury Park, CA: Sage, 1991), pp. 45–79.

77. Nadelmann, "Drug Prohibition in the United States," p. 939.

78. Drug Policy Foundation, *National Drug Reform Strategy* (Washington, DC: Drug Policy Foundation, 1992).

79. Cited in Arnold Trebach, "Thinking Through Models of Drug Legalization," in *The Drug Policy Newsletter* 23 (July/August 1994): 12.

80. These options are discussed by Trebach, "Thinking Through Models of Drug Legalization."

81. Richard B. Karel, "A Model Legalization Proposal," in Inciardi, ed., *The Drug Legalization Debate*, pp. 80–102.

82. Nadelmann, "Drug Prohibition in the United States," p. 944.

83. James Q. Wilson, "Against the Legalization of Drugs," *Commentary* 89 (February 1990): 21–28.

84. See the thoughtful discussion in William Kornblum, "Drug Legalization and the Minority Poor," in Bayer and Oppenheimer, eds., *Confronting Drug Policy*, pp. 115–135.

85. Peter Reuter, Robert MacCoun, and Patrick Murphy, *Money from Crime: A Study of the Economics of Drug Dealing in Washington, DC* (Santa Monica, CA: Rand, 1990).

PART VI

Putting It All Together: Crime and Community

14

Crime and Community: Putting It All Together

THE NEW COMMUNITY FOCUS
ON CRIME CONTROL

What have we learned? After reviewing a wide range of crime control proposals from both sides of the political spectrum, do we know anything about what really works to control crime? We have certainly learned that a lot of ideas don't work out in practice. In the process, we have punctured a lot of popular myths about criminal justice. Simply putting more cops on the street will not deter crime any more effectively than the police already do. Removing procedural restraints on police regarding evidence and interrogations won't result in more convictions of criminals. The alleged loopholes of plea bargaining and the insanity defense do not really exist. Harsher sentences will neither deter crime nor incapacitate offenders any better than we currently do. These are among the most popular conservative crime control proposals. Liberal proposals aren't any better. There is no evidence of treatment programs that consistently correct the behavior of offenders. Alternatives to incarceration—probation and parole—have dismal records with regard to recidivism. Decriminalizing certain behavior might be a good idea, but it won't reduce serious crimes such as robbery and burglary.

We have also learned that the criminal justice system is not "soft" on crime, as many people believe. A lot of dangerous criminals do not "beat the system" through loopholes such as plea bargaining. True, some offenders are released and do commit very serious crimes. These are the celebrated cases we discussed in Chapter 2, and one of the main lessons of this book is that we should not develop policy on the basis of such rare events. At the same time, it is true that some offenders do respond to treatment. Matching a relevant treatment program to the right offender, however, is extremely difficult. The most important thing we have gained is an appreciation for the complexity of crime and criminal justice.

Things have changed over time, however. The first edition of this book, published 25 years ago, ended on a very pessimistic note. There were almost no examples of successful crime control programs. In recent years, however, new thinking, supported by the best research, has identified a set of programs that are very promising. (We will use the word "promising," here. Let's not fall into the old trap of declaring that we have found the key to success before a solid foundation of evidence exists.) We have already covered the most important of these promising new programs. In this final chapter, let's not only review them, and look at some additional programs, but identify the elements they share in common.

The New Operating Principles

A strong consensus has emerged among criminologists that effective crime control requires a focus on communities. This new paradigm is the product of several developments: a new theoretical perspective in criminology, research on criminal behavior, the community policing movement, and applications of community policing principles to courts and corrections. Summarizing this new thinking, Joan Petersilia points out: "Research has long documented how the social organization of neighborhoods—particularly poverty, ethnic composition, and residential stability—influences crime."[1]

The new consensus includes several basic operating principles for crime policies. First, *no single crime policy* holds the key to crime reduction. Effective crime prevention and control requires the simultaneous application of several policies.[2] This is an important departure in crime policy. As we have seen again and again in this book, the advocates of particular policies have focused very narrowly on their particular idea, giving almost no attention to the role of other policies.

A second operating principle is, of course, the *community or geographic focus*. All of the programs discussed in this chapter focus on particular neighborhoods and communities. In policing, the new focus is on community policing, or problem-oriented policing with a specific geographic focus. As we will learn in this chapter, there are also promising innovations regarding community prosecution.

A third principle is a *problem-solving* orientation. Problem solving involves focusing on specific and limited crime and disorder problems: neighborhood gun violence; drug dependence among arrestees. The weakness of so many old failed policies is that they spoke about crime in a global sense. Yet we now know that there are many different kinds of crime, with very different degrees of seriousness, involving different kinds of offenders. Limiting the focus also makes the problem more manageable. By promising less but focusing on specific problems, we believe that this approach is likely to deliver more.[3]

A fourth principle is the *need for partnerships* among different agencies and groups: criminal justice agencies, non–criminal justice government service agencies, nonprofit organizations, neighborhood groups, and private businesses. This idea originated with the community policing movement, which began with the recognition that the police cannot control crime by themselves but need the cooperation of citizens and other groups. What is true with regard to policing, we argue, is also true of other components of the criminal justice system. Later in this chapter we will examine community courts, which also involve partnerships. Prisoner reentry programs also depend on partnerships between parole authorities and a wide range of public and private organizations.

How do partnerships work? Housing code enforcement agencies can help deal with apartments that are centers of drug trafficking; sanitation departments can clean up neighborhoods and eliminate the signs of disorder and neglect (the "broken windows" that invite lawbreaking).[4] Faye Taxman, one of the leading experts on offender reentry programs, explains: "The underlying premise of the reentry partnership is that each component of the criminal justice system … plays a role" in dealing with released offenders and also that "criminal justice agencies cannot do this alone, and must engage family, community-based service providers, the faith community and other sources of formal and informal support in reintegrating offenders."[5]

Fifth, many of the new policies utilize *non–criminal law remedies*. This is particularly true with problem-oriented policing where programs include better street lighting and sanitation services as part of a larger effort to improve the quality of life in a neighborhood. Improving these services necessarily includes partnerships with other government agencies.

Finally, the new community focus embraces the *evidence-based policy movement* (see our discussion in Chapter 1) and insists that policies be supported by empirical research demonstrating effectiveness. It is no longer acceptable to base policies on myths, hopes, and good intentions.

This chapter pulls together the different strands of community-focused and problem-solving crime policies. This includes clarifying the theoretical and practical links between developments in the different components of the criminal justice system: community policing, community prosecution, and reentry programs in corrections.

A final verdict on the new paradigm is not in yet. Many questions remain to be answered. This chapter will hold the paradigm to the standards of evidence-based crime policy. The theoretical basis for this new orientation is clear, and there is evidence that some programs have been effective. But does it all hold together? The supporting evidence to date is preliminary at best. Some programs appear to work, but more research is still needed. Will the successful programs be sustained over time? Will they be effective with regard to the serious crimes of robbery and burglary (the crimes we identified as our focus in Chapter 1), along with murder, rape, and drug-associated crimes? Most important, can all the different elements be coordinated to form a comprehensive crime control effort?

The Theoretical Background

The community focus of crime control is grounded in the most important recent developments in theoretical criminology. Sociologist Robert J. Sampson, arguably the most influential scholar on this subject, argues: "'Community' now reigns as the modern elixir for much of what allegedly ails American society." Sampson proposes the concept of "ecometrics" to measure the social ecology of the individuals being studied. This approach emphasizes direct observation of people in their social environment. The new community orientation represents a turning away from the University of Chicago–style research that emerged in the 1960s. Relying primarily on survey research, it focused on individuals, both as "units of data collection and targets of theoretical inference."[6]

Think back on the issues we have covered in this book, and you will gain a sense of what this has involved. Data on criminal offending, arrests, and the processing of offenders has typically involved "units of data." Don't misunderstand: There is great value in research of this sort. It is the basis of our understanding of the broad patterns in criminal justice—and the complexities involved. It is not wrong, just incomplete. The approach abstracts people from the immediate social environment where they live and all of the factors that influence their behavior.

In terms of crime control, Sampson and others propose the concept of *collective efficacy,* which includes *trust among residents* in a neighborhood and their *shared expectations about their social control,* meaning their capacity to exercise some control over their neighborhood.[7] The importance of collective efficacy represents a radical reorientation of thinking about crime control. As the earlier chapters of this book make clear, the traditional approach places primary responsibility on criminal justice agencies: on police patrol to deter crime, on the courts to convict and punish offenders, on sentencing policy to incapacitate career criminals. The new approach emphasizes the role of citizens as "co-producers" of crime control efforts. Wesley Skogan raised the issue of citizens as co-producers over 30 years ago, and the concept became an important operating principle in community policing.[8]

An important aspect of the theory is that collective efficacy mediates the impact of environmental factors, in the sense of blunting their direct effect. Criminologists have long held that poverty, high rates of unemployment, and other social problems are associated with high crime rates. Recent research, however, indicates that neighborhoods with collective efficacy have lower crime rates than similarly poor neighborhoods with no sense of collective efficacy. In plain English, all poor neighborhoods are not the same.

An important policy implication of collective efficacy is that people need to have trust in local criminal justice agencies. Sampson argues that if people do not trust the police, it will be impossible to develop effective neighborhood crime prevention policies. The same point holds true for the justice system as a whole. As we saw in Chapter 12, Tom Tyler's research on procedural justice indicates that distrust of the justice system increases people's tendency to break the law.[9] The concept of collective efficacy suggests that if they trust the police and other agencies, they will be more likely to cooperate with the police and their neighbors in programs to control crime.

With respect to attitudes toward the police, Sampson challenges the prevalent stereotype that the entire African American community distrusts the police. Forty years of public opinion poll data consistently show that while African Americans are more likely to distrust the police, a majority nonetheless have a positive attitude.[10] This evidence suggests that there is a vast resource that police departments can tap into to develop effective crime prevention programs.

The Empirical Basis

The concept of collective efficacy is supported by empirical research. Sampson's work is based on the Chicago Project on Human Development in Chicago

Neighborhoods. It studied seven cohorts of children and their families, involving about 6,500 children.[11] The project also involved systematic observation of conditions in neighborhoods, including the videotaping and rating of over 23,000 different "street segments" in Chicago. Measures of social and physical disorder were developed and applied to 196 neighborhoods.

Finally, more than 3,500 area residents were surveyed. Collective efficacy was defined in terms of the cohesion among residents and their shared expectations about their ability to control public space. In practical terms, this involved the extent to which residents worked together on neighborhood problems (for instance, to get street lights or broken park equipment repaired) and whether they felt they could exercise some control over areas such as street corners or parks (by calling the police to get rid of drug dealers, for instance).[12]

The data indicate that collective efficacy explains lower rates of crime and observed neighborhood disorder, even after controlling for the economic conditions of neighborhoods.[13] The implications for crime policy are clear and powerful. Poverty alone does not determine crime rates. Within limits, residents have some impact on the level of crime. Collective efficacy emphasizes what citizens believe and do. Traditional crime policies focus entirely on what criminal justice agencies do.

Another study found that domestic violence was lower in neighborhoods where there were higher levels of collective efficacy. It concluded: "Collective efficacy also increases the likelihood that women will disclose conflict in their relationships to various potential sources of support."[14] A study in Detroit, meanwhile, found collective efficacy associated with lower burglary rates in Detroit. "Neighborhoods with active community organizations and a politically active citizenry were better able to control crime than others."[15]

The Basic Model: Operation Cease Fire in Boston

The Boston Gun Project's Operation Cease Fire is the model for community-focused crime control policy.[16] When Boston experienced a surge in gun homicides involving young men in the late 1980s, community leaders brought together a broad coalition of criminal justice officials, neighborhood leaders, and academic experts to seek an innovative and effective response. In the end, it worked; youth homicides dropped dramatically.

Operation Cease Fire incorporated all the elements of the new community focus to crime control. First, it was a highly focused, problem-oriented effort, concentrating on a particular issue—youth gun violence—on particular neighborhoods, and ultimately on particular offenders. Since research indicated that much of the gun violence was associated with particular gangs, those gangs and their leaders were targeted for special attention. This kind of focused effort was quite different from the traditional police "crackdowns" we discussed in Chapter 5, which have generally been unfocused and often involve indiscriminate mass arrests.

Second, it was a multiagency effort, involving partnerships among police and correctional agencies and local and federal criminal justice agencies. In 1995 Police Commissioner Paul Evans convened a working group of representatives from all the relevant agencies to plan a coordinated and innovative effort. This included coordinating the efforts of federal, state, and local law enforcement agencies on gun trafficking and gun crimes. Under the federal sentencing guidelines, prison terms are much longer than under state law. Coordinated efforts referred major gun dealers for federal prosecution.

Third, it involved the active participation of community groups. In this case, religious leaders in the African American community, organized as the Ten Point Coalition, played a major role in working with criminal justice officials and communicating with neighborhood residents. The involvement of these religious leaders—and perhaps more important, the members of their congregations—represent a form of Sampson's collective efficacy which we discussed earlier.

Fourth, it adopted innovative strategies and tactics, rejecting the traditional approach of unfocused arrest, prosecution, and imprisonment. Some of the most important innovations were characterized as "pulling levers": using a variety of legally available sanctions against gang leaders. Gang members with outstanding warrants were arrested; those whose driver's licenses had been suspended had their cars impounded; in Operation Night Light, probation and parole officers made home visits to gang members and enforced violations of the conditions of release; gang members under the supervision of the Department of Youth Services were arrested and taken off the street. (These efforts obviously involved partnerships among criminal justice agencies.) And in another innovative approach, gang members were summoned to meetings and directly told about the enforcement effort and that there would be no deals if they were arrested.

A Justice Department report on an Operation Cease Fire program in Los Angeles, modeled after Boston's, defined pulling levers as "[a] crime deterrence strategy that attempts to prevent violent behavior by using a targeted individual or group's vulnerability to law enforcement as a means of gaining their compliance."[17]

Finally, it included the active participation of academic experts, who not only brought expert knowledge to the program but undertook a rigorous evaluation of its impact. Scholars from Harvard University's Kennedy School of Government were actively involved in planning the project—bringing their expertise in research on problem-oriented policing, gangs, and gun violence—and in evaluating the impact of the project.

The evaluation found a 63 percent decrease in youth homicides per month; a 32 percent decrease in the number of calls to the police regarding shots fired; a 25 percent decrease in gun assaults per month; and a 44 percent decline in youth gun assaults in the district with the highest levels of violence. The researchers controlled for other factors that might explain these results, including changes in the employment rate, the relative percentage of youths in the population, violent crimes in the entire city, homicides among older people, and the level of drug activity. And because the nation as a whole was experiencing a decline in violent crime, they compared Boston's trends with those in other cities. The reduction in violent crime was greater than in the United States generally and in other New England cities. In this respect, Operation Cease Fire met the standard of evidence-based policymaking (see Figure 14.1).

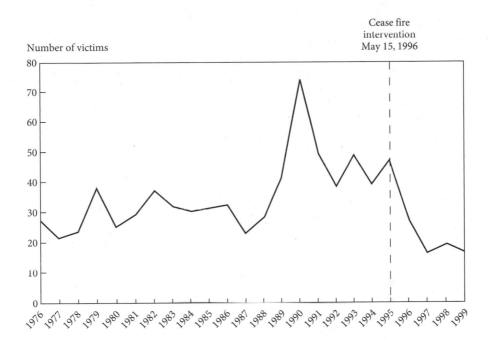

FIGURE 14.1 Youth homicide victims ages 24 and under in Boston, 1976–1999.

SOURCE: Bureau of Justice Statistics, Reducing Gun Violence: The Boston Gun Project's Operation Cease Fire (Washington, DC: Department of Justice, 2001).

Because of its tremendous success, the Gun Project has often been referred to as the "Boston Miracle." It became the basis for a national program sponsored by the U.S. Justice Department, Project Safe Neighborhoods.

Origins of the Boston Project

The Boston Gun Project is one of the most notable innovations in policing labeled *community policing* or *problem-oriented policing* (POP). In many important respects, police innovations are the parent of the other new community-focused crime policies. They have provided the key term and orientation—community—and have defined and tested the basic operating principles we identified at the beginning of this chapter, particularly the idea of developing close partnerships with community groups and other criminal justice and non–criminal justice agencies. (Check the Center for Problem Oriented Policing website for information about recent POP projects.)[18]

Community policing originated in the early 1980s, rising from the ashes of traditional police practices. Research in the 1970s demolished the traditional assumptions underlying preventive patrol (see the Kansas City Patrol Experiment in Chapter 5), the goal of reducing response time, and the myths surrounding the effectiveness of detective work. The key insight was that the police cannot fight crime by themselves but need to work closely with other groups and agencies that ultimately influence crime and disorder.[19] The negative findings from the best research coincided with powerful political pressures to do something about high crime rates and at the same time to improve police/community relations. Police research also contributed the concept of "hot spots," the geographic concentrations of very high rates of crime and disorder. Finally, the concept of "broken windows" emphasized the importance of disorder and its impact on the quality of neighborhood life, as opposed to serious crime, as something criminal justice officials should be concerned with.[20]

Boston-Inspired Innovations

The SMART program in Oakland, California, which we examined in Chapter 5, is based in part on the Boston model. Now let's take a look at similar programs in Jersey City, New Jersey; Cincinnati, Ohio; and Lowell, Massachusetts. After we look at these, we will then examine the concept of community prosecution, which closely resembles these problem-oriented policing programs.

Jersey City, New Jersey.   The POP program in Jersey City first identified 12 pairs of areas in the city where there were high rates of violent crime (hot spots). (We discussed a different Jersey City program in Chapter 5, but there are important overlaps regarding the two programs.) In each pair, one area received focused crime prevention police work, while the other served as a control. In the analysis phase, officers with the Jersey City Police Department identified the specific problems in each of the 24 areas. In treatment and control areas 1, for example, the problem was robbery of commuters; another pair of treatment and control areas, on the other hand, were afflicted by street fights and drug market violence. The analysis phase was consistent with the basic principle of problem-oriented policing: identifying and addressing particular problems in particular places, as opposed to the traditional approach of fighting "crime" in a general sense.

The police employed 28 different strategies in the experimental areas (see Table 14.1). Some of these strategies involved traditional policing: aggressive order maintenance, drug enforcement, and so on. But 8 of the 12 most commonly used strategies involved nontraditional activities: requiring store owners to clean their store fronts, getting the Public Works Department to remove trash from the street, getting more lighting for certain areas. The latter two, of course, involved partnerships with other city agencies.

An evaluation found that the POP program reduced both violent and property crime in the treatment areas compared with their paired control areas. Through direct observation, the evaluation found that observed disorderly behavior declined in 10 of the 12 treatment areas. Signs of physical disorder (uncollected trash, graffiti) also declined in 10 treatment areas, without displacement to neighboring areas.[21]

CIRV in Cincinnati.   The Cincinnati Initiative to Reduce Violence (CIRV) also drew upon the Boston Gun Project example. Small and carefully selected groups of known gang members and offenders are subject to "call in" meetings where they receive a two-part message. Law enforcement officials tell them that after the next

T A B L E 14.1   Police strategies used in Jersey City

Strategy	Number of places used
Aggressive order maintenance	12
Drug enforcement	9
Required store owners to clean store fronts	5
Public Works Dept. removed trash from streets	5
Robbery investigations	4
Increased lighting of areas	4
Housing code enforcement	3
Erected fences around vacant lots	3
Vacant lots cleaned	3
Abandoned buildings boarded and fenced	3
Hung signs explaining rules of behavior (e.g., no drinking)	3
Videotape surveillance of places	3

SOURCE: Anthony M. Braga et al., "Problem-Oriented Policing in Violent Crime Places: A Randomized Controlled Experiment," *Criminology* 37:3 (1999): 544, Table 2. Reprinted with permission.

homicide they will be subject to "swift, targeted enforcement by any legal means available." Apparently, gang members were surprised and impressed with how much law enforcement officials knew about them. Then, representatives from social service agencies described the various services available to them: employment and education services, substance abuse treatment, anger management, parenting assistance, and so on. The service providers' message was, "We will help you if you let us ..." An initial evaluation found that homicides among gang members declined following the first two call in sessions. Further evaluations will determine whether the CIRV program is effective over the long term.[22]

Gangs and Deterrence in Lowell, Massachusetts.   The antigang program in Lowell, Massachusetts, which we examined in Chapter 5 added another potentially rich aspect to the problem-oriented approach to policing. An evaluation of the program argued that it effectively deterred gang-related violence because it delivered the message of possible arrest and punishment in person to a carefully selected target audience: gang members and other offenders who had been identified through a sophisticated data analysis. As we explained in Chapter 6, the problem with most deterrence-oriented crime policies is that the message becomes too diffuse when it is delivered to the entire population, or even a large group of offenders. A focused, problem-oriented approach may overcome that obstacle.[23]

The evidence on the various problem-oriented policing projects is sufficient to support the following proposition.

PROPOSITION 59
Focused, problem-oriented policing programs that involve partnerships and utilize a range of strategies can reduce serious crime.

Unanswered Questions about the Future

Despite the successes reported to date, there are a number of unanswered questions about the future of community policing and POP. These questions are extremely important given the fact that so many of the other community-focused crime policies are modeled after community policing and POP principles and practices.

The first question involves the implementation and continuity of both community policing and POP programs. Skogan's research on Chicago indicates that the city has made a decade-long commitment to community policing.[24] Many other programs reported in the scholarly literature, however, involved short-term, grant-funded experiments that were not continued once the grant ended. And in some programs it is not at all clear whether anything new and distinctive was ever implemented in the first place. Murders in Boston increased in 2003 and 2004. Is Operation Cease Fire continuing? These questions need to be answered.[25]

The problem of maintaining continuity in innovative programs is pervasive in American policing.[26] Over the years, innumerable promising reforms have simply faded away after a few years. The attempt to transfer the Boston Cease Fire program to Los Angeles ran into a number of problems that limited full implementation of the plan, and the impact on crime and gang-related violence was mixed. Additionally, after the initial success of Cease Fire, gun crimes rose in Boston. Sustaining innovative programs and their positive results is a major concern. The reduction in federal funding for innovative programming is an additional obstacle.

A second problem is the impact of powerful social and economic factors that counteract the positive impact of innovative programs. As we discussed in Chapter 1, a serious resource crisis has been affecting the criminal justice system. Police departments are facing personnel shortages because of municipal budget problems. Many public defender agencies are unable to adequately provide competent legal defense to their clients. Probation and parole agencies are understaffed and overloaded with clients, undermining their capacity to serve their clients. Prisons are faced with overcrowding and staff shortages. The result is that throughout the system, agencies are often unable to maintain basic services, much less undertake innovative programs. Finally, the war on terrorism has caused police departments to refocus their efforts. Whereas police chiefs talked about community policing in the 1990s, today they are more likely to talk about preparing for possible terrorist attacks.[27] The capacity to initiate and maintain innovative programs in the current economic climate, in short, is very uncertain.

Community Prosecution

The basic principles of problem-oriented policing have been applied to the prosecution stage of the criminal process in what is called community prosecution. As with community policing, community prosecution represents a new role for prosecutors. Our task here is to take a cold, critical look at it and ask two questions. First, is it really something new and different? Second, is there any evidence that it is effective in controlling crime?

The Concept of Community Prosecution

The American Prosecutors Research Institute (APRI) offers a three part definition of community prosecution: "1. Partnerships with a variety of government agencies and community-based Groups; 2. Use of varied methods including problem-solving to address crime and public safety; 3. Community involvement in the problem-solving process."[28]

It should be obvious that this definition includes the principles of community-focused crime control that we identified at the beginning of this chapter: "partnerships," "problem-solving," and "community involvement." The rhetoric is exactly the same as that of community policing and problem-oriented policing. Community prosecution has redefined to goals of prosecutors' offices. Traditionally, success has been measured in terms of high conviction rates, with a low conviction rate being interpreted as allowing criminals to "get off" and "beat the system." The APRI reports that 90 percent of the media calls to the National District Attorneys Association involve low conviction rates and high plea bargaining rates. It goes on to explain that prosecutors have three goals under community prosecution:[29]

"1. To promote the fair, impartial, and expeditious pursuit of justice;

2. To ensure safer communities; and

3. To promote integrity in the prosecution profession and effective coordination in the criminal justice system."

These goals are very different from the traditional ones for prosecutors, and achieving them may often involve something other than getting a conviction. Ensuring a safer community, for example, might emphasize the treatment of a defendant in a drug court rather than mere prosecution. As we will see shortly with the Manhattan Community Court building a safer community might involve a sentence of community service that involves graffiti reduction and elimination of other signs of disorder.

The idea of community prosecution is extremely popular and has been spreading rapidly. In 1995 there were six programs across the country; by 2010 there were programs in almost every state.[30]

Community prosecution programs are sometimes referred to as "problem-solving courts." According to the National Center for State Courts, the basic elements include a focus on less serious "disorder" offenses, which often get lost in a traditional criminal court, the use of community service and other alternatives to incarceration, strict monitoring of sentence conditions, rapid imposition of sentences (to communicate the message that crime has consequences), close relations with community groups, and a goal of improving the quality of life in the immediate neighborhood.[31]

There are considerable variations in community prosecution and problem-solving court programs. The Center on Court Innovation provides information on specialized Domestic Violence Courts Drug Courts, Mental Health Courts, Sex Offense Courts, and others. Shortly, we will discuss the Harlem Parole Reentry Court, which incorporates many of the practices of drug courts.[32]

The New York Midtown Community Court

Community prosecution originated in 1993 with the Midtown Community Court (MCC) in New York City. (For the latest information, go to the website of the Center for Court Innovation.) The MCC targeted "quality-of-life offenses, such as prostitution, illegal vending, graffiti, shoplifting, fare-beating [not paying subway fares] and vandalism." It grew out of frustration with the failure of the traditional criminal courts to deal effectively with low-level crime. The problem was not that offenders were not punished or punished severely, but that there were often no consequences of any sort for committing quality-of-life offenses. At most, offenders might get a few days of jail time, but often they received probation with no meaningful restrictions.

Court officials and community residents shared the same frustration. A major part of the problem—which affects courts all across the country—is that courts are swamped with major cases and do not have the time or resources to deal with minor crimes.[33] In important respects, this analysis is similar to the one voiced by Morris and Hawkins about the limited sentencing options facing criminal courts (prison or probation), which led to the development of intermediate sanctions (see Chapter 11).

The MCC gives as its guiding principles: (1) restore the community, (2) bridge the gap between communities and courts, (3) knit together a fractured criminal justice system, (4) help offenders deal with problems that lead to crime, (5) provide better information, and (6) design a physical space to match the court's goals. These are lofty goals. Let's see what actually happens in practice.[34]

To implement these principles, sentences in the MCC typically involve a requirement that offenders repay the neighborhood through community service and also undergo treatment. While performing community service (for example, painting over graffiti), sentenced offenders wear bright blue vests. This is designed to "make justice visible" and communicate the message that crime has consequences. To "make justice swift," offenders begin performing their community service within 24 hours of being sentenced.

"Engaging New Partners" involves partnerships with local businesses and agencies in job training, services for the homeless, and so on. The program element of "Offering Social Services" includes providing drug treatment, job training, and other services for offenders. Finally, "Providing Better Information" involves a computerized management information system that provides judges with better information about offenders to help them develop individualized sentences, and also feedback to police officers about the outcomes of their arrests.

Evaluation of the MCC

An evaluation of the MCC by the National Center for State Courts found mixed results. In some important respects, the MCC did achieve its goals. Sentences involving community service were twice as frequent at the MCC compared with the traditional downtown court. Jail sentences were also less common (9 percent compared with 18 percent in the downtown court). This resulted in a reduction of 27,000 jail-days over a three-year period, with the consequent dollar savings.

Interestingly, there was some "feedback effect," as downtown court sentences became closer to MCC's, suggesting that the innovations impressed officials in the other court. Court processing also speeded up, with an average arrest-to-arraignment time of 18.9 hours compared with 29.2 hours in the downtown court. There was also a modest increase in dispositions at the arraignment stage, resulting in both time saved and cost savings.[35]

Offenders who received alternative sanctions (that is, alternatives to jail) were more likely to comply with the requirements (75 percent) than offenders sentenced in the downtown court (50 percent). Additionally, offenders in the MCC who did comply with the terms of their sentences were more likely to receive a secondary sentence than offenders in the downtown court. In this respect, offenders were held to a higher standard of accountability.

With respect to conditions in the immediate neighborhood, observations and interviews with residents of local hot spots in the MCC area indicated "substantial reductions" in the concentration of prostitution and unlicensed vending. There was also a reduction in graffiti on Ninth Avenue, a decline in arrests for prostitution, and a noticeable disruption in the neighborhood drug markets (e.g., fewer individuals, offending less frequently).

The anticipated cost savings were not achieved, and in fact the MCC proved to be more expensive. There were tangible savings of about $1.1 to $1.2 million a year because of speedier court procedures and fewer jail sentences, but the innovative aspects of the program added expenses (for personnel, etc.) of $1.8 to $2.2 million.

The impact on recidivism among sentenced offenders was mixed, however. In the first year a large majority of those sentenced to the mandatory case management/drug treatment program as an alternative to jail did not complete the program. There was a lower rearrest rate for those who did, and in particular lower rearrest rates for those who spent over 90 days in treatment. After three years there was an increase in completion rates in the treatment programs and a reduction in the frequency of rearrest.

A Critical Look at Community Prosecution

Like so many innovations, community prosecution promises a lot: reduced crime, improved neighborhood conditions, and cost savings. Let's take a critical look at this program to see if it meets our standard of dealing with serious crime.

First, it is obvious that community prosecution is directed at less serious, quality-of-life offenses: graffiti, prostitution, and so on. It does not claim to deal with robbery, burglary, or other serious felonies.

The second question is whether the focus on quality-of-life issues helps reduce serious crime. This question lies at the heart of the broken windows and zero-tolerance policing. The advocates of these programs argue that focusing on small crimes and signs of disorder can produce a reduction in serious crime.[36] We need to be fair but also tough-minded here. It is entirely possible that community prosecution does improve neighborhood quality of life. If so, that is a good reason to endorse it. But we also have to ask the tough question of whether it also reduces serious crime. New York City did experience a tremendous reduction in crime that coincided with the operation of the Midtown Community Court. But the direct connection between cracking down on small crimes and a reduction in major crimes remains unproven at this point.

A third question is whether community prosecution effectively treats convicted offenders. For all practical purposes, community prosecution is a form of traditional correctional treatment: probation and parole. The evaluation of the MCC, however, found very mixed results. This leaves us with the same problem we encountered in Chapter 11: Since treatment programs work for those who are ready for treatment, identifying those people and matching them to the right program is the major hurdle. The evidence leads us to the following proposition:

PROPOSITION 60

Community prosecution is a promising alternative to traditional prosecution for minor offenses, but its impact on serious crime remains unproven.

OFFENDER REENTRY PROGRAMS

The Importance of Offender Reentry

Our soaring use of imprisonment has created a new problem for society and the criminal justice system. Every year about 600,000 adults leave prison and return home (this is about 1,600 a day). Joan Petersilia regards the reintegration of released prisoners as "[o]ne of the most profound challenges facing American society" today.[37] The steady flood of returning prisoners has particular relevance for community-focused crime policy and the issue of collective efficacy. As Petersilia points out, it results in "the concentration of ex-prisoners in already fragile communities." The effects are numerous. The concentration of ex-offenders alters the peer culture of the neighborhood, adding one more risk factor to already at-risk young men. It is very likely to overwhelm whatever aspects of collective efficacy exist—bonds among residents, trust and cooperation, neighborhood self-policing efforts, and so on.

The response to this problem is a new set of programs called Offender Reentry. Petersilia defines reentry as "all activities and programming conducted to prepare ex-convicts to return safely to the community and to live as law-abiding citizens."[38] The U.S. Department of Justice launched the Reentry Partnership Initiative in 1999.[39]

Reentry programming embraces the operating principles that guide problem-oriented policing and community prosecution. First, it builds on criminological research indicating that informal social controls, notably family, peer group, and other community factors, have a more direct influence on offender behavior than formal social controls such as probation and parole supervision.[40] Second, it seeks to develop partnerships with both community groups and other criminal justice agencies. Finally, it is committed to evidence-based practice and seeks to base programming on empirical research about what works and what doesn't.

An interesting reentry program is the Harlem Community Justice Center's Parole Reentry Court in New York City. This represents a convergence of innovations in several different areas: problem-solving courts, prisoner reentry (see our discussion later in this chapter), and in part, drug courts. The Reentry Court has a working partnership with parole officials. Clients receive a customized treatment and supervision plan that includes frequent drug testing. In many respects, the program is little different from drug courts across the country, even though it is not officially called one. Offenders appear before a court on a bi-monthly or monthly basis, depending on their level of supervision. The court is presided over by an administrative law judge, rather than a criminal court judge, but the fact that it is a court and a judge adds an element of gravity that is greater than just reporting to a parole officer.[41]

A Closer Look at Returning Prisoners

The reentry initiative has sponsored detailed research on the circumstances of returning prisoners in several cities. The Urban Institute studied 400 prisoners returning to Chicago.[42] Eighty-three percent were African American. Returning prisoners were concentrated in a few neighborhoods with severe social and economic disadvantages. Interestingly, however, only 45 percent returned to their old neighborhood. Some wanted to avoid trouble, while for others their family had moved. Prior to their release, most expressed a strong desire to improve their lives and change their behavior.

Before their release, 87 percent participated in prerelease programs related to such practical matters as finding a job, obtaining a photo ID, and finding a place to live. But in practice, only 25 percent received an actual referral to a job, only 15 percent received a referral to a substance abuse treatment program, and only 22 percent contacted a community program based on a referral from the prerelease program.

Interviewed four to eight months after their return, the parolees reported that family ties and support were the "most important factor" in their adjustment to society. Data on their behavior confirmed this, finding that those with family support were less likely to be reconvicted than those with weak or no support. Almost all suffered from major problems that made readjustment difficult: 81 percent had no health care, and 30 had significant health problems upon release. About half (48 percent) had no close friends; and among those with friends, 40 percent had a friend who had been in prison. They had very limited success in finding jobs, and 70 percent were not employed after four to eight months. The monthly meeting with their parole officers typically lasted between 5 and 30 minutes. After 13 months, one-third (31 percent) were reincarcerated.

The Chicago returnees are typical of parolees nationally. Petersilia reports that half of parolees have less than a high school education, an estimated 19 percent are completely illiterate, and 40 percent are functionally illiterate. Over half (56 percent in 2002) have a prior criminal record, and 53 percent were on probation or parole at the time of the arrest that sent them to prison. Twenty-one percent have some physical or mental condition (such as a learning disability) that limits their ability to work. Most (60 percent) had used drugs in the month before their arrest, and 25 percent were alcohol dependent at that time.[43]

Participation in prerelease programs continues to be low across the country. Prior to release, only about 29 percent participate in a drug treatment program, 35 percent in education classes, and 27 percent in vocational training programs. In prison, a little more than half (56 percent) had any work assignment.[44]

The Urban Institute conducted similar studies of parolees in Baltimore, New Jersey, Ohio, and Texas. The research confirms what we have long known about parolees. They suffer from a number of personal problems, including both a lack of education and histories of substance abuse, and receive weak support in terms of parole services.[45]

WHAT'S REALLY NEW? A CLOSE LOOK AT JOAN PETERSILIA'S RECOMMENDATIONS

On the issue of prisoner reentry, Joan Petersilia is without question the most authoritative voice. Her ideas on this subject are based on over two decades of research on community-based corrections. Her book *When Prisoners Come Home* is the best overview of the important topic of prisoner reentry, solidly rooted in a comprehensive review of official data and the best research.[46] For precisely this reason we should take a very good look at recommendations for reentry programming. She offers four basic policy recommendations. Let's take a close look at them.

Investing in Prison-Based Rehabilitation Programs

Petersilia makes a persuasive case for investing in prison programs that will provide inmates with meaningful work experience and education, and treatment programs that address substance abuse, anger management, and other problems. Today's prisoners suffer from serious deficiencies in all of these areas: About half have less than a high school education; most have very limited employment experience; most have histories of alcohol or drug abuse; many have records of violent behavior, if not involving the crime that sent them to prison, then episodes of violence in their family or among friends.

It hardly needs to be said that all of these factors make it extremely difficult for a person leaving prison to successfully reenter conventional society and establish productive, law-abiding lives. Few employers are attracted to people without a high school diploma and the lack of basic reading comprehension skills that a diploma implies. Even fewer employers are willing to tolerate tardiness or absenteeism. People with histories of drug or alcohol abuse relapse at a very high rate. And people leaving prison generally return to communities where substance abuse is high and consequently will be subject to all of the wrong influences.

The truth of the matter, however, is that all of these things *have been said* before, for many decades in fact. Petersilia's evidence and recommendations evoke a powerful sense of déjà vu, recalling the President's Crime Commission report, *The Challenge of Crime in a Free Society,* from 1967.[47] Many professional associations in the field of corrections have made similar recommendations.

The relevant question is, Why did American society ignore the recommendations of the Crime Commission and other professional associations regarding prison programming and spend the last 30 years just locking up more and more people? This question involves politics rather than criminology. It involves the attitudes of Americans about crime and criminals and how those attitudes are translated into politics. It is fair to ask, What program does Petersilia offer to change the minds of Americans on correctional policy?

A third question is, What evidence does she have that these programs are in fact effective? We might consider the issue of prison industries. There is a long history of the failure to provide meaningful work for inmates. And there are several well-known reasons for this. Restrictive laws limit the kind of industries that prisons can operate. These restrictions reflect the fear among businesses out in the free world that prison industries represent unfair competition. Additionally, many industries provide opportunities for inmate misconduct. Industrial jobs give inmates access to tools that can easily be fashioned into weapons. Contemporary communications jobs, such as telephone calling centers, open the door to telephone abuse. Finally, prison industries that would provide skills relevant to today's job market require all of the basic skills that inmates lack: basic education, work experience, and work habits.

The first edition of this book, published 25 years ago, contained a discussion of prison industries, and in particular a new program called Free Venture that was supposed to overcome the problems that had plagued earlier attempts at developing prison industries. That discussion was dropped, as Free Venture and related 1980s programs proved to be unsuccessful and faded away.

The overriding problem, of course, is the serious resource crisis we discussed in Chapter 1. The severe economic recession of 2008-2010 has forced states to make major budget cuts. This leaves no money for strengthening in prison rehabilitation program. In fact, such programs are most likely to be cut, as prisons have traditionally given priority to security and custody over treatment programs.

Restoring Discretionary Parole Release

Petersilia calls for a return to discretionary parole release. The elimination of discretionary release was one of the most significant policy changes of the past 25 years. Sixteen states have completely abolished discretionary parole release, and because of mandatory sentencing laws only 39 percent of prisoners in 2003 obtained their release through discretionary parole decision.[48] Petersilia's recommendation is based on data indicating that prisoners obtaining discretionary release are less likely to recidivate than those who "max out" their terms. Michael Tonry, a leading expert on sentencing, called for a return to discretionary parole release several years earlier.[49]

In fact, there is some evidence that prisoners released through discretionary parole are more successful—that is less likely to be rearrested—than prisoners released through mandatory release (54 vs. 33 percent, respectively).[50] This is an important finding, and more research on this subject is needed.

At the same time, however, Petersilia's call for a return to discretionary parole release ignores the serious problems that contributed to its demise in the first place. The two major problems are closely linked. The first is a lack of rational, scientifically based standards for deciding when to release a prisoner. We are back to our old friend the prediction problem (Chapter 4 and elsewhere). Parole officials began the search for guidelines to predict success on parole in the 1920s, but we are nowhere nearer that goal today than they were then.[51] The second is that in the absence of rational and scientifically based standards, parole decision making became arbitrary and often discriminatory. These criticisms were raised in the early 1970s and have not been effectively rebutted in the interim.

Front-Loading Postrelease Services

"Front-loading" postrelease services in the first six months after a prisoner's release is Petersilia's third policy recommendation. Common sense supports this idea. The initial weeks upon return to the community pose the most difficult readjustment problems for ex-offenders. They need adequate preparation in the form of job referrals, photo identification, a place to live, and referral to services such as substance abuse treatment. All of these factors are important to their success on parole.[52]

There are several problems with Petersilia's proposal on this point, however. The first is a problem of implementation. Correctional officials have known this for a long time—from their personal experience, if not on the basis of systematic data. The question is, Why have parole agencies failed to do the obvious? This brings us back to the larger problem of organizing and delivering parole services. One answer is that agencies are so overwhelmed by huge caseloads that they really don't have the staff and resources to shift more effort to the first six months. Remember, an estimated 11,000 offenders leave prison every week across the country.

Reallocating resources calls for good management: an ongoing assessment of current operations, an analysis of the evident problems, and a capacity to plan and implement changes. Many parole agencies simply lack good management. Others may have the potential capacity but are simply overwhelmed by the steady flow of new clients.

And then there is a more fundamental question that has plagued both parole and probation since they were invented: Are the services effective? Let's imagine for a moment a parole agency that is well managed and has reasonably sufficient resources. Let's assume that it follows Petersilia and the other recommendations by reentry experts and front-loads its services in the first six months. Do we have any solid evidence that these services are effective? Petersilia's own evidence is pretty grim on this point. As we learned in Chapter 11, the recidivism rates for offenders on probation are depressingly high. And there is precious little evidence that the actual services are effective treatments for the clients. It is appropriate to ask whether front-loading services is really any different than the old idea of intensive supervision. What services, exactly, are being "loaded"?

Petersilia's more recent study of the parole crisis in California—where such a high percentage are sent back to prison through parole revocation—found that most parolees have only minimal supervision. Some categories of parolees, in fact, "report" to the parole officers by mail.[53]

This also brings us back to the more specific problem that has bedeviled community correctional services since the very beginning. It is undoubtedly true that *some* offenders succeed; probation and parole are not 100 percent failures. And it is also probably true that some of these offenders succeed because of the help or monitoring they receive from their probation or parole officer. And it is also probably true that more offenders could be helped if we could match offenders with the combination of services and/or monitoring each one needs. (Some may respond better to a more friendly form of supervision, while others may need the guidance of a sterner form of monitoring.)

And, of course, there is the resource crisis. Cut backs in state budgets leave little room for developing new programs or strengthening old ones.

Eliminate Restrictions on Convicted Offenders

The most devastating section of Petersilia's *When Prisoners Come Home* is Chapter 6, on the barriers society places on ex-offenders ("How We Hinder: Legal and Practical Barriers to Reintegration").[54] An Urban Institute report refers to them as "brick walls," creating enormous obstacles for the recently released offender.[55]

Publicly Available Criminal Records.   Criminal records are increasingly available to the public; 25 states, in fact, make them available on the Internet. While this policy is designed to inform the public and allow crime victims and other people to find out what has happened to an offender, there are potential dangers as well. A report on sex offender notification in Wisconsin found that some offenders had been harassed by neighborhood residents who could find out where they lived.[56]

Employment.   The barriers to employment are sweeping and have been growing in the last decade. For example, California bars convicted felons from holding jobs in law, real estate, medicine, nursing, physical therapy, and education. Even worse, all states prohibit convicted felons from working as barbers, beauticians, or nurses. The cruel absurdity of this practice is dramatized by the fact that hair care vocational programs are the most popular in the New York City Reformatory![57] Six states permanently deny public employment to felons. This means that a parolee cannot hold the most menial city or county job.

The war on drugs has had a special impact. A 1992 federal law requires states to revoke the driver's licenses of convicted drug offenders or lose 10 percent of their federal highway funds.[58] Given the fact that so many jobs have left the inner city and are now located in suburban areas, lack of a driver's license effectively means that a person cannot even look for a job, much less hold on to one. In addition to the legal restrictions, there are serious informal barriers to finding employment. One survey found that 40 percent of employers would never hire anyone with a felony drug conviction.

Housing.   Laws also limit the ability of ex-felons to find housing. Public housing agencies are required to refuse housing to certain categories of offenders (mainly drug or sex offenders).

Welfare.   The 1994 welfare reform law (officially the Personal Responsibility and Work Opportunity Reconciliation Act) requires states to permanently bar drug offenders from receiving federal welfare or public assistance funds (p. 124) (although 9 states have chosen to opt out of this requirement, and 10 have made it available if the offender participates in a treatment program). What this means is that a murderer is eligible for public assistance but not someone convicted of possessing a small amount of marijuana.[59]

The Denial of Federal Benefits Program, established by the 1988 Anti-Drug Abuse Act, provides that anyone convicted of a first-offense drug possession in either federal or state court can, at the discretion of the judge, receive one or more of the following sentences: (1) be ineligible for any or all federal benefits for up to one year, (2) be required to successfully complete an approved drug treatment program that includes periodic testing, or (3) be required to perform community service. For a second offense, the person would be ineligible for all federal benefits for up to five years. The law explicitly grants the judge discretion in applying these provisions, and there is good reason to think that they are not using the law. At the end of 2001, there was a total of 6,938 cases in the Denial of Federal Benefits database, and only 765 had been added in the past year.[60]

Offender Registration and Sex-Offender Notification Laws.   Laws requiring sex offenders to register with local officials and/or that provide public notification of their residence exist in some form in every state. Our discussion in Chapter 6 was very critical of these laws. They include many offenders who are not likely to repeat their crimes; the case overload makes it difficult for law enforcement and parole officials to effectively monitor those who really are high risks for recidivism; and the residence restrictions disrupt peoples' lives (forcing them to live apart from their families, for example) and make it difficult if not impossible for them to establish law-abiding lives.[61]

Voting.   Finally, one of the most serious disabilities is the denial of voting rights to convicted offenders. Every state has some form of voting denial. Several years ago, the Sentencing Project estimated that 4.7 million Americans cannot vote because of a criminal record. That included an estimated 7 percent of all African Americans, and 1.4 million African American males. Denying people the right to vote is perhaps the most dramatic way of telling people that they are outcasts in American society, and an excellent way of keeping them from fully reintegrating into their local communities.[62]

The good news is that there is a small but growing movement to reverse the disenfranchisement trend. The Sentencing Project reported in 2008 that nine states had repealed or revised their lifetime felony disenfranchisement laws, two states had expanded voting rights to offenders under probation or parole, and five states had made it easier for felons to have their voting rights restored.

In the single most dramatic change, repeal of the two-year waiting period in Texas restored the voting rights to an estimated 317,000 offenders. Simplification of the clemency process in Florida, meanwhile, restored the voting rights to about 115,000 people. These are small but important and hopeful steps. If we are serious about achieving successful reentry, allowing people who have been convicted of felonies to vote, and thereby participate in the basic process of democracy and be a part of society is a very important step.[63]

Despite the changes that have occurred regarding voting, numerous restrictions on ex-offenders remain. Denying people access to jobs, housing and social services pose a major impediment to reintegrating recently released offenders back into the community. And if we take seriously the importance of community with regard to crime control, it is necessary to address these impediments.

Summary

When we put all this together, the picture looks almost impossible for the parolee. We take people with very limited education, significant histories of drug and alcohol abuse, criminal records, and mental and physical disabilities and proceed to bar them from many jobs, keep them from getting a driver's license so they could find and keep a job, deny them any possibility of public assistance until they find a job, and bar them from public housing. By denying them the right to vote, we tell them that they are not full members of American society. And remember, they are returning to neighborhoods with high concentrations of similar problems. Is it any wonder that so many fail on parole?

There are reasons why these restrictions exist: Society has demonized criminals for the last 30 years. What Petersilia, the Urban Institute, and others fail to confront

Illustration by Frank Irwin, © Wadsworth, Cengage Learning.

are the political realities that have created these "brick walls." The solution is a technical matter not of correctional programming, but of political action: changing the hearts and minds of the American people and of the officials they elect.

If this sounds bad, the situation for reentering felons is even worse today than it was just a few years ago. The recession of 2008–2010, with its 10 percent unemployment rate, means there are even fewer job opportunities. The high unemployment rate, moreover, means there are many people with far better qualifications than a reentering felon for each job. Additionally, the recession has resulted in major cuts in social service programs—substance abuse treatment, mental health services—that reentry programs need. Can we really expect reentry programs to succeed in this environment?

PROACTIVE PAROLE SUPERVISION

The offender reentry movement has introduced the idea of "proactive supervision" in parole. Rejecting the "passive monitoring" of traditional parole, it is modeled after the proactive approach of problem-oriented policing, and in particular the SARA model (scanning, analysis, response, assessment). This includes a risk assessment of a parolee's problems, an analysis of appropriate responses, implementation of those responses, and an assessment of how well they are working. Faye Taxman explains: "The important part of the risk factor assessment is to use the information to develop a crime prevention plan for the offender."[64]

The Harlem Parole Reentry Court, which we discussed earlier, is an example of proactive parole supervision, combining elements of problem-solving courts and drug courts.

An Indianapolis reentry program applied the problem-solving approach to a group of recently released offenders. The program consisted of a series of neighborhood community meetings for the offenders that also included criminal justice agency officials, community representatives, and social service providers. The goal of the program was to combine deterrence (in the form of parole supervision) with social support from the community and service providers. An evaluation compared a treatment group of 93 ex-offenders who attended between one and five meetings with a control group of 107 ex-offenders released at the same time. The results were not very promising. Forty percent of both groups were rearrested within 10 to 24 months after their release. The treatment group did a little better, lasting an average of 172 days before rearrest, compared with 120 days for the control group.[65]

When we stop to think about the program, there is little reason to expect that it would have much impact. What difference would attending one meeting make to the typical ex-offender? What real difference would five meetings make? Indeed, on closer inspection even the problem-solving aspect of the program seems pretty shallow. The "problem analysis" phase, designed to help tailor the right treatment for each offender, produced the most obvious set of factors: prior criminal histories, employment problems, histories of substance abuse, and so on. The evidence leads us to the following proposition:

> ## PROPOSITION 61
> Without major changes in public thinking about crime and criminals, and accompanying changes in spending and programming, prisoner reentry programs will not reduce crime.

RESTORATIVE JUSTICE

A radically new approach to criminal justice policy involves the concept of restorative justice. As an alternative to the basic ethos of our legal system, it emphasizes both repairing the harm done to the community and building a sense of responsibility to the community in the offender. As the term *restorative justice* implies, it seeks not so much to punish offenders but to *restore* the bonds between the person who has done wrong, the victim, and the community at large.[66] This approach is directly relevant to the community-oriented approach to crime policy.

Instead of the traditional Anglo-American adversarial process, restorative justice emphasizes dialogue, negotiation, and the reestablishment of a positive relationship between victim and offender. In practice, restorative justice programs have often used financial restitution, community service, and mediation, usually in the form of face-to-face acknowledgment of guilt. The restorative justice movement draws heavily on communal peacemaking traditions among Native Americans and other indigenous peoples.

The chief proponent of restorative justice is John Braithwaite, whose book *Crime, Shame, and Reintegration* sparked the movement. Emphasizing shaming as the key to controlling crime, he argues that informal sanctions "imposed by relatives, friends or a personally relevant collectivity have more effect on criminal behavior than sanctions imposed by a remote legal authority."[67] Although Braithwaite is critical of traditional rehabilitation-oriented programs, his concept of restorative justice can be seen as a form of rehabilitation, particularly with its emphasis on reintegrating offenders into the community. Some programs, in fact, operate as diversion programs, referring cases to mediation conferences as an alternative to prosecution.

Restorative Justice in Operation

In a recent elaboration of restorative justice principles, Braithwaite argues that this approach is more effective in controlling crime than policies based on punishment, deterrence, incapacitation, and even rehabilitation. The U.S. Justice Department has recommended incorporating restorative justice into community policing programs.[68]

How well does restorative justice work in practice? Like many of the so-called new intermediate punishments we discussed earlier, the restorative justice programs of financial restitution and community service are nothing new. They have been used for many years but have been seen primarily as alternative sentences within the basic sentencing framework, appropriate for less serious offenses, and not a radical alternative to the basic principles of the justice system.

Evaluations of experimental restitution, community service, and mediation programs have tended to find slightly lower recidivism rates for offenders compared with traditional sentences of prison or probation. The differences are not always consistent, however, and many questions remain regarding the implementation and outcomes of such programs.[69] Some of the most promising findings are closely related to the concept of procedural justice discussed in Chapter 12. In the most ambitious experiment, in Australia, preliminary findings indicate that restorative justice conferences result in lower levels of anger, fear, and alienation from the legal system among both victims and offenders than does traditional court processing.

We have many reasons for being skeptical about restorative justice as a response to serious crime. First, although it may well be appropriate for less serious crimes, especially minor property offenses, many people will question whether, from the standpoint of proportionality and just deserts, it is appropriate for serious crimes. Second, although it may be appropriate for first-time offenders, there are questions about whether it is appropriate for fourth- or fifth-time offenders. And finally, there are questions about whether it effectively reduces serious crime. A careful reading of Braithwaite's long 1999 essay in defense of restorative justice reveals that it is long on theory—and discussions of what it might accomplish—and fairly short on proven results.[70]

The most serious problem with Braithwaite's concept is that the necessary conditions he identifies do not exist in modern urban society. Common sense suggests that the informal sanctions of family, friends, or community are likely to be more effective in controlling behavior than the threats and actions of remote official agencies. But a major part of the crime problem in the United States today is the collapse of families, peer groups, and communities for many people. As Hagan's theory of social embeddedness suggests, some individuals are deeply embedded in lives that encourage lawbreaking rather than law abidance.[71] In our poorest, most economically ravaged and drug-ridden neighborhoods, "community," in the positive sense of the term, has disappeared. The structure of families has collapsed for too many people. The peer group influence too often leads to drugs and crime. The concept of restorative justice may well be appropriate and effective for the juvenile delinquent in a middle-class neighborhood but irrelevant for those aspects of our society that are the center of most serious crime.

Not only does restorative justice draw heavily on Native American traditions of communal justice, but it also reflects a nostalgic view of community in the United States. The informal mechanisms of social control that Braithwaite prizes—disapproval by family, friends, and neighbors—were in fact the primary means of crime control in seventeenth-century colonial New England. They worked because those communities were small and extremely homogenous (almost entirely white, English, and Protestant). As the United States grew into a large and diverse nation, characterized not only by different racial, ethnic, religious, and cultural groups but also by largely anonymous social relations, the old mechanisms no longer worked. That is one of the main reasons that Americans created the

modern criminal justice system in the early nineteenth century. There is no returning to this vanished society.[72] This leads us to the following conclusion:

PROPOSITION 62
The promise of restorative justice remains unproven in reducing serious crime.

CONCLUSION

In the end, what does the new community focus of crime policy offer? Is it a
realistic strategy for reducing crime? Or is it just the latest fad, offering false promises? Remember, this movement is still fairly new, and all the evidence is not
in. But a careful review of the existing evidence suggests the following tentative
conclusions.

First, the most substantial evidence involves innovative police practices following the principles of problem-oriented policing. The Boston Gun Project,
the SMART project in Oakland, and the POP experiments have all been subject to rigorous evaluations by some of the best criminologists, with the results
published in the best peer-reviewed scholarly journals. This meets one of the
basic standards of evidence-based policymaking. The evaluations found all three
programs to be effective. The lessons are that the police can be effective in reducing serious crime if they undertake careful planning, involve outside
experts, focus on particular problems and/or geographic areas, develop partnerships with other criminal justice and non–criminal justice agencies, establish
working relationships with community groups, and allow a rigorous independent evaluation.

Second, the evidence about community prosecution is somewhat weak. The
Midtown Community Court in New York City addressed only quality-of-life
crimes and not serious crimes, which are our primary focus. There was some evidence of successful outcomes, but the anticipated cost savings were not achieved.
A fair conclusion would be that community prosecution is a good idea that can
address some problems of crime and disorder, but there is no evidence yet that
it can address serious crime.

Third, there is at present no persuasive evidence that offender reentry programs are effective in dealing with serious crime by reducing recidivism rates.
The concept of reentry is still in a very early stage; much is promised but the
evidence is still not there. Especially troubling is that reentry advocates offer a
lot of old wine in fancy new bottles. The goal of reintegrating offenders back
into the community is as old as community-based corrections itself. The idea of
preparing prisoners for release through educational programs, counseling, and so
on is equally old. It is simply not clear what is really new here. Even more serious, the advocates of the movement have not faced up to the political realities
that have undermined community-based corrections for the past 30 years.

Restorative justice, moreover, has some potential for less serious crimes, but does not appear to be relevant to the problem of serious crime; this is true especially for robbery and burglary, which we defined in Chapter 1, and which are the special focus of this book.

Finally, two external forces threaten to undermine promising programs that have developed. The larger economic crisis facing American society has greatly reduced job opportunities and sent unemployment to the highest levels in decades. We have long known that unemployment is a risk factor for both juvenile and adult criminality. The economic crisis has further aggravated the resource crisis in criminal justice, straining the budgets of police departments, public defender offices, correctional agencies and social service providers. From this perspective, the picture looks bleak indeed.

We should not end on a totally pessimistic note, however. The main point of this chapter has been to highlight the promising recent innovations in thinking about crime policy. Substantial evidence supports the focus on communities, the role of collective efficacy, and the capacity of carefully planned, well-designed problem-oriented programs in policing, community prosecution and drug courts. A solid evidence-based foundation exists for effective programs that reject the myths and popular stereotypes about criminal justice that have affected so many past crime policies. There is, in short, a basis for programs reflecting sense rather than nonsense.

NOTES

1. Joan Petersilia, *When Prisoners Come Home* (New York: Oxford University Press, 2004).

2. Jeremy Travis and Michelle Waul, *Reflections on the Crime Decline: Lessons for the Future?* (Washington, DC: Urban Institute, 2002). Available on the Urban Institute website.

3. Problem solving originated with Herman Goldstein, "Improving Policing: A Problem-Oriented Approach," *Crime and Delinquency* 25 (1979): 236–258.

4. James Q. Wilson and George L. Kelling, "Broken Windows: The Police and Neighborhood Safety," *Atlantic Monthly* 249 (March 1982): 325–351.

5. Faye S. Taxman, Douglas Young, James Byrne, Alexander Holsinger, and Donald Anspach, *From Prison Safety to Public Safety: Innovations in Offender Reentry* (Washington, DC: Department of Justice, 2002), p. 5. For this and other reports, go to the reentry page on the U.S. Department of Justice website, or the website of the Bureau of Government Research at the University of Maryland.

6. Robert J. Sampson, "Transcending Tradition: New Directions in Community Research, Chicago Style," *Criminology* 40 (May 2002): 213–230.

7. Robert J. Sampson and Steven W. Raudenbush, "Systematic Social Observation of Public Spaces: A New Look at Disorder in Urban Neighborhoods," *American Journal of Sociology* 105 (November 1999): 603–651.

8. Wesley G. Skogan and George E. Antunes, "Information, Apprehension, and Deterrence: Exploring the Limits of Police Productivity," *Journal of Criminal Justice* 7 (Fall 1979): 217–241.

9. Tom R. Tyler, *Why People Obey the Law* (New Haven: Yale University Press, 1990).

10. Summarized in Samuel Walker and Charles M. Katz, *The Police in America: An Introduction*, 7th ed. (New York: McGraw-Hill, 2010).

11. Robert J. Sampson, "Transcending Tradition: New Directions in Community Research, Chicago Style," *Criminology* 40 (May 2002): 213-230.

12. Jeffrey D. Morenoff, Robert J. Sampson, and Stephen W. Raudenbush, "Neighborhood Inequality, Collective Efficacy, and the Spatial Dynamics of Urban Violence," *Criminology* 39 (2001): 517–560.

13. Sampson and Raudenbush, "Systematic Social Observation of Public Spaces."

14. Christopher R. Browning, "The Span of Collective Efficacy: Extending Social Disorganization Theory to Partner Violence," *Journal of Marriage and Family* 64 (2002): 833–850.

15. David Martin, "Spatial Patterns in Residential Burglary: Assessing the Effect of Neighborhood Social Capital," *Journal of Contemporary Criminal Justice* 18 (2002): 132–146.

16. David M. Kennedy, Anthony A. Braga, and Anne M. Piehl, *Reducing Gun Violence: The Boston Gun Project's Operation Ceasefire* (Washington, DC: Department of Justice, 2001). NCJ 188741.

17. National Institute of Justice, *Operation Cease Fire in Los Angeles* (Washington, DC: Department of Justice, 2005). NCJ 192378.

18. www.popcenter.org.

19. These developments are best summarized in David Bayley, *Police for the Future* (New York: Oxford University Press, 1994).

20. James Q. Wilson and George L. Kelling, "Broken Windows: The Police and Neighborhood Safety" *Atlantic Monthly* 249 (March 1982): 29–38.

21. Anthony A. Braga, David L. Weisburd, Elin J. Waring, Lorraine Green Mazerolle, William Spelman, and Francis Gajewski, "Problem-Oriented Policing in Violent Crime Places: A Randomized Controlled Experiment," *Criminology* 37 (1999): 541–580.

22. Robin S. Engel, S. Gregory Baker, Marie Skubak Tillyer, John Eck, Jessica Dunham, *Implementation of the Cincinnati Initiative to Reduce Violence (CIRV), Year I Report* (Updated: April 14, 2008) (Cincinnati: University of Cincinnati Policing Institute, 2008).

23. Anthony A. Braga, Glenn L. Pierce, Jack McDevitt, Brenda J. Bond, and Shea Cronin, "The Strategic Prevention of Gun Violence Among Gang-Involved Offenders," *Justice Quarterly* 25 (March 2008): 132–162.

24. Wesley G. Skogan and Susan Hartmann, *Community Policing, Chicago Style* (New York: Oxford University Press, 1997).

25. National Institute of Justice, *Operation Cease Fire in Los Angeles.*

26. This issue is discussed in detail with regard to accountability-related innovations in Samuel Walker, *The New World of Police Accountability* (Thousand Oaks: Sage, 2005).

An excellent case study of a lack of continuity is the St. Louis consent-to-search program: Scott Decker, *Reducing Gun Violence: The St. Louis Consent-to-Search Program* (Washington, DC: Department of Justice, 2004). NCJ 191332.

27. See the discussion of "Ashcroft Policing" in David Harris, *Good Cops: The Case for Preventive Policing* (New York: The New Press, 2005).

28. American Prosecutors Research Institute, *Just Look What You've Done: Determining the Effectiveness of Community Prosecution* (Washington, DC: American Prosecutors Research Institute, 2007), citing M. Elaine Nugent, Patricia Fanflik, and Delene Bromirski, *The Changing Nature of Prosecution: Community Prosecution vs. Traditional Prosecution Approaches* (Alexandria, VA: American Prosecutors Research Institute, 2004).

29. American Prosecutors Research Institute, *Do Lower Conviction Rates Mean That Prosecutors' Offices Are Performing Poorly?* (Arlington, VA: American Prosecutors Research Institute, 2007).

30. See "Current Programs" on the web site of the American Prosecutors Research Institute, www.ndaa.org/apri/.

31. Pamela M. Casey and David A. Rottman, *Problem-Solving Courts* (Williamsburg, VA: National Center for State Courts, 2004). Available on the National Center for State Courts website.

32. For a description of programs and philosophy, take a look at John S. Goldkamp, Cheryl Irons-Guynn, and Doris Weiland, *Community Prosecution Strategies* (Washington, DC: Department of Justice, 2003). NCJ 195062.

33. John Feinblatt, Greg Berman, and Michele Sviridoff, *Neighborhood Justice: Lessons Learned from the Midtown Community Court* (New York: Center for Court Innovation, 1998).

34. Ibid.

35. Michele Sviridoff, David Rottman, and Rob Weidner, *Dispensing Justice Locally: The Impacts, Costs, and Benefits of the Midtown Community Court* (Williamsburg, VA: National Center for State Courts, 2000).

36. George L. Kelling and Catherine M. Coles, *Fixing Broken Windows* (New York: The Free Press, 1996). William J. Bratton and Peter Knoblach, *Turnaround* (New York: Random House, 1998). James Q. Wilson and George L. Kelling, "Broken Windows: The Police and Neighborhood Safety," *Atlantic Monthly* 249 (March 1982): 29–38.

37. Joan Petersilia, *When Prisoners Come Home* (New York: Oxford University Press, 2004), p. 3.

38. Ibid.

39. Taxman et al., *From Prison Safety to Public Safety.*

40. Michael R. Gottfredson and Travis Hirschi, *A General Theory of Crime* (Stanford, CA: Stanford University Press, 1990).

41. Donald J. Farole, *Harlem Parole Reentry Court Evaluation: Implementation and Preliminary Impacts* (New York: Center for Court Innovation, 2003).

42. Nancy G. La Vigne, Christy Visher, and Jennifer Castro, *Chicago Prisoners' Experiences Returning Home* (Washington, DC: The Urban Institute, 2004). Available on the Urban Institute website.

43. Petersilia, *When Prisoners Come Home,* p. 32.

44. Ibid., p. 95.

45. The reports and other information about prisoner reentry can be found on the Urban Institute website. www.urban.org.

46. Petersilia, *When Prisoners Come Home,* pp. 140–142.

47. President's Commission on Law Enforcement and Administration of Justice, *The Challenge of Crime in a Free Society* (New York: Avon Books, 1967).

48. Bureau of Justice Statistics, *Probation and Parole in the United States, 2003* (Washington, DC: Department of Justice, 2004). NCJ 205336.

49. Michael Tonry, *Sentencing Matters* (New York: Oxford, 1996).

50. Petersilia, *When Prisoners Come Home,* p. 70. Bureau of Justice Statistics, *Trends in State Parole, 1990–2000* (Washington, DC: Department of Justice, 2001). NCJ 184735.

51. David J. Rothman, *Conscience and Convenience: The Asylum and Its Alternatives in Progressive America* (Boston: Little, Brown, 1980). Samuel Walker, *Popular Justice: A History of American Criminal Justice,* 2nd ed. (New York: Oxford University Press, 1998).

52. The Urban Institute report on parolees in Chicago provides valuable data on these issues. See also La Vigne et al., *Chicago Prisoners' Experiences Returning Home.*

53. Ryken Grattet, Joan Petersilia, and Jeffrey Lin, *Parole Violations and Revocations in California* (Washington, DC: Department of Justice, 2008).

54. Petersilia, *When Prisoners Come Home,* pp. 105–137. Office of the Pardon Attorney, U.S. Department of Justice, *Civil Disabilities of Convicted Felons* (Washington, DC: Department of Justice, 1996).

55. Urban Institute, *Prisoner Reentry and Community Policing* (Washington, DC: Urban Institute, 2004). www.urban.org.

56. Richard G. Zevitz and Mary Ann Farkas, *Sex Offender Community Notification: Assessing the Impact in Wisconsin* (Washington, DC: Department of Justice, 2001). NCJ 179992.

57. Petersilia, *When Prisoners Come Home,* p. 114.

58. Ibid., p. 115.

59. Ibid., p. 124.

60. Bureau of Justice Assistance, *Denial of Federal Benefits Program and Clearing House* (Washington, DC: Department of Justice, 2002). NCJ 193770.

61. Human Rights Watch, *No Easy Answers: Sex Offender Laws in the United States* (New York: Human Rights Watch, 2007).

62. The Sentencing Project, *Losing the Vote: The Impact of Felony Disenfranchisement Laws in the United States* (Washington, DC: Author, 1998). Available on the Sentencing Project website.

63. Ryan S. King, *Expanding the Vote: State Felony Disenfranchisement Reform, 1997–2008* (Washington, DC: The Sentencing Project, 2008).

64. Faye Taxman, *Proactive Supervision: Supervision as Crime Prevention* (College Park, MD: University of Maryland, n.d.). Available on the website of the Bureau of Government Research at the University of Maryland.

65. National Institute of Justice, *Applying Problem Solving Approaches to Issues of Inmate Re-Entry: The Indianapolis Pilot Project, Final Report* (Washington, DC: Department of Justice, 2004). NCJ 203923.

66. John Braithwaite, *Crime, Shame, and Reintegration* (New York: Cambridge University Press, 1989).

67. Ibid., p. 69.

68. Caroline G. Nicholl, *Community Policing, Community Justice, and Restorative Justice* (Washington, DC: Department of Justice, 1999).

69. Burt Galway and Joe Hudson, eds., *Criminal Justice, Restitution, and Reconciliation* (Monsey, NY: Willow Tree Press, 1990).

70. Braithwaite, *Crime, Shame, and Reintegration.*

71. John Hagan, "The Social Embeddedness of Crime and Unemployment," *Criminology* 31 (November 1993): 465–491.

72. Walker, *Popular Justice.*

Index

A

Abortion
  crime rates and, 8–9, 294–295
  laws, 316
  legality of, 291
  legally protected choice, 293
Abrahamse, Allan, 100, 127–128
Absolute deterrence, 124
ACLU. *See* American Civil Liberties Union
Acquaintance rape, 48
Active monitoring programmed contact
    systems, 270
Actuarial approach, 81–82
ADAM (Arrestee Drug Abuse Monitoring), 306
Adam Walsh Act (2006), 170
Adaptation by offenders, 102
Administrative license revocation (ALR), 140
Administrative system of justice, 65
Adult crime, 23
Adult criminal justice statistics, 55
Adultery, 295, 316
Adversarial system of justice, 64–65
Affective education, 318
Affirmative defense, 188
African Americans
  Boston's Ten Point Coalition, 342
  conviction rates, 44, 48
  as crime victims, 207–208
  and deadly force, 67
  deterrence, 125
  and dismissals, 61
  and guns, 224, 228
  homicide rates, 13
  and mass incarceration, 24
  as opponents of legalization, 330
  perceived injustices, 289
  and police misconduct, 288
  racial disparities in drug enforcement, 287, 311

racial profiling, 285
reentry programs, 256
and Rockefeller Drug Law, 164
third-strike incarceration rates, 168–169
victimization rates, 13
and voting rights, 17–18, 358
and war on drugs, 17
Aggravated-assault arrests, 48–49
Aging as crime reduction policy, 251
Agnew, Spiro, 190–191
AIDS education programs, 321
Airports, gun control at, 236–237
Akers, Ronald L., 124
Alameda County, California, 39, 204
Alaska, attempt to abolish plea bargaining in, 190–192
Albuquerque, drug use statistics in, 306
Alcohol-impaired driving, 133
Alcohol-related deaths, 304
ALR (Administrative license revocation), 140
American Bar Association
    Standards for Criminal Justice, 156
American Bar Foundation
    Two Million Unnecessary Arrests, 290
American Civil Liberties Union (ACLU), 326
    The Rights of Crime Victims, 204
American criminal justice system
    complexity of, 36
    prosecutors' discretion, 190
American Probation and Parole Association, 19
American Prosecutors Research Institute (APRI), 349
American Psychiatric Association Insanity Defense
    Work Group, 185
Anger management programs, 272
Announcement effect, 134–135
Annual offending rates, 87, 88, 157
Anti Drug Abuse Act (1988), 356
Anti-smoking education programs, 322
Appeals, postconviction, 194–196